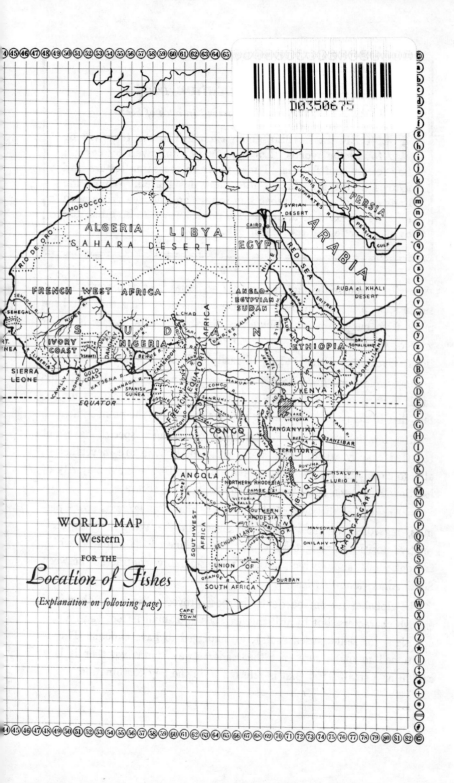

WORLD MAP
(Western)

FOR THE

Location of Fishes

(*Explanation on following page*)

How to Use Location Maps

"Western" in front, "Eastern" in back of book

UNDER the heading given each fish in the text will be found the words "Location Map," followed by certain key letters and figures. These refer to the same letters and figures in the margins of the maps designated. Where the lines extending from those key letters and figures cross each other is an exact or approximate point known to be inhabited by that particular species of fish.

It will, of course, be understood that a species is seldom confined to a single spot, although in many instances collections have thus far been made from but one point. Where the distribution of a species is either wide or scattered, there are sufficient location-points (and text explanations) given so that the reader will easily understand what is meant.

Most collections have been made from streams and pools quite too small to show on anything less than a huge map. This accounts for the fact that in many places no water appears to be near the point indicated.

In a few instances commercial collectors of new species have not reported exactly where fishes were gathered, but we are, nevertheless, able to closely approximate where they are found. The great majority of locations have been described by scientists, and are accurate.

Continents, for the sake of clearness, are shown as large as space permits, regardless of their respective sizes. In the Western Map their relative positions are ignored, except for the line of the Equator, which is continuous and correct, although considerably contracted between South America and Africa.

The alphabet for our particular purpose proved to have less than half enough characters, but by utilizing capitals and small letters (and a few odd signs for seldom-used spots), we managed to have enough. This is mentioned to make sure that the reader always notes whether it is a capital or a small letter that is referred to in the key combination.

FOREWORD TO THE REPRINT EDITION

William T. Innes, more than any other man living or dead, made the tropical fish hobby what it is today. More than thirty years ago Dr. Innes wrote, financed and published this book, *EXOTIC AQUARIUM FISHES*, and it was a milestone in the hobby. It is with great humility that my company reprints this book, for it has great historical as well as practical value.

Though the original edition of the Innes masterpiece had a substantial number of color photographs, we have elected to reproduce all of the Innes photos in black and white. I have, with Dr. Innes' permission, added some of our color photographs, mostly of fishes which Dr. Innes did not include in his original book because they had not been discovered at that time. So, for the reader, it is easy to differentiate between the original Innes plates and those which we have added.

Even as this book is being printed, T.F.H. is planning a new edition of the Innes work. The forthcoming edition will feature every species illustrated in full color.

Dr. Innes, now in his 92nd year, has written a new foreword (see page 2) for this edition. I can only thank him for his great kindness in authorizing us to republish a work which will live on forever.

Dr. Herbert R. Axelrod
President
T.F.H. Publications, Inc.

Jersey City, N. J.

Rasbora heteromorpha

EXOTIC
AQUARIUM FISHES

A Work of General Reference

By WILLIAM T. INNES

Distributed in the U.S. by T.F.H. Publications, Inc., 211 West Sylvania Avenue, P.O. Box 427, Neptune, N.J. 07753; in England by T.F.H. (Gt. Britain) Ltd., 13 Nutley Lane, Reigate, Surrey; in Canada to the book store and library trade by Beaverbooks, 953 Dillingham Road, Pickering, Ontario L1W 1Z7; in Canada to the pet trade by Rolf C. Hagen Ltd., 3225 Sartelon Street, Montreal 382, Quebec; in Southeast Asia by Y.W. Ong, 9 Lorong 36 Geylang, Singapore 14; in Australia and the South Pacific by Pet Imports Pty. Ltd., P.O. Box 149, Brookvale 2100, N.S.W., Australia; in South Africa by Valiant Publishers (Pty.) Ltd., P.O. Box 78236, Sandton City, 2146, South Africa; Published by T.F.H. Publications, Inc., Ltd., The British Crown Colony of Hong Kong.

THE AUTHOR'S FOREWORD 1966

The first edition of my book *Exotic Aquarium Fishes* naturally gave me a very exciting experience, but as all copyrights must, this one finally expired; but, with additions of his own, Dr. Herbert Axelrod is reprinting it herewith.

Turning aside from the main point for a moment, Dr. Axelrod recently published a masterwork, *Encyclopedia of Pigeon Breeds,* the most sumptuous work I have ever seen on any kind of pet. On receipt of a gift copy I exploded with these carefully chosen words to the publisher, "Your vaulting ambition is only equalled by your apparently exhaustless energy."

That praise now goes double since his determination to print my book.

For my part, I am very pleased that the work has fallen into the hands of a person who does everything well. Witness how he taught himself to be one of the world's foremost color photographers of aquarium fishes.

It gives me satisfaction indeed to be associated with him in this pleasant undertaking, and it seems that our readers will profit, too.

William T. Innes

February 18, 1966

Author-Publisher's
Introduction

THE AUTHOR has to thank his thousands of correspondents for their part (mostly unconscious) in letting him know what kind of an aquarium book they need and want. In sifting their letters, it is not difficult to tell.

The call is for something different, especially as to the selection, proportion and arrangement of material.

Particularly is more detail wanted regarding those practical principles, which, when applied, keep the aquarium and the fish in health. In responding to such needs we have devoted a great deal of space to that general topic, so arranged and cross-indexed that any subject may be quickly located. In the end this does not add bulk to the book, for we have gained paper by omitting many species of fishes which are of no value to aquarists for the simple reason that they cannot be had, although their pictures continue to appear in aquarium literature with time-honored regularity.

Next, aquarists want to be able to recognize and classify species. With proper help this is simpler than it seems. Photographs, taken for clearness of detail, without regard to pictorial effect, furnish the best and truest medium of expression. They are especially useful when the author has himself taken the photographs and places them before him when writing, so that he can, when necessary, intimately interpret them to the reader, explaining various points—and sometimes, shortcomings. We began photographic portraiture of aquarium fishes in 1905 and first introduced it as a basis of illustration in 1917. As nearly all our plates up to 1930 showed only single specimens, we discarded the work of a quarter century and began all over in order to show fishes in pairs, here and in our magazine, "The Aquarium," both in black-and-white, and in color.

The placing of the illustration and the text together in every instance is one of the main features of this book.

A point to which we attach importance, and which has received much care, is one that the casual reader might easily overlook. This is the arrangement of the fish families in their correct order of precedence, those lowest in the scale of development being first, and the highest, last. The reasons for this are very interesting. They are explained as simply as possible under the heading, "Classification of Fishes." This is followed up by short notes given at the heading of each family. A little study of this subject will dispel much of that fog in which aquarists usually find themselves when attempting classifications. They will know just why each fish is placed in its own family. Yes, they will themselves be able to correctly place many species which had previously puzzled them. This feature is capable of being used in schools as a primary course in the systematic study of fishes.

While such points as the pronunciation of scientific names, the 7 family distribution maps and the 2 master location maps are new features, they are so easily understood that no elaboration on them is necessary. They are offered as our solution to many questions we constantly receive.

It will be noted that greatly varying amounts of text accompany different fish illustrations. This is deliberate. Where little is known of a species, or where its habits have just previously been described for another member of the same family, we believe blank paper is better than needless repetition or any literary "padding." Those species which are especially interesting or popular, or whose life habits require extra space to describe, receive it.

"Exotic" has been used because in every way it is a better word than "tropical." Tropical gives the false impression that all these fishes come from torrid climates, and that they must be kept at a steaming temperature. In many instances this idea works to their injury and also creates in the public mind the belief that they are delicate, and difficult to keep. "Exotic" expresses that charm and strangeness we expect of anything from distant parts, and which our aquarium fishes possess in such full measure. This much better word is in use by French and other aquarists. The German "ausländische" is a synonym for it.

It has not exactly been our object to write so that "he who runs may read," but rather to express ourselves so simply at all times that any who take the trouble to read can understand. Scientific terms have been avoided whenever common words would serve the same ends.

By fully setting forth every detail which the beginner wants to learn, we may at times bore the advanced aquarist, who "knows the answers." However, a truth already known, but freshly stated by another, may be given new life. In any case, it is well to remember the words of a certain wise old Frenchman, who wrote: "If you would be thought agreeable in society, you must consent to be taught many things you already know."

Appreciations

THIS BOOK, written and planned by an aquarist who is not an ichthyologist, would have lacked accuracy in names, classifications and locations without help from a competent authority. It is most fortunate for the author and his readers that this help was forthcoming from one who knows his science and who at heart is himself an ardent aquarist. This friend in need who is a friend indeed is Dr. George S. Myers, assistant curator in charge of fishes at The National Museum, Washington, who studied under Drs. Carl H. Eigenmann and David Starr Jordan. Dr. Myers has corrected names, dug up locations, placed the pages in their correct order of precedence and supplied virtually all of the material regarding classifications. He filled in the areas on the 7 family distribution maps and made important corrections on the 2 master maps. In the summer of 1934 he gave up most of a needed vacation to help the author in every possible way. Words cannot express our appreciation.

The master maps, which look quite simple when finished, are the product of much thought and of many hands. The actual drawing and lettering were done by Miss Betty Innes and Miss Clara M. Titus. We have profited by the assistance of The National Geographic Society, and by the use of official Mexican Government maps, furnished by Dr. Myron Gordon.

Sections of our manuscript have been read before aquarium societies, both by secretaries of distant organizations and by the author himself where they are within a day's travel. The discussions which followed the readings sometimes brought out illuminating comments which are reflected in the finished work. Thanks are due the secretaries who reported back the substance of those observations.

Dr. John M. Fogg, Jr., of The University of Pennsylvania, has helped in pronunciation problems, and we are also indebted to Messrs. G. E. Merriam and Company, publishers of Webster's Standard International Dictionary, for valued suggestions.

In the general construction of this book, precedent has been disregarded. This does not at all mean that the valuable writings of others have been ignored. On the contrary, they have been carefully read, compared and checked against our own conclusions, often with benefit to the final result.

As perfection in a work of this character would be too much to hope for, despite every care, it is anticipated and hoped there will be suggestions from readers. To them we extend thanks in advance. It is largely through such sources that we hope to improve succeeding editions.

Contents

Aquarium Principles

"The best way to be free of the law is to obey it."

PRIMARY PRINCIPLES

THE principles of correct aquarium management are based on a few, easily-learned natural laws. To take advantage of them is to succeed. It is our hope to explain these laws so simply that none who follow them can fail.

The ideal aquarium is one which is self-sustaining, except, of course, for feeding the fishes. It should stay in good condition with little care. This is possible if four fundamental factors are observed. They are:

Sufficient oxygen	**Right temperature**
Enough light	**Correct feeding**

Let us take the four factors in order and see how they apply.

Oxygen

Fishes to live must, like land animals, breathe oxygen. They can get along on much less of it than do warm-blooded animals. That is why they can live on the small amount they get by absorbing dissolved oxygen from water as it passes through their gills; lungs to them. As they exhaust the oxygen from the water, more is absorbed, mostly from the contacting air. Water has an affinity for it. The cooler the water, the more air it can absorb. The larger the air surface, the more rapidly it can replenish the oxygen used. *It is the window of the aquarium.* It will, therefore, be seen that the actual fish capacity of any body of water is dependent mainly on the area of the *water surface*. Depth counts for nothing in that respect, nor cubic capacity.

There are two other ways in which oxygen is supplied. It is given off by healthy growing aquatic plants while they are under the influence of good light, or it may be supplied by artificial aeration. Each of these subjects will be considered separately.

7

The soundest principle is to have only enough fish in an aquarium so that the air-surface-per-fish is sufficient to give them ample oxygen without depending on any other source.

Aquarium Proportions From what has been said, it will be seen that those aquariums which are designed so as to give liberal air-surface to the water are best for the fishes. Tall, narrow tanks for window-sills or for special spots in decorative schemes should be populated only on the basis of water surface measurement, disregarding the depth altogether.

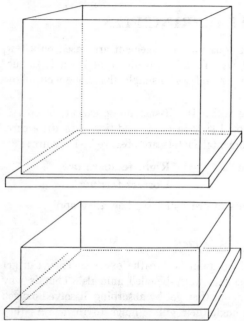

These aquariums have equal water surface areas. In theory, without the aid of plants or artificial aeration, each can maintain the same number of fishes.

The larger one, due to its extra capacity, has a greater initial supply of dissolved oxygen held in the water. In this tank the evil results of overcrowding would merely be longer postponed.

It will also be clear that when ordinary "fish globes" are used they should be filled only a little more than half way, so as to get as much water in contact with air as possible.

Aeration This is one of the modern developments in aquarium convenience. A small electric pump forces the air through a tube connected to a liberator at the bottom of the aquarium, sending up a spray of small bubbles. It is a common impression that some of this air is *forced* into the water, but such is not the case. It is all picked up by absorption, some from the bubbles, but mostly at the surface, which is steadily circulated by the rising column of bubbles, thus circulating the fresh oxygen through the whole aquarium.

Aeration is particularly valuable to turn on at night in aquariums partly depending in the daytime on the oxygen from plants, for at night

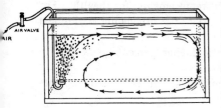

they make no oxygen and give off carbon dioxide, a gas that should be gotten rid of. It is also particularly valuable in hot weather, when the natural oxygen capacity of the water is low. Then, again, when overcrowding of fishes is unavoidable, a stream of air through the water has the effect of practically doubling the fish capacity of the aquarium. Sometimes a cloudy gray (not

Indicating the beneficial circulation of water which is set up by aeration.

green) tank can be cleared in a few days by constant aeration.

The chief disadvantage of aeration is that, if applied continuously and freely, it makes the fishes so dependent upon it that they are apt not to do so well when removed to still water. Usually a thin stream of bubbles is sufficient for ordinary purposes. Small bubbles, using a given quantity of air, are more efficient than large ones.

Number of Fish per Aquarium? Most of our exotic fishes will take a lot of punishment before coming to the surface to whisper their complaints by breathing atmospheric air. They can be overcrowded without any such demonstration. The author is in constant receipt of letters stating that the correspondent's aquarium is in beautiful condition, but that the fishes do not grow. Inquiry nearly always brings out the fact that the fishes have neither enough "elbow room" nor oxygen. (They are also often underfed. That point is covered under the heading of "Feeding," and in the paragraph on "Forcing Growth.")

After making a series of studies of aquariums under average conditions, it is believed the following will form a satisfactory but flexible basis of computation. For fish the size of grown pairs of Guppies, 3 square inches of air surface per fish. That is to say, an aquarium 9 x 20 inches, with an air surface of 180 square inches, can safely support 60 grown Guppies, giving each 3 square inches. Roughly, this would apply to all other exotic fishes of about the same size, except the labyrinth fishes or air-breathers (Betta, Paradise, etc.), which require much less.

Fishes the size of grown Swordtails, large Platies, etc., need about 8 square inches per fish (4 x 2 inches, or equivalent).

The medium Barbs, like *conchonius*, in 3½-inch size, and other fishes of equal weight should have 20 square inches per fish (4 x 5 inches, or equivalent).

Large Barbs, like grown *everetti*, and Cichlids of 5-inch length require a minimum of 54 square inches per fish (6 x 9 inches, or equivalent).

The foregoing figures are minimum requirements for health. For growth and first-class condition, the air-surface per fish should be doubled or even trebled.

A large aquarium can support a little higher percentage of fish in proportion to its size than a small one.

The computations are made from aquariums that have neither plants nor aeration.

Effects of Plants   While the subject of plants is a very important one in itself, the reader will notice that it is treated here as a sub-heading under "Oxygen." This is as it should be. Their main purpose is to supply oxygen, which they do under the influence of light. At the same time they absorb the injurious gas (carbon dioxide) which the fish (and all other animals) give off in breathing.

Besides their decorative value they serve another important end. That is the absorption of certain concentrations which are bound to accumulate where animal life is maintained in any confined space. For that reason alone an aquarium with healthy plants is better than one without them. It is this reciprocal reaction between plants and fishes, each to the benefit of the other, that gives rise to the very good, if not accurate, expression, "balanced aquarium."

Plants, besides being one of the most important subjects, is also one of the largest. To dwell in detail on it at this point would interfere with giving a reasonably brief outline of the main features of "Aquarium Principles." Having shown their place in the scheme of things, we will defer details for the present and place them in a later section on "Plants and Planting."

Light

Aquarium Location   Location depends upon whether or not the aquarist intends to use plants. If not, then the problems of placing are simplified. All that is needed is a spot where the temperature does not go to extremes and where there is enough light for the fishes to easily see their way about. While some few species (top fishes) require light for health, most of them can live satisfactorily in quite a subdued light. It should be kept clearly in mind, however, that no plants should be used where the light is very poor, for there they are a positive detriment. By "very poor" is meant a location where a newspaper cannot easily be read by daylight.

For plants of mixed varieties there should be a medium light. A position by a window where there is a good diffused light and about 2 hours of direct sun is ideal, but not indispensable. A strong north light without sun is satisfactory and, on the other hand, a position by a south window is likely to give too much sun, and a certain amount of shading becomes necessary. The great difficulty about excessive light is the growth of too much algae, resulting either in green water or a green mossy coating on glass and plants. Also too much summer sun is apt to overheat small aquariums. Altogether it is really a nice problem securing just the amount of light needed to stimulate the plants into that action which is so valuable, and yet not develop other unwanted growths. Light is like many virtues. In excess it may become a liability.

Of course, it is better being over- than under-equipped with illumination, for we can always find means of cutting it down.

Exotic fishes should not be placed in draughty locations, nor where room temperature varies greatly, such as in ventilated bedrooms.

To those who do not mind the use of electricity, the question of location, so far as light is concerned, is an easy one, for with our modern electrical equipment, daylight may be completely ignored.

Artificial Light Artificial light in the aquarium has one great advantage. It gives us accurate control, so that it is easier to furnish needed plant stimulation without encouraging algae.

The ordinary artificial illumination of a living-room, even though it penetrate into the aquarium, is worthless to plants. Electric light, to be of value to them, must be *very close,* and *preferably overhead.* Various devices are manufactured for holding bulbs in position over aquariums. Some of them have reflectors completely covering the frame. A home-made job will do. A socket can be fastened to a board to be laid across the aquarium, the bulb pointing downwards and the wires coming through holes in the board from the top. The light may be just above or in the water, so long as it is not in up to the socket. Bulbs will not break in the water unless placed there while heated. The life of filaments in submerged bulbs is greatly increased.

Roughly the amount of electric light needed per aquarium per day is as follows: For a 10-gallon tank of ordinary shape, 40 watts for 8 hours or 75 watts for 4 hours. For a 15- to 25-gallon tank, 60 watts for 6 to 8 hours. For a 25- to 50-gallon tank, 75 watts for 8 to 10 hours. These figures must be reduced if there is help from weak daylight, but increased if frosted bulbs are used. Clear bulbs are much the better.

Ultra-violet lights have no more effect on plants than ordinary bulbs. Plants are influenced more by the red end of the spectrum.

There is one important thing about artificial light which may be either an advantage or a disadvantage. It supplies heat. This is very good when needed, but in warm summer weather when the temperature is already in the eighties, it is dangerous to the fishes. At such times the light must be raised well above the water, and perhaps the aid of an electric fan called upon, arranged to blow across the water surface.

Temperature

The name "Tropicals," as has before been remarked, places too much emphasis on the idea of high temperature for all exotic fishes. A number of them are not from the tropics and quite a few of them from the tropics do *not* come from particularly warm water. It is true that most of our exotic aquarium fishes can not stand chill, but, on the other hand, many of them do not prosper in the higher temperatures because they need more oxygen than such waters carry. Placing them all in the neighborhood of 80 degrees is not sure to be the kindness that is intended by the aquarist who is a high-temperature fiend.

Nor should it be believed that there is an exact degree of heat which is best suited to each species. Most of them have a toleration of at least 10 degrees, and can stand a 5-degree change over night without injury. That is to say, if a fish has a safe toleration range of from 70 to 80 degrees (and most of them have), it would be all right for them to experience a drop from 75 to 70 spread over a period of several hours.

The one practical thing to work out, as far as individual species is concerned, is to place the tender fishes in the warmest and most uniform places, and the hardier ones in the cooler spots. Which these species are is indicated in the descriptive list.

The author believes a great deal of needless worry and expense is given to trying to keep aquariums or aquarium rooms within 2 degrees of a fixed point. Almost nowhere does Nature supply such an environment, and it has often been observed that fishes are stimulated by a reasonable change of temperature.

Nor should aquarists be too seriously concerned about the variation between the heat at the top and the bottom of the aquarium. This difference in native waters is often considerable, but the fishes negotiate it without trouble. They have the choice of selecting the level they like.

It is to be hoped that these unorthodox opinions will give no one the idea that it is a workable idea to naturalize fishes to a new climatic range. That is an old experiment which has always failed.

Fishes Outdoors In many temperate parts of the world, certain fishes from tropical countries can be placed outdoors in pools to advantage during the summer months. They can stand a greater temperature variation in large bodies of water where the general conditions are virtually perfect. Fishes that, in an aquarium, are in danger at 65 degrees, can stand 60 in a good pool. Of course, it is not wise to tempt fate too far, but the fishes are so benefited by an outdoor vacation, and often breed so beautifully, that it is a temptation to try it. The great dangers are in placing them out too soon and leaving them too long. Also, of course, they must be placed in pools where they can be caught. The setting of aquariums outdoors in a changeable climate is not recommended.

In returning the fish to indoor tanks after being outdoors for the summer, it is *most important that the same water in which they have been during the summer be used in the indoor aquariums.* Later, if desired, this can gradually be changed.

The Nest Builders all breed profusely in warm lily ponds, as do most of the Cichlids. Separation of breeding pairs from their young in large bodies of water is unnecessary. The mixing of different kinds of breeders, however, is inadvisable.

Some professional breeders, mostly south of the Mason and Dixon line, set wooden tubs in the ground and place single pairs of fishes in them for summer breeding. The tubs are covered on cold nights with sashes.

In practice, it all comes down to this: The average exotic aquarium fish is perfectly happy at an average temperature of 72-76 degrees. For short periods it can go down to 68 or up to 85 degrees without trouble. Even these extremes may be safely passed in aquariums which are in extra fine condition, and where the fishes are not crowded. If, through uncontrollable causes, the temperature drops to the extreme danger zone of the low 60's, or even the 50's, the thing to do is to slowly raise the temperature to about 80 and keep it there for 24 hours or more.

Sudden Changes While fishes may safely swim from warmer to a cooler strata in an aquarium, it is an entirely different matter changing them from a tank at one temperature to another having a difference of several degrees—either up or down. This is one of the things that just *must not be done.* The effect may not be apparent at once, but it is seldom escaped. It usually brings about the "shakers" or "shimmies," Ichthyophthirius ("ick"), fungus or a general decline. Changes should be made within 2 degrees of the same temperature.

Thermometers As average thermometers are liable to be wrong to the extent of 4 degrees or more, they should all be checked.

Feeding

"Now, good digestion wait on appetite, and health on both."

How fishes are fed is quite as important as *what*. A poor food properly handled may give better results than an excellent one used without judgment.

How Often to Feed   Temperature and oxygen directly influence the amount of food a fish can properly consume. The life processes (metabolism) of all cold-blooded animals are very much affected by temperature. The warmer they are, within their own established limits, the faster they breathe, digest, eliminate and grow. Such animals as frogs, turtles and alligators offer extreme examples of this law. With a few degrees deficiency in temperature they will refuse food for months on end. Lizards, lightning-fast in the sun, are torpid in the cool of the morning and can be picked up. An ordinary aquarium fish has an indifferent appetite at 67 degrees, a good one at 72, and a ravenous one at 77. It does not increase above 80 degrees because of the diminished oxygen content of the water at the higher temperature. Digestion and appetite are twins, and both require oxygen, as well as warmth.

Upon reflection it will be realized that exotic fishes, mostly from tropical countries, and normally leading a life that is well speeded up, need a fair supply of fuel, delivered frequently. The practical application of this thought is to feed at least twice daily instead of once. This will double the pleasure of most aquarists (for they like to feed their charges), increase the sales of the food manufacturers and make fishes bigger, better and happier.

If it is possible to feed but once daily, the morning is the best time, especially if the aquarium contains healthy, growing plants. The oxygen they develop during the day aids digestion. At night they give off carbon dioxide, which does the opposite.

Should an aquarium be kept at the lower end of its allowable scale— say 67 to 70 degrees—one feeding daily is sufficient. It is only when we get up into the 73-80 range that we need be concerned about extra feedings.

Frequent small feedings of live Daphnia are even more important than of prepared foods. The Daphnia compete with the fishes for the oxygen in the water. When their numbers are too great over a period of several hours, they do more harm than good, in extreme cases even suffocating the fishes, for they can live in more impoverished water. Give only enough Daphnia at one time so that they will all be eaten in 2 hours or less. Five feedings of a half hour's supply each is ideal, if convenient.

Mosquito larvae are different. They breathe atmosphere and take no oxygen from the water. A fairly large supply may be given the fishes, provided one is prepared to deal with the Mosquitoes which are likely to hatch from the uneaten larvae.

How Much to Feed Regardless of all other rules, theories, practices or printed instructions, the aquarist should stick tenaciously to this one: *Feed only enough prepared food at one time so that ALL of it is consumed within 5 minutes.*

The rigid application of that rule will avoid many mysterious ills, and much clouding of water.

On the other hand, light feeding is another one of those virtues which may easily become a vice. The writer favors frequent feedings, especially in well heated aquariums, but more especially if ALL of the preceding meal has been eaten and the fishes show signs of real hunger.

Floating feeding rings for dry foods have the advantage of concentrating the food within a small area, so that it does not scatter about the aquarium.

As all dried foods swell considerably when moistened, it is just as well not to at once give hungry fishes all they can eat. The fishes may experience the same disastrous results as the boy who bolted a pound of dried apples and then drank a pint of water. It is better to feed them slowly. If there are several aquariums, make two rounds of the feeding when using dried food. Some aquarists wet the food beforehand, but it always seems that the fishes prefer the flavor before it has been soaked.

Care During Absence If one must be away for a few days it seems to be safer to let the fishes go hungry rather than entrust their feeding to some one without experience. It is quite extraordinary what a number of things can go wrong when aquariums are in unfamiliar hands. In leaving the fishes unfed it may relieve the mind to remember that when they are shipped and are on the road several days they arrive without signs of starvation. Should the aquarist be away a week or more and it is necessary to call in a substitute, let the person first do an actual feeding, under instructions.

When fishes must be kept without food for several days it is better to maintain them at a temperature of 70 rather than the high range.

Substitute caretakers should err on the side of underfeeding, and of extra care (if possible) in replacing covers.

A very good plan is to leave with the novice caretaker a set of one-meal packets of food, designating the aquarium in which each is to be used.

There is a wide range of flake foods on the aquarium market, and each different food has some special value to recommend it in terms of food value or appeal to the fishes. By choosing a number of different food bases and brands the aquarist can make a very good approach to supplying a balanced diet.

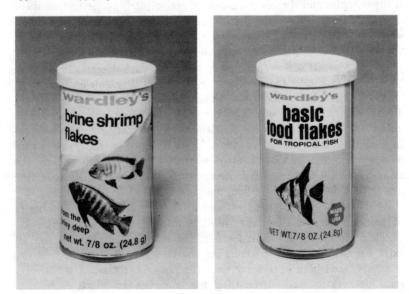

Today foods for aquarium fishes come in many different consistencies, including flakes, pellets, granules, chunks and cubes, and in dried, frozen and freeze-dried forms. The variety of good foods offered makes it easy for aquarium hobbyists to give their fishes a varied and nutritious diet.

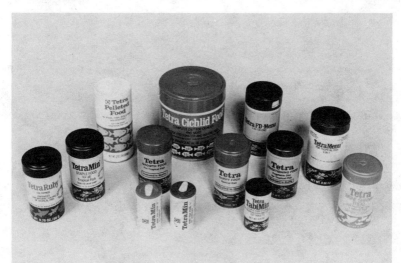

Beautiful Cardinal Tetras, **Cheirodon axelrodi**, attacking a piece of Freeze Dried Tubifex worms which have been pressed against the aquarium glass. Photo by Dr. Herbert R. Axelrod.

Both freeze-dried and frozen foods are available in a number of different food bases of both animal and vegetable origin.

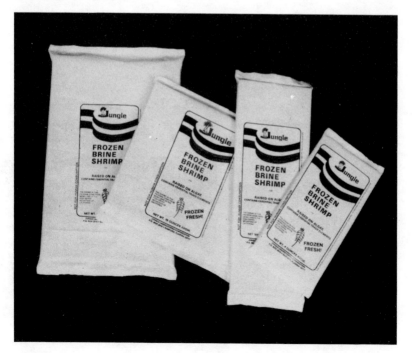

In addition to the standard types of foods to feed on a daily basis, tropical fish hobbyists also have available to them specially formulated feeding items designed to release eating materials slowly so that they can be consumed by the fishes while the aquarist is away and unable to feed them.

FISHFOODS

"The stomach is a helpless slave, but, like a slave when abused,
it takes sly and sometimes deadly revenge."

LIVE FOODS

Daphnia   Except in a few cases, live foods are not indispensable, but they are always desirable. They are important to baby fishes and they round out a needed something which few, if any, prepared fishfoods possess.

Daphnia are the best known of the living foods. They are of almost universal distribution. However, one can not go to any body of water anywhere and get what the fish might describe as a delicious dish of Daphnia. It is not as easy as that.

Daphnia pulex, About Twice Natural Size

While it is true that this little aquatic crustacean (about the size and general shape of a flea) occurs in fresh water almost everywhere, it only appears in concentrated numbers in a comparatively few places—rather unpleasant places, as a rule. It is at the margins of the pools sometimes present on city dumping grounds that we find the true "fish fan," enveloped in a cloud of mosquitoes, patiently swirling a net through evil-looking water, hoping to land a few million of the "bugs." What none but the initiated can understand is that they *like* to do it.

Collecting Daphnia   It is always difficult to tell a person what Daphnia look like and how to gather them, but let us try. The one best short-cut to this knowledge is to go out once with an experienced collector. Perhaps a member of a local aquarium society would oblige. But let us assume the worst, and start from scratch. Our photograph shows Daphnia as well as a photograph can, which is none too well. They vary in color through green, gray and red. We like them red—the redder the better. We always *hope* to find them in colonies sufficiently thick so that the mass colors the water. From a few feet away, if red, they look like a dull red or rusty cloud in the water. Perhaps the cloud will be only 2 inches across. If we are lucky, it will be 2 feet; or, if luck is running high, the whole surface of the water will be red with them, "like liver," as the Daphnia hounds gleefully describe it.

The cloud formation is not unusual, but often there are plenty of "bugs" with none in sight, and again there really are none. The Daphnia gatherer provides himself with a special kind of net, made of cheesecloth (see next page). It should be about 10 inches across, 14 inches deep and of seamless pattern, with rounded bottom. Some are made with a seam and pointed at the bottom like a reversed foolscap, but this design injures the Daphnia by concentrating their weight into a ball, if the catch is a good one. For convenience in carrying, the net should be attached to a stout, jointed pole, usually to be had in sporting goods stores or departments. A 9-foot length in 3 sections is about right.

The net is dipped into the pond and its contents reversed into a large carrying pail of water, which should be liberally iced if the weather is hot. If the Daphnia are in sight in masses, the net need only be dipped, but usually a little gentle churning is necessary. The net is moved in a figure 8 at the surface of the water for perhaps a half minute. If the Daphnia are at the bottom, this brings them up.

The uncertainty as to whether Daphnia will be found, and where, is both the vexation and fascination of the collector. Ponds go through cycles. They may be good for a time and then die down, to again ripen later. *When,* none can predict.

Daphnia need a fair amount of oxygen. Like fishes, when it is deficient, they rise to the surface. This is apt to be the case in hot weather or on humid days. Early morning, before the wind has started to stir, also finds them at the top. Where collecting competition is sharp, the true fish fanatic starts out for live food at daybreak. Future generations may smile at our working hours, but· this schedule also enables Mr.

Collecting Daphnia from a Characteristic Pond

Fancier to get to his salaried occupation at 8. At any rate, the point of this paragraph is that on crisp days the Daphnia are apt to be down, while on heavy days and early mornings they are up where they are more easily taken. When overcrowded they will come to the surface, no matter what the weather.

In cities like Philadelphia, having the average mixed temperate zone climate, Daphnia begin to be plentiful in April. They diminish in hot midsummer, do well again in October, and in favorable years can be had in reduced numbers in mild periods through the winter.

Ponds, of course, can be fished-out of Daphnia, but it is believed that moderate fishing prolongs the cycle rather than shortening it. It prevents the Daphnia from overcrowding themselves.

There are many species of Daphnia. A few kinds live in acid water, but they are not the kinds which multiply by the billion. Those gathered by aquarists live in neutral or slightly alkaline waters.

Storing Daphnia Again, like fishes, Daphnia should be given as much air surface to their water as possible. They should also be kept as cool as convenient. If not overcrowded, they will last about 2 to 3 days in summer and about a week in April or October.

Daphnia for Sale The keeping of aquariums has become so popular that the aquarium departments of many stores now sell live Daphnia. A portion twice a week will go a long way towards keeping the fishes in a small aquarium in good condition. Nearly all professional fish dealers and breeders also sell live Daphnia. Some collectors have routes which they serve. Most of us, therefore, may have live food for the fishes without the trouble (or the fun) of collecting it.

Food Value of Daphnia Daphnia, named for a beautiful Greek goddess, receives blind homage by many aquarists. It is considered to be the one perfect food, and the more of it that can be fed, the better. In riding a theory, as well as a hobby, it is well to keep the eyes open. Daphnia is truly an important fishfood, but it is not magical, nor without defects, nor even dangers. Owing to its soft but insoluble shell it acts as a laxative, and too much laxative produces a fish which is not plump. This tendency can be overcome by alternating with fishfoods containing starchy substances, such as wheat or oatmeal. Occasionally fishes die from gorging on Daphnia. This can be true of other foods, but it is more likely to happen with Daphnia, for they are excessively fond of it. As has been pointed out, fishes may be robbed of necessary oxygen by the presence of an excessive number of Daphnia.

The most serious objection to Daphnia is the company they keep. In those pools, feeding on the Daphnia, are many enemies of fishes. They are mostly larvae of small size, impossible to detect, but which grow apace when feeding on valuable aquarium fishes. Some of these are described under "Enemies." Furthermore, in recent years we are observing more and more of strange maladies attacking our exotic fishes: lumps on the body, open sores, bloody excrescences, worms emerging from the bodies or eyes. Possibly some of these distressing (and as yet incurable) maladies are brought in with the fishes from the tropics in a state of incubation, but it seems more likely that they come from some ripe Daphnia pond where thousands of forms of life swarm. In the majority of instances where these rare diseases appear, Daphnia are being fed. Having pointed out the disadvantages of Daphnia, the fact remains that their merits far outweigh their faults.

Dried Daphnia   On the assumption that Daphnia is perfect fishfood, some believe that in dried form it must be *nearly* perfect. The experience of competent aquarists does not confirm this. It is troublesome to dry, expensive, and of doubtful value except, perhaps, as a laxative, for the shells remain insoluble, while the fleshy parts dry out to practically nothing.

Artificial Propagation of Daphnia   While Daphnia is raised in large quantities by wholesale breeders having outdoor pools, and although we sometimes hear claims of persons who have raised enough in a tub to supply their fishes over winter, it may be put down for a fact that with our present knowledge of the subject it is not possible to breed enough in a tub, either summer or winter, to satisfy an average amateur's collection of fishes, even though they were fed 50 per cent on other food. It would be quite an achievement to comfortably feed a pair of 2-inch fishes for a year entirely on Daphnia grown in a tub. If we do not look for too much and are satisfied to take out an occasional light feeding, the thing can be done and it is interesting to try. An old wooden tub or trough is best. It should be in a bright light.

The best food for Daphnia is green water. This can be produced in unlimited quantities when not wanted! However, slightly alkaline water, plenty of light and a little sheep manure mixed with rotted leaves will produce either green water or other conditions favorable to the growth of Daphnia.

Open ponds may be enriched by the decomposition of almost any vegetable or animal substances.

Wholesale breeders requiring large quantities of Daphnia often have several culture ponds for the purpose. They are approximately 2 feet deep and have soil bottoms. Average size, about 50 feet square. In order to be assured of a constant supply, they are fertilized and used in rotation. The dry soil is heavily fertilized with liquid manure and soy bean flour. This is exposed to the sun until dry, thus eliminating most aquatic enemies. The pond is then filled. If Daphnia have previously been in the pond, they will soon start breeding again. If not, a few breeders should be introduced as soon as the water has turned green. Multiplication will be rapid. Ponds may be fertilized with stable litter and dead leaves, partially covered by earth.

Daphnia introduced into a duck pond usually do very well.

Drainage from a barnyard or pig-sty emptying into a pond produces a rich culture for Daphnia.

Midsummer heat is hard on Daphnia. Some protection from it would be an advantage. A source of fresh water to be used during dry periods is desirable, as the water becomes too "thick" at times.

In the fall dark little egg capsules form on the bodies of the females. These are easily seen. They drop off and hatch in the early spring. Neither frost nor drying affects them.

Mosquito Larvae   Here we consider a living food which is often present in Daphnia pools, but in many others besides. In season it is found in almost any pool that is free of fishes, especially in water containing decaying vegetation, such as old leaves. In many instances Mosquitoes place their eggs in rain puddles, which is the reason we have more Mosquitoes in rainy seasons. The larvae hatch in a few days and become "wrigglers." They are usually dark, straight, have a big head at one end and a Y-shaped ending at the other. In length they average perhaps a quarter inch when fully developed. When not eating they congregate in masses to breathe at the surface of the water, but ready to wriggle to the bottom when alarmed. For this reason it is necessary to approach them rather carefully and make one quick sweep with the net. They can be carried in water in a crowded condition. Ice is unnecessary.

Figure to left is Mosquito larva; to the right, the pupa, ready to be transformed into a Mosquito; in center is a pair of eggs. Below these is the "egg raft." It actually looks like a small bit of floating charcoal. If lifted and placed in a jar, every egg will hatch into a larva that would make a choice morsel for fishes of half-inch length or larger. *Figures greatly enlarged.*

Mosquito larvae are good food for fishes large enough to swallow them readily. Fishes about an inch in length have been known to strangle, and larger ones to overeat on them. As previously stated, this is liable to occur with other good foods. Suicide by eating is common enough in the world.

Our opinion of dried Mosquito larvae is the same as that of dried Daphnia—not worth the trouble. Drying Mosquito larvae, however, has the added merit of killing millions of prospective bloodthirsty mosquitoes.

When larvae is collected from suspiciously foul pools it is just as well to give it a rinsing in fresh water before feeding or storing.

Flies   House-flies, freshly swatted, are very fine food for larger fishes. Once they become used to them, they are always on the lookout for their owner to give them a few as a special treat.

Tubifex Worms Sometimes in Daphnia pools we find a rusty edge around the shore that looks hopefully like Daphnia, but which turns out to be a mass of wriggling, threadlike worms called Tubifex. When they are alarmed they become quiet and draw back into their cases for a short time. These are the worms that sometimes infest the soil of aquariums. They are good fishfood.

In some localities where they are more plentiful than Daphnia they are utilized as a substitute for them. It is only practicable to collect Tubifex Worms where they occur in numbers so that they form a mass. The best places for collecting are on the muddy flats of streams about a half mile below the point at which sewage is discharged. The surface mud is lifted by a shovel and placed in coarse cheesecloth or fine wire net. A stream of water is then run through the mass so that the mud is washed away and a lump of solid worms is left.

The best way to store these worms for use is to place them in a pail under a small stream of water from a tap. The worms remain in a mass in the bottom of the container. The colder the water, the longer they last. Obtainable the year round, but their collection is more a job for the professional than for the amateur. If they start to die they become dangerous fishfood, and should be disposed of.

TUBIFEX WORMS
(*Magnified, and as They Appear to the Naked Eye*

Earth Worms Having considered various natural foods from the water, let us give some attention to that choice morsel from the land, the lowly worm. It is known as the Earth Worm, Garden Worm, Rain Worm, or Fishing Worm. It is the one grand food of practically all fresh-water fishes. Nature's gift to them. Man cannot improve upon it. Even vegetarian fishes take it with relish. Game fishes probably suspect the hook but cannot resist the worm.

Not much need be said about collecting this choice food. That is a matter for local experience. The one thing to avoid is taking the evil-smelling Dung Worm, usually inhabiting manure piles, and exuding a disgusting yellow secretion. Even wild fishes will not touch them.

Small worms are more tender and generally preferable. Most of them should be chopped for aquarium fishes, except for such as large Cichlids. A pair of old scissors does it very well. These worms are fine for putting fishes into breeding condition. Gather a big supply of them in the fall for winter use. Keep in damp earth, but not wet. Feed lightly on mashed potatoes, corn meal or rolled oats. They also will eat dampened dead maple leaves placed on the surface of the soil. In many of our large cities there are live-bait stores, having Earth Worms the year round.

Glass Worms In many lakes and ponds throughout the land one may break the ice in midwinter and net out a liberal supply of live food called Glass Worms. They are the larvae of a fly, are about half an inch in length and are nearly transparent. From a top view

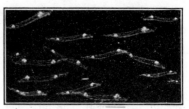

GLASS WORMS

they look something like a miniature Pike. Although popularly called Worms, they are not worm-like in appearance. They keep remarkably well in crowded conditions and will last for weeks if stored in cool water. Food value, fair.

Blood Worms Often in Daphnia ponds and other bodies of water one sees deep red, jointed worms, about half an inch long, wriggling awkwardly through the water. They are Blood Worms, the

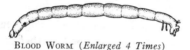

BLOOD WORM (*Enlarged 4 Times*)

larvae of Chironomus midges. Wild fishes eat them ravenously and they are good food for all except the smaller varieties of aquarium fishes. Instances have been reported of their eating their way out of fishes that had not chewed them. These worms build themselves cases, especially on decomposing wood.

White Worms These little relatives of the Earth Worm are about an inch long. They are cultivated. Cultures may be had commercially. Under proper conditions they may be multiplied copiously. Keep in covered damp soil of a light character, containing plenty of leaf-mold, etc. Every 2 days stir in as much raw oatmeal as it is found they will consume in that length of time. Or they may be fed a variety of foods placed in small holes in the soil, and covered. Mashed potatoes, cheese, bread soaked in milk, are a few of the things they like and prosper on. Overfeeding sours the soil. Mite-like creatures usually accompany them, but do no harm, nor are they related. These mites are suitable fishfood. The principal enemies of White Worms, or Enchytrae, are ants, mice and heat. It is difficult carrying them over the summer. Most amateurs buy a new culture each fall. There are many methods of getting out the worms for feeding, but a pair of tweezers dipped into a mass of them seems to be about as good as any. The worms will live for hours in the water, but it is well not to overfeed, especially in situations where the worms may crawl between stones, die and decompose.

Cyclops Almost always in Daphnia ponds we find Cyclops, a slightly smaller animal which moves rapidly in a straight line by a series of jumps. Sometimes there is a double tab on the end of the body. It is the egg-pouch of the female, and presently drops off. There is much discussion about this crustacean. In many German publications we are told to feed "sifted Cyclops" to young fishes. In this country we could not ordinarily gather a large enough mass of Cyclops to sift, and if we could, we would not use them. Leading scientific authorities assure us that Cyclops are vegetarian and that they have no jaws with which to attack fishes. Nevertheless we have found Cyclops on young fishes, and it is the almost universal opinion among successful American breeders that they are dangerous in breeding tanks. To such fishes as can catch them they are good food. Efforts at tub cultivation of Daphnia usually end by the disappearance of the Daphnia and survival of the Cyclops.

Other Live Foods While there are many good live foods other than those here described, such as Asellus, Fresh-water Shrimp, Fairy Shrimp, May Fly larvae and others, they only amount to interesting conversation for aquarists when other subjects give out—if they ever do. They cannot ordinarily be gathered in quantity. Some cereals, such as pancake flour, are apt to get wormy. If one wishes to take the trouble to sift out these fat little white worms, they are enjoyed by the fishes.

Larger Meal Worms, such as are sold in pet stores for feeding to birds, are good food for strong-jawed fishes like the Cichlids. If placed in plenty of bran in a large, covered tin box, and allowed to go through their natural beetle stage, they will multiply greatly in a few months.

Crushed small aquatic snails of any kind are good fishfood, and are especially valuable in winter when other living foods are scarce. Newly hatched Ramshorn Snails (Planorbis) are greedily eaten whole by almost any fish.

Brine Shrimp A distinct innovation in live foods is newly hatched Brine Shrimp (*Artemia salina*). The eggs, about the size of table pepper, are collected, dried and sold commercially. Unbelievable as it seems, these eggs when placed in marine water (natural or artificial) hatch in a day or two, even though they have been dry for over a year! When hatched they are miniature shrimp, about half the size of a pin head. Netted and placed in a fresh-water aquarium with baby fishes, they are greedily eaten. If the shrimp are kept in marine water containing a small amount of vegetal decomposition (lettuce, etc.) and some algae growth they may be grown to adult size of about ⅜ inch.

Infusoria   To the fish-breeder the word "Infusoria" means almost any aquatic animal organism that is of a suitable size to feed young fishes before they are large enough to negotiate small Daphnia. Many of these little animals, such as the important group of Rotifers, are not Infusoria at all, but we aquarists are used to making scientific blunders without embarrassment, so without apology we are going to use the word in its popular sense.

Averaging in size something like small dust, a finer net is needed to catch them. Fine bolting cloth is very good for the purpose. Fine muslin is also very good. Infusoria in quantity is even more uncertain of being present than Daphnia. The spring, up till hot weather, is usually a favorable time, but it appears intermittently through the summer and fall, and some species live through the winter. The larger kinds are apt to form into misty groups that can be seen as a kind of haze in the water. One of the most important species (*Brachyonus rubens*), a Rotifer that sometimes attaches itself to Daphnia, can be seen as a rusty film at the surface of the water. Often this little fellow encrusts the Daphnia so completely that it takes on a rounded appearance and keeps up its hopping motion with apparent labor. Under these conditions, if the Infusoria are not swimming through the water, it is a simple matter to collect them by first getting the Daphnia, placing them in a very fine sieve and running water through them. The Infusoria are knocked off and pass through the screen, which is too fine for the Daphnia to go through. Another important species containing much solid substance, and on which young fishes grow prodigiously, is *Hydatina senta,* which appears in its greatest profusion in the very early spring before the Daphnia have a good start. Both of these species are large enough that a muslin net will hold them.

Cultivation of Infusoria   The spores which form Infusoria are present in the air everywhere. When they land in water in which decomposition is going on, they find a favorable environment and multiply. The practical way to get a culture is to set up a little decomposition and await results, which usually appear in a few days. A variety of materials are used for this purpose, including some commercially prepared articles. One method is to dry lettuce leaves either in the sun or over a radiator. Crumble them and sprinkle enough on the surface of the water to cover it. Lettuce, spinach or other leaves may be used raw, but no Infusoria develop until these start to decay. Aquariums containing snails which eat heavily, like the four-horned Ampullaria, soon develop Infusoria. The snails gorge on lettuce or other leaves. Their partially digested droppings make an ideal medium of culture.

An old laboratory method of developing Infusoria is to pour boiling water on hay and allow it to stand a few days. Established aquariums which have not been kept too clean always contain some Infusoria, but only enough to give the baby fishes a start.

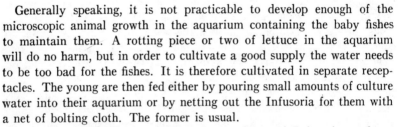

To the left is the "Slipper Animalcule" or Paramœcium (pronounced Para-mee'see-um), much the commonest organism produced in the artificial culture of Infusoria. It thrives on the products of organic decomposition and can live in either foul or good water. Its food value to newly hatched fishes is fair.

At the right is the Rotifer, *Hydatina senta* (pronounced High'da-tie'na sen'ta), one of the best of microscopic live foods. It occurs in Daphnia ponds and elsewhere; most abundantly in the early Spring months. The two figures are shown in their relative sizes.

Generally speaking, it is not practicable to develop enough of the microscopic animal growth in the aquarium containing the baby fishes to maintain them. A rotting piece or two of lettuce in the aquarium will do no harm, but in order to cultivate a good supply the water needs to be too bad for the fishes. It is therefore cultivated in separate receptacles. The young are then fed either by pouring small amounts of culture water into their aquarium or by netting out the Infusoria for them with a net of bolting cloth. The former is usual.

It has been found that aeration in a culture of Infusoria tends to prevent that foulness which is often present. This both prolongs the life of the organisms and makes them better food for fishes.

Mr. Lee Ayres, chemist at the Shedd Aquarium, recently developed a method of feeding selected cultures of Infusoria, so as to produce them in succession, or when wanted.

The ingredients of the food are split green peas, Ralston's Breakfast Food and clean timothy hay, finely chopped. To make a week's supply of food for 7 one-gallon culture jars, take 1 level teaspoonful of split peas, 2 like measures of Ralston's and 2 heaping tablespoonfuls of chopped hay. Boil slowly until peas are disintegrated. Add boiled water to make a gallon. In each gallon jar place a pint of this liquid and its settlings. Fill the balance of the jar with boiled water. Set exposed to air for 3 days and then add one of the commercial cultures of Infusoria. Cover with glass and in a week the culture will be ready.

If a specific culture is not being worked with, prepare the food as directed, use raw water and leave the mixture exposed continuously to the air. Medium temperature and mild diffused light are best.

At the time the harvest of live food is taken from the first jar, prepare a new lot of boiled food if a continuous supply of Infusoria is desired. Siphon off half the culture jar (from the top), replace with a pint of boiled and cooled mixture, and fill up the jar again with tap water. The next day follow the same procedure with jar number 2, and so on. In a week jar number 1 has cleared up and is ready with a new crop.

While this formula calls for the use of a pint feeding from each jar, it should not be assumed that a pint is in all instances the correct amount to be used. We would estimate that a pint placed in a 10-gallon aquarium containing a fair number of fry would be sufficient. A simple microscope should be used to check on the success of the cultures.

ENEMIES

Fortunately there are few serious enemies of fishes in the aquarium. The three outstanding ones all smuggle themselves in with our supply of live foods. Since one of these enemies is far more destructive than all others combined, we will give it first consideration.

Water Tiger This sleek, spindle-shaped creature is the larval form of a large Water Beetle (Dytiscus), which itself is also a powerful enemy of fishes. There are several species, but in effect, as far as the aquarist is concerned, they are all one. Our illustration gives a clear idea of its formation, but the great difficulty is that in its smallest size it is hard to pick it out from among the Daphnia upon which it feeds. The pincers, or mandibles, are hollow, and through these they rapidly suck the blood of their victims. Growth is rapid and they soon attain a size where they attack tadpoles, fishes or any living thing into which they can bury their strong bloodsuckers.

Water Tiger and Victim

Theirs is one of those appetites which "grows by what it feeds upon," and they move steadily from victim to victim. In a size such as illustrated they would soon clear an ordinary aquarium of its fishes, but these big ones are not so dangerous because they are easily detected. It is the half-inch fellows, moving quietly about among young fishes, that do the wholesale damage. In a few days entire hatchings are liable to disappear, and all that remains is a Water Tiger, which, by that time, is probably an inch in length. What helps make these larvae so deadly is that they are good swimmers.

Vigilance is the only protection against them. Large, hard-mouthed fishes will eat them. Destroying them gives double pleasure to parent Cichlids while tending their flocks of young.

The victim in our illustration was a medium-sized female Guppy. She was dead in a matter of seconds and within a minute was shriveled and pale. The Water Tiger breathes air through its rear end and, therefore, must occasionally come to the surface. This one maintained a breathing position during the bloodsucking.

Dragon Fly Larvae Although not nearly so deadly as Water Tigers, these larvae have a more widely heralded reputation as killers. Their disadvantage is that they have to lie in wait for their victims and seize them from below with a much smaller and less

Dragon Fly Larva With "Mask" Extended (Viewed from below)

effectual pair of pincers. These pincers are on the end of a "mask," a contrivance having hinged joints, so that it normally lies folded just below the head, but ready to be extended in an instant when within striking distance of a victim. When attacking a fish as large as that in the illustration, the pincers frequently fail to penetrate the scales, and slip off. It was not until they finally caught on the lower edge of the gill plate that a fastening was secured. While holding the fish with the pincers, the larva slowly chewed at the side of the fish with a mouth better equipped for swallowing small victims. After a minute in this position the fish was released by the photographer and it soon recovered from two slight wounds. This account is not intended to minimize the danger from these larvae, for in a little longer time the fish would have been killed and consumed. Smaller ones are effective in proportion.

Dragon Fly Larva Holding Live Fish
(*The Floating Plants Are Duckweed*)

Although there are more Dragon Fly Larvae than of Water Tigers, they are less likely to be collected with Daphnia, for they usually lie half concealed in the mud, whereas the Water Tigers are swimming about.

Aquarists having outdoor pools are the principal sufferers from Dragon Fly Larvae. Strange as it may seem, there are many persons who do not know what a Dragon Fly looks like. We therefore show one of those beautiful and otherwise useful creatures—useful because they are among the best of mosquito catchers. When seen hovering over a pool, there is danger that they may deposit eggs there. Careful breeders often

Dragon Fly, or "Devil's Darning Needle"

screen their outdoor water to exclude this and other visitors. The Damsel Fly, much smaller in size and with wings that come to rest along the body, have larvae that are similar, smaller and less dangerous.

Hydra These low forms of life are enemies of any small water creatures that can be caught by their peculiar method. So far as the aquarist is concerned, Hydra catch baby fishes up to a size of $\frac{3}{16}$ of an inch. They also devour Daphnia.

In form they are extremely variable. The fact that they can contract themselves almost to the point of invisibility makes it impossible to detect them in a can of Daphnia. Even worse is the fact that any broken bit of a Hydra soon develops into a new, complete specimen.

The usual appearance of a colony of them is like pendant, slowly swaying gray or green hairs, about a half inch long or less. From the main thread are from 3 to 7 tentacles, spread starlike. They are usually found attached to the glass and the plants. It is rather surprising to find that they can move about. They use alternately their tentacles and their suction foot in a clumsy kind of locomotion, but they eventually arrive.

The body, and especially the tentacles, contain many sharp barbs, filled with a numbing poison. As a prospect passes near, the apparently inert Hydra springs into action, injects a "shot" into its victim, draws it into a mouth from which the tentacles radiate, digests it and presently discharges the undigested portions from the same opening. When business is brisk, a Hydra may have a Daphnia or a young fish held by each tentacle, to be swallowed at leisure.

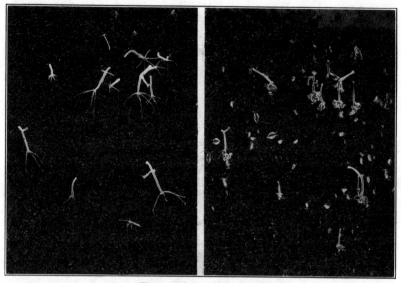

HYDRA (*Slightly Enlarged*)

Difficult as it may be to realize, the same Hydra are on both sides of the illustration, unchanged in location. To the right they have just been fed Daphnia.

Immediately following a "strike" the creature undergoes a marked change in form, becoming much more compact. This lasts until digestion is completed. Multiplication usually takes place by budding, and under the influence of plenty of food, is rapid.

The larger young live-bearers, like Mollienisia, are a little too big for them to negotiate. Their favorites are the babies of the different egg-laying species.

The easiest and safest way to get rid of this rather interesting pest is by introduction into the aquarium of a few Three-spot Gouramis (*Trichopodus trichopterus*). Give them no other food and they will soon devour the Hydra. *Trichogaster leeri* will do the same service. If these fishes are not available the Hydra may be killed by removing the fish and raising the aquarium temperature to 105 degrees for a quarter hour.

Hydra has been successfully eliminated without injury to plants or fishes by the use of quinine sulphate. Prepare a stock solution of 7 grains dissolved in a pint of warm water. Of this solution use 4 teaspoonsful to each gallon of aquarium water. It is effective in 4 days.

Other Enemies   Two questionable intruders which sometimes enter with Daphnia are Water Boatmen (Corixidae) and Back-Swimmers (Notonectidae). They may be introduced while very small or in larger sizes. It is a well established belief that they are enemies of young fishes. The writer has conducted experiments with a view to settling the question. To date the verdict is "Not guilty," but in view of the generally accepted contrary opinion, we include a picture of one of them in our Rogues' Gallery. There is no doubt whatever that some of them can inflict a severe bite when

BACK-SWIMMERS

handled. Plenty of herbivorous animals can do the same thing. They swim with a rowing movement of the two long, oar-like legs.

Beetles   Most Water Beetles live on other insects or animals. They seldom get into the aquarium, but should be immediately removed when discovered, whether small or large.

Fish Lice (Argulus)   These very efficient arthropods are like a thin, nearly transparent wafer, almost a quarter inch in diameter. In culture ponds they have become a serious menace to Goldfish and have also been found on other aquarium fishes when introduced on the Goldfish. They are free-swimming, but in a moment can attach themselves tenaciously to the body or fin of a fish, where they proceed to drink blood at leisure. As this parasitic animal becomes prolific only in ponds or pools, we will not go further into the subject than to say that it can be carefully scraped off the fish with the point of a knife. The reason for mentioning it here is to aid in identification. Many owners erroneously believe their exotic fishes to be infested with "lice" when they are observed to scratch or rub themselves against objects in the aquarium. It should be said that Argulus is not a louse. That is merely a popular name. A thorough article on the subject, including a method of destroying the pests in pools, appeared in the September, 1933, issue of "The Aquarium."

Anchor Worm   A distressing parasite appeared a few years ago on Goldfishes from Japan, and they have multiplied in certain wholesale hatcheries, so that they are now spread in the United

States. Some South American fishes, especially Cichlids and large Characins, have arrived bearing similar unwelcome guests. They are threadlike worms, over a half inch long, fastened into the body of the fish with a cruel anchor that tears the flesh when extracted. They, too, require pool conditions in order to prosper. There is no known chemical treatment which will kill the worms without injury to the fish. With large fishes they may be extracted and the spot touched with mercurochrome. In small fishes it is better to allow the worm to die naturally over a period of some weeks. The fish has some chance of surviving. This disgusting parasite has a free-swimming, microscopic stage, when it can be killed by permanganate of potash, using the same treatment as for Fish Lice.

Outdoor Enemies In outdoor ponds or pools the fishes have to contend with special enemies. Frogs will eat any moving thing nearly as large as themselves. Then we have Snakes, Rats, Cats, Kingfishes, Blackbirds, Starlings, Water Turtles and Boys. Ground-level ponds are, of course, the more susceptible to several of these invaders.

Such enemies as the adult sizes of the Predaceous Diving Beetle, Giant Water Bug (Electric Light Bug), Dragon Fly Larva and Water Tiger, which are easily detected in the aquarium, are much more difficult to control in planted ponds, or where the water is not clear. Here, again, vigilance, helped by screening, is our best weapon.

DISEASES

Fortunately, far fewer diseases and parasites attack our fishes in the aquarium than they do in Nature. This is probably because the aquarium does not furnish favorable conditions for the life cycles which many of them undergo.

Ichthyophthirius The only very common disease which gives us much concern is popularly called "Ick," being short for Ichthyophthirius, the name of the parasitic protozoan causing the trouble. The malady by some is aptly called the "pepper and salt disease," because in the advanced stage the small white specks on the fins and body of the victim resemble seasoning. At first only a few specks are seen, but unless treatment is given they multiply rapidly until the body and fins are almost covered. A coating of fungus follows, and death soon follows the fungus.

The cause of attacks of Ichthyophthirius and closely similar parasitic diseases is nearly always chill. Chill works doubly against the fish. Its own resistance becomes reduced, while the vitality of the parasite is increased at lower temperatures. Sudden temperature change is dangerous, even without cool water, say in reducing from 78 to 72 degrees.

The organism causing the trouble is one of the low forms of animal life, being a simple cell covered with swimming hairs. It burrows just below the outer skin of the fish, the irritation causing a tiny pimple. In this the parasite prospers on the fluids and tissues of its host, causing an itching, which is evidenced in the early stages by the efforts of the fish to scratch itself against objects in the aquarium.

A Tilapia Attacked by Ichthyophthirius

In a few days it has reached its maximum size of one millimeter, leaves the fish, drops to the bottom, forms a cyst and breaks up into from 500 to 2200 young. Not all these young succeed in reaching a host, but enough do so that the progress of the disease sweeps on "like wildfire."

The important thing, of course, in checking the parasite is to break into its life cycle at the weakest point. This is in the early free-swimming stage. Several successful methods have been developed. They all call for heat, either with or without the addition of medication. Many men of experience are of the opinion that simple heat is not only the best, but the only effective remedy. However, the consensus of thought, after a great deal of observation, is that the addition of 2% Mercurochrome helps, using about 4 drops to the gallon of aquarium water. Fishes can stand twice that amount, but where greater strengths have been employed, there has been suspicion of later signs of mercurial poisoning. The plants do not seem to be injured by a reasonable amount of the drug.

The use of Methylene Blue, 2 drops of 5% aqueous solution to the gallon of water, in conjunction with 85-90 degree temperature, is one of the newer treatments. It has no injurious after-effects, of which Mercurochrome is suspected.

After either of the foregoing treatments have effected a cure, which should be within a week, it is well to siphon from the bottom about half the aquarium depth and replace with unused, seasoned water.

Acid water of 6.2 reading (see "What is pH?") is said to make life hard for the parasites. Also sea salt, one level tablespoonful to the gallon of water, helps, but this is strong enough to injure plants.

Regardless of what treatment is used, the temperature of the water, if possible, should be slowly raised to 85 degrees and kept there for several days.

The germs of this organism are not carried through the air like the spores of fungus or of green-water algae. In an absolutely sterilized aquarium, fishes will die of chill without developing Ichthyophthirius, but in ordinary practice it is difficult to produce or to maintain water in that condition. Biologists state that the microscopic young die in 60 hours if they fail to find a host, but if this is true there must be some unknown way in which the life of the organism can be indefinitely suspended, for an epidemic has often been produced by chilling an aquarium that had been subject to no recent contamination, and which for a long preceding period had not been attacked. In any case, all aquarium implements should be well sterilized and water splashings into other tanks avoided when handling a case.

Aquarists are often puzzled as to why, in a tank of mixed species, only certain kinds may be affected by "Ick." This is for several reasons. The parasites prefer certain hosts. Some fishes withstand chill better than others. Certain species in an aquarium will be in better health than their companions, due to the aquarium conditions and food being more suited to themselves.

It should be remembered that it is by no means a sure indication of "Ick" if fishes scratch or rub themselves against objects. It could very well be "Flukes" or some other parasitic disease. Treatment for Ichthyophthirius should not be given unless the little white spots are observed. When these are seen, no time should be lost.

Dropsy   One of the strangest of our fish diseases is dropsy. It is also one of the most unpleasant in appearance. The fish becomes puffed and the scales stand out at an angle to the body. Sometimes the eyes have a tendency to bulge. The puzzling thing about the malady is the unaccountable way in which it singles out individual fishes. It is never epidemic. Although some aquarists believe that the trouble arises from faults in diet, the fact remains that it strikes without apparent regard to what the fish has been fed, and it is just as likely as not to single out a fish in a pool where the conditions seem to be perfect, and where nothing but the best live food has been used.

Some species seem to be more subject to dropsy than others. *Colisa lalia, Danio malabaricus* and *Brachydanio rerio* are among the more susceptible.

The disease is fatal in from one to three weeks. Most fanciers destroy the unfortunate victims at once. Reports of cures by the use of extract of digitalis have persisted for many years, but apparently without a basis of fact.

Flukes Why this disease is so named we do not know. It is caused by a parasitic animal called Gyrodactylus, which lodges in the skin and gills. The fish dashes wildly about and comes to a sudden stop, exhausted. There are other maladies which cause fishes to act in this way, but since we know little or nothing about them, the treatments here described may as well be applied.

Flukes can be cured in a bath of one part of glacial acetic acid to 500 parts of water (one drop to an ounce), the treatment lasting 20 seconds and being repeated in two days.

Another treatment is 20 drops of formaldehyde to a gallon of water. Leave the fish in this bath until it shows signs of exhaustion, which is usually in from 5 to 10 minutes. Repeat as in previous formula.

A third remedy consists in a 2-hour bath in a solution of permanganate of potash, ¼-grain-to-the-gallon-of-water, used in a perfectly clean, bare receptacle. A 1-grain permanganate tablet, in 4 gallons of water, makes the correct strength. First dissolve completely in a pint of warm water.

The disease is highly contagious and the aquarium should be sterilized after removal of fishes by a 2-hour treatment of permanganate of potash, ¾ grain to each gallon of aquarium water. Siphon and refill.

Itch This is different from "Ick." The fishes seem to itch, but do not develop white spots, nor do they dash about as with Flukes. Neither is it usually fatal. The cause arises from numerous organisms which develop from too many settlings and uneaten food in the aquarium. Remove nothing and give the aquarium a ¼-grain-to-the-gallon permanganate treatment for 2 hours. Siphon the bottom, drawing off about half the water, and replace with clear, seasoned water. The remaining permanganate will soon clear itself.

Fungus A white, slimy coating on fishes, usually following the first stages of Ichthyophthirius, but it sometimes appears independently. In either case it is caused by a Fungus called Saprolegnia. Mild salt water is effective, using 3 level teaspoonsful to the gallon of water or one part of sea water to 5 of fresh. This is the best form of salt treatment, with genuine sea salt the second best. Treat for several days at a temperature between 75 and 80, preferably with aeration.

The permanganate treatment as for the Flukes is also good. Mercurochrome is sometimes used. Salt seems to be the best.

Fishes are made susceptible to Fungus by bruises, attacks of other fishes, sudden temperature change, chill, overfeeding and poor general condition.

Mouth Fungus This is a wicked disease, of which we know little. A cottony fluff appears at the lips, gets into the mouth and soon starts eating the jaws away. Unless action is taken very quickly it is likely to kill all the fish that have been exposed to it. The progressive salt treatment should be given. If possible, use seasoned water in a clean receptacle. Dissolve one heaping teaspoonful of sea salt in each gallon of water and put in the fish. Increase the salt content by the same amount twice more, 2 hours apart each time. That is to say, that in 6 hours there will be 3 teaspoonfuls of salt to each gallon of water. Leave the patients in until cured (if!) and gradually reduce salt in water so that the change on being returned to the aquarium will be only slight. If the fish live a week they are likely to recover. Aeration during treatment helps.

Wounds Nothing seems to be better for wounds than touching them with 2% Mercurochrome, which is the strength supplied commercially.

Recovery is further helped by keeping the fish in slightly acid water, about pH 6.6, or else in water which has been boiled, cooled and aerated. The container should also be sterilized.

Shakes or "Shimmies" A description of this trouble is not easily made, but most aquarists have seen it, and once seen it is always remembered. The fish usually stays stationary, wabbling its body from side to side, in a slow, clumsy motion. It is like swimming without getting anywhere. There are several causes, but the principal one is chill. Many aquarists declare their fishes to have been afflicted in this way without having been chilled, but probably they are mistaken. A short drop in temperature may do it and the effect lasts long.

Fishes with Ichthyophthirius are apt to "shimmy." This shaking is merely a manifestation of trouble and is not a definite disease in itself, any more than chills are with us. Aside from the remedy already mentioned, the usual successful treatment is a persistently applied temperature of about 78-80 degrees.

Indigestion is, no doubt, another cause. There is reason to believe that a too dirty aquarium gives rise to quantities of microscopic organisms which cause the fish to act in this way, for cases have often been instantly cured merely by a complete change of water, the new water, of course, having been duly seasoned. This is the best thing to try first, unless the cause is either chill or "Ick."

Wasting When a fish falls away and becomes hollow-bellied, it is just too bad. Sometimes it is caused by too light feeding, or unsatisfactory food. Persistent overcrowding is another cause. Continued overheating can do it, as well as prolonged low temperature. It must be remembered that fishes, like all other animals, die of old age. In that case they waste away.

Whatever the cause, an emaciated fish seldom survives, although it may last for some time. The only hope is to give the fish plenty of room, as much nourishing food as it can eat, and a temperature of about 76 degrees. A change in diet to something like scraped raw fish, chopped earth worms or live Daphnia, alternated with scrambled egg, may help.

Swim Bladder Trouble The great majority of fishes are equipped with a very wonderful mechanism which enables them to remain balanced, almost without effort, in any reasonable depth of water. It is a flexible bladder, filled, not with air, but with gas generated by the fish. It may be seen elsewhere in our picture of *Ambassis lala*. For this balancing system to be effective the amount of internal pressure must be precisely right. With too little gas the fish sinks; with too much it floats. Sometimes floating is temporarily caused by intestinal gases. Usually floating or sinking is caused by some derangement of the swim bladder, and is incurable. It seems to be caused by a constitutional weakness, often due to chill. Warmth and the laxative effect of a diet of Daphnia or chopped earth worms may give relief.

Other Troubles There is a list of rare troubles of which we aquarists know little or nothing. Cysts, lumps on fishes, blindness, partial paralysis, worms eating through from the inside, sudden death with no outward sign of disease, are all things we hear of and hope some day to learn more about. No doubt there are internal parasites which defy treatment. Many of them must have free-swimming stages in which they can be killed. Just on general principles, when we do not know what to do, we try an attack from that side, either by placing the fish in acid water (about pH 6.4) for a week or two, or else for 4 hours in a bath of permanganate of potash, $\frac{1}{8}$ grain to the gallon of water, repeating every few days until the fish is either better or "better off" dead.

Check-ups It not infrequently happens that aquarium conditions seem to be ideal, the aquarist has been careful about feeding and temperature, yet the fishes are low in vitality or otherwise ailing.

All conditions have their causes, however obscure they may be. Sometimes these causes are beyond the range of our knowledge, but there are several important points on which a re-check can be made. Here are some of them:

Is there a possibility of concealed dead fish or snails?

Has the water an unpleasant smell? If so, it should be partially changed and aerated, either by pump or hand pouring. A sprinkling pot serves temporarily. If the cover is down tightly, raise it a little.

Is there enough light for the plants? Have they a good green color? Are they growing? Are there plenty of them? Plants which are not prospering are a detriment.

Is the pH of the water within a range between 6.6 and 7.4? For ordinary fishes that is the allowable variation.

Is there much accumulation of sediment? If so, try siphoning it off.

Has the water been green and then turned yellow? In that case it should be changed.

Have the fishes been chilled within a month, or are they being kept at 68 degrees or a little lower? Persistent heat (about 76 degrees) will probably pull them up.

On the other hand, there are heat fanatics who never let the aquarium water drop below 80. If and when the fishes weaken in this tropical temperature, try something about 74-76.

Are others successfully using aquarium water from the same source as yours? Sometimes the water of a whole community is unsuited to fishes, particularly if sulphur is present, or if the water is highly alkaline. In that case, get water from another source. Distilled water containing a teaspoonful of cooking salt to the gallon is satisfactory. Avoid non-caking table salt. Distilled water can be corrected by adding a small lump of ordinary chalk, or with lumps of marble, or broken oyster-shell.

Are the fishes overcrowded? This is possible without their coming to the surface to announce it. See paragraph, "Number of Fish per Aquarium?"

Is the food right? Finding no other clue to trouble, try a change, especially to a live food, or to scraped and finely minced raw fish.

Have the fishes been underfed? It is possible to be over-conservative in this. At a temperature of 72-80 degrees they should have two meals per day.

How about metal poisoning? Sometimes nickel-plating on electric heaters chips away and exposes brass. Condensed water on covered brass aquariums can trickle down and do damage. Brass, copper or aluminum in contact with aquarium water will eventually cause trouble.

What about coal gas, paint fumes, or even excessive tobacco smoke?

General Management

Green Water The facts about green water appear to be so simple that this should be an easy matter to control, but it is not. The green cloudiness unaccountably rises to confound the ablest aquarists and the humblest of authors—even those who tell others how to keep water clear.

We know that the color is produced by microscopic vegetal cells that must have food and light in order to develop. By taking away either or both of these stimulants, we would have no green water, but that is not easy when we have fishes present which enrich the water both by their breathing and their droppings, and which themselves, along with plants, require light.

Yet, on the other hand, it is perfectly true that there are numberless aquariums which are healthy and clear, year after year. It would seem we should be able to reproduce the same condition at will. To a great extent, we can. In such aquariums we nearly always find plenty of strong, growing plants, usually Vallisneria or Sagittaria. The reason is that they successfully compete with the green cells (suspended algae) for both food and light.

In these perpetually clear tanks, two other things will be observed. The fishes are not crowded and there is only enough light to keep the plants in good condition. That is another way of pointing out that if there is only enough supply of life elements to keep the plants going, and with practically no excess left, then the green organisms are kept in subjection.

Slightly acid water tends to check most vegetable growth. While it produces cleaner water, it also discourages the plants.

Many of these green water cells go through periods of activity. If allowed to subside naturally, the water may remain clear for a long time.

Oppositely, many of them are only stimulated by a partial change of aquarium water, and start out on a fresh rampage.

To briefly condense the reasons into practice: When green water appears, remember it is not an unmitigated evil. It is healthy. It oxygenates the water. It will disappear if left alone. It *does* ruin the

44

scenery. Therefore cut down the light. Papers placed on the light side of the aquarium will aid. A floating mantle of Riccia, Duckweed or Salvinia in the aquarium supplies an agreeable means of cutting down the light and of furnishing added vegetal competition. *It is the most effective single factor in keeping the water clear.* Such a mantle will *not* cut down the oxygen-absorbing capacity of the water surface. Difficult to explain, but true.

Remove some fishes if crowding is suspected. Feed less. Every scrap of food becomes fertilizer. Siphon the bottom frequently. Use only enough water for replacement.

When green water reaches the "soupy" stages and is very opaque, it is dangerous, especially in hot weather. It is liable to suddenly decompose and kill the fishes. A change to a slightly yellowish tinge is the danger signal. This calls for an immediate change of water. Minutes count.

Cloudy Water Green water is cloudy, but cloudy water is not necessarily green. There is a difference with a distinction. Both are frequently caused by unabsorbed organic matter in the water, due to too many fishes and an excess of fish waste. Suspended algae feeding and prospering on it causes green color, while gray cloudiness is produced by bacteria doing the same thing. Nature is always trying to balance the water. In light places algae are used; in darker ones, bacteria. The treatment for both, up to a certain point, is the same. That is, the use of more plants to absorb the organic matter, and a reduction in the number of fishes producing it. On the other hand, there may already be enough plants but insufficient light to stimulate them into action, so that in this case *more* light is needed.

Newly set aquariums are likely to be clouded from sand that is not well cleaned. Also they are particularly subject to gray cloudiness because the plants have not yet begun to fully function. For every reason it is better to have an aquarium planted and in a favorable light a week before the fishes are introduced. Even then the aquarium should not be taxed with its full limit of fishes in the beginning. A small start is better, adding a few from time to time.

Clearing Water Correction of underlying causes has been indicated for the different kinds of cloudy water, but there are ways in which clearing can be hurried. Gray cloudiness can be reduced in a few days by constant aeration. If fishes are removed from a green-water aquarium, it can be cleared by the introduction of Daphnia. Filtering, described elsewhere, will improve conditions caused by larger particles of organic matter in the water. No aquarium filter will remove green-water algae nor cloudy-water bacteria, but they can be precipitated chemically. One method is to dissolve ⅟₆ grain by weight of permanganate of potash into each gallon of aquarium water. At this strength nothing needs to be removed. The water clears in a day or two, but it will cloud again if the same conditions continue.

Filters   The days of making your own filter have long passed. There are many types of filters on the market. Many are placed under the gravel, some are boxes inside the aquarium, while others are boxes outside the aquarium. For the beginner, the best filter is an undergravel filter. The first undergravel filter was invented by Norman Hovlid. He called his filter the "Miracle" filter. It was advertised as *"You never need change the water in your aquarium."* This is certainly the type of filter for most aquarists. It is available in all sizes for every shape of aquarium. While many imitations have appeared on the market, they have all had to make changes from the original design to "get around" the Hovlid patent.

Power filters, such as the famed Eheim filter made in Germany, are recommended only for tanks of 10 gallons or larger. They filter the water so thoroughly that they remove almost everything in suspension, even Ich! They have the unique advantage of being able to be hidden under the aquarium, or placed away from the aquarium, so the tank doesn't look like a jumbled mess. They are absolutely silent, too.

Metals in Water   Metal in contact with aquarium water should be avoided where possible, although a well plated chromium job is considered safe. Lead and block tin have little effect. Aluminum disintegrates, while copper and copper alloys (chiefly brass and monel) are poisonous. Galvanized iron is dangerous. Iron is not poisonous, but its rust is unsightly.

Sometimes the cement chips away from the corners of a brass-framed aquarium and exposes the metal to the water. Re-cementing is needed.

A thing to be particularly avoided is having two different kinds of metal present in aquarium water, especially in contact.

Trouble sometimes occurs when water of condensation collects on defectively plated or aluminum top reflectors, and runs down into the aquarium. Even such water that gathers between glass covers and the aquarium frame can, in time, poison the water, especially if brass is exposed. Nickel plating does not last well in water.

Water Quality The household water supplied by most cities and towns is satisfactory for aquarium use. It should be nearly neutral as to acid or alkaline quality and reasonably free from objectionable minerals like sulphur. There are whole districts where the water is not suitable. These are usually in strong alkaline districts, or where certain types of artesian water are used, for they, too, are apt to be alkaline, or to contain objectionable algae. We re-state the fact that distilled water is satisfactory for aquarium use, but a little rock salt should be added to it; about a level teaspoonful to the gallon. Also, when the quality of city water is suspected, it is a good idea to try water from some pond or stream known to contain plenty of fishes.

What is "pH"? The letters pH, which are sometimes seen in connection with certain problems regarding aquarium water, are symbols. Just what they mean and why these particular letters are used is a subject entirely too technical to be attempted here. An explanation of the practical application is a simpler matter.

A reading of the pH of any water means that we apply a test to it showing its acidity, neutrality or alkalinity. Acids and alkalis are two great classes of chemical compounds. They are in a sense opposites, like positive and negative electricity. They tend to neutralize each other when mixed. A neutral balance can be established by placing the correct amounts of acid and alkali together; or any strength in either direction can be had by varying the amounts of the two opposing substances.

Remarkably sensitive and easily applied tests have been developed, which not only tell whether water is neutral, acid, or alkaline, but also the degree of acidity or alkalinity. This degree is known in science as "hydrogen-ion concentration" but this is another technical term with which we need not be concerned.

The test for aquarium water is to add one drop of bromthymol blue to 20 drops of the water to be tested. If it turns pale green, the water is neutral. If yellow, acid. If blue, alkaline. The depth of yellow or blue shows the concentration in either direction. Color comparison scales, necessary for correct readings, are supplied by manufacturers of test sets. Very simple and inexpensive sets are made especially for use by aquarists. A scale has been adopted by scientists in which 7.0 is the neutral point. Below 7.0 is acid, and above is alkaline. The higher the figure, the more alkaline; the lower, the more acid. In the tabulation below it will be seen that for the purpose of accurate determination, numbers have been subdivided into fractions of two-tenths. Color matching standards are provided for each of these subdivisions.

Acid	Neutral	Alkaline
6.0, 6.2, 6.4, 6.6, 6.8 (Yellow)	7.0 (Green)	7.2, 7.4, 7.6 (Blue)

APPLICATION. One of the necessities in the life of many organisms is that they be in an environment having a pH suited to themselves. For example, it is accepted as a fact that the germs of some common colds need an acid condition, and that they die in one that is alkaline. Plants have proven preferences. Agriculture has profited tremendously by knowledge of that fact. F. J. Myers has pointed out that a pH reading of any water in Nature will indicate which of the many species of rotifers are liable to be found at that point. We know that our important friend, *Daphnia pulex,* can prosper in a big way only in alkaline water.

And now aquarists are turning serious attention to the subject, with the double hope of disease control and the propagation of certain species of fishes which up to now have proven difficult. Most of our aquarium fishes can tolerate a range of from 6.4 to 7.6, although possibly they may be able to breed only at some point between these extremes. The majority of their microscopic enemies have no such toleration. Most of them die in acid water, some in alkaline. On the other hand, it must not be overlooked that nearly all of our aquarium plants are naturally associated with alkaline conditions and that they slowly decline in acid water.

As yet we have little definite knowledge as to the effect of pH variations on different species of fishes and on their breeding. In Nature, owing to rains, the condition of water changes without apparent injury to the fishes, and it must also be admitted that certain species are found at different points where the pH readings are not the same. Undoubtedly some species have more toleration than others.

We believe we have arrived at conclusions of value regarding the pH requirements of a few species, and the probable needs of others. These few are noted later, under their individual headings.

Fishes should not be subjected to pH changes of more than 4/10 on the scale per day, taken in 2 steps of 2/10 each.

A testing set will prove interesting to serious aquarists, and will be found to have several applications. Some of these are mentioned under the heading "What to Do With Newly Received Fishes," and in the chapter on "Diseases."

The testing sets made for aquarists contain the necessary chemicals for changing water in either direction — bicarbonate of soda for the alkaline side, and acid sodium phosphate (mono-basic) for the acid. This sometimes forms a harmless precipitate which may be drawn off. No attempt should ever be made to change the pH of aquarium water without the use of a testing set.

"Medicine Balls," containing, principally, plaster of Paris and chalk, keep water on the alkaline side. They should not be used unless a test shows the need of the minerals they supply.

Algae on Glass A green film of Algae on glass is one of the aquarist's greatest griefs. It is bound to occur if strong daylight is used. In weak light, even when augmented by electric illumination, it is negligible. Active snails keep down the soft kinds, but presently

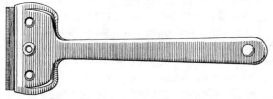
Razor Blade Aquarium Glass Cleaner

a hard species develops which they can not touch. A razor blade scraper can be used to remove it in a few moments. Also a piece of stiff felt or a ball of steel wool is good for the purpose. Many of our fishes, especially Mollienisias and Swordtails, are extremely fond of Algae, and it is undoubtedly a beneficial food. These fishes do much towards keeping the glass and plants clear.

It should be remembered that Algae is not an unmixed evil. It is an active oxygenator and a shield against too much sun. In this respect it has a tendency to keep the water clear. Judgment should therefore be used in its removal.

Brown Algae sometimes infests an aquarium, particularly in a dull light. Neither snails nor fishes seem to care for it. The only known corrective is stronger light, and this is not always successful. The best treatment is to clean the aquarium and start over, using, if possible, water of a different character.

One of the great unsolved problems is what to do about a smelly blue-green alga (*Oscillaria*) which frequently infests tropical tanks. Neither snails nor fishes like it—except the Goldfish. As it is easily wiped off, the question resolves itself to a choice as to whether the aquarist is going to do the work himself or have a team of small Goldfish for the purpose. If left alone, it suffocates the plants, runs its own course and dies out.

Scavengers Many aquarists, especially beginners, demand too much of so-called "scavengers." It is unreasonable to expect any creature to take all undesirable matter out of an aquarium and utterly destroy it—or to keep the glass cleaner than the aquarist himself would.

The original aquarium "scavengers" were Fresh-water Snails. Other important assistants have appeared in the persons of Weather-fishes, Armored Catfishes, Tadpoles, Fresh-water Mussels and Fresh-water Shrimp. All except the Mussels hunt out and eat particles of food which have been missed or rejected by the other occupants of the aquarium. This is a very important service. It prevents the evil chain of conditions and events following the decomposition of that food. It has foolishly been argued that they only convert it into humus. True, but it is then practically harmless. Snails, in addition, keep down the film of green algae from glass and plants, but none of them get *all* of it. They can not, unassisted, make a polished plate-glass parlor of the aquarium.

The great disadvantage of snails is that many of our exotic fishes kill them. Also they can be a nuisance by eating fish spawn. They never attack live fishes of even the smallest size.

Tadpoles and Weather-fish are not much favored because they agitate the water too strenuously.

Mussels to some extent remove suspended green algae from the water, but they require watching to see whether they are alive. Altogether we are inclined not to recommend them, especially as heat does not agree with them. The risk is hardly worth their doubtful benefits.

We have novelties in everything; why not in aquarium scavengers? The Fresh-water Shrimp is a bottom feeder and will find neglected small bits of fishfood. It can live with the milder mannered small fishes and makes an interesting pet, but the larger fishes regard it as a choice morsel of food.

It is generally conceded that several species of the fishes called Corydoras are the best aquarium scavengers. These are illustrated and described under their own headings.

Snails The popular EUROPEAN RED RAMSHORN SNAIL (*Planorbis corneus*) continues to hold interest. Bright red ones, free from chippings or blemishes, are always in demand, and their breeding is a matter of some commercial value. In order to get them clear red, they must be grown rapidly, and to be grown quickly they must have plenty of room, warmth and food, together with slightly alkaline water. The preferred foods are spinach, lettuce and boiled oatmeal containing powdered shrimp. They should be fed as much as they can possibly eat. This has a tendency to foul the water, which, in turn, produces erosion of the shells. Therefore, the bottom of the tank should be siphoned off frequently and fresh water added. Daphnia tends to clear the water and to prosper at the job. The flat, amber egg masses appear freely in the early spring. If properly raised, they will be ready for the market in October, although the demand is greater in midwinter. The eggs hatch in anywhere from 10 to 40 days, according to temperature. Nearly all fishes destroy newly hatched Red Ramshorn Snails. Great care should be taken not to allow dark snails of the same species

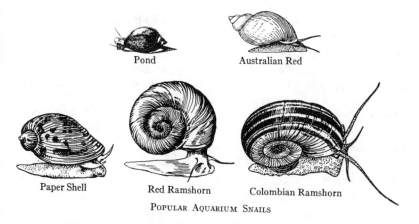

Pond   Australian Red

Paper Shell   Red Ramshorn   Colombian Ramshorn

POPULAR AQUARIUM SNAILS

to cross with the reds, as this ruins the stock for generations. They do well in outdoor ponds, especially lily pools, for they like to lay their eggs on the under-side of the lily pads.

POND SNAILS (*Physa*) are the best of all, in the writer's opinion. They are rather hard when hatched and will be eaten only by hard-mouthed or large fishes. Some consider this snail a pest, it multiplies so freely.

COLOMBIAN STRIPED RAMSHORN (*Marisa rotula*), reaching a diameter of 1½ inches, is the best of several South American introductions. It is very handsome, is moderately active and does not destroy plants. The stripes shown in the illustration are alternating ivory and brown. The large "foot" is blue-white. It breeds only in warm weather, laying bunches of large eggs at the water's edge.

THE AUSTRALIAN RED SNAIL is a most prolific breeder outdoors, and a handsome creature, but it seems to have few friends.

Among aquarium snails, those which can remain outdoors under a reasonable sheet of ice are the Ramshorn (Red or Black), the Japanese Live-bearing Snail, and the formerly popular Paper-shelled Snail, also incorrectly known as the "African" Snail—from Florida!

Covers Principally owing to the tendency of many fishes to jump out of the water during excitement, it is necessary to keep them covered. Sheets of glass are usually used, but fine screen is satisfactory. The cover is usually laid directly on the aquarium frame, which not only makes sure that no swift-leaping fish can find an opening, but also keeps the water a little warmer.

The idea of tight-fitting cover glasses usually causes the beginner aquarist some mental suffering, for it seems opposed to all our theories about oxygen. The answer is that the amount of dissolved oxygen in water is extremely small, and it would take a long time for an aquarium to exhaust or appreciably diminish the amount in an inch layer of air in the top of the aquarium.

The writer personally believes in having the glass very slightly raised or else using screen covers, not for a fresh supply of oxygen, but to better carry off some of the stale gases, and at the same time promote a beneficial circulation of water caused by evaporation and its consequent cooling. The young of a few species need tight covers, but these cases are mentioned under their own headings.

Screen covers are particularly good in summer. Rustless fly screen (not copper) is best, attached to a light wooden frame, or with edges bent down over the aquarium top.

Fishes are especially apt to jump after transfer, or other fright. They are less likely to leap from an aquarium when they enjoy the safety of dense vegetation.

In our many fish problems we should try to *think like a fish,* much like the wise simpleton who found the lost horse when others had failed. Asked how he did it, he answered, "I started from the barn and tried to think like a horse."

Gases Water absorbs not only the beneficial oxygen, but injurious gases and fumes as well. One of the worst and commonest is coal gas, prevalent in many homes at night when coal stoves are improperly banked. Often human noses fail to detect the presence of this poison. Polished silver is very sensitive to it. If this oxidizes in a few days, there is too much coal gas in the house and something should be done about it. Tight aquarium covers help in such situations. Fumes from varnishes, varnish removers, paints, turpentine, shellac, or anything containing wood alcohol, are all injurious to aquarium water. Not infrequently they are fatal. An excess of tobacco smoke does no good.

Rockwork Beautiful effects in the aquarium can be had by the clever arrangement of rocks. They can be used to construct terraces, grottos, arches, or other natural formations. Smooth, weather-worn stones are much to be preferred, for fresh broken surfaces are likely to injure the fishes. Coral is extremely rough and should only be used with such marine fishes as are used to it in Nature.

Catching Fishes Approach the task with confidence but not conceit; also with a determination not to lose patience, nor to ruin the plants. Any fish can be outwitted and out-waited by man. Each species has its peculiarities. Once captured, all individuals of that species can be caught by the same method. Many species yield to very slow movement. It is the first thing to try. A net in each hand often helps, a large one for a catcher and a small one for a persuader. In large greenhouse pools or other places where it is almost impossible to catch the fishes without drawing off the water, it is surprising to find what can be done with a minnow trap. It is an article sold in sporting goods stores. It is made of glass and is about the size of a rat trap. Bait is placed in it and it is laid on the bottom of the pool, attached to a cord. After perhaps a quarter hour, it is lifted and is likely to contain a number of fishes, which may be removed without injury.

Very small newly hatched fishes had best not be handled at all, but if it must be done, a good way is to raise them near the surface with a fine net and then dip fish and a little water out in a spoon. Sometimes they are lifted in a dip-tube, in the same manner that dirt is drawn from the bottom of an aquarium.

Nets Except for use in globes, all nets should have straight edges. Fine bobbinet is preferable to coarse knotted threads. Nets rot rapidly in a moist atmosphere, especially when laid down wet on a sheet of glass. They should be hung up when not in use. It is a good practice

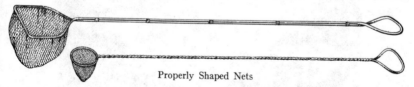

Properly Shaped Nets

to rinse all nets in clear water before drying. Every aquarist loses fishes by having them leap while being transferred from a net. We can only suggest extreme care. A net should be deep enough so that a little bag enclosing the fish may be made by the free hand. Oppositely, a net ought not be deep enough to entangle the fish so that in its struggles it will tear its fins. Small nets, up to about 3 x 4 inch frames, should be about as deep as they are wide. Larger nets ought to be a little shallower.

"Glass nets" shaped somewhat like large clay smoking pipes, are used by careful German aquarists in catching small fishes. They can be purchased from some American dealers. In certain situations the author likes them very much. With them, young fish can readily be lifted without danger, and at the bottom of plant thickets, where netting is almost impossible, the "glass net," being nearly imperceptible, can often be slipped over 2-inch adult fish without difficulty. The water and fish are removed as in the use of a dip-tube, by placing the thumb over the end of the tube.

With large aquariums a large net is almost indispensable. Professionals who must catch their fishes without wasting too much time about it often have a square net nearly the full width and depth of the tank. With this the fishes are raised to the surface and then removed by a smaller net. Splendid large net frames (about 8 inches square) of heavy aluminum wire can be purchased cheaply.

Effective Net for Use in Large Tank

What to do with Newly Received Fishes If fishes come from healthy tanks where they were thoroughly acclimated, and have not traveled more than half a day, and have had no marked change in temperature, then they need no attention beyond two very simple things. One is to see that the new water in which they are placed is within 2 degrees of the same temperature as that in which they traveled. This applies to all transfers under all circumstances. If the new fishes come in small containers and there is a noticeable difference in temperature between the two waters, it is a very good plan to float the container in the aquarium until the temperatures are equalized before making the transfer.

The second point is one that may be neglected without great risk, but careful aquarists should take it into account. Most fishes are injured by a too sudden change in the degree of acidity or alkalinity of the water. Fishes from other aquariums, especially those from a distance, are liable to be used to water which is quite different in that respect. Therefore, if the aquarist is equipped to take a pH reading and make needed adjustments slowly, it is the prudent thing to do. Such simple precautions sometimes prove to be the well-known "ounce of prevention." For many years experienced aquarists have utilized the water of shipment to mix with the aquarium water. Unknowingly they have been adjusting the pH. This is a very practical way of doing it if there is sufficient volume to make it count. See remarks under "What is pH?"

While the same things apply to fishes that have traveled one or more days, other points must also be taken into consideration in their behalf. Experienced shippers do not feed fishes prior to expressing them. After this fast they should be fed *lightly* for a few days, preferably making Daphnia or other live food a part of their diet.

New arrivals from a distance should be looked over as to general condition, particularly as to their fins and any indication of Ichthyophthirius, the "Pepper and Salt" disease. If there are suspicious signs the new arrivals should be quarantined, given a dose of permanganate of potash, ¼ grain (by weight) to the gallon of water, and have their temperature slowly raised to 85 degrees, keeping it there a few days.

Many aquarists aerate cans of fishes for several hours before making the transfer. This both refreshes the travelers and gives the water time to become equalized in temperature with its new surroundings.

It is generally a good policy to introduce new fishes among others *after* feeding those which are already established in the aquarium. This is especially true in placing small fishes with larger ones. The world over, a good meal makes for mellowness.

Emergency Aquarium It takes resolution to resist regularly using any well-planted aquarium in beautiful condition, but it pays in the long run to keep at least one emergency tank. In such a container all new arrivals should be placed, regardless of apparently clean bills of health. Too often do we hear the mournful tale of an aquarium that was a paradise until some new fish or plants were introduced, and, along with them, disease. Strangers ought to have at least 2 weeks' probation, but, in justice to them, under the best of conditions.

A healthy aquarium, balanced with plants, containing no other fish, is the very best place to put one that is a little out of condition, or that has been bullied; or for a female live-bearer needing protection and rest after delivery of her young.

Bullies Sometimes an individual fish, possibly of a peaceful species, learns that other fishes will flee if chased. This becomes a sport with that fish, to the misery of its fellows and the discomfiture of their owner. It should either be disposed of, partitioned off (perhaps in a corner, like a dunce), or placed in another aquarium with larger fishes, where, among strangers, it may reform. Like the rooster taken out of its own barnyard, it will not fight so well.

Seasoning Tanks New wooden or concrete tanks to be safe must be seasoned. Without artificial help it takes at least 3 months to season wood by occasional changes of water. This may be hurried by slaking a large piece of lime in the tank while it is filled with water, stirring it and allowing it to stand a few days. After a good rinsing it is ready for use. Theoretically, any mild alkali, such as bicarbonate of soda, should serve the same purpose. We have only tried lime.

Wooden tanks should not be painted, either inside nor out. Cypress is the best wood.

Probably the best medium for neutralizing the free alkali in concrete pools is phosphoric acid. An ounce to 50 gallons should be sufficient. Stir well and allow it to stand about 48 hours. Wash well and use. Otherwise the pool may be made safe for fishes by 4 changes of water over a period of a month.

New wooden tanks and concrete pools may be tested by introducing tadpoles. The water is safe if they will live 3 days.

Tapping on Glass There seems to be about as much sense to tapping an aquarium glass to gain the attention of the fishes as there is in speaking in a loud tone of voice to someone who does not understand our language. The result is the same—fear and confusion. Many fishes have sensitive nervous systems. They can be stunned or even killed by clapping stones together under water. Tapping on their aquarium is a needless cruelty and never produces the desired result. A small net or stick in the water is more likely to persuade them into a desired position.

Sudden Light Along with the petty cruelties to fishes which might be mentioned is the thoughtless practice of suddenly placing them in powerful light when they have gotten used to darkness. This is done both by switching on full electric light at night, and by suddenly lifting the lid of a shipping can in bright sun. The fish give every evidence of experiencing the same distress we ourselves would feel under like circumstances. A little care in this matter is a kindness that is not misspent.

A THICKET OF ITALIAN VALLISNERIA

Showing characteristic reproduction by runner; common also to the Sagittarias and other grass-like aquatic plants. The depth of this aquarium is 16 inches.

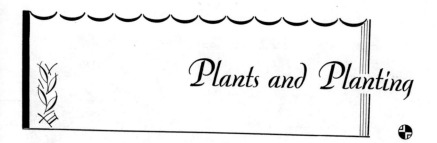

Plants and Planting

$\mathcal{W}$E now come to the point of considering plants, not only as oxygenators, but as purifiers and beautifiers. As it is with garden flowers, a few old friends are the ones we find to be best. In 80 years of organized aquarium study, only 5 kinds of plants (with their variations) have come into general use.

Three of these favorites have running stems, to which leaves are attached. These are Myriophyllum, Cabomba and Anacharis. The other two are in grassy form, Vallisneria and Sagittaria. Each has its own uses and its admirers. Each is easily obtained and propagated, two of the qualifications for any popular plant. Enormous quantities of all of them are marketed annually. As those 5 plants are the most important, we will consider them first, and follow with others which have special uses.

VALLISNERIA SPIRALIS

(Eel Grass, Tape Grass)

Perhaps the author allows himself the pleasure of personal preference in heading the list with this beautiful plant. Its tall, graceful, grass-like form with narrow, silken, light green leaves, rises vertically in undulating lines, and gives a charm to an aquarium which is both aquatic and artistic. The plant in moderately good light multiplies rapidly and forms a dense but not impenetrable thicket or screen. It is one of the very best oxygenators and its roots tend to purify the soil.

Propagation is principally by runners. The plants are male and female and, peculiarly enough, the plants from runners are all the same sex as the parent. Nearly all of them are female. Their little floating, white, cup-shaped flowers are on the ends of long, thin spirals, rising from the crown of the plant. The word *spiralis* refers to the shape of these flower stems. The flowers of the rare male plants are close to the crown. Pollen rises from them and fertilizes the floating female flowers. The seeds from these fertilized flowers may produce both male and female plants, but very few of the seeds ever germinate. In planting Vallisneria care should be taken to keep the crown just at the surface of the sand.

THREE KINDS OF SAGITTARIA

The larger plants are Giant Sagittaria; the small ones in the foreground are Dwarf, while the single plant above the arrow is Subulata. The two stems of reddish leaves at the top are the red phase of Ludwigia.

As this is the first successful natural-color photograph of a populated aquarium interior, a few words regarding it may prove of interest. It is the outcome of original experiments proposed by Mr. Arthur J. Sweet, of the Westinghouse Lamp Company, and which were carried out by the author at the Company plant at Bloomfield, N. J.

Photographing only a pair of fish by the natural color process (Agfa) requires a great amount of light, but to do an aquarium interior in detail with the lens "stopped down" there must be an enormous flood of illumination.

Carefully-placed flashlight bulbs were used, generating 18,000,000 lumens for a period of about 1/50 second. Mr. Sweet worked out this interesting comparison in order to present to the popular mind what that volume of light means. He says: "It would require 1,200,000 ordinary paraffin candles to produce this amount of light. Placed close together they would occupy a space of 90 square feet. If they were lighted at the rate of one every 2 seconds, it would take a man 27 days, working 24 hours a day."

The photograph is taken in a size of about 1/4 diameter. The young Scalares are 65 days old and were raised with the parents, although that is not common practise. The adult to the left is the female.

While we have a native variety which grows to great length in places like mill races, it is not well suited to the aquarium because it insists upon keeping up its old habit of dying down to the tuft in winter. The Italian strain, 10 to 15 inches long, which grows without interruption, is the one almost always seen in aquariums.

A giant species with leaves about five-eighths of an inch wide and several feet long, with bristly edges, is propagated in Florida. It is splendid for aquaria of 50 gallons and upward.

There is a band down the center of Vallisneria leaves dividing them into 3 nearly equal stripes of 2 shades of green. This makes an easy way of distinguishing it from Sagittaria.

SAGITTARIA
(Arrowhead)

This famous old aquarium plant is also one having a grass-like form. It comes in many more species than Vallisneria, most of them being bog plants, rather than pure aquatics. Their barb- or lance-shaped aerial leaves, common along watery borders almost everywhere, are responsible for the naming of the plant after the mythological Sagittarius the Archer.

About half a dozen species, some of them of doubtful identity, are being successfully used as aquarium plants. The 3 most important are *Sagittaria gigantea* (believed to be a cultivated form of *Sagittaria sinensis*), *Sagittaria natans,* and *Sagittaria subulata.*

The strong green leaves of *Sagittaria gigantea* are a half inch or more wide, and from 7 to 14 inches in length. They are rather firm and withstand a fair amount of buffeting by nets, once they are well rooted. As their roots are eventually quite vigorous, they should be planted in sand about 2 inches deep. The plant is a comparatively slow grower in the aquarium, but aquarium-grown specimens are best. These are easily distinguished by a large mass of yellowish roots, whereas those grown in ponds have fewer, shorter and white roots. It takes about a year to get pond-grown plants acclimated to the aquarium.

Sagittaria natans. This is the original Sagittaria of the aquarium, and was at one time very popular, especially in the early days of the fancy Goldfish. In the Goldfish tank it was largely replaced by *Sagittaria gigantea,* which was better for that purpose. Since the advent of "tropicals" it has again come into its own, for it has advantages which make it welcome in the small aquarium. The main point is that it does not grow very long and, therefore, does not easily get into a tangle. The 6- to 8-inch leaves are tough and the plant is a long-lived, good oxygenator.

The leaves of this species, as well as those of *gigantea,* arch over

Cabomba   Myriophyllum   Anacharis

THREE POPULAR FAVORITES

Among those aquarium plants having leaves attached to a running stem, these 3 are
by far the best known and are in the most general use.

considerably, so that singly the plants do not appear at their best in a photograph.

Several Sagittarias are shown in the accompanying natural-color photograph. The pointed leaves in the frontispiece are *Sagittaria natans*.

Sagittaria subulata. This is a species which has in recent years become very popular. It is different from the 2 foregoing kinds in 3 respects. The leaves are narrower and thicker. They are straighter and they are darker green. Under favorable conditions this plant propagates rapidly. The leaves are from 5 to 10 inches long, and are rather wiry.

All these truly aquatic species of Sagittaria throw up summer stalks which develop long, oval leaves above the water. Flower stems bear trusses of pretty cup-shaped white flowers with a yellow ball in the center.

CABOMBA
(Washington Plant, Fanwort, Watershield)

While we by no means claim this to be the best of aquarium plants, it is the most largely sold, and has its good points. It fell out of fashion in the Goldfish aquarium because those husky fishes picked it to pieces, for it is brittle. Very few of our exotics munch on plants, and so that objection to Cabomba is removed, as far as they are concerned. Certainly when in good condition it is one of the brightest and most beautiful of aquarium greens. It is used chiefly on account of its attractiveness, coupled with the fact that it is always in supply.

The fan-shaped, light green leaves on a running stem form good refuge for young fishes, but they are not sufficiently dense to make a satisfactory spawning plant. Cabomba is apt to become long and stringy unless kept in a strong light. It is a fair oxygenator.

ANACHARIS
(Elodea, Ditch Moss)

Early dealers claimed that Anacharis was the best of oxygenators. This was generally accepted and has become something of a tradition, although the claim is open to question. It is probably based on the undoubted fact that it is the most rapid-growing of all aquarium plants. An inch-a-day for a long strand is not unusual. However, growth and oxygenating power bear little, if any, relationship to each other. Rapid stem growth occurs in poor light, producing plants lacking vigor.

It is the author's observation that Anacharis is only at its best in outdoor ponds that are partially protected from the full light of the sun. There it grows into gorgeous, firm, thick-leaved masses. In the aquarium it gradually becomes thinner and softer, and is eaten by some fishes.

MYRIOPHYLLUM

A plant of delicate beauty. Its fine leaves, attached to a stem, make a perfect maze for the catching of spawn from the egg-dropping fishes. For that purpose it is equally useful for those that spawn at the top or the bottom of the aquarium. It naturally floats just below the surface, but can easily be fastened in masses at the bottom. Ordinarily it is planted and grows upright. Broken bits of its feathery leaves precisely suit the uses of those fishes which like to introduce pieces of plant into the construction of their breeding nests.

There are several species of submerged Myriophyllum, but their botanical differences are of little interest and less value to the aquarist.

PARROT'S FEATHER, A SPECIES OF MYRIOPHYLLUM, IN GREENHOUSE PROFUSION

The long-leaved species (*verticillatum,* shown in previous illustration) are the better spawning plants, but the short-leaved ones are the more durable. It is a plant that varies in form according to growing conditions, especially in the matter of light. The more light, the more compact. There is a submerged variety of a coppery red color, which is very pretty.

Parrot's Feather (*Myriophyllum proserpinacoides*) is an interesting species mentioned here only on account of its decorative quality. The feathery plumes of the ends stand above the edges of pools in magnificent masses. Good in the greenhouse.

PLANTS FOR SPECIAL PURPOSES

Here are listed plants which are not so commonly obtainable, but which have their own values in utility or beauty. Choice bits not always found in the highways of trade.

Ludwigia This is not a true aquatic, but a bog plant which does fairly well under water. It never completely forgets its habit of having some leaves above the water-line. There are about 25 species in North America, usually growing at the shallow edges of ponds and streams, somewhat similar to Watercress, but, unlike that plant, not requiring cool water. The native kinds are not as well suited to the aquarium as a South American species, *mullerttii*. This is also handsomer, being more robust and not having as many rootlets along the stem. A very beautiful red strain of this species is cultivated in Florida, where conditions exactly suit it, but elsewhere it soon loses most of its peculiar character. This is shown in the color plate with the Sagittarias.

For best results Ludwigia should be rooted in earth and placed in strong light. Otherwise the leaves drop prematurely. It is easily propagated from end cuttings. Nurserymen stick these in small pots containing earth and a top layer of sand. This is not done under water, but on trays of saturated sand or ashes. As soon as growth starts, the pot may be placed in the aquarium. This is a very satisfactory method.

Cryptocoryne Aquarists who like decorative plants which are out of the ordinary have been using Cryptocoryne more and more, so that now it is quite well known. As will be seen, it has leaves shaped like terrestrial plants, rising from a crown at the surface of the soil. When in a particularly happy situation, it sends up a flower to the surface, which in shape resembles a thin, very elongated Jack-in-the-Pulpit.

This plant has two very good points in addition to its interesting appearance. It does well in subdued light and the leaves are tough. There are a number of species, but only two are commonly used by aquarists. The larger, with broad, oval pointed leaves that are silky dark green on top and pink underneath, is *griffithii*, and is suited to aquariums a foot or more in depth, while *willisii*, with narrow, wavy leaves, is at home in either large tanks or in aquariums not shallower than 7 inches.

Cryptocoryne willisii

Propagation is by runners and is rather slow, especially if in too strong a light. It does not like direct sun. Not a cheap plant, but obtainable from many commercial sources. Its origin is in tropical Asia.

Ceratophyllum   Ceratophyllum, or Hornwort, has a delicate beauty that would make it one of our standard aquarium plants, but for two fatal faults. It is brittle and it has no roots. It is like a thinned-out Myriophyllum. Illustrators of fishes never seem to tire of placing a spray of it in backgrounds. Our own color photograph of *Etroplus maculatus* shows a bit of it to advantage. Placed in a concrete pool in summer, where it will receive about 3 hours of sunshine per day, it grows into magnificent scrolls, floating just below the surface.

A Spray of Ceratophyllum, or Hornwort

Our illustration is an end broken off of a 4-foot runner. It is so brittle that a piece of this size is difficult to lift intact from the water.

But why, then, mention it as an aquarium plant at all? Because when confined it grows into dense masses which make excellent refuge for young fishes. Also it is a good oxygenator. So common is it that some of our southern shippers use it as filler in packing, or it may be found in many country ponds in eastern North America. In nature it is usually much more compact, and is quite hard to the touch.

Spatterdock One of the forms of this plant from southeastern United States makes a striking centrepiece in the aquarium. The large, long leaves are of a delicate, translucent light green. Propagation is from a heavy, trunk-like root-base called a rhizome. Unfor-

SOUTHERN SPATTERDOCK

tunately, when this is broken off a creeping decay sometimes sets in and eventually destroys the plant. The break heals over better if placed in soil, rather than sand. In summer the leaves become quite long, but they are always submerged.

Seedlings from northern Spatterdocks produce smaller plants with much more rounded leaves. While the parent stocks of most of those seedlings have aerial leaves, seen by the million along the edges of rivers, they seldom, if ever, become sufficiently robust in the aquarium to reach that stage of development. Usually they are pretty little submerged plants not over 6 inches in height.

Fontinalis, or Willowmoss Our readers have noted that there are several species of fishes that spawn on plants at the bottom of the aquarium. While Fontinalis is not easily obtained, it is one of the best mediums for that purpose. Its long, willowy filaments, covered by extremely small leaves, are found attached to a stone or a bit of waterlogged wood in some small, swift, cool stream. Professional collectors

Fontinalis gracilis, or WILLOWMOSS

usually have it for sale from May until November. It grows in long masses which are torn from their anchorage by moving ice in spring.

Never has the writer met with any other plant which harbors such a host of tiny creatures of the water, principally Crustacea. Most of these animals are fine fish food, but safety demands that plants from the wild be *"de-bugged."* They may be rinsed, or, better still, placed in an aquarium with an adult Betta. It will enjoy some pleasant pickings.

Fontinalis holds its own in the aquarium for a long time. It does not actually prosper, but puts forth a few fresh green leaves in contrast with the old sage-brown ones.

The usual fine-stemmed species is *gracilis.* A much thicker, more rope-like species, *antipyretica,* is not so useful for spawn-catching.

Heteranthera

The very opaque quality of the light green leaves of this plant almost serves as a means of identification. If the reader will imagine a modified Anacharis, with the long leaves coming alternately from two sides of the stem, he will have a fair idea of Heteranthera. It is a rather limp plant, but does well in a good, strong light.

HETERANTHERA

HAIR GRASS (*Actual Size*)

Hair Grass Growing along the edges of many ponds and streams in the Eastern and Southern parts of North America are short, hair-like grasses suited to aquarium culture. The majority of them propagate from runners, such as the one shown here. Others divide on the leaves, and send down rootlets.

Plants of this character offer not only interesting variety in contrast with other aquarium vegetation, but they make perfect thickets for harboring baby fishes finding themselves in a dangerous world.

This or a similar species may usually be had from dealers or specialists in aquatic plants.

Naias (*Surface View*)

A plant which serves both man and fish. Its close yet open mass formation at the surface of the water makes it useful as a hiding place for tiny fishes. Apparently a good oxygenator. Brittle and not rooted.

Found in fresh water from Florida to Labrador, and in Europe. In places it grows so luxuriantly that it is dried and used as packing.

FLOATING PLANTS

Riccia To the breeder of aquarium fishes, this is one of the most valuable of plants. Its green, crystal-like formation produces masses which are compact enough to catch and hold the spawn of the surface egg-layers, yet open enough for new baby live-bearing species to use as a perfect refuge. When it is desirable to produce top shade in an aquarium, we can depend upon Riccia to do it in any desired degree.

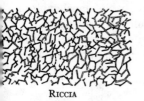

RICCIA

For some aquarists it grows tremendously, but the surplus never should be thrown away, for there are always those in need of it. When a mass grows over an inch thick, so that the sun can not force light through it, a thinning out must be effected, or it will turn yellow and soft and pollute the water.

Under the influence of sun these little plants are enormous oxygenators. Large bubbles of that precious gas become imprisoned among the massed leaves and stay there until absorbed by the water. This takes several hours and favorably affects the fishes long after the sun has disappeared.

The great enemy of Riccia is algae, which get among the leaves and choke it. A plentiful supply of small snails with it usually keeps it clean, although when it is to be used for spawning purposes, no snails should be present.

While Riccia is native to the fresh waters of the middle and southern Atlantic States, it appears to grow better in a well-lighted aquarium than it does outdoors. The sun seems to shrivel it.

Water Fern This is an interesting floating plant, anywhere in size from an inch to a foot in diameter, according to the conditions under which it is kept. It likes greenhouse moisture and temperature. When so favored, it grows in great masses and piles itself up several inches out of the water. It is viviparous, the young plants forming on the large parent leaves. In an aquarium it keeps down to a moderate size and makes a very pretty shade plant. In this respect it is one of the enemies of green water. Bettas and other bubble-nest builders delight in placing their nests below one of the plants. It is shown in the colored plate of Paradise Fish.

Duckweed A despised pest in Daphnia ponds, but not without its use in the aquarium. Some of our fishes like to eat it, and it is a good producer of shade where a tank gets too much top light. No fear need be entertained about introducing it in aquariums where it can be kept under control, but in large containers and lily pools it is apt to gain too much headway and prove difficult to get rid of.

For so tiny a floating leaf, it develops quite long roots, if they are not nibbled by fishes. Shown in the illustration of Dragon-fly Larva.

An almost solid mantle of any of these little floating plants seems to have little or no effect in preventing the water from absorbing oxygen at the surface. Dried Duckweed is a good producer of Infusoria.

Salvinia This is a floating plant much larger and handsomer than Duckweed, the leaves being about a quarter inch across. The upper surface is covered with vertical hairs, which are probably unpalatable to fishes. At any rate, none of them eats it. It multiplies rapidly in a warm, moist atmosphere, but does not do so well outdoors, and will not survive icy winters. The heart-shaped, velvety leaves are very ornamental.

Azolla A peculiar little floating plant, native to our Southern States, sometimes used as an aquarium plant. It forms a dense covering, varying in color from dull sage green to dark red.

AZOLLA (*Life Size*)

WATER LETTUCE

A beautiful floating plant about 4 inches in diameter, having fluted, velvety, light green leaves and long roots. Requires warm, moist atmosphere and diffused light.

PLANTING

Sand or Pebbles? Coarse sand is best, or a mixture of sand and small pebbles, such as Jersey gravel. Washed building sand is satisfactory. Fine sand packs too hard and allows no beneficial circulation of water.

Pebbles, stones, shells or marbles alone are bad because they have open spaces which catch and hold fish food where no scavengers can reach it, thus causing the water to turn foul. Large and small stones, well selected, may be very ornamental and natural in an aquarium, but they should be set in sand, for the reason given.

Depth of Sand This is a more important subject than is generally recognized. The planting medium should be only deep enough to be certain of holding down the rooted plants. Vallisneria and the smaller Sagittarias need only about 1½ inches, while Giant Sagittaria requires 2 inches or more. It is a good plan to root the larger plants in deeper sand in the back of the aquarium and then let the level slope lower towards the front. This serves the double purpose of giving the smaller plants a place in the light and of working the aquarium sediment forward, where it is more easily removed. Some aquarists place a glass bar or other stop about an inch wide between the front edge of the sand and the front glass of the aquarium, making an inch trench the entire length. An excellent dirt trap. The stop may also be made of well selected small stones, placed in the form of a semicircle.

Use Earth? No. Theoretically it might be a good idea to provide soil substance in the form of a sub-stratum for plants, but in practice it does not work out well. It is apt to become foul, and any accidental stirring up clouds the aquarium. Besides, we expect the plants to get their livelihood by absorbing the waste products of the fishes. This they do. To those who feel they must try soil, we recommend clean, old earthy settlings from some stream, rather than garden soil with all its fresh organic matter.

How to Plant Enough has been said as to the characteristics of available plants for the aquarium, so that here we are concerned with the mechanics of the job.

The first thing is to make sure that the plants are kept moist while the work is being carefully done. A half-drying may set them back for weeks. If they are laid in water and covered with a wet newspaper, there will be no danger.

The water in the aquarium should be about 5 or 6 inches deep while most of the work is being done. If the sand is fairly clean, the water can be kept clear by placing a piece of paper over it while filling. Pour on the paper. When rockwork is to be used, it should be placed before the plants are set. The only real difficulty is in nicely planting the grasses having spreading roots, but it is not very troublesome when the water is shallow. Spread the roots of Sagittaria and Vallisneria as widely as possible and cover them well with sand, being careful not to bury the leaves. If there are tall, stiff leaves, partly in the air, be sure to sprinkle them often during the balance of the work. Sometimes a large plant is so buoyant that it is necessary to place a small stone or two on the sand over the roots. Each rooted plant like Sagittaria or Vallisneria should have sufficient space so that there will be room for the new runners to expand.

The smaller plants and those with long strands like Anacharis should be placed last. Old yellowish leaves should be removed before planting.

Planting Sticks   If plants must be added after the aquarium is filled, or if any of them ride up, a slender pair of sticks will be found most useful. Push the plant into the sand with both sticks, then withdraw one, and with it heap the sand about the roots. The other

PLANTING STICK

stick may then be withdrawn and usually the plant will stay down. It is well to slightly notch and round off the sharp edges of the pushing ends of the sticks. A pair of rulers will serve in an emergency.

Bunched Plants   Plants when received in wired bundles look so attractive and it is so easy to plant them as they are, it is indeed a temptation to do so. They never naturally grow that way and it should not be done. Stemmed plants, like Anacharis, Cabomba and Myriophyllum, ought to be slightly separated so that water and light may pass between the stems at the base.

Fertilizing Plants   This is a "noble experiment," but a dangerous one. It belongs in the same category as placing a layer of soil under the sand, only it is a few degrees more dangerous. It has been proven many times that *Fish Fertilize Plants*. If there are enough fish present, the combined effects of their breathing and their droppings give the plants all the chemical stimulation they need. The author has seen many well-planted aquariums degenerate without the presence of fish life, only to revive beautifully upon the reintroduction of fishes. However, if any readers feel that their plants are in need of added stimulation, the most approved method of supplying it is by making a liquor from pulverized sheep manure (a standard commercial fertilizer) and shooting it into the sand about the roots by use of a pipette like a fountain pen filler, but larger. Different fertilizers have been introduced in the sand in capsules, but this makes it rather strong in spots. Rabbits and guinea pigs supply natural fertilizer lozenges in convenient form for inserting in the sand near plant roots.

Plants in Trays Planting in trays is practised by many of our foremost aquarists. The idea has advantages. They may be lifted from the aquarium without the slightest disturbance. This is a great convenience either in house-cleaning the aquarium or in catching elusive fishes that hide among plants, for the tray can be removed and leave the bare aquarium in which to work. Many a planting has been wrecked by the net of a desperate and maddened aquarist whose patience has been exhausted by the chase.

Earthenware trays made for the purpose are sold in many of the aquarium supply shops. These have an inside measurement of about 2½ x 5 inches and are about 2 inches deep. This size is suited to small aquariums only and allows no space for runners. Seedsmen sell propagating pans about a foot square and 3 inches deep. Also glass drip pans, used in electric refrigerators, make splendid plant trays. These larger sizes allow room for propagation. Beautiful thickets of Sagittaria and Vallisneria can be raised in this way. They are the best plants for use in trays.

The same principles of planting may be employed as in the bottom of the aquarium itself. The tray can either be set on the plain aquarium floor or hidden in sand or rockwork.

In general, plants do better in neutral or slightly alkaline water, in preference to an acid condition.

Selecting Plants As in other branches of horticulture, it is best to select young or half-grown plants rather than fully developed specimens that have arrived at the zenith of perfection. The young adapt themselves better and last longer. Avoid plants covered with algae, or "moss" as some know it. It chokes the plants and spreads through the aquarium.

Disinfecting Plants When it becomes necessary to clear plants of germs that may have been attacking the fishes, we naturally look for something which will be effective without harming the plants. This is a chemical nicety not easily found. The best thing we know for the purpose is a solution of permanganate of potash, in a strength of ½ grain (by weight) to the gallon of water. A treatment for 2 hours is sufficient. This may also be used for disinfecting an aquarium, first removing all fishes and snails. If the aquarium is very dirty with settlings, a bit stronger solution may be used. The sand should be stirred. A little permanganate remaining after the water is drawn off and the aquarium refilled will do no damage.

Filling There is an art to even so simple a thing as filling an aquarium. In the first place, it should have even bearing or support all around. If the slightest rocking can be produced by raising or lowering any corner, it should be equalized before filling. An uneven strain is liable sooner or later to crack the glass or cause a leak, unless the base is of heavy slate.

We have already suggested covering the plants with paper during the final filling. A sprinkling pot for the pouring serves the same purpose.

Large aquariums, particularly new ones, should be filled slowly, say half the first day and the balance the next, provided no leaks appear. Here is a valuable point seldom mentioned. Like fishes, plants really ought to be placed in *old water,* especially in winter when new water is surcharged with oxygen. This is injurious to plant tissue. In winter, hot water should be drawn the day before and used in the aquariums when it has come down to house temperature. Hot water, of course, should not be placed in the aquarium. It can safely be stood for cooling in a bathtub or other enamel container, or in stone laundry tubs.

Leaks An ordinary slow leak in either a new or an old aquarium should be given a chance to cure itself. This it often does by the suspended matter in the water choking the crack. A handful of earth mixed in the water and stirred occasionally will hurry the process. This may take a week.

In the case of a slow seepage, attach a strip of news or tissue paper (about 5 inches wide) to the wet spot at the bottom of the aquarium. Let it reach nearly to the floor. Most or all of the water will evaporate from this wick before reaching the end. A pan placed below will catch any drops.

Repairs to a leaking aquarium must be made from the inside. If it is an old aquarium, first thoroughly dry for a week, tip on edge and pour any good spar varnish the length of the edge, seeing that it runs into the cracks. Repeat with the other edges as each one dries. Use in a week.

Any of the tacky modern cements placed like putty in the well-dried corners of an aquarium will make a quick, safe and fairly durable repair. Usually it is best to treat all edges.

Fishes

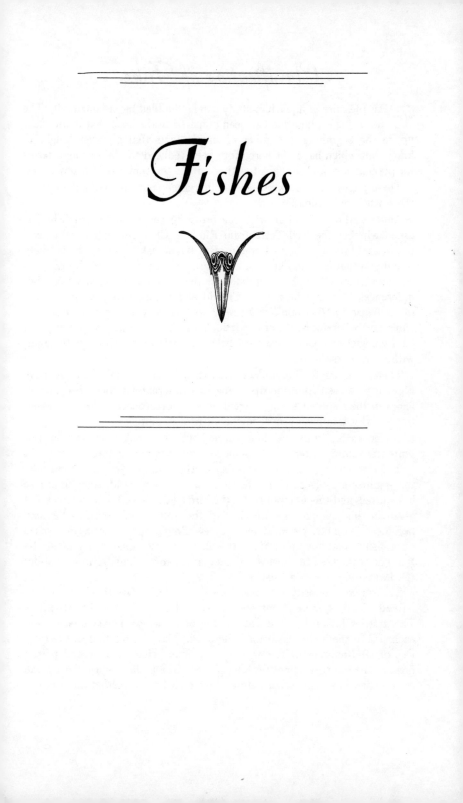

Classification of Fishes

THE pleasure of aquarium study can be doubled by organizing it. The following explanation has been prepared in the hope that it will clear up, in the beginning, a number of simple facts that aquarists ought to know, but which have not heretofore been reduced to plain enough terms for popular use, and brought together within the compass of a few pages.

These pages may be skipped without regret (but not without loss) by those who are science-shy.

Anyone who is familiar with the ordinary run of aquarium fishes, if asked whether the Red Tetra from Rio is a Characin or a Cichlid, will not hesitate to say it is a Characin. But if you ask him why, he is likely to tell you that it is similar to other Characins, that it has an adipose fin— and stop right there. Very probably he has never considered what other differences there are between a Cichlid and a Characin; *he has learned to recognize the two families by sight* without attempting to analyze the whys and wherefores. In this particular he is just like the professional ichthyologist who can place most fishes in their proper families by sight, without recourse to books.

There is more to the subject than this, however, and since we have decided to present, for the first time, the different families of aquarium fishes in their correct ichthyological order-of-precedence, a brief explanation of why this has been done should prove helpful.

Under each family heading throughout the book there are a few sentences calling attention to some of the external features which will help the aquarist recognize a member of that group. To understand *why* the families are placed in the order in which they stand, something else is required, and this is supplied by the bird's-eye-view of fish classification given in this chapter. Before this, or the notes under the families can become intelligible, we must learn a few simple names for certain parts of a fish's anatomy, especially the fins. Every aquarist ought to be familiar with these few terms, for they are used continually in describing the form and color of all fishes.

The great majority of fishes have 7 fins. Of these 7, 4 are **paired.** That is, there is one on each side of the body opposite its mate. The first, or forward paired fins are the **pectoral, or breast fins,** one on each side of the body just behind the head. These correspond to the fore-legs of land animals or the arms of a human being. The second paired fins are the **ventral** or **pelvic fins,** placed close beside each other on the under-side of the fish, either before, directly below, or behind the pectoral pair. Aquarists frequently misname these the breast fins. The ventral fins correspond to the hind legs of land animals and the legs of man. The remaining 3 fins are **unpaired,** or single, being placed exactly on the midline of the fish as viewed from the top or front. The most important

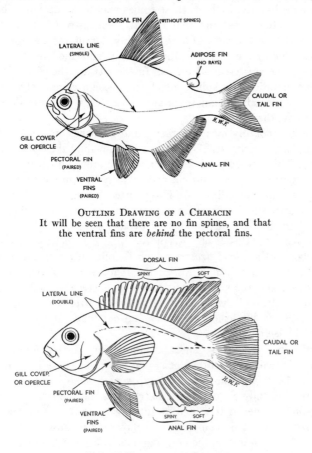

OUTLINE DRAWING OF A CHARACIN
It will be seen that there are no fin spines, and that the ventral fins are *behind* the pectoral fins.

OUTLINE DRAWING OF A CICHLID
Note presence of 2 sets of fin spines, and the forward position of the ventral fins, *under* the pectoral fins.

of the unpaired fins is the **caudal,** or **tail fin.** With most fishes it is the caudal fin that provides the chief propelling power in swimming. It may be forked, as in most swift-swimming fishes, cut off straight, rounded at the end or pointed. On the back of the fish is the **dorsal,** or **back fin,** and on the under-side **behind** the vent, is the **anal fin.**

These fins are formed of a delicate **fin membrane,** supported by fairly stiff, but jointed **fin rays** which usually branch somewhat as they approach the outer edge of the fin. In certain fishes the front rays of some of the fins are bony, unjointed, and sharp. These bony rays are called **fin spines,** and in groups like the Cichlids these spines may make up more than half of the rays of the dorsal and anal fins. In such cases it is usual to refer to the two parts of the dorsal fin as the **spiny dorsal** and the **soft dorsal,** and fishes which have several spines in the dorsal and anal fins form a group called the **spiny-rayed fishes.** In the Gobies, the Silversides, and some other families, the spiny dorsal has become completely separated from the soft dorsal, so that there are two entirely separate dorsal fins, the first spiny, the second soft.

Other fishes, notably most Characins and Catfishes, as well as Salmon and Trout, have another small fin on the back, behind the dorsal and near the tail fin. This, the **adipose fin,** is unlike the other fins in that it is not usually supported by rays, but consists of fatty or adipose tissue. In the Armored Catfishes the adipose fin is supported by one stiff spine.

The similarities and differences in these fins, as well as in other, mostly internal, characters are utilized by ichthyologists in classifying fishes.

All the fishes in this book, except the lung fish, belong to the great group of bony fishes, or *Teleostei,* which is split up into a great number of **orders,** the orders into **families,** the families into **genera** (singular form, **genus**), and the genera into **species.** There are good reasons for this arrangement, and the aquarist who takes a little time in spying out the similarities in his fishes can easily find out much about fish classification for himself.

The order in which the species and families are treated follows rather closely that in which the ichthyologist places fishes. Those families which resemble most closely the primitive types of fishes of bygone ages, as revealed by the study of fossils, are placed first, and the rest are arranged in an ascending order, determined by the advancing degree of complexity of their structure. This complexity is shown externally chiefly by the greater number of spines in the dorsal and anal fins and the more forward position of the ventral fins. For instance, a Characin has no spiny dorsal fin and there are never any spines in the anal fin. Furthermore the ventral fins are set well back along the belly of the fish. These are relatively "primitive" fishes and belong well towards the beginning of the series. On the other hand, the Cichlids have well-developed spiny dorsal and anal fins, and their ventrals are placed well forward, under the pectoral fins. The Cichlids are highly developed "spiny-rayed" fishes. The Cyprinodonts (egg-laying tooth-carps) and Pœciliids (live-bearing tooth-carps) are about midway between the Characins and the Cichlids in their make-up. They have not developed any spines in their fins, but their mouth structure and other points show that they are measurably nearer the end of the series than are the Characins. Some families, like the Snakeheads (Channidæ), lack fin spines, but we know from their anatomy that they are close relatives of the spiny-rayed Gouramis, so we place them next to that group, something like poor relations who lack much that their immediate relatives have.

We now proceed with a few notes on the **orders**, in which the families in this book are placed.

The Herring-like fishes (order *Isospondyli*) are "primitive" bony fishes, lacking fin spines, and having the ventral fins well backward. Only one species is included in this book, the Butterfly-fish, *Pantodon*.

The true fresh-water fishes (order *Ostariophysi*) include probably three-fourths of all fresh-water fishes throughout the world. The Characins, the South American Gymnotid Eels, the Carps or Minnows, the Loaches, and the Catfishes all belong to this order. As a group, they closely resemble the Herring-like fishes, but differ from them and from all other fishes, in having a complicated series of bones (the Weberian ossicles) connecting the air-bladder with the inner ear. The exact function of this complex organ is not certainly known, but it is probably of use to its possessors as an accessory organ of hearing or in detecting differences in water pressure.

The Bill-fishes (order *Synentognathi*) are mostly salt-water fishes, but a few of them, like *Dermogenys*, are from fresh water. The Half-beaks, salt-water Gars, and salt-water Flying-fishes belong to this order. In the structure of the mouth and other characters they are more advanced than the foregoing groups.

The egg-laying and live-bearing Tooth-carps, together with some lesser families, are placed in the order *Cyprinodontes*, generally known as the Cyprinodonts. These are much like the Bill-fishes in the fins, but differ in the mouth and other points.

The Sticklebacks belong in the order *Thoracostei*, together with the Sea Horses and Pipe Fishes. They are remarkable for their gills and for the free spines in front of the dorsal fin.

The Flatfishes (order *Heterosomata*) include the Fresh-water Soles, to which group our common Sole belongs. This is the most easily recognizable order of fishes. All its members lie flat on the bottom on one side and both eyes are on the same (upper) side of the head. All Flat-fishes start out in life upright, with an eye on each side, as we think it ought to be, but when still small they lose their balance, so to speak, flop over on one side, and the underneath eye migrates either over the top of, or directly through the head to join its fellow on the "seeing side."

The Silversides belong to the order *Percesoces,* an intermediate group with the spiny and soft dorsal fins separate, and with a mouth structure resembling that of the Cyprinodonts. Most of the species are salt-water fishes. The Barracudas and Gray Mullets belong to the same order. Fresh-water species are represented in aquarium fishes by the Australian Rainbow Fish.

The order *Percomorphi,* or Perch-like fishes, includes the majority of spiny-rayed fishes. Among our aquarium fishes, the Cichlids, the Pomacentrids, the Perches, the Ambassids, the Sunfishes, the Theraponids, the Nandids, the Monodactylids, the Archer Fishes, and the "Scats" all belong here. All of them have well-developed spiny dorsal and anal fins and ventral fins placed forward under the pectorals.

The Labyrinth fishes (order *Labyrinthici*) are close to the last group, but differ in having a chamber above the gills with which they breathe atmospheric air. The 3 families, Anabantidæ, Luciocephalidæ, and Channidæ, form this order. All of them are Old World fresh-water fishes.

The order *Gobioidei* includes only the Gobies, the Eleotrids, the Periophthalmids, and a few little-known families, peculiar fishes found on the coasts of all the continents. A few inhabit fresh water. The spiny and soft dorsal fins are separate, giving the appearance of a double dorsal, and the ventrals are far forward, either set very close together or united into a sucking disk.

The order *Opisthomi,* or Spiny Eels, includes elongate, long-snouted fresh-water fishes of the Old World with a great many free spines in front of the dorsal. The only fish in the book belonging to this order is *Rhynchobdella.*

Finally, we have the order *Plectognathi,* which includes the Puffers and Trigger-fishes. Most of them have the teeth fused together into a beak, with which they can give a bad nip. Nearly all are salt-water fishes, but a few of the smaller puffers come up into fresh-water streams. A few are used as aquarium fishes.

If the reader has scanned the foregoing with care, he will see at once that the terms "order," "family," "genus," and "species," all mean something definite in fish classification. The term "family" is the one most frequently misused by aquarists. We see many references to the "Panchax family," the "egg-laying family" or the "live-bearing family." Such uses of the term family have no meaning and will not be followed by the careful aquarist. Instead of the *"Panchax* family" or the *"Barbus* family" one should say the "genus *Panchax"* (which belongs to the Cyprinodont family) or the "genus *Barbus*" (which belongs to the Carp family). Further, all live-bearers do not belong to one family; witness the live-bearing Half-beak, *Dermogenys*.

The first word in the name of a fish is the genus to which it belongs; the second is the species, and ordinarily is the last sub-division, although sometimes a less important peculiarity is taken into account and made into a sub-species, race, or variety; for instance, *Platypœcilus maculatus*, var. *ruber*. The first name indicates the genus; the second, the species; the third, the variety. "Variety" should never be used in any other sense. It is always *within* a species, and crosses between varieties and not hybrids.

When no specific name is given a fish, but the word "species" is used, it means that we know the genus to which it belongs, but not the species. An example would be "Corydoras species" or "spec." as it is often written.

It should also be noted that the singular of species is species, not "specie."

Sometimes after a fish has just been referred to by its full scientific name, the generic name is abbreviated on following repetitions, such as *Scatophagus argus* being repeated as *S. argus*.

Last of all, we turn our attention to that bugbear of aquarist and scientist alike, scientific names. The best we can say on this point is that "names do change" in accordance with the progress of ichthyological research. The chief source of confusion has been the hurry and carelessness of some aquarists in clapping any name on a newly imported fish before it has been carefully identified. Later check-up usually shows such names to be erroneous, with consequent aquaristic brain-ache. Sometimes modern research has made changes necessary, but where the job has been done well, we may expect relative permanence before a particular group is again subjected to revision.

In the main heading for each fish is given the name of the scientist who first described it. This is in accord with universal practice. There is one point in connection with this which is not always understood. It will be noticed that sometimes this name is in parentheses. This means that there have been developments since the original naming which require that the fish be moved into some other genus (the first name) than that in which it was originally placed. When this is done, the original describer is retained, but his name is placed in parentheses.

Pronunciation
of the scientific names of fishes

AS "rare Ben Jonson" expressed it, most of us have "little Latin and less Greek," yet we aquarists would like to be able to acceptably pronounce the scientific names of our fishes.

We have therefore consulted leading scientists and scholars. In the main, all agree. The few differences of opinion occur principally as to which syllables in compound words take the accent.

Generally speaking, there is an accepted standard of pronunciation of scientific names. This, however, is not inflexible, nor without its exceptions. As with all languages, it is influenced by popular usage.

And now a word about the modern system. English botanists, so far as we can learn, were the first large group of scientists to address themselves seriously to this matter. Nearly a century ago they decided to modernize Latin and Greek names by giving English pronunciation to the vowels. At the same time they devised a method of simultaneously indicating the vowels to be accented and whether those vowels take the long or short English sound. The very simple system consists of the use of the French acute mark (′) over the vowel to indicate the short, and the grave (`) to indicate the long sound. This system proved so satisfactory that it has continued and is now in practically universal use in all works or books of science written in English. The phonetic spellings, just below the marked titles, are for the benefit of those readers who have not acquainted themselves with the system of accents just referred to.

It will be noted that in the phonetic spellings, both single and double accents are used. The double mark shows which syllable takes the stronger accent.

The pronunciation of the vowels, long or short, according to the marks are as in the following words:

Long à as in hay; short á as in hat.

Broad ä as in bar.

Long è as in key; short é as in met.

Long ì as in tie; short í as in hit.

Long ò as in toe; short ó as in top.

Long ù as in cue; short ú as in nut.

Aquarists will be relieved to know that the consonants C and P queerly used in the beginning of such words as *Ctenobrycon, Ctenops* and *Pterophyllum* are silent. They represent Greek sounds which have no English equivalents.

Spawning the Egg-layers

$\mathcal{T}$HERE are three general classes of Egg-layers: those which drop non-adhesive eggs, those which scatter or drop adhesive eggs and those which carefully place adhesive eggs. The first of these classes is pretty well covered under *Brachydanio rerio*. The last is fully described under the general heading, "The Cichlids."

We dwell here principally on that large and important class which scatters adhesive eggs, and particularly on the culture of all newly hatched fishes which are very small in size. That includes nearly all the classes of Egg-layers just referred to. It takes in most of the Characins, the Carps or Minnows, the Egg-laying Tooth-carps and others.

In general the requirements for breeders of this type are similar. The aquarium should have a reasonable amount of open space, but with thickets of plants having finely divided leaves, such as Myriophyllum.

For this purpose such plants can be added to an already established aquarium containing Sagittaria, Vallisneria, etc. Myriophyllum, in addition to its excellent form for egg-catching, also has the advantage of being easily removed, either with or without the eggs attached. Plenty of the floating plant, Riccia, is perfect for some of the species which like to spawn near the surface.

Many fishes are more apt to spawn if separated for a few days from their mates. "Absence makes the heart grow fonder." It is usually best to place the female in the breeding aquarium half a day in advance of the male. Feed well on live food if possible, or on chopped earthworms.

If spawning does not take place within a few days, give them about 1/5 of new (but seasoned) water every other day. Aeration helps.

Remove breeders after spawning, or take out the plants bearing the eggs, and place them in seasoned water of equal temperature.

The greatest problem in fish culture is the feeding of newly hatched fishes. The tiny ones, like baby *Ambassis lala,* should at first have green water given them, if possible. Usually the practice with the average young is to feed Infusoria (see "Infusoria Culture") until they are large enough to take small sifted live Daphnia, or the finest sizes of prepared foods. It helps them grow if able to pick among natural algae in the tank.

Young fishes should have a constant supply of food, but if any prepared article is used, snails ought to be present to eat the surplus. They will not harm the smallest fish.

Except where noted, breeding tanks should be in good light.

Ordinarily young fishes should not be placed with their parents until they are too large to be swallowed!

PANTODONTIDAE
Pronounced Pan to don' ti dee

This family includes only one species, the Butterfly-fish of the aquarist, which comes from West Africa. Its nearest relatives are the members of the Osteoglossidæ, a family of large fishes which includes the Pirarucú of the Amazon, one of the largest of fresh-water fishes. The chief distinguishing features of Pantodon lie in the large ventral fins and in certain peculiarities of the skull.

Pántodon buchhòlzi PETERS

Pronounced Pan'to-don book'holts-eye   *Popular name,* Butterfly-fish

MEANING OF NAME: *Pantodon,* with teeth everywhere (in the mouth); *buchholzi,* after the naturalist, Buchholz

W. Africa   Western Location Map A57; x61; C64; E65   Length, 5 inches

NO finely drawn description of this bizarre fish is needed to help the reader single it out from close relatives, for it has none. However, when we see the picture of so extraordinary a fish, we wish to know something of its peculiarities, and whether there is any known reason for its fantastic fins.

This is in reality a fresh-water flying fish, the immense pectoral fins being even larger and more extended than a side illustration can show. The fish spends much time at the surface of the water, and is said to skim along it for at least 6 feet at a leap. Whether this power is used in catching food or avoiding enemies is not known. We do, however, know that the fish is nocturnal, remaining still most of the day; that it is carnivorous and must be fed on worms, large insects or small fishes; that it does not eat the young of its own kind; that its aquarium must be covered.

The pectoral fins, reminding one of the wings of an aeroplane, are blackish, deeper towards the edges. Body silvery, no bright colors. Mouth enormous. The species is, and is likely to remain, expensive.

One would hope to see something unusual about the spawning of so strange a fish, but, so far, the act has not been observed. Small eggs have been found in the morning among the leaves of such floating plants as Riccia. They hatch in 2 days at a temperature of about 78 degrees, and look like microscopic mosquito larvae at the surface of the water.

Pantodons will not eat anything which falls to the bottom. Success in getting them to spawn seems to depend largely on patient and plentiful hand-feeding of live tid-bits. An aquarium of 15 gallons or more is satisfactory.

Top View of *Pantodon buchholzi*

THE FAMILY MAPS

*A*S THE following is the first of our seven family maps, showing the world distribution of the principal groups of fresh-water aquarium fishes, a few comments may prove of interest.

What constitutes a family and its sub-divisions has already been explained. It will therefore be understood that the black areas indicate the distribution of all genera and species included in that family for which each map is made.

One of the first questions that naturally presents itself on viewing any of the maps showing a family which inhabits both the Old and the New Worlds is whether there are identical fresh-water species found on both sides of the Atlantic. The answer is that there are not any. Whether they have once been the same and then changed, owing to millions of generations under different environment is, and is likely to remain, an open question. There are scientists who believe that the Old and the New Worlds were once one, and then split apart, the Atlantic Ocean filling the vast intervening space. A glance at the map easily shows the basis for this theory. Push the Americas and Greenland eastward and the fit is not bad.

Various kinds of life, especially plants with fish eggs and microscopic organisms attached to them, have undoubtedly been introduced into new waters while clinging to the feet of aquatic birds. To span the Atlantic in its present size by this means would, of course, be out of the question on several counts, the one that would first occur to the aquarist being that the eggs would have dried long before their hatching period had been reached.

In some parts of the world, such as S. E. Asia, it is quite certain that man himself has increased distribution by carrying fishes from point to point.

The boundaries of distribution of many forms of life, including fishes, are now so well known that if a species is found far outside its natural family range, it would be taken for granted that it had been artificially introduced, the same as an Oregon Fir tree being found in England, or an African Lion discovered in the neighborhood of Hollywood, California!

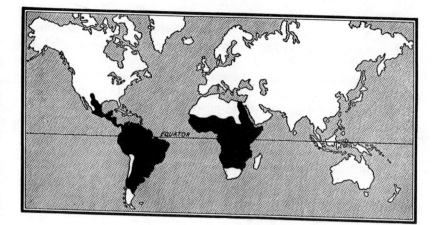

THE CHARACINS
FAMILY CHARACIDAE
Pronounced Ka ra'si dee

The Characins (pronounced kà ra sins) form one of the largest families of fishes in the world. They are all from Tropical America and Africa, as will be seen from the accompanying map. They belong to the great order Ostariophysi, together with the Carps and Catfishes. Many Characins look much like some species of Carps (Cyprinidæ), but the aquarist seldom has trouble distinguishing members of the two families. No Carp ever has any teeth in the jaws, or any adipose fin. Most Characins possess both teeth and an adipose fin. Some lack one or the other, but few or no species lack both, and if aquarists will remember this "one-or-the-other" combination, they will seldom be puzzled. The presence of teeth in a small live fish is easily determined by running a pin or needle lightly along the upper jaw of a fish held gently but firmly in a wet cloth or net. (Some Characins have teeth only in the upper jaw.) Internally they differ from the Carps in the bones of the throat. All Characins have scales, excepting one very rare species from Argentina.

While there is considerable variation in members of the family as to size, shape and habits, ranging from the dainty water-skimming little Carnegiella to the blood-thirsty Piranha, there is usually a suggestion of uniformity that is not hard to discover.

Most of them are fairly hardy, considering that they come from tropical regions.

Generally speaking, they are not fighters, although any fish with good teeth is liable to use them. This sometimes results in a little sly nipping of fins. It takes place so seldom, and without any outward appearance of fighting, that it is hard to detect. On the whole they are peaceful and seldom kill.

In the matter of food most of them are easily pleased with an average fish diet. They appreciate variety, especially when it tends towards live foods and fleshy substance, such as minced fish or shellfish, either boiled or raw.

Breeding and Care
Very few of the species are easily bred. They offer an interesting challenge to the aquarist in that respect. A number of them yield to skillful handling, yet several of the most desirable species, such as *Hyphessobrycon heterorhabdus* (better known as *Hemigrammus ulreyi*), still oblige us to import native specimens in order to keep up our stocks.

With the exceptions to be noted, the Characins drop adhesive or semi-adhesive eggs, to which they pay no attention, except, perhaps, for the doubtful compliment of eating them. Failing this, they are likely to make up for the oversight by devouring the young. None of them fight in defense of their fry, as do the Cichlids and Bubble Nest-builders.

In general the Characins are not fishes requiring very "tropical" temperature. They do very well in water at from 70 to 75 degrees, although for breeding, it should, in most instances, be raised to 80. If kept at constantly high temperatures, the diminished oxygen content of the water seems to have a weakening effect on these and many other "tropical" fishes.

Gnathonemus petersi (GUENTHER)

Pronounced Nay'tho-nee'mus peters-eye

MEANING OF NAME: *Gnathonemus*, jaw-thread; *petersi*, for Dr. Wilhelm Peters,
Berlin zoologist

Niger River to Congo River   Western Location Map A56 to G61   Length, up to 9 inches

THIS species shows up occasionally in African imports. Its downswept snout is admirably adapted to grubbing in the bottom gravel for worms, of which it seems to be very fond. It should be kept in a well-planted tank, where it will frequently hide among plants or behind rocks. Breeding habits are still unknown, and there do not seem to be any external sex differences. A temperature of about 76 degrees is well suited to this species

Gymnocorymbus ternetzi BOULENGER

Pronounced Jim'no-ko-rim"bus ter'nets-eye   *Popular name*, Black Tetra

MEANING OF NAME: *Gymnocorymbus*, naked nape; *ternetzi*, after Carl Ternetz, who collected them

Mato Grosso region of Brazil   Western Location Map T21   Length, to 3 inches

ALTHOUGH this species was named by Boulenger as far back as 1895, aquarium hobbyists in the United States and Germany did not get to see them until 1935, at which time they scored an immediate hit. Most specimens sold are only one-third grown or a little less, at which size they show their deepest black. As maturity is attained the black fades to a deep gray and the fish loses much of its beauty.

Hobbyists who intend to spawn these little gems must wait until they have attained maturity, which does not come until they are about 2 years old. A spawning temperature of 78 degrees is recommended, and a tank of about 15 gallons in capacity is about right. Males are not only more slender in the body, but considerably smaller than are females. Gravel on the bottom is not absolutely essential, but a bundle or two of bushy plants weighted down at the cut end is an advantage at one end of the tank. The species spawns like almost all of the other characins, with the pair releasir g and fertilizing about 10 eggs at a time among the plants. The eggs are not highly adhesive, and some fall to the bottom. The parent fish seldom eat their eggs, but should be removed in any case when spawning is over. The young are easy to raise. They may be fed finely powdered dry food until they can take newly hatched brine shrimp.

Anoptichthys jordani HUBBS & INNES

Pronounced An-op-tick'thiss jor'dan-eye   *Popular name*, Blind Cave Fish

MEANING OF NAME: *Anoptichthys*, fish without eyes; *jordani*, after C. B. Jordan

San Luis Potosi, Mexico   Western Location Map n13   Length, 3 inches

HERE is an excellent example of what can happen to a fish if it finds itself in a cave where there is absolutely no light and no escape for many thousands of generations. The eyes, which at first were just as efficient as those of any fish, became useless and gradually atrophied until there were only the almost-empty eye sockets left. As is also the case with many persons who have lost their sight, the remaining senses are greatly improved. So here we have a fish which is totally blind but far from helpless. The sense of smell, touch and taste are developed to a remarkable degree, and this fish never takes a back seat at feeding time. Sexes are easily distinguished, the males being considerably slimmer than the females, and if a spawning is desired it is best to use a tank of about 15 gallons in capacity. A temperature of 75 to 78 degrees is good. Do not use plants during breeding; they would serve no purpose. It is advisable to bring the water down to about 6 inches and cover the bottom with several layers of glass marbles to prevent the pair from eating their eggs. Hatching takes place in 1 or 2 days, and the young are easily raised.

Osteoglossum bicirrhosum (VANDELLI) SPIX AND AGASSIZ

Pronounced Os'tee-o-gloss"um by'seer-ro"sum   *Popular name*, Aruana' or Arowana

MEANING OF NAME: *Osteoglossum*, bony tongue; *bicirrhosum*, with two barbels

Amazon River and Guyana   Western Location Map z16 and J8 to G30   Length, to over 3 feet

EVERY year when the young of this fish become available we receive shipments of 2- and 3-inch youngsters, which find a ready market among our fish hobbyists. They are usually kept in a tank of their own where they will not be tempted to swallow smaller fishes, of which they are capable to an amazing extent. They are very fond of gulping down smaller fish that are fed to them alive, but soon become tame and accept strips of raw fish dangled before them. Once they have become accustomed to their surroundings, they will do much better if they are kept there and not moved unless absolutely necessary. A striking feature of this fish is the pair of barbels which project from the mouth. The species does very well at a temperature of about 76 degrees and if not given a large tank individuals will outgrow a smaller one in short order. They make excellent "conversation pieces" and are often featured exhibits at fish shows.

Rhodeus sericeus PALLAS

Pronounced Roe′de-us ser-iss′see-us   *Popular name*, Bitterling

MEANING OF NAME: *Rhodeus*, rosy red; *sericeus*, silky

Central Europe   Western Location Map c59 to f59   Length, 3 inches

IT is indeed an unusual European aquarium textbook on aquarium management that does not devote a great deal of space to the Bitterling, and for a
very good reason: Although not a tropical species, it may be kept at the
same temperatures as are generally given to Goldfish, and it has a strange
symbiosis with the freshwater mussel that permits the fish to lay its eggs
within the protection of the mussel's gill cavity. A pair seeks out a freshwater
mussel, and the female extends her unusually long ovipostor tube and inserts
it into the gill cavity of the mussel. Forty to 50 eggs are released there.
These eggs lie in the cavity where the water that the mussel inhales circulates,
and when the female removes her ovipostor the male, who is waiting close
by, releases his sperm where it will be sucked in with the water and fertilize
the eggs. When the eggs hatch, a process which takes 4 to 5 weeks at a
temperature of 65 to 70 degrees, the fry swim out on their own.

The insertion of the female's ovipostor must be done with a great deal of
finesse and very gently, so that the mussel never becomes disturbed and snaps
his shell tightly shut.

Another interesting fact was uncovered in the middle 30's: It was found that an inexpensive and simple human pregnancy test could be performed with the aid of these fish. When the urine of a woman who suspected that she might be pregnant was put in with a pair of Bitterlings and nothing happened, she was not a candidate for motherhood. But if the male turned rosy pink with his breeding colors and the female extended her 2-inch-long ovipostor tube, it was time to think about ordering birth announcements and begin shopping for infants' wear.

This relatively simple system sounded like the answer to a gynecologist's prayer, but it had a tremendous flaw: it was not always infallible, and after many failures, it was discarded as untrustworthy.

There are several species in this genus, all of which breed as described for *Rhodeus sericeus*. Breeding them is said to be a rather simple operation, and certainly a very interesting one. It might be an easier task for the hobbyist to locate a pair of these fish than to get a fresh-water mussel. These mussels are sometimes sold to be added to the aquarium and provide a convenient means of filtering the water. There are some drawbacks which have turned most dealers away, however. The most important is that, even as you and I, a mussel must some day come to the end of his rope and die. Unless he is watched very closely for signs of life, a dead mussel very closely resembles a live one, with the important difference that decomposition soon sets in, and the aquarium water is quickly fouled. The trained eye will always watch for signs of water circulating at the mussel's intake opening, which is always left above the gravel although the creature is completely buried otherwise.

Hóplias malabáricus BLOCH

Pronounced Hop'lee-as mal'a-bar''ee-cuss

MEANING OF NAME: *Hoplias,* heavily-armed (teeth); *malabaricus,* an erroneous name, as the fish does not come from Malabar, as might be inferred

South America   Length—Aquarium size, 5 to 6 inches; in Nature, 20 inches

Western Location Map y7 to F28 and V22

A SUITABLE popular name for this voracious fish would be the "Surplus Destroyer." One of them might properly have a place in every well-regulated collection of aquarium fishes in order to relieve the aquarist of the problem of what to do with the runts, the cripples, the invalids and the inevitable surplus. Each may be dropped in with the *Hoplias malabaricus,* and if they are not more than half his size (and he is usually large), he will dispose of the subject head-first, with neatness and dispatch. Live food, however, is not an absolute necessity.

This savage has occasionally been in the catalogs of dealers for many years, and as it is totally unsafe to associate with other fishes, one must suspect that it has been used for the purpose here suggested. The teeth of the gentleman can be slightly seen in the illustration. The markings in the fins are gray, while the general body color is brown. The several dark streaks radiating from the eye give an appropriate malignant expression. Breeding habits unknown. Temperature, 70 to 84 degrees.

Copeìna ärnoldi REGAN
Pronounced Ko-pie'na   ar'nold-eye

MEANING OF NAME: The generic name *Copeina* after Edward Cope, the Philadelphia
scientist; *arnoldi* after Johann Paul Arnold, of Germany; formerly
known by aquarists as *Pyrrhulina filamentosa*

Brazil   Western Location Map G24   Length—Male, 3 inches; female, 2½ inches

THIS is one of the most extraordinary of all aquarium fishes, and one
of the most desirable, for in addition to its unbelievable breeding
habits, it is of attractive appearance, is peaceful and easily kept.

The pair illustrated could have been better selected, as the male (the
upper figure) is commonly larger than the female. The principal color
features are a suffused red in the anal and ventral fins, a red tip on the
lower lobe of the tail fin and the brilliant white spot at the base of the
back fin of the male, which is given added effect by contrast with the
black area just in front of it. This fin in the female shows a reddish spot.

The perpetuation of all animal life is obviously dependent upon the
preservation of the young. This preservation is accomplished in three
principal ways. First, we have parents which are so prolific that the
fraction of their young which escape their natural enemies is sufficient
to carry on the species. Such young receive no parental protection. Second, we have parents, not so prolific, which fight in defense of their
young. Third, we have parents which are neither prolific nor fighters,

but which depend upon clever ways of protecting their offspring. Of this class *Copeina arnoldi* is a perfect example, and all the more outstanding for being an animal in water, where cannibalism is more prevalent than on land.

Mating them is a simple matter. Place a pair together in a covered aquarium of about 10-gallon capacity, using water which is neutral or slightly acid, and at a temperature of about 73 to 75 degrees. Feed well on live Daphnia, chopped earthworms or mosquito larvæ. Presently love play and tremblings will begin, and soon we may look for action. The water should be about 7 inches deep. Into this stand a sheet of sanded glass, large enough to stand several inches out of the water. Lean this at a moderate angle against the end of the aquarium which is nearest the light. It is on this glass, about two inches *above the water line* that the spawn should be deposited. When the female is ripe she not only shows fullness, but the yellowish eggs can be seen by transmitted light through her abdominal walls.

The male soon busies himself looking for the most favorable place for the spawning and then drives the female to it. Here, in a sudden action they partially lock fins (her right side to his left) and leap together out of the water to the chosen spot. By fin suction they adhere to the glass and remain in this position for about 10 seconds, depositing a jelly-like mass containing about 10 eggs. This is repeated at intervals for perhaps an hour, until approximately 100 eggs are laid. None are placed over the others and usually the whole is evenly joined into a solid, flat mass about the size of a silver half dollar. Notwithstanding the difficult gymnastics involved in the act of spawning, every egg is fertilized.

Now begins the second stage of this remarkable procedure. With the eggs placed well out of the reach of other fishes, the problem of keeping them moist arises. The male ingeniously supplies the answer. In order to attract as little attention as possible to the eggs or maturing embryos, he stations himself a distance away. Every 15 to 20 minutes he rushes to a position below the eggs and splashes them by several rapid lashings of his tail. He then retreats to the other end of the aquarium, where he likes to have a few floating plants in which to hide. The embryos can be seen in 24 hours and hatch in about 72 hours, when they burst their thin egg shells and fall into the water, where, for nearly a week, they seek shelter at the bottom, after which they rise in a school and swim about. Infusoria and the regular feeding program for egg-layers will soon develop a fine lot of fish.

There is no object in keeping the parents present after the young have hatched, but it has been done successfully as an experiment.

The pairs in spawning are able, if necessary, to leap at least 4 inches out of water and deposit their eggs on the cover glass, but unless this surface is roughed, the eggs cannot adhere, and will not hatch if they fall into the water.

The young have a peculiarity common to several species. A narrow fin develops above the top edge of the tail fin, which appears as though the main fin were split, and that the split section had grown longer. This is known in science as the urostyle, and is present in this species between the ages of 2 and 5 weeks. The appendage is rounded (not flat like a fin).

It would be difficult to imagine, much less find, a fish to equal *Copeina arnoldi* in its interesting and resourceful life habits, yet there is nothing about the appearance of the fish to lead one to expect the unusual.

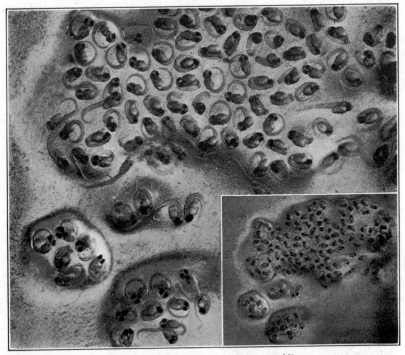

Masses of Embryos of *Copeina arnoldi*

The insert in the lower right-hand corner is from the original photograph, and is a little larger than life size. The larger picture will be recognized as a further magnified section from the same negative.

The eggs were on a sheet of sanded glass, and were above the water line, where they were placed by the fish. A few embryos had burst their shells and were ready to drop into the water. Within an hour after the photograph was taken, every one had plunged to its native element.

Copeina guttàta   (STEINDACHNER)
Pronounced Ko-pie'na gut-tay'ta
MEANING OF NAME: The generic name is for the Philadelphia scientist, Edward Cope;
the word *guttata* means spotted, as with rain drops; also known as *Pyrrhulina guttata*
Central Brazil   Western Location Map H14 to G24   Length, 3 to 4 inches

*W*ITH many species of aquarium fishes we never get them quite as large as they grow in their native waters. An extreme instance is the case of *Osphronemus goramy*. In aquarium specimens we seldom see one over 5 inches long, yet in Nature they arrive at the magnificently impossible size of 24 inches.

Copeina guttata reverses all this, in moderate degree. We grow it to 4 inches, yet collected specimens from the wild have thus far not exceeded 3 inches. The difference may not be great, but the exception is notable.

The fish is a long-established one in the fish fancy, and always has a few good friends, but for some reason has never become popular. In outline it is not particularly pleasing, and for periods the colors become pale, but when at full color and viewed in the right light, it is really a show-piece.

The reader will have little trouble in selecting the upper fish as the male. The female has few, if any, red dots; her fins are paler, but she has a much more intense black mark in her dorsal fin.

Breeding habits are quite simple. Spawns are large and the young are easily raised. The pair fans a depression in the sand, often in the fore part of the aquarium. Into this the eggs are deposited and fertilized. Very few other Characins pay any attention to eggs or young, except to eat them. In this instance the male drives the female away and fans the eggs with his pectoral fins. It is common practise to remove the female after spawning. The eggs, at 75 degrees, hatch in about two days. Ordinarily the male does not eat the young, but it is safer to remove him when they are a few days old. They should have the regular feeding prescribed for egg-layers.

The fish is apt to be just a little sluggish in its movements, which perhaps in part accounts for its lack of general popularity.

This species has a wide range of temperature tolerance. Anything between 60 and 90 degrees. Quite peaceable. Easily fed. Not timid. A good egg-laying fish for the beginner who is willing to give it a space of not less than five gallons to the pair. They have been known to breed in a community aquarium.

Pyrrhulìna rachoviàna MYERS
Pronounced Pir-oo-lie′na rak-ko′vi-a″na
MEANING OF NAME: *Pyrrhulina*, little red; *rachoviana* for Rachow, the German
aquarist and author

Argentina   Western Location Map ‡21   Length, 1¾ inches

*H*ANDSOME as is this little fish, the meaning of the name might mislead. "Little red" originally referred to the red spot in the dorsal fin of *P. filamentosa*. Anals and ventrals of the species are edged orange. While this color is lacking in the female, she has an orange tip on the anal fin. The dark spot at the tip of the dorsal fin in the male is black. It will be noticed that a similar spot is on the female, more towards the centre of the fin. The general color of the back is brown to olive. Belly white. A rather clear saw-tooth band of blue-black traverses the entire length of the body, about the middle, dividing the back and belly colors. Red dots appear in the male in the V spaces in the upper half of this line. The fins are slightly yellow, being a trifle deeper shade in the male. Also his anal and ventrals are lightly edged with orange. The fish to the right is the male.

This species likes to spawn on the leaves of broad aquatic plants, such as Giant Sagittaria, The male guards and fans the eggs, which hatch in about 24 hours at a temperature of 75. The young sink to the bottom for a few days. The leaf bearing the spawn may be removed and hatched independently, as described for hatching the eggs of *P. scalare*. Otherwise standard culture for the young of egg-layers.

Astẏanax bimaculàtus (LINNAEUS)

Pronounced As-ty'an-ax by'mac-you-lay"tus

MEANING OF NAME: *Astyanax,* see following species; *bimaculatus,* two spotted
Formerly known as *Tetragonopterus maculatus*

Eastern S. America   Western Location Map z8 to J38 and V22   Length, about 4 inches

A RATHER robust species. In nature it reaches a length of 6½ inches, but we aquarists have never seen it in such a size. It is a fine breeder and the young grow rapidly, even on prepared food, if fed small amounts frequently. As with all other species, however, good growth can only be had when the fishes have reasonable room and warmth.

Breeding habits the same as the other large Characins, such as *Ctenobrycon spilurus.*

The species, an active and graceful swimmer in the aquarium, is distinguished by the black spots on shoulder and tail. These, it should be added, are responsible for the specific name, *bimaculatus,* two spotted. Both sexes are silvery, with a decided yellow overcast. In the male the dorsal, anal and tail fins are yellow-to-red, according to the locality from which the stock was collected. He is smaller and slimmer than the female, even out of breeding season. Temperature range, 65 to 85 degrees. Breeds best at about 74 degrees. A peaceful fish.

Astỳanax mexicànus (FILIPPI)
Pronounced A-sty'an-ax mex'i-kay'nus
Formerly known to aquarists as *Cheirodon arnoldi*
MEANING OF NAME: *Astyanax,* son of Hector, a figure in Greek mythology, possibly
because of resemblance of silvery scales to armor; *mexicanus,* Mexican
Eastern Mexico and Southern United States   Length, 3 inches
Western Location Map d-e, 8-10 to q20

IT IS on account of this species that the northern area of the Characin
map is drawn upward, even into New Mexico, being the only member
of the family found in the United States.

In color it is silver, suffused light yellow. The anal and tail fins are apt
to be thinly tinged with red.

There are two markings which do not show very well in the illustration,
a backward-sloping darkish bar just behind the head and a black, dia-
mond-shaped spot at the tail base, extending into the tail fin. A suggestion
of this is seen in the lower fish. The dark portions of the lobes of this
fin are pale red.

Its hardy nature and free breeding quality are points that have made
it popular in the past, but since the advent of so many of its more colorful cousins it is not seen as often as formerly. Breeding habits similar to
those of *Hemigrammus caudovittatus*. The male is smaller than the
female, to a greater degree than shown, the male being the lower fish.

A generally satisfactory aquarium fish. Being of a peaceful nature and
of lively movements, it is well suited to life in the community aquarium,
especially as it will take any food. Temperature range, 65 to 85 degrees.

Hyphessobrỳcon bifasciàtus ELLIS

Pronounced Hy-fess'o-bry"kon by'faș-see-a"tus   *Popular name,* Yellow Tet

MEANING OF NAME: *Hyphessobrycon,* small Brycon; *bifasciatus,* two-banded

S. E. Brazil   Western Location Map U31 to Z26   Length, 2¼ inches

A FORMER favorite that of recent years has been outshone by its more colorful relatives, and by its other self, the Brass Tet.

It is a rather plain fish, overcast with dark yellow, yet not lacking in a pleasant, variable iridescence. On the sides, just in back of the head, are two vertical dark bars, of variable intensity, reminding one of well-known markings on *Hyphessobrycon flammeus.* These show more plainly on the fish to the left (the male).

In addition to being a good aquarium fish, suited to the community tank, it is one of the few Characins that breeds readily. Formerly the species was multiplied here in large numbers, so great was the demand for it. Breeding conditions are the same as those described for its cousin, *Hyphessobrycon flammeus.* The male has the broader anal fin.

A peculiarity of the young is that at the size of an inch or less, they look like very fine Bloodfins, so fiery are their fin bases. A young one is shown in the inset.

This species shares with other "Tets" in a lesser degree, the lengthening, with age, of the points of the lower fins, especially the ventrals. The extra growth begins at from one to two years of age, and continues throughout the life of the fish. Temperature range, 68 to 85 degrees. Peaceful.

Hyphessobrycon callistus BOULENGER

Pronounced Hy-fess'o-bry"con cal-lis'tus *Popular name*, Serpa Tetra

MEANING OF NAME: *callistus*, pretty sail, referring to the dorsal fin

Formerly known as *Hyphessobrycon serpae*

Parana-Paraguay system   Western Location Map S27 to W22   Length, 1½ inches

THIS lovely little fish has been the cause of much controversy among our ichthyologists in late years. There have been many similar species which have been called "Serpae Tetras" by dealers which are actually something just a little different.

It is very unlikely that we will ever see them in large numbers, because breeders are having some trouble with them: Many females do not develop eggs and remain sterile. It may be necessary to use a number of females before a successful breeding can be achieved. They spawn in standard Tetra fashion, the male flitting before the female to get her into the plant thickets, after which, amid a lot of quivering, the eggs are laid. They will be eaten quite promptly if the pair is not taken out right after they are finished.

Hyphessobrycon eos DURBIN

Pronounced Hy-fess'o-bry"kon e'os   *Popular name*, Dawn Tetra

MEANING OF NAME: *Eos*, Greek Goddess of the dawn

Guyana   Western Location Map A21   Length, 1¾ inches

THE Dawn Tetra is one of the lesser-known species, although it was identified by Durbin in 1909. This is not one of the highly colorful species, but it is peaceful and hardy in the aquarium. The body has a sort of golden overtone, with a bit of yellow at the dorsal base and throat. There is an intense black spot at the caudal base. There is a weakly indicated shoulder spot just behind the head. Breedings have been accomplished, but it is highly unlikely that this little fish will ever take the aquarium world by storm. This unfortunately is true of many species which would be highly interesting in the aquarium but lack vivid colors. Collectors won't touch them, and the only ones the hobbyists ever get to see are the ones which were included in the shipping bags by mistake.

Hyphéssobrỳcon flámmeus MYERS

Pronounced Hy-fess'o-bry"kon flam'me-us (Hy-fess-ob're-kon is allowable)

MEANING OF NAME: *Hyphessobrycon*, little Brycon; *flammeus*, flame-like

Popular names, Tetra from Rio, Red Tet and Flame Fish

Brazil   Western Location Map U31   Length, 1½ inches

𝓑EAUTY has no relation to bulk. It only needs be large enough to be seen and appreciated. For that reason the smaller exotic fishes have gradually increased in popularity, because the little ones make small demands for space.

An inch-and-a-half size is, by many aquarists, regarded as ideal. The "Tet from Rio" is just that kind of a fish, and has all the other points of merit that could well be asked for. Its color pattern is brilliant and so simple that nothing is sacrificed to its small size; it is harmless, reasonably hardy, easily cared for and can be bred—but not so easily as to become uninteresting.

Professional breeders, especially in Europe, produce these fishes in such numbers that we are independent of direct importations for our new stock. The price is never in the dirt-cheap range.

Like many of our exotic fishes, *H. flammeus* needs favorable conditions in which to develop its best colors. Plenty of room in a well-planted aquarium, an occasional extra meal of Daphnia, or other live food, and a temperature of 75 degrees or over will soon bring it into "show condition."

The sexes may be told in several ways. The males have the Characin hooks on the end of the anal fin, which stick to a fine-mesh net when the fish is turned out. The anal fin of the male is fuller than that of the female. Its outline is more nearly straight. Hers is more concave, and pointed. In our illustration there are three males and two females, judged by this standard. It is said that the abdominal sac, when viewed *through* the light, is more pointed in the male than in the female. Color is not a dependable index.

This species is one that should be bred where at least a part of the aquarium has a thicket of finely divided leaves, such as Myriophyllum. After lively driving by the male, the fishes take a close parallel position among the plants. Accompanied by a little trembling, about 10 eggs are dropped and fertilized. This is repeated until 100 or more eggs are produced. They are small, nearly transparent and slightly adhesive. If not disturbed, they will remain fairly well on the plants, but those which fall may hatch. The young, at a temperature of 75 degrees, appear in three days. They are almost as transparent as the eggs. Green water is a good first food for them, but fine infusoria will do. Should no live food be available, a flour made of ordinary fishfood may serve the purpose. Considering the almost microscopic size of the young when hatched, it is surprising to find that when well fed they will be two-thirds grown in less than six months.

As a matter of practise, it is found that a higher percentage of eggs hatch when two males are used with a female.

The spawning fishes do not usually eat their eggs until the egg-laying is finished, at which time the breeders should be removed. As most fishes prefer eating Daphnia rather than their own eggs, it is a good plan to have a few Daphnia present during spawning, but not enough of them to create a problem after the young are hatched, for too many can crowd out and suffocate the baby fishes and the infusoria, too.

The temperature range for the species is from 70 to 85 degrees. They will eat prepared foods, but, as already stated, an occasional meal of live food is very stimulating, and is absolutely essential to bringing them into breeding condition.

For small fishes they are rather long-lived, attaining a ripe old age of from 3 to 4 years.

Hyphessobrycon innesi MYERS

Pronounced Hy-fess'o-bry"kon in'nis-eye   *Popular name*, Neon Tetra

MEANING OF NAME: Named for the author, Wm. T. Innes
Brazilian-Peruvian border: far western Brazilian Amazon;
extreme eastern Peruvian Amazon

Western Location Map H14 to J11   Length, 1¼ inches

THIS little beauty took the aquarium world by storm back in 1936, and Dr. George S. Myers did his old friend the great service of naming them *Hyphessobrycon innesi* in his honor. A few facts about the fish's interesting history are given here.

In 1936, word was received from France that M. Rabaut, a French collector of butterflies and orchids had found a very beautiful aquarium fish; the man he had sent them to in France offered to send two pairs, and, although the story was not a new one, the offer was accepted. They arrived, and caused much astonishment to all who saw them.

When more followed, aquarists all over the country as well as in other foreign countries indulged in fond dreams of getting the little jewels to spawn for them. It was soon found that this was no small feat. An interesting thing happened in this connection: Breeders in Germany were of course running into the same difficulty as those here in America. But in certain parts of the country, notably in Saxony, a few breeders were turning them out with startling regularity, and they were accused of harboring some deep, dark secret in their me'hod. An analysis of the water in this district provided the answer: The tap water which was being used was not only soft, but acid as well! When these conditions were duplicated, breeders in other places enjoyed their first successful spawnings. Unhappily, though, there were not enough fish to satisfy the ever-growing demand; it was found to be much cheaper to import huge quantities of them from the upper Amazon than to hand-raise home-bred specimens.

It has been found most important to use very clean water and containers when breeding this little fish. Eggs are quite fragile and easily destroyed by bacteria. For breeding, a 3- to 5-gallon aquarium is sufficiently large. It should be cleaned out thoroughly and meticulously, then rinsed thoroughly with distilled water. The use of plants is not recommended, but a bundle of nylon fibers which has been boiled first can be added. Distilled water in which has been brought to a pH of 6.5 by adding peat moss may be used to fill the tank. This water should be allowed to stand until it is perfectly clear, and then a small amount of salt added, about $\frac{1}{2}$ teaspoonful to the gallon of water of Turk's Island or kosher salt. When the water is again perfectly clear, bring it to a temperature of 76 degrees. You are now ready to add your breeders: select a female which is well rounded, and a vigorous, active male. Do not light the tank brightly while they are spawning, and add a lightly bubbling airstone. When the female has become depleted, remove the pair and cover the tank with a towel. Leave it covered for 2 days, then shine a flashlight through the opposite side to check for youngsters. If you find any, keep them out of bright light for the first 2 weeks. They may be fed sparingly on hard-boiled egg yolk squeezed through a clean cloth, then finely ground prepared food. In a couple of weeks they can take newly hatched brine shrimp. Rapid growth will follow.

Cheirodon axelrodi   SCHULTZ

Pronounced Ki'ro-don axel-rod'eye   *Popular name*, Cardinal Tetra

MEANING OF NAME: *Cheirodon*, with hand-shaped teeth; *axelrodi*, after the famous publisher, Dr. Herbert R. Axelrod

Upper Rio Negro, Brazil   Western Location Map E16 to F18   Length, 1½ inches
to Eastern Colombia

THERE was a great deal of confusion at first when this fish was named, for the reason that it was the recipient of *two* names: *Hyphessobrycon cardinalis* by Myers and Weitzman, and *Cheirodon axelrodi* by Dr. L. P. Schultz. The International Commission on Zoological Nomenclature decided to assign the latter name because of a priority of only one day. To this day we still see some German references to the Cardinal Tetra as *Hyphessobrycon cardinalis*, which they popularly call the "Red Neon." This beautiful fish is found in the upper Rio Negro, and, like the Neon Tetra, which it greatly resembles, it is native to streams where the water is soft and acid. Seen at a distance these waters are black as ink, but close by they look brown and very clear, but not black.

Spawning these fish takes just as much painstaking care as must be given to Neon Tetras. Good results can be achieved with the same steps, and it will be found that this species is not a bit more prolific.

Hyphéssobrỳcon heterorhábdus (ULREY)

Pronounced Hy-fess'o-bry"kon het'er-o-rab"dus
MEANING OF NAME: *Hyphessobrycon*, small Brycon; *heterorhabdus*, differently striped
Incorrectly known as *Hemigrammus ulreyi* (see the following)

The Amazon   Western Location Map F29 to G28   Length, 1¾ inches

GIVE this fish its proper setting, and its charm is hard to equal.
Certainly it is the most attractive gem of all the beautiful cousins
comprising the Hemigrammus group.

What it needs for setting off its fine points is a rather dark background
and a strong overhead light, preferably artificial, shielded from the eyes
of the observer. The red line almost disappears in an unfavorable light.
Probably it is prismatic, and not dependent upon pigment. The difficulty
of catching the fish in just the right light may be in part responsible for
the author's feeling that this is perhaps his finest set of color plates, for it
shows the group at its best.

Unfortunately we are almost entirely dependent upon importations of
native stock, because practically no results have come from the few
recorded spawnings.

The males are easily told by the hooks on the anal fin, which cause the fish to stick when lifted from the water in a fine-mesh net. When the net is reversed it takes several light shakings to loosen the fish. As has been elsewhere remarked, these little hooks are imperceptible to the eye. It is something of a vexation that the sex is so easily told in a fish that is so difficult to breed.

The species is moderately hardy and does well in an aquarium containing the smaller sized fishes. Many a fish is not appreciated because it is cast into company out of scale with its own size.

Feedings of live Daphnia are not only much appreciated by them, but are also very beneficial. White Worms or Tubifex Worms are the next-best substitutes.

This fish likes a temperature of about 75 degrees. A slow 5-degree variation either way does it no harm.

The purchaser of this species may need to exercise a bit of patience waiting for the fish to develop its full color. In being transferred from one water to another it is liable to take on a "washed out" appearance, but in a healthy, well-planted aquarium its original beauty will soon return.

Hemigrammus ulreyi (Boulenger), a very similar species, is deeper in body and lacks the translucent quality of *H. heterorhabdus,* and has no black spot at the tail base. See the following.

Hemigrámmus úlreyi   (BOULENGER)
Pronounced Hem'i-gram"muss ul'ree-eye

MEANING OF NAME: *Hemigrammus,* half-lined, in reference to the incomplete lateral line; *ulreyi,* after the ichthyologist, A. B. Ulrey

Paraguay   Western Location Map Q21 to 22   Length, 1¾ inches

HIS fish is almost an exact duplicate of *Hyphessobrycon hetero-rhabdus* except that it is deeper bodied and less translucent. It is from Paraguay and only occasionally appears in this country. Aquarists usually confuse the two. We give it a separate heading because many will look for the more slender fish of this name. Personally we have never seen the true *ulreyi* that we know of, and therefore have no photograph. For facts regarding the fish popularly known as *H. ulreyi,* see the illustration and description of the foregoing fish.

Hyphessobrỳcon rosàceus DURBIN

Pronounced Hy-fess'o-bry"con   rose-a'see-us

MEANING OF NAME: *Hyphessobrycon,* little Brycon; *rosaceus,* rosy

British Guiana and Brazil   Length, 1¾ inches

Western Location Map A21, G24 and P20

A FISH flying a black flag, but by no means a pirate. In fact it is one of the gentlest and best of aquarium species.

The handsome, over-arching dorsal fin with its great, black blotch, made more vivid by contrasting whites, is nearly always carried with military erectness as the fish darts about the aquarium in its busy way.

It is somewhat translucent, and the body color consequently varies according to whether it is viewed by transmitted or reflected light. At one time it is pale yellow; at others it is gently suffused with red. The red shown along the spinal column seems to be an internal color. Like other species of this type it appears best under strong overhead artificial light. Our photograph was so lighted.

The male (top fish in illustration) at maturity develops the longer dorsal fin, while the female shows a brighter red tip atop the white edging. Breeds the same as *H. flammeus.* Difficult to spawn. Temperature range, 72 to 82 degrees. Ahl identifies a similar fish as *H. ornatus.*

Hyphéssobrỳcon sérpœ DURBIN
Pronounced Hy-fess'o-bry"con ser'pe

MEANING OF NAME: *Hyphessobrycon*, little Brycon; *serpœ*, after Serpa, a town
on the Amazon, Brazil

Brazil   Western Location Map G22, N17 and Q22   Length, 1½ inches

A FISH that ought to be the flower of its family, but, unfortunately,
it does not display its wares to advantage. Except at moments it
does not "spread" itself and show the color of its fins. It is just a little
lacking in spirit, that important ingredient in going to make up beauty.

Allen Moody aptly says that in appearance the fish is a cross between
Pristella riddlei and the Flame Tetra, and that the colors are brighter
than in either. There is a strong glow of red over the body and into the
fins. The anal is strikingly edged with black. Enamel white edgings on
the fins give a sparkle to the fish.

This is one of the species which shows its colors to best advantage
under a strong, overhead, artificial source of light.

The species was introduced into Germany from Brazil in 1931. It was
a new importation into the United States in 1933. A few of them came
direct, but the majority were young that had been bred in Germany.
Although difficult to induce to spawn, they have, on several occasions,
been bred here. The breeding is similar to that described for *Hyphessobrycon flammeus*. An inoffensive species, easily cared for.

We suggest here, as well as at a number of other points, that small
fishes, such as these, look and do best among others of approximately
their own size. Large fishes, even of the mildest natures, have a way of
jostling smaller ones away from the food—indeed they sometimes even
chase them away.

Temperature range, 70 to 85 degrees.

Hyphessobrycon scholzei AHL

Pronounced Hy-fess'o-bry"kon shol'ze-eye

MEANING OF NAME: *Hyphessobrycon*, little Brycon; *scholzei*, in honour of the aquarist Scholze

Popular name, Black-line Tetra

Lower Amazon   Western Location Map G28   Length, 2½ inches

THIS species is one of the easiest of the Tetra group to get to spawn, and while it is not extremely colorful a tankful of half-grown youngsters is a very pleasant sight, always on the move to be sure they don't miss whatever is going on. They are not demanding as far as water conditions are concerned, and while live foods are preferred, the fish are not above accepting frozen or prepared foods and thriving on them.

Males are distinguished by a more slender body. If it is desired to get a spawning, a pair should be put in a thickly planted tank of about 10 gallons or bigger and the temperature raised to 78 degrees. The male will pursue the female, and if she is ready to spawn, a number of eggs are hung on the bushy leaves of the plants. Remove the parents when spawning is completed, or they will eat their eggs. Hatching takes place in about 24 hours. After they have become free-swimming, the youngsters are fed easily on finely ground foods.

Hyphessobrycon peruvianus LADIGES

Pronounced Hy-fess′o-bry″con pe-roo′vee-ay″nus   *Popular name,* I oreto Tetra

MEANING OF NAME: *peruvianus,* Peruvian

Peruvian Amazon   Western Location Map H14 to I11   Length, 1¾ inches

*H*YPHESSOBRYCON PERUVIANUS comes to us from the same waters that harbor the Neon Tetra, the upper Amazon on the Peruvian border. For this reason the collectors are likely to pass them up and concentrate on the much more marketable Neon Tetras, and we seldom get to see Loreto Tetras, even though they are fairly numerous in these accessible areas.

The Loreto Tetra is a small, mild-mannered fish that should not be kept in the same tank with larger, more aggressive species. The black area of the lower part of the body forms a pleasing contrast to the reddish fins.

We have not yet seen a breeding account of this nice little fish, but we have no doubt that it has been spawned on occasion. It will be interesting to know exactly how it spawns. A good guess would be that the same procedures followed with Neon Tetras would get results.

Hyphessobrycon pulchripinnis AHL

Pronounced Hy-fess-o-bry′kon pul′kre-pin″nis   *Popular name,* Lemon Tetra

MEANING OF NAME: *pulchripinnis*, pretty-fin

Incorrectly known as *Hyphessobrycon erythrophthalmus*

Amazon basin   Western Location Map H20   Length, about 1¾ inches

THE Lemon Tetra has several outstanding points: the bright yellow edging in the front part of the anal fin and the intense black of the lower edge of the same fin, but most of all the brilliant red in the upper part of the eye. These fish have an unusually perky bearing, and to see them at their best it is advisable to keep three or four pairs together in a well-planted tank. They are very good community fish, never picking on their neighbours. Spawning poses a slight problem: The fish are greedy egg-eaters, and their breeding tank should be well planted. Lowering the surface to a depth of about 6 inches helps, too. They should be spawned only in pairs, so that there will be no extra fish around when a female begins laying eggs.

Females of this species are sometimes a bit slow when it comes to developing their eggs, and should be well conditioned beforehand. The aquarium water temperature should be raised to 78 degrees for breeding, and the male will very soon go into a regular frenzy, dancing in front of the female and trying to coax her into the plants. When he does, they come to a quivering stop and a few eggs are expelled. You will never get all of the eggs. Some will always be eaten, no matter how thickly planted the tank may be. They should be carefully watched and taken out when spawning is finished. The fry are easily raised.

Hemigrammus erythrozonus DURBIN

Pronounced Hem′i-gram″mus er′y-throw-zo″nus   *Popular name,* Glowlight Tetra

MEANING OF NAME: *Hemigrammus*, half-line; *erythrozonus*, with a red stripe
Formerly known as *Hyphessobrycon gracilis*
Potaro and Mazaruni Rivers, Guyana   Western Location Map X19 to D26   Length, 1¾ inches

THE Glowlight Tetra is a justly popular species. The fish are small and very peaceful, and a small school in a well-planted tank with a dark background, lighted from above, is a sight to behold. The brilliant red stripe that runs the length of the body actually seems to glow as if the fish were carrying a fluorescent tube and lighting it with a tiny battery. This color, of course, is merely a reflection of the light coming down on the fish and disappears when the light is turned off.

Spawning this beauty is not as difficult as it was first believed to be. The important thing is to use a pair that is mature; maturity does not seem to come to this fish until it has reached the ripe age of 2 years. Water chemistry is not a too-important thing, but the pair will spawn more readily if the water is slightly acid and moderately soft. The best temperature for spawning is 76 to 78 degrees. A clump of fine-leaved plants is placed at one end of the tank. The observer, if he is fortunate enough to see a spawning, will witness an unusual thing. The two fish will cuddle close together and turn over completely on their backs while about a dozen eggs are released. Then they will return to their original position. When the female is depleted, remove the pair and cover the tank with a towel. After 2 days the fry are swimming, and the towel can be removed.

"Brass Tets"

JUST what the above name means to science is anybody's guess. To aquarists it conveys a fairly definite idea. In about 1929 a number of opaquely bright, slightly brassy, glistening "Tets" were imported. They were very distinctive and took fish fanciers by storm. None knew their scientific identity. The body seemed a little deeper than in the "Yellow Tet" (*Hyphessobrycon bifasciatus*), and the fins spread more saucily. Our photograph is from one of the characteristic early importations, and is approximately life size.

Now let it be said that the multitude of variations in closely similar plain "Tets" is a problem remaining to be unravelled. "Brass Tets" with other shaped bodies began to appear—four apparent kinds in all. It is now the settled conviction that the brassiness is purely an individual (and a rare) variation. It does not in any case seem to be a species, nor even a race, for of the thousands of them that have been bred in captivity we have not heard of one that showed the peculiar color, even when bred from two first-class parents.

One of the peculiarities of this and many of the "Tets" is that with **age they develop** long, streaming points on the ventral fins.

Hemigrámmus rhodóstomus AHL

Pronounced Hem'i-gram''muss row-dos'to-muss   *Popular name,* Red Nose

MEANING OF NAME: *Hemigrammus,* half-line; *rhodostomus,* red-mouthed

Brazil   Western Location Map F to G on 28   Length, 2 inches

TWO things about this species strike the eye at once. The first is the parallel light and dark lines running through the tail fin, reminding one just a little of the pattern of *Brachydanio rerio* or *Prochilodus insignis.* The second, if the fish is in happy surroundings, is the cherry-colored glow over the entire snout. This is particularly in evidence under top artificial light.

The fish is a comparatively new importation, but seems to live well, and to attract favorable attention. We have not heard of its being bred, but there is no reason to suppose that it has different habits from those of the other members of its family.

The species has proven itself to be an ideal inhabitant in the mixed aquarium, especially among fishes of approximately its own size. We hope some day to reproduce it in color plates. It likes a temperature of about 76 degrees.

Hemigrammus nanus   LUETKEN

Pronounced Hem′i-gram″mus nan′us   *Popular name*, Silver Tip Tetra

MEANING OF NAME: *Hemigrammus*, half-line; *nanus*, dwarf

Eastern Brazil   Western Location Map L36   Length, 1¼ inches

IN a bare tank such as you would find in a dealer's establishment, you would be very likely to pass this species by without a second glance. But put it in a well-planted tank with a dark background, and it makes a very attractive appearance.

This species has provided quite a bone of contention among the world's ichthyologists. Some say that *Hemigrammus nanus* has an adipose fin and that the species which has none is *Hasemania marginata*. Others contend that this latter name is not valid and that *Hemigrammus nanus* sometimes occurs with an adipose fin and sometimes not. This should not be too difficult for taxonomists to resolve, and we should be hearing from them with a definite identification before too long.

The Silver Tip Tetra is a fairly hardy proposition and is quite easy to spawn in the standard Tetra fashion. It accepts almost any kind of food, but should have an occasional meal of live or frozen food for diversity. Males have slightly larger fins with silvery tips that are just a little bigger and brighter.

Hemigrammus pulcher LADIGES

Pronounced Hem'i-gram"mus pul'ker   *Popular name,* Pretty Tetra

MEANING OF NAME: *Hemigrammus,* half-line; *pulcher,* pretty

Middle Amazon   Western Location Map G20   Length, 1¾ inches

THIS species has a body that is a trifle less compressed than the others in the genus, but the feature that makes it really look different is the large wedge-shaped spot that reaches from the caudal base to a point in line with the last dorsal ray. Because of this spot, some dealers have called them "Rasbora Tetras". In addition to the black spot, they have a perky bearing that makes them look for all the world like *Rasbora heteromorpha*.

Hemigrammus pulcher, unfortunately, are not "easy" spawners. For one thing, they take several years to attain full maturity. It seems that the males are frequently the ones that must be changed until a successful spawning is achieved. A pair that can be counted on to spawn successfully is a valuable acquisition. The fish spawn like the other small Characins, and fry growth is rather slow. These fish are attractive and always mind their own business. They never attack others. Although they take prepared foods readily, live or frozen foods should be given frequently.

Hemigrámmus caudovittàtus AHL

Pronounced Hem'i-gram"muss cau'do-vi-tay"tus *Popular name,* Tet from Buenos Aires
MEANING OF NAME: *Hemigrammus,* "half-line"; *caudovittatus,* with tail stripe
(through middle)
Argentina   Western Location Map V22   Length, 3½ inches

THIS is the largest of the Hemigrammus known to aquarists. Although it has its defenders as a community tank fish, there are known cases where it has been convicted of fin-nipping, particularly after it becomes large. The fish is not so attractive in appearance after it exceeds the size shown in the illustration.

Breeds similarly to the Goldfish, the male chasing the female to thickets, where she drops rather adhesive eggs. Parents must be removed after spawning. Not difficult to spawn, but ought to have a tank of at least 15-gallon capacity. Breeding temperature should be in the neighborhood of 72 to 74 degrees. The species is easily fed and cared for, as may be surmised from its wide temperature range.

The female is slightly the larger and is fuller in outline. She is the aggressor in chasing the male, sometimes killing him. Temperature range, 60 to 85 degrees.

Hemigrámmus océllifer   (STEINDACHNER)

Pronounced Hem'i-gram"muss o-sell'if-er   *Popular name,* Head-and-tail-light Fish
MEANING OF NAME: *Hemigrammus,* half-line; *ocellifer,* with eye-like spot
British Guiana and Amazon Western Location Map A21, F29 to H13 Length, 1¾ inches

𝒜DMITTING that this is one of our most popular aquarium fishes
on the basis of its own merits, there is little doubt that the clever
name, "Head-and-tail-light Fish," did much to give it a vogue. The
inventor of this label is Mrs. C. H. Peters. It would seem she ought to
be in the advertising business, for she has seized upon the most attractive
feature of the species, and dramatized it. The "lights," of course, are the
repetitions of a glowing coppery color in the eyes and at the top of the tail
base. So compelling is the illusion under a top light at night that a legend
has become established, here and there, that these mysterious points are
really luminous. The prosaic reality becomes apparent when all lights
are turned off and the fishes are left in darkness, for then they have no
lamps, like ancient watchmen or deep-sea fishes, with which to explore
the night.

Males are distinguished by a faint, light spot on the anal fin, shown
in the color plate. Also the dorsal is slightly more pointed. Breeding

similar to *Hyphessobrycon flammeus.* A vigorous, satisfactory aquarium fish, not very difficult to breed. Temperature range, 68 to 84 degrees. These are easily suited as to diet, but should have an occasional meal of live Daphnia, or treated to a suspended shrimp, as illustrated under "Feeding."

"Head-and-tail-light Fish," but not *Hemigrammus ocellifer*

The identity of this species yet remains to be determined. It is so similar to the true *Hemigrammus ocellifer* that ordinarily one of them passes for the other. The kind pictured here is the one more commonly found in aquariums.

For quite some years a very similar species was innocently, but none the less mistakenly, sold as *H. ocellifer.* In fact there are today more of the wrong than the right kind being handled in trade. However, from the aquarist's standpoint, it makes very little difference, for one shows the "lights" quite as prettily as the other. The easiest point by which to tell them apart is the pair of white dots at the base of the tail in the fish which is not *H. ocellifer.* The accompanying illustration, when compared with the color plate, makes the point clear. Just what this fish is we do not yet know.

In 1933 in our monthly magazine, "The Aquarium," we asked our subscribers to indicate which fishes they would most like to see in color. The "Head-and-tail-light Fish" and the "Tetra from Rio" led the field by a comfortable margin, the third choice being the Black Mollienisia. Experience, however, teaches us not to take these tests too seriously. Public taste changes rapidly and if the vote were taken a year later the results would no doubt have presented a different order of favorites. Still, there is little question that this interesting fish will continue for a long time to hold a secure place well up in the pageant of popularity.

Hemigrámmus unilineàtus GILL
Pronounced Hem'i-gram"muss un'i-lin'ee-a"tus
MEANING OF NAME: *Hemigrammus,* half-line; *unilineatus,* one-lined
N. E. South America   Length, 2 inches
Western Location Map x between 18 and 19; y19 to A22; F29; O19

HIS Hemigrammus is easily distinguished from the others (and remembered) by the straight black-and-white line down the front edge of the anal fin. The word unilineatus meaning "one-line," makes one of those useful memory helps.

The tail fin is faintly suffused with brownish red. Otherwise the fish carries no color, other than the black-and-white shown in the illustration. It is, nevertheless, popular, and is one of the old-time favorites. The body is silver, shading upward to olive. Eye, warm silver. Breeds like *Hyphessobrycon flammeus,* but is much more easily spawned, and the young, being larger, do not require excessively small food at the start. The female is slightly larger than the male.

The fish has those cardinal virtues of being willing to eat practically anything, and of keeping at peace with its companions, whether they are of its own species or not.

This is one of the more hardy of the small Characins, and, owing to its lively ways and easy adaptation to the aquarium, it is in steady demand. It can be found in the stocks of most dealers. Temperature range, 68 to 85 degrees.

Creagrùtus beni EIGENMANN
Pronounced Kree'a-gru"tus bay'nee
MEANING OF NAME: *Creagrutus,* tearing off flesh; *beni,* from the Rio Beni,
Bolivia, where first caught
Bolivia, Upper Amazon, Venezuela   Length, 2¼ inches
Western Location Map x15 to B12; O15, O29

*A*N overhanging nose is characteristic of this species, introduced to aquarists in 1934. It is a silvery fish, yellowish towards the tail. Adipose fin absent. The dorsal has a tracing of fine dark lines and a small spot of faint red, which is brighter in the male.

As to breeding habits, this is one of those species regarding which **we** must not be too sure. It has been bred in Europe quite freely, but there is an important point about their method of fertilization that has not been worked out. It belongs in that same uncertain borderland as Mimago-niates, Corynopoma, and Pseudocorynopoma, in which it appears that in some way the eggs are either fertilized prior to spawning, or else the female in some manner receives the sperm from the male and carries it about with her until she is ready to spawn, for it is apparently true, at least with this species, that eggs may be fertile, even though not deposited in the presence of the male. A problem remaining to be solved.

An average spawning consists of about 40 eggs, which are hatched in 24 to 36 hours at a temperature of 74 degrees. Males, if present, eat the eggs. The young, after 24 hours of hanging on plants, seek the bottom when they become free-swimming. Their growth at first is rapid, but this does not continue. Full size is attained in about 7 months.

The species seems to enjoy a temperature from 73 to 76 degrees.

Pristélla ríddlei   (MEEK)
Pronounced riddle-eye (not riddley-eye)
MEANING OF NAME: *Pristella,* a little saw, referring to the teeth;
riddlei for Oscar Riddle, the collector
N. E. South America   Western Location Map y19 to A22   Length, 1¾ inches

(O)RDINARILY this species does not show much warmth of color, yet it is one of the most outstanding of small aquarium fishes. This is because of its black-and-white contrasts in fins, particularly in the dorsal. As the fish nearly always bears itself well, like a miniature yacht with sails spread, it can be depended upon to look its best. Without any loss to itself, it sets off some of the more colorful species.

There are not many fishes in which white decorations in the fins form such an outstanding feature. This comes out best when seen against a dark background, such as is produced by plenty of foliage, like the leaves of Sagittaria, Vallisneria or Cryptocoryne. The fish looks most attractive when playing in and out of the shadows. When against lighter grounds the *black* markings become prominent.

At breeding time the tail fin has a blush of pink, somewhat as shown here. On the whole we do not feel that our color plate does the subject full justice. It has lost some of that peculiar, translucent quality which is a characteristic of the fish.

Sexes may be told by the fact that in the male the black spot in the anal does not completely cross the fin, whereas in the female it does.

Like most of the small Characins, *P. riddlei* is a "school fish." It is happiest when moving in unison with a group of its own kind. When a pair is discovered to be in spawning condition, they may be removed to an aquarium in a sunny situation, where they will deposit their eggs after the manner of *H. flammeus*. Hatching takes only 2 days at a temperature of 77 degrees.

The commercial production of *Pristella riddlei* is one of the more important phases of wholesale breeding, as the demand is a steady one.

This species comes from clear, running streams, and has a distinct preference for clear aquarium water at a temperature not lower than 70 and not above 85 degrees. Given proper conditions it will live 4 years or more—a long life for a small fish.

It should have mostly live food or else that good substitute, scraped and minced raw fish, for instance. Other live food substitutes mentioned under "Fishfoods" are acceptable. Prepared foods are taken, but these should not be used too long without a change to fresh or live diet.

A fish that one never seems to tire of.

Moenkhausia oligolèpis   (GUENTHER)

Pronounced Monk-hous'e-a ol'ee-go-lee''pis (ol'ee-gol''ee-pis is allowable)

MEANING OF NAME: *Moenkhausia,* after W. J. Moenkhaus; *oligolepis,* with few scales

S. E. Brazil   Western Location Map G14 to I28 and A21   Length, 4 inches

A FLASHING red upper half of the eye, contrasting with a leaden gray body gives this fish an individuality easily remembered. It has other features, too. The large, black spot at the tail root and the black edging of the scales, presenting a laced effect, are pleasing points. The front rays of the anal fin, as with so many of the Characins, is white. There is a small golden spot in back of the adipose fin (just above the tail).

The market is mostly supplied by foreign breeders, who send quantities of them here at a size of about 1½ inches. Purchasers are usually surprised to find how large and how rapidly they grow.

In 2-inch size it makes a fairly good community-tank occupant, but as it reaches maturity it is not to be trusted among other fishes.

The species is not easily spawned, but when it does breed, large numbers of fertile eggs are produced. Breeding habits similar to those of *Hemigrammus caudovittatus.* Temperature range, 70 to 85 degrees. Breeds best at about 75 degrees. Should often have chopped worms or minced raw fish, but will take any food.

Moenkhausia píttieri

Pronounced Monk-house'e-a pit'te-er-eye

MEANING OF NAME: *Moenkhausia,* for Dr. W. J. Moenkhaus, Indiana University; *pittieri,* for H. Pittier, a scientist in the employ of the U. S. Government

Venezuela (Lake Valencia)   Length, 2½ inches

Western Location Map 15 between x and y

𝒫ROBABLY color is the first thing that is looked at in an aquarium fish, but of almost equal importance is the size and shape of the fins. In particular a characteristic dorsal fin makes a quick and lasting impression. The accompanying illustration demonstrates the point. The dorsal is bold, striking and different from that on any other aquarium fish that we are able to recall. The magnificent anal fin matches it.

Otherwise the fish is a beautiful glistening silver, with iridescent small sparkles of green. The ventral area of the body, in certain lights, displays a light shade of blue. Contrasting with these generally cold colors is an eye of fiery red, especially in the upper half of the iris. Altogether we would say that this is a fish of distinction.

In adult specimens the sexes may be distinguished by the males having longer and more pointed dorsal and anal fins. The lower fish in the illustration is the female. The species has been bred by European aquarists, and the habits are the same as for similar Characins. It is a good community tank fish. Temperature range, 70-82 degrees.

Ctenobrỳcon spilùrus   (CUVIER AND VALENCIENNES)

Pronounced Ten'o-bry"kon spy-lew'rus   *Popular name,* Silver Tetra from Guiana

MEANING OF NAME: *Ctenobrycon,* rough-scaled Brycon; *spilurus,* with tail spot (at base)
Guiana   Western Location Map y19 to B24   Length, 3¼ inches

A FLASHING, silvery fish of flattened shape, very much as shown
in the illustration. The only relieving bit of bright color is a glow
of red in the rear portion of the anal fin in the *female.* She is the larger.

This is a hardy, peaceful fish, and is one of the stand-bys in a community tank of larger species. It is one of the most easily bred of the
Characins. Writers have described "circular and spiral dances" during
the mating season, but the author and local breeders of experience have
not observed anything different from the ordinary breeding habits similar
to those of *Hemigrammus caudovittatus.* However, we must always keep
open minds as to the actions of the fishes. They have an interesting way
of doing the unexpected. Incidentally, notice the above correct pronunciation. Unnecessary effort is sometimes made to pronounce the *C.*

The deserved popularity of this species is due not only to its glittering
appearance in the aquarium, but largely to its hardiness and the small
demands it makes for care. Eats anything. Temperature, 68 to 80 degrees.

Gephyrochàrax átracaudàtus MEEK AND HILDEBRAND

Pronounced Jee-fy'row-kay"rax at'ra-caw-day"tus   *Popular name,* Silvertail

MEANING OF NAME: *Gephyrocharax,* a bridging over Charax; i.e., intermediate between 2
   related forms; *atracaudatus,* with black (marks) on tail (the outer borders)

Panama   Western Location Map between w28 and x29   Length, 3 inches.

THE characteristic which stamps this attractive fish as being different
   from the many Characins known to aquarists is a pair of difficult-
to-describe silvery spots at the base of the tail fin. These are neither
white nor green nor blue, but have an elusive satiny silver sheen that
seems to reflect different cold tints according to the angle of the striking
light. On the outside edges of the tail fin, just above and below the
silvery spots, are narrow dark streaks. These show best in the lower fish.

A lively, graceful, gentle aquarium fish which has not yet been bred.
Temperature range, 70-84 degrees. Eats anything.

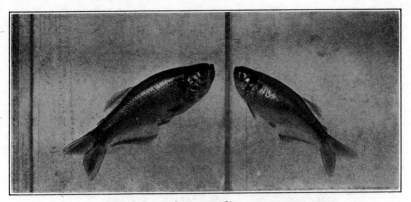

Glandulocauda inequälis EIGENMANN

Pronounced Gland'u-lo-caw''da   in'e-qual''iss

MEANING OF NAME: *Glandulocauda,* with a gland on the tail (base, in the male);
inequalis, unequal, with reference to the male's tail fin

S. E. Brazil   Western Location Map ★26   Length, 2½ inches

GUN-METAL blue is a very fair color description of this interesting and rather tender fish. The dark portions seen in all the fins are yellow to dark greenish. The dorsal, tail and anal fins are tipped white. Shoulder spot just back of gill plate is black or dark blue. Eye, red in upper part, silver below. A chunky but graceful, nicely rounded fish.

This is one of a number of species having some modification of the gills in order to hold atmospheric air. It is not as developed in this respect as is the Betta, for instance, but it often comes to the surface for a bubble of air, making a little clicking noise each time. Meinken describes a noise they sometimes make at the surface of the water as being like that of a fly caught in a spider's web.

Although this fish has been successfully bred a number of times, there remains some question as to just how fertilization takes place. The fishes do a side-by-side love dance, but no eggs seem to appear at the time. Reliable observers claim that the female several hours later deposits fertile eggs without the presence of the male. Possibly she draws into her egg duct water that has been charged with the sperm of the male. The author has never proven the process and there is not sufficient confirming evidence for him to make positive statements regarding it. The male may be distinguished by a more bulging outline to the outer edges of the tail fin, particularly of the lower lobe.

The species has a kindly disposition, is easily fed and does well in a temperature range from 65 to 75 degrees.

Mimagoniates microlèpis   (STEINDACHNER)

Pronounced Mim'a-gon-eye'a-tees mike'ro-leep''iss   *Popular name,* Blue Tetra

MEANING OF NAME: *Mimagoniates,* similar to Agoniates, a genus of Characins; *microlepis,* with small scales

Incorrectly known as *Paragoniates microlepis,* and *Coelurichthys microlepis*

S. E. Brazil   Western Location Map V30 to U31   Length, 2¼ inches

THERE are some fishes which aquarists know to be difficult to keep alive, yet they repeatedly accept the challenge because the charm of the species justifies it. Such is the "Blue Tet," the hope and despair of many a fancier.

Let us hasten to correct any idea that the fish is bright blue. It gives an impression of dark bluishness, produced mainly by a broad, dark blue lateral band, some blue on the rear part of the body and in the margins of the dorsal and anal fins. The lines seen through the dorsal fin are yellow to orange. A fine line of gold tops the broad blue band along the body. Fins otherwise clear, with a yellow-green hue. A peculiarity of the species is a fullness of the *upper* edge of the *lower* half of the male's tail fin.

This fish has been bred in the aquarium, but neither the author nor his associates have ever been fortunate enough to witness the act; nor do we know of a strictly authentic account of what happens. Rumors place it in the same breeding category as *Glandulocauda inequalis.*

With these egg-layers that are supposed to produce internal fertilization, we know of no physiological peculiarity making this possible.

Their weakness is a tendency to contract "Ick" as a result of a slight chilling of the water. They should be kept between 75 and 80 degrees.

Pseudocòrynopòma dòriæ PERUGIA

Pronounced Soo'do-ko'ree-no-po"ma do'ry-ee   *Popular name,* Dragon Fin

MEANING OF NAME: *Pseudocorynopoma,* false Corynopoma; *doriæ,* after the
Marquis G. Doria, the collector

Paraguay, S. E. Brazil   Western Location Map Z26 to V22   Length, 3½ inches

A VERY outstanding fish on account of the spectacular dorsal and anal fins of the male. The scales are silvery to blue and green. The tail fin of the male is split to the root. A jumper.

The male in breeding encircles the female with spasmodic, trembling movements in which he assumes the queerest positions. Presently both fishes dart off abruptly and about 20 eggs the size of millet seed are dropped. This is repeated at intervals for half a day. They should be bred in a large aquarium, not too deep—say 8 inches. An inch layer of marbles or large pebbles, as for Brachydanios, will save most of the eggs from the devouring parents. Hatching time 2 days at 75 degrees. The aquarium should be free of algæ, as the young become entangled in it. The young look like splinters of glass, and may be raised as per directions for egg-droppers.

There have been claims made that this is one of the species where a form of internal fertilization takes place, but this is doubtful. Temperature range, 70 to 85 degrees. They are peaceful.

Corynopòma riisei GILL

Pronounced Ko'ree-no-po"ma rees'ee-eye   *Popular name,* Swordtail Char

MEANING OF NAME: *Corynopoma,* with a spatula attached to gill plate; *riisei,* aft
A. H. Riise, the Danish zoologist of St. Thomas, West Indies. Also known
Stevardia albipinnis

Trinidad and E. Colombia   Length (exclusive of tail), 2 in
Western Location Map x between 19. and 20; also B12

*A*S AN aquarium fish *Corynopoma riisei* is unique in at least two
respects—its unusual breeding habits and the paddle-like extension
from the outer edge of the gill plate. This is most peculiar, and we have
no idea of its purpose. Perhaps it is ornamental from a fish standpoint,
comparable to the grand comb of a rooster, or, in lesser degree, to the
gaudy spread of a peacock's tail. Without the accompanying photograph
this feature would be rather difficult to explain. A very thin white line
will be observed on the lower (male) fish, beginning at the edge of the
gill plate and extending to the spot midway between the dorsal and anal
fins. Strange as it may seem, this is actually an extension of the gill
plate, and a tough, wiry one. Delicate as it appears, and difficult to see,
it is seldom injured in handling. The flattened disc at the end is iridescent, and is more easily seen than the thread-like connection that holds
it. The whole extension is seen best by a top light.

The lengthened lower lobe of the tail fin of the male gives the fish its
popular name, Swordtail Characin. The same lobe in the female is only
slightly thickened and pointed. Needless to say, the fish is *not* a cross
with Xiphophorus, although that theory has been expressed.

This and similar species have long been known to science and they are
easily collected, but for some reason they were not brought in for aqua-

rists until recently (1932). In color, *Corynopoma riisei* is translucent silver. It is not touched by any warm tints.

There is one step in the breeding method of this fish that mystifies us. It will need some clever observation or actual dissection to learn the exact truth. Courtship begins by the male circling the female in approved fish fashion but the "paddles," ordinarily held close to the sides, are occasionally extended at an angle to the body, and the long anal fin is curved towards, but not in contact with, the female. It is at this point that something occurs which we are not clear about. There is no embrace and the eggs do not appear at this time, but from what subsequently happens, it seems as though the female is now carrying the sperm of the male in her mouth. She selects spots, preferably on broad leaves like Cryptocoryne or Sagittaria, and after rubbing them with her mouth, presses about half a dozen or more eggs there. This is repeated at different points until the spawning of about 75 eggs is completed. The male does not approach either the female or the eggs at this time. The female very soon begins to move the eggs from one point to another, taking them in her mouth and sticking them on a new spot on a leaf. She constantly swims about them and guards them, refusing all food until several days after they have hatched. Hatching period, about 26 hours at 75 degrees. The male does not need to be removed, as he does not eat either eggs or young.

The babies are quite small, but are not difficult to raise by the methods described for egg-droppers. Breeding should be in a well-established and planted tank of 10- to 15-gallon capacity. Adults are easily fed, but should have live Daphnia prior to breeding. A fish of gentle habits, whose temperature range is 68 to 85 degrees.

Aphyochàrax rubripínnis PAPPENHEIM

Pronounced Af'ee-o-kay''rax rub'ri-pin''niss   *Popular name,* Bloodfin
MEANING OF NAME: *Aphyocharax,* small Charax; *rubripinnis,* with red fins; formerly
well known as *Tetragonopterus rubropictus*
Argentina   Western Location Map ‡21   Length, 1¾ inches

$\mathcal{A}$N early objection to exotic fishes was that most of them could not withstand chill. One of the first notable exceptions to this rule was the species we are here describing. The writer first saw it in the office of a business man, who assured him that these fishes successfully withstood the cool temperature common to week-ends in most office buildings in New York City. This proved to be true, and it is not very surprising, for its home in Argentine is not strictly tropical. This hardiness, combined with a distinct beauty, has long kept it to the fore as one of our most popular of aquarium fishes.

Its unique manner of breeding has seldom been observed. Two males and a female are placed in a thickly planted tank not less than 24 inches long, containing a depth of about 6 inches of water, drawn from the tap one day previously. The water is kept agitated by liberal aeration.

In their mad pursuit the fishes jump clear of the water, their bodies coming into contact in the air. Tiny transparent eggs are tossed in all directions. Being non-adhesive, they do not stick to the plants, which are useful only as a screen to hide the eggs until the fishes can be removed after spawning is completed. The young are reared according to the standard directions for egg-droppers.

This is one of the species which plays mostly about the middle of the aquarium. It seems to like being in a group or school of its own kind, but associates pleasantly enough with other fishes. For effect it shows best in numbers.

While the fish survives a temperature of 50 degrees, no such harsh treatment should unnecessarily be given. A range of 65 to 80 degrees is safe, but the best average to maintain is in the neighborhood of 70. Takes any food.

Prionobràma filígera (COPE)

Pronounced Pry'o-no-bray"ma fill'idge"er-a   *Popular name,* Translucent Bloodfin

MEANING OF NAME: *Prion,* saw tooth; *brama,* bream (a fish); *filigera,* bearing a filament (on anal fin)

Formerly but incorrectly known as *Aphyocharax analialbis*

Amazon Basin   Western Location Map H14 to G20 and M17   Length, 2 inches

O THE careless observer this fish might easily be mistaken for the much better-known *Aphyocharax rubripinnis.* A closer examination will show it to have distinct, beautiful characteristics of its own. The body has a very beautiful translucent quality that is almost glass-like. The anal fin in adults is long and pointed, the first ray being opaque white. The red in the fins is confined to the base of the tail fin in the female, the coloration in the male extending well into the lower and partially into the upper lobe. The red color is not as vivid as in the fins of *A. rubripinnis,* and the fish is a little longer. At the end of the spinal column will be seen a little heart-shaped design which can be noticed in many fishes having bodies that are partially transparent.

Probably the breeding habits of both species are similar, but at this time no spawning of this fish has been recorded.

Temperature range, 66 to 85 degrees.

Phoxinópsis týpicus REGAN

Pronounced Fox'in-op''siss tip'i-cuss

MEANING OF NAME: *Phoxinopsis*, similar to Phoxinus, the European minnow; *typicus*, typical. Also known as *Spintherobolus broccæ*

Vicinity of Rio de Janeiro   Western Location Map U31   Length, 1½ inches

*A*BOUT the only part of the illustration needing any interpretation is the light marking just at the tail base. This is an encircling golden ring and gives somewhat the same luminous effect as the spot on *Hemigrammus ocellifer*. There is no adipose fin. One authority describes the fish as having light red fins. Those we have observed were colorless. The horizontal band extending into the tail fin is dark brown. The body is partly translucent.

A meek little fish for which one is apt to feel sorry, yet in company of approximately its own size it seems to get along very well. The aquarist should always keep in mind the fact that fishes with small mouths ought to be supplied with sizes of food that they can easily swallow. Otherwise they are liable to decline and die.

The species is not particularly interesting in appearance and has not been bred. Temperature, about 74 degrees.

Crenùchus spilùrus GUENTHER

Pronounced Kren-oo'kus spy-lew'rus

MEANING OF NAME: *Crenuchus,* with a notch on the nape of the neck; *spilurus,* with a
spot on tail (root)

Amazon   Length—male, 4 inches; female, 3 inches

Western Location Map B21 to F26 and G20

IT IS quite a common thing for fishes to undergo great changes in
appearance between what we might call infancy and the adult form.
In fact, there are scientists who specialize on the study of these differences.

We have here one of those more uncommon instances where a pronounced change occurs between half-grown and full-grown specimens.
When the male, in its second or third year, passes the 2½-inch length,
his dorsal and anal fins, which previously had been only a little fuller
than on the average fish, suddenly sprout into luxurious elegance, so
that he is scarcely recognizable as the same individual. There are no
distinctive colorings aside from the long black dot at the tail base.

They have been spawned a few times, but none were reared and we
know nothing of their breeding habits, beyond the fact that their behavior
seems to be about the same as that of the usual Characin. They have
been successfully maintained for several years at a temperature of about
75 degrees. Easily fed. Not a good community tank fish.

Chalcìnus elongàtus GUENTHER
Pronounced Kal-sigh'nus e-lon-ga'tus

MEANING OF NAME: *Chalcinus,* diminutive of Chalcis, a slender bird; *elongatus,* elongate, referring to extension of tail fin.

N. E. South America   Length, aquarium specimens, 4 to 5 inches
Western Location Map Z17; G22

IT would be proper to place this species among the aquarist's rare fishes. Although pictured in European books and catalogs for some years past, live specimens did not reach the United States until 1933. There have since been several importations of this interesting novelty, the outstanding feature of which, as will readily be seen, is the dark spike extension through the centre of tail fin. Where these fishes were photographed, in the Shedd Aquarium in Chicago, they attracted considerable attention, especially from visiting aquarists.

The species has large pectoral fins and is related to the Hatchet Fishes, but lives better than they do in the aquarium. It has not been bred in captivity.

They will take any ordinary fishfood, but this should be alternated with animal substance, such as chopped earthworms or bits of shrimp.

No color translation of the photograph is called for, as it is simply a silvery fish. The dark lines on the sides are grayish to black. The middle tail spike is definitely dark, and seems like a thing apart. Judging by the deeper anal, the lower fish is probably the male. Does well at 75 degrees.

The Hatchet Fishes

STRANGE little creatures, these Hatchet Fishes, with their bulging bellies, yet so thin from the front view. They seem to be built on some highly specialized plan, not unrelated to the principles employed in aeroplane construction. They are indeed known as Dwarf Freshwater Flying Fishes, for in their native waters, when alarmed, they skim lightly over the surface for considerable distances. Although in the aquarium they will eat Daphnia and even prepared food that floats, it seems to be their nature to catch insects on or near the surface of the water. They do not like to pick food from the bottom.

It has been found rather difficult to keep most of the few species we aquarists have had, probably on account of the lack of their natural foods. Few have been bred in captivity, and importations surviving over a year are considered to have done well. This review does not sound very encouraging, but they are attractive novelties, well worth a place in a mixed aquarium, provided one does not hope to breed them nor to be their host for a very long visit.

They are not related to a well-known genus of marine Hatchet Fishes, nor to the famous Flying Fishes of the seas.

In the matter of temperature they seem, on the average, to prefer water in the neighborhood of 75 degrees. Like most fishes that hang about the surface of the water, they are not very active, but can move fast enough when occasion demands.

Gasteropelecus levis   EIGENMANN

Pronounced Gas'ter-o-pel"e-kus lee'vis   *Popular name*, Silver Hatchet Fish

MEANING OF NAME: *Gasteropelecus*, axe-belly; *levis*, smooth

Lower Amazon region   Western Location Map G24   Length, 2¼ inches

THE Hatchet Fishes have been referred to as "Fresh-Water Flying Fishes." Their structure is unusual and seen from the front the deep, keeled belly is very much in evidence. In their natural waters they are frequently seen skimming along the surface, with their bellies barely cutting through the water. As may be assumed, their natural food consists of insects that have fallen on the surface, or are flying a short distance above it. As it is difficult for the average aquarist to provide such foods, this fish group is frequently not as long-lived as it might be in the aquarium, and we have not yet heard of any successful spawning attempts. The tank in which they are kept should of course be covered at all times, and care should be taken to avoid frightening them, because if they jump they are very likely to become injured by bumping against objects. A perfect food would seem to be wingless fruit flies, or *Drosophila*. These would give an approximation of the same values found in the fish's natural food, and may well provide some substances which would be missing from the usual everyday fish food diet.

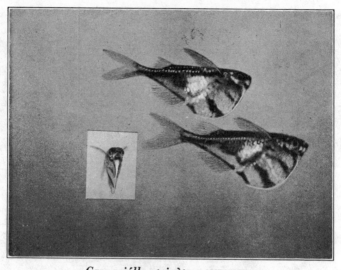

Carnegiélla strigàta GUENTHER
Pronounced Kar'nee-gee-ell'a stry-gay'ta

MEANING OF NAME: *Carnegiella,* named for Miss Margaret Carnegie; *strigata,* streaked
N. E. South America   Western Location Map A15; G20   Length, 1¾ inches

CONSIDERABLY smaller, more wisp-like and colorful than the fore-going. Highlights seen about the head are metallic, olive green, while the one traversing the broad belly (lower fish) is translucent gold. The dark parallel markings decorating the belly are brown or black. It will be noticed that no adipose fin is present. While not hardy, it is more durable than *Pterodiscus levis.* Requirements the same.

One breeder reports several large spawnings. These took place at a temperature of 83 to 87 degrees. Courtship of the male consisted in circling the female and dashing closely past her. The pair did much leaping out of the water, but the actual spawning took place in a side-to-side, head-to-tail position, the small transparent eggs being scattered among floating plants, such as Riccia.

The sexes can be told only by the broader body of the female (top view).

Carnegiélla märthœ MYERS

Pronounced Kar'nee-gee-ell'a mar'thee   *Popular name,* Black-winged Hatchet Fish

MEANING OF NAME: *Carnegiella,* for Miss Margaret Carnegie; *marthœ,* for
Martha Ruth Myers (Mrs. G. S. M.)

Amazon and Orinoco Rivers   Western Location Map A15; G20   Length, 1¼ inches

(O)F ALL known Hatchet Fishes this is both the smallest and the hardiest. In fact it is the only one to which the word "hardy" could be
fairly applied. It has been known to survive severe chill and bad treatment. One of the photographed specimens successfully got over the effects
of a dash to a dry concrete floor. Also the species readily takes dried,
prepared food. Minds its own business, but this can also be said of its near
relatives (as well as of the ladies for whom the species was named).

The "Black-Wing" part of the popular name is due to the fact that at
night the centres of the long pectoral fins are black. The silver sides of
the belly and up towards the head are heavily sprinkled with small black
markings. The halftone plate loses the clearness of these, but they may
be distinguished in the upper fish. Adipose fin (behind the dorsal) is
absent. It will be noticed that the lower body black outline is much
stronger than in *Pterodiscus levis. Carnegiella strigata* has no marginal
edging at all. Its dark parts are only portions of its patterns and its long
lower stripe does not come to the edge of the body.

C. marthœ seems to have a temperature range of 65 to 85 degrees, but
it appears to be happiest at about 75. Owing to its quaintness, as well
as its hardiness, this little fish should become a fairly popular aquarium
species.

Chàrax gibbòsus (LINNAEUS)
Pronounced Kay'rax gib-bo'sus
MEANING OF NAME: *Charax,* an old Greek name of some fish; *gibbosus,* gibbous, with
reference to the projecting nape
Amazon, Guiana   Western Location Map A21 to K10 and G25   Length, 4 inches

A NUMBER of South American genera seem to have a natural balance in which the head is down and the tail up. This is one of them, but with an added peculiarity. The head itself, taking a line through the nose, eye and gill plate, is about horizontal, while the body from this point shoots unaccountably upward.

The color is an interesting, translucent brownish amber. In the right light fine scales scatter an assortment of opalescent colors.

The fish takes kindly to captivity, and is easily fed, but has never shown the slightest intention of breeding. It is not very active. There are a number of very similar species among the genus Charax. The genus Roeboides, with several species, is also much the same.

The similarity of related fishes sometimes gives rise to the belief that the owner has a pair, whereas he has only single fish of two species, possibly both being of the same sex. A count of fin rays by the aid of a good photograph will often establish a difference in species, for in most instances males and females of a kind have the same number of rays in the fins, especially in those of the dorsal and anal.

This and similar fishes seem to be quite harmless. One might say they are harmless to the point of dullness. They are easily fed and seem to be contented in any temperature between 72 and 82 degrees. Since first appearing on the market in 1932, they have been in fairly continuous supply, although there is no prospect of their ever becoming popular.

Exodon paradóxus MUELLER AND TROSCHEL
Pronounced X'o-don pa'ra-dox''us
MEANING OF NAME: *Exodon,* with teeth projecting outward; *paradoxus,* paradoxical
Amazon   Western Location Map B21 to G22 and N29   Length, 3 inches

ERE we momentarily depart from our avowed principle of listing only such fishes as have become fairly well established in aquaria, and which aquarists may reasonably expect to secure, at least from time to time. Although this fish has been known to science since it was named by Mueller and Troschel in 1845, only a single living specimen has reached our shores. This was in 1932. So favorably did it impress our aquarists that efforts at securing a large shipment still persist. The species is not difficult to transport nor maintain, but is said to be very elusive. By its graceful, rapid swimming in the aquarium this can easily be believed.

From the general appearance and the presence of the little adipose fin near the tail, together with the knowledge that it is a South American fish, the aquarist will easily perceive that it is a Characin. Obviously the huge, intense black spot on the silver sides and the smaller one at the tail are the outstanding characteristics. The larger spot covers over 30 scales. As no other known fish closely resembles this one, the lucky aquarist who obtains specimens will have no trouble in identifying them.

The fish was first described and illustrated for aquarists in "The Aquarium," for June, 1932.

Postscript. As we go to press (March, 1935) we are able to report 2 recent small importations of this attractive species. Now that a source of supply has been definitely found, we may hope for its general introduction.

Stethaprion innesi MYERS
Pronounced Steth'a-pry"on in'ness-eye
MEANING OF NAME: *Stethaprion,* with a saw on breast; *innesi,* after Ye Author
Amazon   Western Location Map 28 between F and G   Length, 3 inches

*F*OR a time this fish, on account of its more pointed fins, especially the forward part of the anal—was regarded as the male of *Mylossoma aureum* (popularly and erroneously, *schreitmuelleri*). The aquarist Troemner early pointed out the difference in fineness of scales, and when Dr. George Myers examined one of the so-called "males," he found it to be an entirely new species that aquarists had brought to science. Just in front of the dorsal fin is a small slot into which is laid a little spine, as though it were the first dorsal ray. Repeated observation has failed to show this spine raised, and its purpose, if any, is unknown.

The fish has much less color than *M. aureum,* the fins and eye being plain silver. A flash of faint red adorns the three unpaired fins. In body shape it is quite flat, belonging to what aquarists call the "pancake" type. Breeding habits unknown. Best average temperature, about 74 degrees.

Mylóssoma aureum

Pronounced My-loss'so-ma o're-um   Popularly and incorrectly, *schreitmuelleri*

MEANING OF NAME: *Mylossoma,* shaped like a millstone; *aureum,* golden

Amazon   Western Location Map Z16 to F26   Length, 3½ inches

ONE of the most attractive and enduring of the disc-like, or "pan-cake" Characins. It is so flat that it seems emaciated. The fact that it keeps living happily on in what appears to be a thin condition reminds one of the old saying, "a lean horse for a long race."

The dark portion of the anal fin is a rich, golden brown. Note that the broadest part is in an exceptional place—up towards the tail. In life, and even more so in the photograph, it is difficult to tell just where the body edge ends and the anal fin begins. An imaginary continuation of the curve of the lower belly line approximates it. The scales are very small and very silvery. The soft vertical bars are gray, and the back is light olive. A speck of color will be noted in the adipose fin, the little projection just above the tail. The dark portion is reddish. Eye, warm golden.

The anal fins are unbelievably small. They are indicated by the white spot on the lower part of the body. Sex differences not known.

A good community fish, especially when kept with companions that are not diminutive. Comfortable between 72 and 85 degrees. Easily fed. Never been bred.

Colóssoma spec.
Pronounced Co-los′so-ma

Amazon Basin

Length, 4½ inches

*I*F THE reader, in looking at the photograph will bear in mind that the dark portions about the head and gills and the entire ventral and pectoral fins, as well as the markings in the anal fin, are deep red, it will be readily realized what a striking fish personality is pictured. The rest of the lower half of the body is delicately suffused orange. Tail edging, gray to black. Note the fine scales for a large fish.

The pectoral fins are nearly obscured because of their deep red color, matching the body color in their vicinity. Aquarists will recall that, regardless of how brilliantly a fish may be colored, its pectoral (breast) fins are nearly always transparent. Possibly this is a matter of protection, for these fins are usually in motion, and, if bright, would attract the attention of enemies. "See but don't be seen" is a good motto in a cannibalistic world. This fish is so well able to take care of itself that it can afford to flaunt an extra bit of color. Never bred. Canned shrimp is taken with apparent relish. A good average temperature for the species is about 75 degrees. As earlier stated, "spec." is an abbreviation for "species." When "spec." or "species" is used it means the species is unidentified.

Metýnnis ròosevelti EIGENMANN
Pronounced Me-tin′niss rose′velt-eye
MEANING OF NAME: *Metynnis,* with a plough; *roosevelti,* after the late ex-president,
Theodore Roosevelt
Amazon   Western Location Map G between 20 and 24   Length, 4 inches

JUST before going to press we photographed what seemed to be a new
species, resembling *Metynnis roosevelti,* having a deeper body, a different dorsal and more color than the well-known fish we have been
calling "Roosevelti." Imagine our shock to find that *this* is the true
M. roosevelti, and that for the present we must label our old friend
"Metynnis species," and move it forward to the next page!

In addition to the extra depth of body, the tail fin is different in shape
and in color. The outer edge is black. Next is an inside edging of warm
orange, the same color appearing in the anal fin and in the upper centre
of the dorsal, slightly indicated in the photograph. The tip of the dorsal
is black. In angle the fin almost tips forward. Another difference is in
the spotting on the body. In this species one of the forward spots is
larger and stronger than the rest, whereas in the other fish they are of
about equal strength.

This true "Roosevelti" is very handsome and is in fairly good commercial supply at the present writing.

The several specimens we have seen are considerably larger than observed individuals of the species next to be described.

Metynnis species

WHILE this and the preceding species are probably of similar habits, our observations are based on the actions of this fish.

Looking pugnacious, with jutting lower jaw, it is a surprisingly peaceful fish, with a decided liking for vegetation. It is especially fond of nibbling Vallisneria, to the extent of the plant's complete ruin. It will take ordinary prepared fishfood, but should also be supplied with Duckweed, chopped lettuce, or some other greens, as well as a portion of live food. A few have been bred, but we do not know how.

The only color is yellow in the anal fin. The interesting body spots are gray. A deeper cut anal fin is shown in the male (upper) fish. Some believe that the males also have a longer hooked point on the dorsal fin. We doubt this. Our observation is that the long point develops in both sexes after an age of about 3 years. Temperature range, 70-82 degrees.

A physical peculiarity of the species is the presence of an uneven sprinkling on the body of little lumps, the size of a small pin head. They look like the effects of a parasite, but they neither disappear nor increase.

Metýnnis schreìtmülleri (?) AHL

*A*S there is some uncertainty regarding this species, we will not attempt to make a guess at the locations to which it is native, except we are sure it is from the Amazon district.

In trade circles this fish, or one very close to it, has long enjoyed popularity, under the name "Schreitmüller," although our illustration does not precisely fit the original description by Ahl.

In the photograph the dark portion of the anal fin represents bright orange. The same color shows in the dark crescent to be seen on the gill cover. The elongated dots in the dorsal fin are black. Shoulder spots of dark gray and similar edgings on the tail fin are present in most individuals. The oblique dark mark on the centre of the body is a shadow, and not a marking. It is a silvery fish, and one of much beauty. Very peaceful and easily cared for. Temperature range, 70-82 degrees.

We know of no instance where the species has been successfully bred.

The statement has been made that in Brazil this is a food fish, and that its export has been banned. We cannot confirm this.

Serrasalmus spilopleura KNER

Pronounced Ser′ra-sal″mus spy-low-plu′ra   *Popular name,* Piranha

MEANING OF NAME: *Serrasalmus,* saw-toothed, salmon-like; *spilopleura,*
with spots on the sides

Throughout tropical S. America

Western Location Map W between 5 and 38   Length, up to 12 inches

THIS is one of the best known of all South American fishes. Many a horror tale has been told of these savage little fish which are said to endanger anyone who as much as puts his hand in certain waters. Actually, the Piranha is a rather shy, somewhat timid fish when kept in an aquarium by itself. As with coyotes, Piranhas' courage seems to grow with their numbers. In their native waters they travel in huge swarms and the natives find them easy prey to a hook baited with a piece of raw meat. When they want to attract them they beat the water with their fishing-rods. A caught Piranha, whether it is on a hook and line or in a hobbyist's net, must be handled with extreme caution. When the fish senses that he is in danger, he snaps with his razor-sharp teeth at everything he can sink them into. The aquarist who keeps a Piranha in his collection is, therefore, warned to keep his tank where children cannot get at it.

There have been reports of spawning this species, but such spawnings are very rare. A tank of at least 50 gallons in capacity is used, with heavy planting of bushy plants. Piranhas spawn like most Characins, and some large spawnings have been raised. A temperature of about 76 degrees is recommended. Many hobbyists feed their Piranhas small, living fishes which, once they get used to them, seem to be the best food. Piranhas can also be trained to eat strips of raw fish or pieces of clam, oyster, mussel or shrimp.

144.1

Nematobrycon palmeri

Pronounced Ne-mat'-o-bry"kon palm-er"eye   *Popular name,* Emperor Tetra

MEANING OF NAME: Named after Palmer

Colombia   Western Location Map B13   Length, Male 2 inches; Female 1¼ inches

THIS is one of our later introductions to the aquarium hobby, although it has been known to science for some time. Its name *Nematobrycon* (a Brycon with threads) refers to the three-pronged tail the males have, as well as the dorsal fin which ends in a threadlike elongation. The first thing one is likely to notice with this fish are the eyes which shine like jewels of the deepest blue.

Spawning, while not as difficult as with other fishes in the same group, is not very easy, either. A well-condition pair is put into a tank of about 10 gallons capacity with a clump of bushy plants near the top. The temperature of the water should be brought to about 78 degrees, and the composition of the water does not seem to matter very greatly. The male does a graceful dance in front of the female, luring her into the plant thickets. Eggs are expelled in the plants, after which the parents should be removed. The fry are quite hardy and easy to raise.

Leporinus fasciàtus (BLOCH)
Pronounced Le-po-rye'nus fas-see-a'tus
MEANING OF NAME: *Leporinus*, with a snout like a rabbit; *fasciatus*, banded
Amazon and Guiana   Western Location Map Z15 to B24 and H33   Length, 4 to 6 inches

ALTHOUGH this very striking fish has long been kept by aquarists, it has never become commonplace. This is for two reasons: It is extremely difficult for collectors to gather, and it has not been bred in captivity. It is an enormous leaper and jumps over the nets of the natives. Just to give an idea both of its acrobatics and its toughness, an incident in the Battery Park Aquarium in New York will demonstrate both. One of them jumped obliquely upward a distance of 5 feet, landing in a marine aquarium of a different temperature. After several hours it was returned undamaged to its own tropical fresh-water aquarium.

As the fish is rather sluggish in its movements, the aquarist is apt to become careless about keeping the aquarium covered. Reflection, however, will recall that the worst jumpers, such as Pantodon and Blue Gularis, are apparently slow movers.

The light bands in the photograph represent ivory yellow, while the dark bars are black. The fish has and needs no other colors. An interesting feature is that with age the number of bands increases. The young have 5, while fully grown adults show 10. In the upper fish it can be seen where 2 bands are beginning to split so as to add 2 more. The species usually maintains a slightly head-down angle, common to the family. Never bred. Eats anything. Harmless. Temperature, 70-80 degrees.

Abramìtes microcéphalus NORMAN
Pronounced A-bray-my'tees mike'row-sef"al-us
MEANING OF NAME: *Abramites,* like Abramis, the bream; *microcephalus,* small headed
Lower Amazon   Western Location Map F26   Length, 3 inches

DISTINCTLY a novelty, and with its assortment of markings, ranging from white, through shades of gray and into heavy black, it catches and holds the eye as being something unusual. The crescent in the tail fin is white. The other parts are mostly grays and blacks, pretty much as the photograph shows. Too few have yet been imported for us to know much about them, but from familiarity with its relatives, we could hardly expect to learn a great deal, even though their numbers were greater.

While this fish is not a member of the Leporinus family, it is closely related, and, no doubt, has many of the same characteristics. Going about with the fore part of the body tilted downward is one of them. From this peculiarity one would expect them to be bottom feeders, but from their manner of taking food in the aquarium, this does not appear to be the case.

The fish has been kept with other species and no harm was done on either side. At an exhibition in Brooklyn in 1933 this species took a prize for being "the rarest" fish shown.

Judging by its near relatives it should be happy in an average temperature of 75 degrees.

Anóstomus anóstomus (LINNAEUS)
Pronounced An-os'to-mus an-os'to-mus
MEANING OF NAME: turned-up mouth
Common in Guiana, rare in Amazon   Length, 4 inches
Western Location Map z21 to G23

*W*HEN one is used to seeing *Nannostomus trifasciatus* this fish seems like a large and rather sluggish cousin to it. The dark portions of the forked tail root are deep blood-red. Also the dark parts in the dorsal, the adipose and the beginnings (at the body) of the ventrals and anal are red. Aside from these strongly characteristic markings the broad black stripe along the body is very striking. There are two narrower dark stripes on the sides and one down the middle of the back which do not show in the illustration. These dark stripes are set off by being placed against a background of metallic gold.

The fish is related to the genus Leporinus and swims in somewhat the same head-down fashion. Although this species was described by one of our earliest great ichthyologists, it was not imported for aquarists until 1933. As yet we know nothing of its breeding habits. It is peaceful and easily cared for.

In the matter of food it will take either prepared dry food, boiled shrimp, white worms or the unfailing Daphnia. Temperature of 75 degrees is recommended. Never bred.

Prochilòdus insígnis SCHOMBURGK

Pronounced Pro'ki-low"dus in-sig nis

MEANING OF NAME: *Prochilodus,* with teeth on the forward-projecting lips;
insignis, distinguished

Amazon Basin   Length—Aquarium, 5 inches; Nature, 11 inches

Western Location Map C20 to G24

THE particular feature of this fish which captures the eye is, of
course, the flag-striped tail. A visitor at an exhibition dubbed it the
"Flag Fish," but as this name has already been preempted for the
Jordanella floridæ, we can hardly bestow it on both. Thus the advocates
of popular names for fishes may get some idea of the importance of having an organized naming system.

Prochilodus insignis has no bright colors, but the belly is rose-tinted
and the lighter parts of the tail fin between the dark stripes are opaque
ivory. Dorsal and darker portions shown on the lower fins are yellow.

The mouth is peculiar and can be used as a sort of sucking disc, with
which it digs in the soil. Likes algæ and boiled spinach. Quite peaceful.

It is necessary that this fish be carefully covered, as it can leap high
out of the water. Fortunately for the author and his readers, this one
landed back at the same spot where it left the photographing aquarium
on an aerial excursion. The owner of the fish reported a similar experience, without the photography.

Neolèbias species
Pronounced Nee'o-lee"bee-ass

MEANING OF NAME: *Neolebias,* new Lebias (an error, since Lebias is not a Characin)
West Africa; exact locality not known   Length, 1¾ inches

A HANDSOME little creature, overcast with a rich, deep red in the male. .The female (upper fish) has only a suggestion of the bright color of her mate. This fish has been imported as *Neolebias landgrafi,* but does not check up with that species in body proportions and other features. We are not yet sure of the correct name.

The species, while very attractive, has the fault of going into hiding among the plants and remaining still for long periods. Also it is sensitive to lower temperatures. Like most Characins, it is difficult to spawn. We know of no real success with the species in this respect. Temperature, 77 to 85 degrees.

Neolèbias ansòrgii BOULENGER
Pronounced Ñee'o-lee"bee-as an-sorge'e-eye
Named for W. J. Ansorge, of England

West Coast Africa   Western Location Map H60   Length, 1¾ inches

THE same error of name exists here as with the preceding. The fish is a Characin, but Lebias are not Characins. It will be seen that the form of both species is quite similar, and, so far as we know, their characteristics are the same. In life they may easily be told apart, as the broad line down the body of the male is, in this species, a metallic green when seen in a favorable light. There is a good, though slightly exaggerated, color picture of it in the National Geographic Magazine for January, 1934.

Very little is known about the fish, except what may be inferred by its family connections. It has been said that a man is known by the company he keeps. A shrewd guess may be made about a fish if we know its family. Although this idea may at times lead us astray, it is at least a good starting point.

Chilòdus punctàtus MUELLER AND TROSCHEL
Pronounced Ky-low'dus punk-tay'tus
MEANING OF NAME: *Chilodus,* with teeth on lips; *punctatus,* spotted

Guiana   Western Location Map A21 to B25   Length, 3 inches

THERE are those fishes which, without possessing any actual bright-ness of color, are nevertheless brilliant. An arrangement of contrasts or of designs in blacks, grays, olive or brown tints, combined with sparkles of silver can be very effective. Such a fish is *Chilodus punctatus.* The middle band is clear black, while the spots on the scales and the markings in the dorsal fin are brownish. This is one of those species that maintains an oblique balance most of the time, head downward. Whether absorbed in thought or merely looking on the bottom for food is a question any aquarist can answer for himself, without fear of contradiction.

The photograph of the lower fish might at first glance give the impression of its having a very long pair of pectoral fins, reaching well above the back. This is an illusion caused by the line of the dorsal and pectoral fins being momentarily held at the same angle.

The species, to the best of our knowledge, has never been bred in captivity. It seems, however, to be content with aquarium life at a temperature of about 75 degrees and is readily fed. The mouth is rather small, so when dried prepared food is used it is advisable to select something composed of small grains. Peaceful and not very lively.

Hemiòdus semitœniàtus   KNER

Pronounced Hem'ee-o"dus sem'ee-tee'nee-a"tus

MEANING OF NAME: *Hemiodus,* half-toothed (as there are teeth only in the upper jaw);
semitœniatus, half striped, referring to the short body stripe

Guiana and Amazon Basin   Western Location Map A21 to P17   Length, 4 to 5 inches

THE sharp, black spot on the side of this silvery fish, followed by the dark line extending without interruption to the tip of the lower lobe of the tail is something unique among aquarium fishes. Below the black line, and also faintly above it, is a stripe of ivory tint. The upper tip of the tail fin is touched with black, a point our camera missed, likewise a bit of white on the first anal ray. The only suggestion of color in the fish is an iridescent green along the spinal line.

Not a species commonly obtainable, but well worth securing when occasion offers. Not a very active fish, but moves easily about the centre of the aquarium. It is something to add to a miscellaneous collection, rather than to acquire enough of them to make a "school." Some fishes appear best in numbers, but this is not one of them. It is what might be called a "contrast fish."

It lives well but we have never heard of its being bred in captivity. Suggested temperature, 75 degrees. Varied diet.

Nannóstomus anómalus STEINDACHNER
Pronounced Nan-os'to-mus an-om'al-us

MEANING OF NAME: *anomalus,* abnormal, referring to lack of adipose fin; also known as *N. beckfordi,* a similar species having a dark spot on the lower half of the gill cover

Amazon and Rio Negro   Western Location Map G20 to G24   Length, 1½ inches

ONE might be justified in recording two separate color descriptions of this fish, one made by day and the other by night when a light has suddenly been turned on. The latter would be the more alluring, for the colors seem to be brightest at night when there is no one to appreciate them, like the violets that blush unseen.

Our photograph was taken against a dark background with the idea of bringing out on the male the blue-white tips on the ventrals and a tiny tip of it on the anal. This was secured at the cost of losing the effect of red ornamentations in the dorsal, tail and anal fins, which would have shown against a lighter background. The long, dark body band is intense black, bordered above by gold, which glistens vividly. The eye is light gold, divided by the black line which extends to the tip of mouth. The back is "fish olive." Belly, bright white. It is sprightly in its movements, standing still momentarily and then moving forward briskly.

Difficult to induce to spawn. Their procedure is like the average egg-dropper, depositing spawn among rootlets and plant thickets. The babies adhere to plants and glass sides rather longer than do most fish babies, taking about 5 days before they become free-swimming. The temperature at which they do best ranges from 73 to 80 degrees. Any food for this species, living or prepared, should be small, for they have tiny mouths.

Nannóstomus marginātus
Pronounced Nan-os'to-mus mar'jin-a''tus
MEANING OF NAME: *marginatus,* margined

N. E. South America   Western Location Map A21; G28   Length, 1½ inches

SMALLER and more chunky than its cousins, it has somewhat the same coloring. The broad dark band, showing more plainly on the upper fish (the male) is finely edged below and above with red. The light band above that is golden, followed again above by a dark line, and finally the olive-colored back, margined at the top by a thin black edging. Belly, silver. Dark areas will be noted in the fins in the illustration. These are deep, rich red.

The 2 fish in the insert are the young of these parents, and are magnified a little more than twice size. The difference in the tail fin, as compared with that of the parents, is very pronounced. Also the body color and shape would make identification difficult.

This spawning occurred in 5 inches of water having a surface measurement of 8 x 14 inches. The eggs were deposited in Riccia and hatched in 3 days at a temperature of 77 degrees.

The species is quite peaceful, but seems to be ill at ease in an aquarium of mixed fishes.

Nannóstomus trifasciàtus   STEINDACHNER

Pronounced Nan-os'to-mus   try'fas-see-a"tus

MEANING OF NAME: *Nannostomus,* little-mouth; *trifasciatus,* with 3 bands

Amazon   Western Location Map H13 to G28   Length, 2 inches

A COMPARATIVE newcomer in the aquarium, having been introduced as late as 1933, but it is one of the most satisfactory and
beautiful of fishes, its only drawback being that it is difficult to breed.
Some may regard this as a favorable point, for have we not seen many
fine species that were too free with their favors become commonplace
and unappreciated?

We expect some day to do this fish in natural color, for it is well worthy
of it. For the present it is easy enough to translate our photograph into
terms of color. The dark spots in the fins are blood red. Otherwise except
for enamel white on the front rays of the lower fins, they are all clear.
The two bold, dark stripes and a smaller lower one are black. Spaced
between the large stripes is a broad, beautiful ribbon of pale metallic
gold. In the male this is lightly dotted red.

We know little of its breeding habits, but what little we do know is
comparable to those of *N. anomalus.* A most satisfactory aquarium fish,
its only special requirement being food of small size. It seems to stand
a temperature range of 72 to 85 degrees without difficulty.

It will be observed that members of the genus Nannostomus do not
have an adipose fin, a fatty little projection on the back just forward of
the tail.

Pœcilobr̀ycon auràtus Eigenmann

Pronounced Pee-sill'o-bry"kon o-ray'tus   *Popular name,* Pencil Fish
Meaning of name: *Pœcilobrycon,* Pœcilia-like Brycon; *auratus,* golden
Guiana and Amazon   Western Location Map A21 to G28   Length, 1¾ inches

THE name, "Pencil Fish," is popularly applied to all the Pœcilobry-cons. Whether this is due to someone thinking that the first half of the name resembles "pencil" or it is the rounded and pointed shape of the fish which looks like a pencil, would be hard to say. In either case it is a memory help for recalling the name.

The Pœcilobrycons are very similar to the genus Nannostomus, but they have an adipose fin, which is absent in Nannostomus. Most of them tend to go about with their bodies tipped up at an angle, skygazing, just an opposite angle from their near relatives, Leporinus, which adopt a pensive posture of looking down on the world.

None of them we have ever seen have been very active fishes, although it must be said they are interesting in appearance. For some reason the writer unconsciously accords them a place among the aristocracy of the aquarium. Perhaps it is because they are unique and never very plentiful. They seem to have that indefinable something called "class."

This species has a golden brown color with several narrow brown stripes and one broad black one traversing the length of the body, ending in a splendid spread over the entire lower half of the tail fin. The light line seen just above this is metallic gold, and the dots below are dark. Anal fin, brown with a red spot next to body.

As breeders the Pœcilobrycons are not much of a success in the aquarium. They deposit about 40 scattered single eggs on the under side of such leaves as Sagittaria or Cryptocoryne. These are guarded to some extent and are not eaten. The young appear in about two days at a hatching temperature of 80 to 84 degrees. The species does not at other times require so high a temperature to remain in health. It is best to remove the parents after spawning, as their services to the young seem to be principally sentimental, and there is no telling when sentiments are going to change. Infusoria, especially the kind from ponds, is needed for several weeks. Once the babies reach the stage where finely sieved Daphnia can be taken, they are fairly safe. The main difficulty is in getting the fishes to spawn at all. For breeding purposes they should be kept in an aquarium of at least 10-gallon capacity. It ought to be well planted and contain old water, part of which may occasionally be changed in order to stimulate spawning. At no time should these fishes be kept below 70 degrees. As their mouths are small, they should have suitable sized food.

This species has been erroneously sold as *P. eques,* which has a maroon stripe instead of a black one, has red in the tail fin where this is black, and stands in a horizontal position, instead of being tipped upwards.

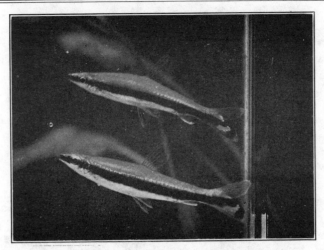

Pœcilobrỳcon unifasciàtus (STEINDACHNER)
Pronounced Pee-sill'o-bry"kon　u'ni-fas'see-a"tus

MEANING OF NAME: *Pœcilobrycon,* Poecilia-like Brycon; *unifasciatus,* one-banded

Amazon　　　　　　　Western Location Map G17 to G20　　　　Length, 2 inches

HE general remarks on *P. auratus* apply also to this species. It is longer and more graceful in form. There is a marked elegance about its simple color arrangement. The illustration tells its own story except that the two light spots in the tail fin are brilliant red. Were it not for the black line cutting the red field in unequal halves, it would be an oval, sloping upward. The narrow line on the body above the black is a metallic iridescence.

The upper fish, as judged by fins and body shape, is the male. Temperature range, 74 to 82 degrees. This species is not easily obtained. It lives for years.

Thayeria sanctae-mariae LADIGES

Pronounced Thay-er'ee-a sank'tee-mar-ee"ee *Popular names,* Penguin or Hockey-Stick Tetra

MEANING OF NAME: *Thayeria,* for Nathaniel Thayer; *sanctae-mariae,* for the town Santa Maria on the River Tocantins in Brazil, its habitat

Tocantins River in Brazil   Western Location Map K27   Length, 2½ inches

THE *Thayeria* genus is easily recognized, with its deep black stripe which runs horizontally from the gill cover to the tail base, then turns down to run to the tip of the lower tail lobe. They have an odd manner of swimming as well: when moving they are on a fairly even keel, but whenever they come to a stop, their tails' ends droop. Our British aquarist friends invariably refer to them as "Penguins." In the United States, some imaginative dealers have taken the unusual formation of the black line into consideration and called the fish "Hockey-Stick Tetras."

This is not a very prolific breeder, but sometimes a successful spawning can be achieved. They seem to prefer to lay their eggs in the open spaces and allow those that they do not snap up and eat to fall to the bottom. A layer of pebbles or glass marbles will prevent the parents from finding these fallen eggs, and they should be removed when they have finished. The fry are very small and should be given the finest sizes of foods at first.

Phenacogrammus interruptus BOULENGER

Pronounced Fee-nack″o-gram′mus in″ter-rup″tɯs   *Popular name*, Congo Tetra

MEANING OF NAME: *Phenacogrammus*, false line; *interruptus*, interrupted

Congo River   Western Location Map G61   Length, 3 inches

THIS is one of the showiest of our Tetras. Its body has an opalescent sheen which is very difficult to capture in a photograph. A group of these lovely fish with the sun shining on them from behind the observer is a sight which is guaranteed to make the most hardened "fish-nut" stop and take notice. An interesting feature of this species is the way the center rays of the tail in the male seem to sprout what looks like feathery growths. These are often broken off or bitten off, but they regenerate again.

Congo Tetras have been spawned on occasion, using large tanks and soft, acid water. They propagate in the usual Tetra fashion.

A proper temperature is in the neighborhood of 76 degrees. The water should preferably be well aged and, of course, filtered so that it is clean.

Characìdium fasciàtum RHEINHARDT
Pronounced Ka'ra-si"de-um fas'see-a"tum
MEANING OF NAME: *Characidium,* Charax idea, *i.e.,* similar to Charax; *fasciatum,* banded
E. Central Brazil, Orinoco, Amazon, Paraguay, Rio Sao Francisco
Western Location Map A15 to ‡21 and L36   Length, 2½ inches

*A*LTHOUGH to the unpractised eye this fish does not look particularly like the Leporinus family, it is closely related to it. It comes from cooler water than do most of our exotics, and is comfortable at 67 to 73 degrees.

There are no very distinctive colors. A dark stripe decorates the sides, while a number of vertical bars cross it at times. The male has longer anal and tail fins, as well as a higher, broader dorsal. In the illustration he is the fish to the left. The species is rather carnivorous, although it will eat prepared foods containing a large percentage of animal substance.

Spawning takes place in the lower part of the aquarium. Fontinalis is a very good receiving plant for the eggs. The young must have small live food. Not commonly for sale, as it has no outstanding appeal to the eye. It is a fish for those desiring a comprehensive collection, especially as it is an important connection between families.

Nannaèthiops unitæniàtus GUENTHER
Pronounced Nan-e'thee-ops u'ni-tee'nee-a''tus

MEANING OF NAME: *Nannaethiops,* small African; *unitæniatus,* single-lined
Nile, Congo, Niger   Length—Male, 2½ inches; female, 3 inches
Western Location Map B56; B53; C58; w69

THE lateral stripe shows an attractive golden line just above it. As this proceeds towards the tail, it becomes coppery. Continuing into the upper half of the tail fin it spreads into a reddish area. The centre of the lower half of the tail fin is a subdued red. This, however, along with the brighter red in the central lower portion of the dorsal fin, becomes very bright at times, especially at the breeding season. The forward part of the dorsal is edged black.

After viewing the fish closely, one is aware of a body shape that is different from that of our other aquarium fishes. It has a sort of rounded plumpness, seeming to denote a good supply of vitality. The fins are always erect and well spread, which gives an appearance of well-being to any fish.

A 15-gallon aquarium planted closely with Myriophyllum is ideal for breeding. Any plant thicket will do. Eggs are numerous and hatch in 2 days at a temperature of 78 to 82 degrees. Parents should be removed when spawning is completed. Follow standard directions for rearing young of egg-layers.

A hardy, peaceful, attractive aquarium fish. Temperature range, 70 to 85 degrees. Eats anything.

THE GYMNOTID EELS
FAMILY GYMNOTIDAE
Pronounced Gym no' ti dee

THE Knife Fishes, as aquarists call the Gymnotid Eels, are not Eels at all, but close relatives of the Characins, as has been determined by anatomical studies. From the Characins, and, in fact, most other fishes, they differ in having the vent placed at the throat, rather than immediately in front of the anal fin, and by their elongate body and long anal fin. All of them are from South America or southern Central America. Most aquarists confuse the Gymnotids with the African and Asiatic "Knife Fishes" (Notopterus and relatives) which are occasionally brought in as aquarium fishes. The Notopterids have the vent in the normal position and do not even belong to the same order as the Gymnotids. Most Notopterids have a well-developed dorsal fin, while the Gymnotids, if they have one at all, have only a long thick filament held close down along the back, so that it is not easily seen.

These Knife Fishes, so-called on account of their blade-like appearance, are for the most part entirely too large for the household aquarium, the adult size in Nature being 2 feet or more. It is therefore only the young which we aquarists occasionally possess.

There are many species looking closely alike, so that positive identification is not easy. However, they are so similar in their ways that, so far as the aquarist is concerned, they may be treated as a group.

The most interesting thing about them is their ability to swim forwards or backwards, seemingly with equal ease. A graceful rippling of the long anal fin propels them in either direction, slowly or rapidly as occasion requires. The way in which they instantly reverse themselves in the aquarium when pursued by a net is most interesting.

All of the species are cannibalistic and had best be kept by themselves.

Nothing is known of their breeding habits. We do know that they are tough and can live in pretty bad conditions. They seldom die. The great trouble is that even despite the stunting influence of a small aquarium, they presently become larger than aquarists like.

Gymnòtus cárapo LINNAEUS
Pronounced Jim-no'tus kar'a-po

MEANING OF NAME: *Gymnotus,* with naked back; *carapo,* a native name
N. South America   Length, as in preceding description
Western Location Map t19 to s21; z8 to v22 and F29

THIS brown fish is fairly well distinguished by the approximately 20 backward-sloping bars, the centres of which are gray and the edges black. In life, these markings give the impression of being slightly s-shaped. The pectoral fins are clear, with a dark spot where they join the body.

It is nocturnal in its habits and is regarded as a suspicious character in an aquarium with other fishes, especially when it has grown large.

The fish may be fed on raw meat, fish or large aquatic crustaceans. Temperature, 65 to 85 degrees.

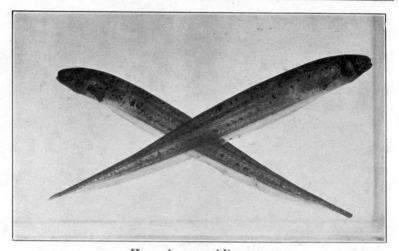

Hypopòmus artédi KAUP

Pronounced High'po-po"mus are'ted-eye

MEANING OF NAME: *Hypopomus,* with the (gill) cover underneath; *artedi,* after
Peter Artedi, the father of ichthyology

Guiana   Western Location Map A22 to G24 and X22

ONE of the several peculiarities of many of the Knife Fishes is that
some have no dorsals nor tail fins. Both representatives of the type
shown have those deficiencies, but this is apparently no handicap. In
fact considering the described gift these fishes have for swimming backwards, and possessing no eyes in the rear to guide them in avoiding
collisions, it would seem better to have a plain stump, such as we see
here, rather than a fragile fin.

The body of this species is gray-green, dotted black, and with a thin
dark line parallel with the spinal column. Fins clear. Eye almost imperceptible, being rather small and of the same color as the body. The
peculiar pose in the photograph is accidental and means nothing.

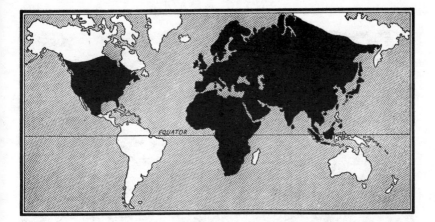

THE CARPS OR MINNOWS
FAMILY CYPRINIDAE
Pronounced Sy prin'i dee

The Carps form the largest family of fishes known. Nearly all have scales, but none has teeth in the jaws. In place of jaw teeth, they have curved pharyngeal bones in the throat which bear grinding teeth. Many Carps have barbels (whisker-like structures about the mouth) but none of them have more than 2 pairs. No Carp ever has an adipose fin, and no Carp ever occurs naturally in South America or Australia.

The Carps vary in size from the giant Mahaseer of India, which grows to 6 feet in length, to such tiny creatures as our little *Rasbora maculata,* of scarcely more than an inch. They are particularly numerous in tropical Africa and Southeastern Asia. Many of our best small aquarium fishes belong to this group.

Dànio malabáricus (JERDON)

Pronounced Dan'e-o mal'a-bar"i-cus   *Popular name,* Giant Danio
MEANING OF NAME: *Danio,* after a native name Dhani; *malabaricus,* from Malabar
India   Eastern Location Map x18 to A20; C22   Length, 4 inches

THIS is in many ways an admirable fish. Always on the move, easily
fed and bred, rather long lived and ordinarily peaceful, this species
is considered to be one of the standard members of a "happy family"
tank. We have heard of their eating much smaller fishes, but this is
liable to occur with many species when the difference in size is great.

Brachydanios were formerly known as Danios. On this basis it will be
seen that this species is entitled to be called a giant.

Distinguishing the sexes is not easy except at breeding time, when the
female is fuller in belly outline. The ruddy hue shown in the fins and
anal region is a breeding color, and ordinarily does not appear. It is
stronger in the male. On the sides of mature fishes the golden vertical
and horizontal bars and stripes are more broken in the female. Also the
lower jaw of the male protrudes slightly. The illustration shows all three
of these points, the lower fish being the male. The size of the sexes,
however, should be reversed, the adult female being slightly larger than
the male. They have *adhesive* eggs and breed like Barbs. Temperature,
68 to 80 degrees.

Upper left, *Brachydanio rerio;* upper right, *Brachydanio nigrofasciatus;*
lower, *Brachydanio albolineatus.*

Bráchydànio rèrio (HAMILTON-BUCHANAN)

Pronounced Brack'i-day"ne-o ree're-o   *Popular names,* Zebra Fish, Zebra Danio
MEANING OF NAME: *Brachydanio,* short Danio; *rerio,* a native name; also known
as *Danio rerio*
Bengal, India   Eastern Location Map w22 to p28 and p33   Length, 1¾ inches

OF THE various small egg-layers this fish is, no doubt, the most
permanently popular, and with good reason. In an exceptional
degree it has all the points which make an ideal aquarium occupant.
It is unusually active without being nervously annoying, and as a fish
to show to advantage moving in schools, it scarcely has an equal, for its
beautiful horizontal stripes, repeated in each fish, give a "stream line
effect" that might well be the envy of our best automobile designers.

The sexes can be distinguished, but not at a glance. As is usual in
many species, the females are noticeably fuller as spawning time
approaches, and this is particularly true of all of the Brachydanios, but
it is possible to tell the sexes of adult Rerios by the fact that there is a
more yellowish cast over the female, and particularly in the tail fin.

The spawning of the Brachydanios is interesting because it challenges our ingenuity and resourcefulness in overcoming the strong tendency of these active fishes to eat their own eggs as they fall.

The scheme is to have the water so shallow that the fishes have no chance to spear them as they sink, and to then have the eggs fall into a trap where the fishes cannot follow. The trap consists simply of small marbles or pebbles to a depth of about an inch. The eggs are non-adhesive and drop between the marbles to the bottom. One danger with marbles is that the fishes in fright are liable to wriggle among them and be unable to get out. In that respect, quarter-inch rounded stones are

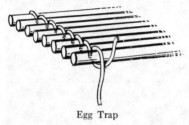

Egg Trap

better. A mat of glass bars, such as illustrated, serves the purpose well. This is fastened together with 16-gauge soft aluminum or solder wire. It is raised off the bottom by resting on 2 bars laid at right angles to those in the mat. The water should not be higher than 4 inches above the pebbles or glass bars.

As spawning time approaches it is well to separate any promising-looking female and feed her for a week on choice food. Have the trapped aquarium prepared and seasoned, ready for her and 2 or 3 lively males. Place the aquarium where it will get good light, introduce the female a day ahead of the males, and if there is no spawn in 3 or 4 days, separate and try again. The spawning action is easily recognized. It is a wild chase, similar to that indulged in by Goldfish. The business man does not need to stay home to save the eggs, for with the arrangement described he can be assured that few will be lost. If a glass-bottom tank is used, the aquarist can look up through the base to see whether eggs are scattered among the marbles. To a practised eye the shape of the female is sufficient indication as to whether there has been a spawning.

The fishes, of course, are removed after spawning, and at this time an Infusoria culture should be started as directed under "Egg-layers," for the young will hatch in about 2 days. They at first adhere in odd positions in their first efforts at moving about, but in 2 more days they act like fish and have appetites. As the spawns average about 200 eggs, it is desirable to give the babies plenty of room. They should be continuously pushed in growth. It is the only way in which to produce fine, large specimens, and they are well worth the pleasant effort. While it is possible to raise them entirely on prepared foods, graded according to size, the result does not produce a robust fish. They are apt to be small, and even deformed. Live food is better. The best age for breeders is about one year. At two years they are old. They seldom live beyond an age of three years.

While *B. rerio* has a temperature range of 65 to 85 degrees, it should be bred at about 77 to 80. Takes any food.

Brachydànio nigrofasciàtus (DAY)

Pronounced Brack'i-day"ne-o ny'grow-fa'see-a"tus
MEANING OF NAME: *Brachydanio,* short Danio; *nigrofasciatus,* black-lined
More popularly known as *B. analipunctatus,* or *Danio analipunctatus*

Burma   Eastern Location Map v between 32 and 33   Length, 1½ inches

THIS species is a little smaller than *rerio,* and while it has a similar horizontal golden line, edged by two blue ones, all three of them passing through the tail fin, its distinguishing characteristic is a group of rows of blue dots along the light belly, and extending into the anal fin.

It is indeed a beautiful little fish, but has never been as popular as *rerio,* nor is it as easily bred, although the method of collecting the spawn is the same. The females seem more liable to become egg-bound. After much chasing the sexes assume a vertical position towards each other, the eggs being dropped during a partial embrace. Their temperature should be 70 or above, and 80 for breeding.

Brachydànio albolineàtus (BLYTH)

Pronounced Brack'i-day"ne-o al'bo-lin'ee-a"tus   *Popular name,* Pearl Danio

MEANING OF NAME: *Brachydanio,* short Danio; *albolineatus,* white lined, an
erroneous designation due to description from a preserved specimen
which had changed color; also known as *Danio albolineatus*

Burma   Eastern Location Map v33, w35 and D34   Length, 2½ inches

MANY fishes in order to be seen at their best should be viewed by reflected light. That is, with the light coming from the observer towards the fish. This is especially true of *Danio albolineatus,* whose exquisite mother-of-pearl colors can only be appreciated under those conditions. This is particularly true of the interesting colors in the anal fin, which ordinarily pass unnoticed. It has been claimed that this fin shows colors in the male only, but this is not in accordance with the observations of the writer, who finds that both sexes possess it. Possibly it is a little stronger in the male. Also the ruddy glow about the lower rear part of the body is deeper in the male.

Breeding, feeding and other requirements the same as for *B. rerio.*

Brachydanio Hybrids
B. rerio x *B. nigrofasciatus*

THE Brachydanios offer some possibilities in hybridizing, but the progeny is sterile. Crosses have been made between *rerio* and *abolineatus*, and *rerio* and *nigrofasciatus* (*analipunctatus*). The young from the latter cross, illustrated above, are longer and more slender than either parent. In life the resemblance to both parents is a little more apparent than is shown in the photograph. A few of the *nigrofasciatus* (*analipunctatus*) spots may be, seen on the central fish. In the *rerio* x *albolineatus* the resulting progeny are more like *rerios,* but with the warm, purplish glow of *albolineatus.*

These hybridizations have been produced both by natural and artificial spawnings, the latter being brought about by what professional culturists of food fishes call "stripping." This consists in gently expelling, or "expressing" the eggs from the ripe female by a stroking pressure down her sides. After they are secured, the spermatic fluid of the male is forced in the same manner, and is stirred up with the eggs, thus fertilizing them. With tiny aquarium fishes it is almost impossible, even with the most delicate touch, to bring about this fertilization without killing the fishes.

The experiment is chiefly one of scientific interest, as there is nothing about these species that would be likely to be improved by crossing.

THE RASBORAS

OF THE approximately 25 species of *Rasbora* known to science about 10 have been tried in aquariums. Those listed here are the only ones that have become established in any degree of popularity. They have only been bred semi-occasionally and more or less accidentally, for there has been no secret discovered that can be depended upon to consistently produce results. Those who were fortunate enough to propagate them can seldom repeat.

The fact that most of the species are, at seasons, observed in large schools leads the author to suspect that they are what are known as "community breeders" in which large numbers take part, and the action requires liberal space. In aquariums we get them into seemingly perfect condition, loaded with spawn, yet nothing happens. The same theory applies to the hard-to-spawn Characins. Certainly we have missed some trick, for in natural conditions both of them are tremendous breeders. What makes it all the more puzzling is that they both take kindly to aquarium life and live for years in splendid health.

They can live on prepared foods, but do much better on live ones or such substitutes as finely minced raw fish, clam, oyster, crab, shrimp, etc. In the matter of temperature they should be kept at about 73 degrees or above. Not lower than 70.

Female (lower fish) in upside-down position, rubbing leaf preparatory to spawning.

Rasbòra heteromòrpha DUNCKER

Pronounced Raz-bo'ra het'er-o-morf''a

MEANING OF NAME: *Rasbora,* a native name; *heteromorpha,* varying in shape
(from most members of the genus)

Malay Peninsula and Sumatra   Length, 1¾ inches
Eastern Location Map F39; D34; X38

ALTHOUGH until recently an expensive and rather rare fish, *R. heteromorpha* has for many years occupied a prominent place in the minds of all advanced fish fanciers. It has been the open or secret ambition of many a one to own this little beauty, so outstanding in its appearance. This writer, over a quarter century ago, was "converted" to exotic fishes when viewing the collection of Mr. Isaac Buchanan, of Elizabeth, N. J. The principal agent of this conversion was *Rasbora heteromorpha.* It must be confessed that this fish and the Sailfin Mollienisia are all that are remembered out of a collection of 300 species, easily the best in America at that time, and not since surpassed. These personal allusions are made in honor of the fish being described, for the beautiful black wedge of this little gem has opened the mind of many another confirmed goldfish fancier. It is a pleasure to be able to accord the fish the place of honor as the color frontispiece in our first edition.

So outstanding is this species among its cousins that the popular and trade name, "Rasbora," takes it for granted that *R. heteromorpha* is meant, just as though no other species existed!

The lure of financial returns has spurred collectors and importers to such elaborate efforts in bringing them alive from far Asia that they now (1934 to 1935) arrive by thousands, where before dozens were considered an event. This state of affairs has its disadvantages as well as advantages, so that one is not certain whether to be glad or sorry about it.

Many an expert has set himself to the task of breeding them. A few have had partial success. Reports of spawnings vary somewhat in detail, but in the main they agree. The successful temperature is from 78 to 82 degrees, and the action takes place within a day or two after a ripe pair has been placed in a planted tank containing water that has aged only a few days. The male swims over the female for a time. She often assumes an upside-down position, contacting her belly with the under side of leaves, such as Cryptocoryne or large Sagittaria, apparently searching a suitable place on which to spawn. Possibly she is doing something to prepare a place so that the eggs may adhere. Our photograph gives a true picture of this action. She may be coaxing the male, for presently, but not immediately, he joins her under a leaf and quickly clasps her in the crescent he makes of his body, the female continuing in an upside down position. During the momentary, trembling embrace several small crystal-clear eggs appear. These are attached to the under side of the leaf. The action is repeated under different leaves at intervals, for a period of about two hours, at the end of which time there are from 30 to 80 eggs. It is probable that clean, new leaves best serve the purpose. If they are coated with algæ the eggs are apt to fall and be eaten. At a temperature of 80 degrees they hatch in 18 hours. They are like tiny splinters of glass, but do not seem to be difficult to rear by the ordinary method used for small egg-droppers. Some have successfully reared them in the same aquarium with the parents, but this is taking a needless risk with precious babies. The largest recorded successful rearing of young is 65. At one month of age they are ⅜ inch long and begin to show the dark triangular spot so characteristic of the species.

A 3-gallon aquarium is large enough for breeding purposes. If larger, the water should be shallow.

The surest method of telling the sex in breeding size fish is by the golden line along the top edge of the black triangle. It is more brilliant and deeply colored in the male, especially by overhead artificial light. This is partially shown in our natural color photograph (frontispiece), the upper fish being the male. He also happens to show another sex indication, this one not being regarded as dependable. That is the forward-pointing of the bottom of the vertical side of the triangle. Also the intensity of the darkness of the triangle is without meaning. This dark area varies in size, form and intensity in different strains, no doubt due to the location from which they are collected. A large, blue-black triangle with clearly defined edges is regarded as the best form.

Rasbora heteromorpha moves about the aquarium easily but not nervously. It is neither timid nor aggressive, It is adaptable both as to food and temperature, a range from 68 to 88 degrees producing no ill effects, if brought about slowly. Lives about 5 years. A splendid little fish.

Rasbòra maculàta   DUNCKER
Pronounced Raz-bo′ra   mac′you-lay″ta   Known incorrectly as *R. kalochroma*
MEANING OF NAME: *Rasbora,* a native name; *maculata,* spotted
Malay Peninsula   Eastern Location Map F39   Length, 1 inch

THIS rare and dainty little fish at first glance reminds one of a male Guppy, partly on account of its size, but more especially owing to the large, rainbow-edged spot on the fore part of the side. The bearing of the fish, however, is more perky, with the fins always well spread. It is also more slender, and the fins are differently shaped.

It seems to be the destiny of certain of our aquarium fishes to come into prominence only at long intervals, like the visits of a comet to our skies. *Rasbora maculata* is one of that kind. We have seen it pictured and described perhaps 3 times in 20 years. It was not until 1933 that enough of them were imported to offer us much opportunity for observation. Although these were eagerly bought and widely distributed into a large variety of conditions, few of them survived long enough to become really acclimated to the aquarium. This is to be regretted, for it is a beautiful little creature, and especially attractive to those who like their fishes small.

The general color is reddish, but the abdominal area is a greenish white, separated from the color of the upper body by an arching line of gold. The dark portions of the fins are red and there is a smaller ocellated spot at the tail base. Males may be distinguished by their whiter bellies, and the large spot on the side is more distinct. Also they have one small black spot above the anal fin, while the females have two. The central figure in the illustration is a female, the others being males. The "ghost" in the background is that of the owner of the fishes, who unintentionally got into the picture at the instant of exposure.

The species has been bred a few times in small numbers. The eggs are deposited on the under side of a leaf, much the same as with *R. heteromorpha*, but there is no embrace, the male fertilizing the eggs immediately after they are attached. Being extremely small, the young must be fed on the finer sizes of Infusoria and rotifers.

The adult fishes will eat anything, but should be given a liberal proportion of live food of suitable size. Temperature range, 73 to 80 degrees.

Rasbòra élegans VOLZ
Pronounced Raz-bo'ra   el'e-gans
MEANING OF NAME: *Rasbora,* a native name; *elegans,* elegant
Sumatra and Malay Peninsula   Eastern Location Map F39; J40; H46   Length, 5 inches

𝒜 CENTRAL black body spot below the first dorsal ray, more or less oblong in shape, and varying in intensity, roughly distinguishes this species. Besides the ocellated dot at the tail base, there is a horizontal narrow dark line just above the anal fin. This mark and a dark nick in the upper part of the silvery iris, for some reason, fail to show in our illustration. The fish does not have the glittering appearance of burnished silver common to such individuals as *Ctenobrycon spilurus.* It is more of a leaden gray. There is just a touch of warmth to it, as in the interesting shade called French gray. The dorsal fin is light brown.

In the female the central body spot is paler, and she is the more aggressive. Anal yellow in male, clear in female. Seldom breeds. Spawns on fine plants. The species is in fairly good commercial supply.

As will be seen from the length given, this species grows to be a rather large fish, the illustration representing it at just about half size. While it is always a pleasing fish to see, it makes an especially attractive show fish when fully grown. The rather large scales, edged dark gray, show like a sleek coat of armor, which, of course, is what they are.

In the small streams of Sumatra, Singapore, Malacca and Borneo, where it is generally found, it occurs in large numbers.

The species enjoys a mixed diet, will live at peace in a community and will do well in any ordinary temperature of from 70 to 80 degrees.

Rasbòra einthòveni (BLEEKER)
Pronounced Raz-bo'ra eint-ho'ven-eye
MEANING OF NAME: *Rasbora,* a native name; *einthoveni,* for Dr. J. Einthoven,
the collector
For a time erroneously known by aquarists as *R. daniconius*
Malay Peninsula and Archipelago   Length, 3½ inches
Eastern Location Map x36 to F39; I40; I42; E47

A STRIKING stripe of black running the length of the body, clear through to the tip of the protruding lower jaw, characterizes this species. It divides the golden eye in equal upper and lower halves. The stripe is wider in the male, which in the illustration is the upper fish.

The general color of the scales is gray, with darker gray edges. The male is slightly suffused purple, while the female is more greenish. There is also a difference in the fins, the male having reddish ribs in the tail fin, as well as a touch of warmth in the dorsal. All fins in female are clear, except for a tinge of yellow in her tail fin.

An attractive, vigorous, fairly well-known aquarium fish. Although this fish has large spawns, many of the eggs fall to the bottom, and are attacked by fungus. The eggs had best be moved to shallow, clear water. The young vary greatly in size, and should be sorted to prevent cannibalism.

Like practically all of the Rasboras, they are fishes easy to get along with and mind their own business. Temperature range, 72-82 degrees.

Rasbòra danicònius   (HAMILTON-BUCHANAN)
Pronounced Raz-bo′ra   dan′e-cone″e-us
MEANING OF NAME: *Rasbora,* a native name; *daniconius,* from a native name
India, Ceylon   Eastern Location Map W19 to Q29   Length, 3 inches

RECORDS of size of this fish, a very common one in all sorts of pools, ditches and streams in India and Ceylon, run as high as 5 inches, but no aquarium specimens give any hint of such length.

It is not a particularly outstanding species as to color. The central body stripe is blue-black, delicately edged, above and below, by a thin, metallic golden line. Back olive; belly white, fins tinged with yellow. It will be noted that a narrow stripe on the body, just above the anal fin, is dark. The lower fish is the female. There are no exterior signs of sex, except shape. They spawn on fine plants, much the same as *R. tæniata.* Temperature range, 72 to 85 degrees. Active and peaceful.

Rasbòra taeniàta AHL
Pronounced Raz-bo'ra tee-nee-a'ta
MEANING OF NAME: *Rasbora*, a native name; *taeniata*, with narrow stripe
Malay Peninsula   Sumatra, exact locality not known   Length, 2¼ inches

A RATHER plain fish, light olive to brown in color, with the scales edged black. The dark body stripe is edged above with dull gold. Fins clear except tail fin. There is a dark edging on the lips.

A moderately lively fish and one of the few Rasboras that is not so difficult to breed. They spawn much in the manner of the Barbs, on the finely divided leaves of plants, depositing about 250 eggs.

The fuller body of the lower fish correctly suggests the female. The male shows orange in the base of the tail fin. He is not usually smaller, as here shown. Subject to the parasitic disease, Ichthyophthirius, at any temperature below 70 degrees.

On the whole we would say that the species is better looking and more lively than the photographic illustration seems to indicate.

Rasbòra leptosòma   BLEEKER
Pronounced Raz-bo'ra   lep'to-so"ma
MEANING OF NAME: *Rasbora,* a native name; *leptosoma,* slender body
Malay Peninsula   Eastern Location Map H39   Length, 2½ inches

*A*S IN many other fishes, the horizontal body stripe divides an olive
back from a more or less white belly. The line itself frequently
has interesting character, such as in this instance. It is a pretty band
composed (from bottom to top) of red, gold and black, and runs through
the eye to the tip of the nose. The top of the eye is red gold. Fins all
clear. Breeding habits not known. An attractive fish in a quiet way, and
one not often seen in collections.

The lower fish is the female. They are quite playful in chasing each
other about, but no damage seems to get done, nor does the fish population
seem to be increased as a result of playful pursuits.

They are adaptable as to food, but, as with other members of this family, they are much benefitted by an occasional meal of live food, such as
Daphnia or mosquito larvæ. In the absence of these an occasional bit of
minced earthworm or scraped fish is acceptable. Temperature range, 72 to
80 degrees.

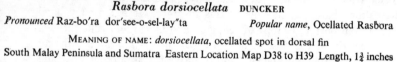

Rasbora dorsiocellata DUNCKER

Pronounced Raz-bo'ra dor'see-o-sel-lay"ta   *Popular name*, Ocellated Rasbora

MEANING OF NAME: *dorsiocellata*, ocellated spot in dorsal fin

South Malay Peninsula and Sumatra Eastern Location Map D38 to H39 Length, 1¾ inches

THIS is one of the small Rasbora species, certainly not distinguished by any bright colors. Its one outstanding characteristic is a distinct black spot with a white circle around it on the dorsal fin. This fin it carries stiffly and proudly erect at all times. An interesting sight is about six or 12 of these little beauties swimming in a well planted tank under a dimmed light. The fish's bodies are not too distinct, but that white circle with the deep black spot is very much in evidence!

At first it was considered quite a feat to spawn Ocellated Rasboras, but it has since been found that they are quite prolific. Their water should be definitely acid, pH about 6.5, and the temperature 78 degrees. A few sprigs of *Myriophyllum* or *Ceratophyllum*, or even a bundle of nylon fibers, are weighed down in a small aquarium. Eggs are scattered into this, after which the parents should be removed. Hatching occurs in 24 to 36 hours, but the youngsters do not absorb their yolk sacs for 3 to 5 days. They are easily raised with fine prepared foods or hard-boiled-egg yolk pressed through a fine cloth.

Tanichthys albonubes LIN

Pronounced Tan-ick'thiss al-bo-new'bees   *Popular name*, White Cloud

MEANING OF NAME: *Tanichthys*, Tan's fish, after the Chinese boy who found it; *albonubes*, White Cloud

White Cloud Mountain, near Canton, China   Eastern Location Map p44   Length, 1½ inches

THIS very attractive fish is a sort of paradox. It was introduced to hobbyists at just about the same time as the famous Neon Tetra. Both fish were of about the same size and shape, with one big difference: White Clouds were found to be ready breeders, spawning under a great variety of conditions, while Neons were the very devils to propagate. For this reason, Neons sold at astronomically high prices while White Clouds, which were being turned out by the thousands everywhere, went begging at "bargain" prices.

Since those days, the pendulum has come to the other end of its swing: Neons are still hard to breed, but they are being imported in such numbers from their native waters in the Peruvian Amazon region that their price has plummeted to ridiculously low levels. Meanwhile the White Cloud, which at first was called the "Poor Man's Neon," commands a higher price by far.

The White Cloud is one of the easiest of aquarium fishes to propagate. Water chemistry is not at all important, but the water should be reasonably clean. A temperature of 70 degrees is about right; a few degrees either way is not important. The pair should be adequately fed for about a week on living crustaceans such as daphnia or brine shrimp, frozen if the live ones are not available. They will then proceed to lay eggs among the plants or scatter them all over the bottom if there are no plants. Amazingly, fry are not touched by the parents.

Rasbòra meìnkeni DE BEAUFORT

Pronounced Raz-bo'ra mine'ken-eye

MEANING OF NAME: *Rasbora,* a native name; *meinkeni,* after Herman Meinken,
German aquarist and ichthyologist

East Indies Sumatra, exact location unknown Length, 3 inches

EXCEPT for this fish having a marked yellow-brown cast all over, the same remarks apply as to *R. daniconius,* except that it is not so common. The difference in color and the less clear side stripe in this fish are the two main points by which the aquarist may tell the two species apart. In this illustration it is the upper fish that is the female.

Esòmus danrìcus (HAMILTON-BUCHANAN)

Pronounced Ee-so'mus dan-ry'cus   *Popular name,* Flying Barb

MEANING OF NAME: *Esomus,* slender body; *danricus,* after native name; also known as
Nuria danrica

Northern India and Burma   Length, 4 to 5 inches
Eastern Location Map 119 to p29 and y21

A GRACEFUL, active fish, spending much of its time at the surface.
It has a wide spread of pectoral fins, as indicated in the figure to the
right. These fins enable it to make sizable leaps from the water, giving
rise to the popular name, Flying Barb. There are two pairs of barbels,
or "whiskers," the lower pair being extremely long, reaching to the
middle of the body. The line along the body is black, with an upper
ribbon of gold, dividing an olive back from silver sides. The line goes
faintly into the tail fin. At breeding time the male develops a reddish
hue towards the end of his body, and the triangular red speck at the base
of his tail stands out more clearly.

They breed prolifically, somewhat in the manner of the Barbs. They
should be provided with a large, thickly planted aquarium, with water
not over 6 inches deep. A layer of natural settlings, or of large pebbles,
should be on the bottom, in order to conceal such eggs as fall, for they

are only partially adhesive and do not hold very well on the plants. The spawning situation should be a sunny one, and the temperature about 78 degrees. The breeding action has an unusual variation from most of the egg-droppers. The male strikes against the sides of the female to induce her to spawn and then she returns in kind and pokes him so as to assist him in fertilizing the eggs with his sperm. Remove breeders after spawning.

The small, pale yellow eggs hatch in 2 days and Infusoria should be supplied the fry 2 days later. The young are not easily raised.

Owing to the ability of Esomus to leap, it is important to keep their tanks well covered. An interesting characteristic of the species is that each fish seems to have a sense of property rights, patrolling back and forth over a selected spot, attempting to keep away any intruders that do not look too formidable.

This sounds rather unfavorable if the fish were a candidate for a community aquarium; but, as a matter of fact, these threats result in no damage.

Temperature range, 70-84 degrees.

Esòmus malayénsis AHL

Pronounced E-so'muss may'lay-en"sis

MEANING OF NAME: *Esomus,* slender; *malayensis,* from the Malayan region

Malayan Region   Location not exactly known   Length, 3 to 3½ inches

*V*IRTUALLY all that has been said about the general habits of the foregoing species also applies to this one. The only further instruction the reader needs is to be able to distinguish one fish from the other. *Malayensis* is about an inch smaller, it has not such a clear side stripe, but the decorative spot at the base of the tail is larger and prettier. Also it has a small black spot at the base of the anal.

Both of the Esomus shown are popular and are in fairly good supply, especially *malayensis,* which is a very pretty little aquarium fish, waving its dark tail-spot through the water.

Notròpis hypselópterus (GUENTHER)
Pronounced No-tro'pis hip'sel-op"ter-us
MEANING OF NAME: *Notropis,* with keel-shaped back; *hypselopterus,* deep, or long-finned
Generally known as *Notropis metallicus*

ONE of our beautiful American minnows. It has more than once been
used as the medium of a practical joke on some seasoned fancier
of exotic fishes. When it is shown him as a "new importation from
Timbuctoo," or elsewhere, he is thrilled by its beauty, and must have
some at any price. His ardor soon cools when informed that it is a
home product. However, the fish is never what might be called "dirt
cheap," for it is not found in large quantities, and is not easily captured.

The former specific name, *metallicus,* gives some hint of its general
color. It is a coppery, warm-brown with yellow in the fins. The base
of the dorsal is red, shading to black. These colors make a fine setting
for the broad, golden-topped, blue-black band extending the entire length
of the body.

This is really a most attractive fish, and is easily domesticated, but
it can hardly receive full approval as a "tropical." It should be kept
in a well-planted aquarium of not less than 10-gallon capacity, and at
a temperature of 65 to 70 degrees. The males have all the color and
much the larger fins. Never bred in close confinement. Aeration desirable.

Notròpis lutrénsis   (BAIRD AND GIRARD)

Pronounced No-tro'pis loo-tren'sis   *Popular name,* Rainbow Minnow

MEANING OF NAME: *Notropis,* with a ridge on back, the original specimens having been
dried; *lutrensis,* from the Latin word *Lutra,* meaning Otter, referring to the fact that
the fish was first recorded from Otter Creek, Arkansas

Central and Southern Mississippi Valley   Length, 2¾ inches
Western Location Map f10 to e19 and Northward

ONE of the most beautiful of our native fishes, especially in the spring
and early summer months when the males are at the height of their
rainbow colors. The reds and blues on the body are not sharply defined,
but melt softly with each other. There is great variation in effect, according to the angle of the light striking and leaving the scales.

In a large aquarium at a temperature of 65-75 degrees the fish lives
happily, especially if plenty of plants are present, or their equivalent
in mechanical oxygenation.

While this species likes an occasional meal of Daphnia or chopped
worms, it does well on almost any kind of food. Very tame, active and
quite harmless. Never bred in the aquarium. To be had of dealers in
our central southern states.

THE BARBS

*T*HE Barbs give gaiety and grace to an aquarium. Their large, mirror-like scales constantly catch the light and flash it back from many angles, for they are seldom still.

A sparkling appearance is only one of their merits. They are peaceful, playful, most of them are easily bred and they prosper at moderate temperatures, being quite happy within a range of 68 to 76 degrees. It might be added that most of them are of popular aquarium sizes. Despite their general similarity, it is not difficult to detect the interesting differences in the many species known to the aquarist.

Nearly but not quite all of them have short whiskers or barbels about the mouth, a characteristic for which the genus is named.

A sunny situation not only suits them, but shows them off best. Old water and plenty of plants should be provided.

As to breeding Barbus, this is a simple matter. The female, naturally a little bigger than the male in many species, becomes noticeably larger as she fills with spawn. When this evidence is apparent, she should be placed with one or two males in a thickly-planted aquarium as described under "Egg-layers." The breeding is very much the same as that of the Goldfish, to which it is related. The males chase the female and when she becomes sufficiently excited, she scatters or sprays adhesive eggs on the plants or wherever they may fall. As both sexes soon eat what eggs they can find, it is well to have the plants densely arranged so as to defeat this destruction. Naturally, with that thought in mind, the aquarist will promptly remove the fish when spawning is finished. The eggs hatch quite quickly, requiring only about 38 to 40 hours. The young are easily reared by the described formula for egg droppers.

So simple are the temperature requirements of the Barbs that it is one of those exotic fishes which may be bred in outdoor pools in the Summer climate of most of our states. If placed in a large, well-planted space and constantly supplied with live food, they will prosper and breed without further attention.

They will accept any kind of food. Another point of value is that they are not "scary" fishes.

Fortunately aquarists are not obliged to board all Barbs. Some of them weigh one hundred pounds! Several hundred species of them are known from Europe, Asia, and Africa, but most of the little fellows we know as good aquarium fishes come from India and the Malayan region. They belong to a section of Barbus called Puntius by ichthyologists, but the name Barbus is so firmly fixed in aquarium parlance that we make no effort to institute a change.

Bärbus binotàtus   CUVIER AND VALENCIENNES
Pronounced Bar'bus by'no-tay"tus
MEANING OF NAME: *Barbus,* from the barbels present in some, but not all species;
binotatus, two-spotted

Malayan region   Length, 5 inches
   Eastern Location Map w37 to F39; D35 to K41; L42 to N49; I45 to B50; and y52

THE size of the dark markings on fishes must not always be taken too seriously in the matter of identification. This fact is mentioned here because this fish is a case in point. Apparently all of the German books show quite large black spots on the species, especially the one on the back, which, according to these illustrations, is comparable in size to the spots on *B. everetti.* The writer has seen a few Barbs so marked, but of the hundreds owned by aquarists in our Atlantic states, all seem to be like our illustration. The spots become less distinct with age. Except for dull gold to brown eyes, the color is confined to silver and black. Inset in illustration shows characteristic markings on young.

The sexes are much alike, but breeding is not difficult. A large aquarium at 70 to 80 degrees is advised, and standard treatment for Barbs. A fairly popular species.

Bärbus chòla   (HAMILTON-BUCHANAN)

Pronounced Bar′bus ko′la

MEANING OF NAME: *Barbus*, with barbels; *chola*, after a native name

India   Eastern Location Map z19 to p29 and w36   Length, 4 inches

THERE is a strong family resemblance between this species and the better-known *B. conchonius.* It is slightly more slender and the dark spot is nearer the base of the tail. This species has a small pair of barbels, whereas *B. conchonius* has none. A further point of identification is a rosy spot on the gill plate. This is suggested in the illustration, a little in back of the eye, and almost in a line with it.

The sexes are distinguished by the orange-tinted anal and ventral fins of the male. All fins in the female are quite clear. While she is slightly the larger, the difference is not usually as great as shown here. The species does not breed so freely as its neighbor in Nature, *B. conchonius,* but requires the same treatment in all respects.

This is one of those species which, while not rare, can only be obtained from time to time. Those who own it like it very much, and find that with moderately good treatment it enjoys robust health and lives for years. Experimental efforts have been made to cross the species with *B. conchonius,* but without results.

Bärbus conchònius HAMILTON-BUCHANAN

Pronounced Bar'bus kon-ko'nee-us   *Popular name,* Rosy Barb

MEANING OF NAME: *conchonius,* after a native name

India   Eastern Location Map 119 to q31   Length, 3½ inches

TAKEN over a period of years, the Rosy Barb is easily the best known and most popular of the genus, as far as aquarists are concerned. In selecting it as our color subject, we do so because it is typical of the many species.

Anyone with just a little experience will identify the lower fish as the male, but from the colors shown it should not be assumed that the sex is always so easily distinguished, for when love-making is over, he lays aside his gay courting costume. Even outside breeding season the tops of those fins shown dark here have a tendency to be darker than those of the female. On the average, he is also a little smaller.

The dark spot on the body is slightly ocellated, a point which our color plate has failed to pick up. That is to say, it should be edged with a lighter color, gold—in this species. Through an error, barbels were added to the photograph.

Usually in good supply and is one of the hardiest of the Barbs.

Bärbus dúnckeri AHL
Pronounced Bar'bus doonk'er-eye
Named for Georg Duncker, the German ichthyologist
Malay region, Malayan rivers   Eastern Location Map about D37   Length, 4½ inches

NOT many aquarists keep this species, for the reason that it has no outstanding beauty to offset the disadvantage of its large size, such, for instance, as that possessed by *B. everetti.*

The one feature which will help the amateur ichthyologist identify the species is the large spot on the body, just below and nearly the size of the dorsal fin. This spot becomes rather indistinct at maturity. In color the fish is olive silver, with a yellow undertone. The dorsal is dirty yellow. The other fins have a yellow cast, and, in the case of the anal, it shades to a reddish-brown at the end. Eye, silver with a dark ring outside. There are 2 pairs of barbels, the lower pair being long.

Breeding and care conform to instructions for Barbus. They are quite hardy, but are seldom bred. Not easy to spawn.

The female (upper fish) is apt to be just a little the larger, about in the proportion shown in the illustration. There are no other known sex indications.

Bärbus éveretti BOULENGER

Pronounced Bar'bus ev'er-et-eye   *Popular name,* Clown Fish

Named for the collector, Everett

Also widely, but incorrectly, known as *Barbus lateristriga*

Malay Peninsula and Borneo   Eastern Location Map F39 and F45   Length, 5 inches

THIS fish is a good proof of the importance of introducing a species under its correct scientific name, or of promptly changing it when we discover a mistake. For quite a while the beautiful *B. everetti* was known as *B. lateristriga,* but when the true *B. lateristriga* was brought on the scene, and in its own right turned out to be a fish of importance, something had to be done about the awkward situation. By a study that could have been made earlier we would have found that what we were calling *B. lateristriga* is really *B. everetti.* After a bit of mental adjustment, we are now giving each of the two species its correct name.

The "Clown Fish," as it has been called on account of its characteristic, conspicuous spots, is one of the bigger Barbs and one of the more difficult to spawn. Aeration, a little fresh water and plenty of live food help put it in breeding condition.

The colors develop when the fish is about 2 inches long, and at that size, or a little larger, the big blue-black spots are more clearly defined than in the fully mature fish. They have 2 pairs of barbels. A large, well planted aquarium should be given them, and a temperature range of 72 to 78 degrees.

On account of its rather robust size and striking markings, *Barbus everetti* makes one of the best of exhibition fishes.

Bärbus lateristrïga   CUVIER AND VALENCIENNES
Pronounced Bar'bus   lat'er-iss-tri'ga
MEANING OF NAME: *lateristriga,* with lateral stripes
Malay Peninsula and East Indies   Length, 5½ inches
Eastern Location Map F39; I40; L43; I45

TO aquarists this species was a new introduction in 1932. The first ones we saw were about the size of our illustration, and were very interesting, with their shield-like arrangement of vertical and horizontal stripes. Since then they have grown apace and now rank with the largest of our Barbs in the aquarium. There are no bright colors to be seen, and as the fish becomes large, it loses that crispness of the black pattern which makes them more interesting in their smaller sizes.

See the foregoing (*B. everetti*) as to requirements, and also regarding confusion of the two names.

Bärbus gélius (HAMILTON-BUCHANAN)
Pronounced Bar'bus jel'ee-us
MEANING OF NAME: *gelius,* after a native name
India   Eastern Location Map r27 to p30   Length—male, 1¼ inches; female, 1¾ inches

A RATHER rare and odd Barb is shown here. It is characterized by
three features; its diminutive size, its slim shape and its oddly
sprinkled black spots. A fourth point is that it is expensive, but that
means nothing, for tomorrow it may be cheap. In this instance we doubt
that possibility, for it is a difficult little fish to breed, and imports have
to come from a great distance. Furthermore, being without bright color
spots anywhere, it can hardly be expected to attain popularity. The
broad dark stripe along the body is brownish, while the nearly translucent
fins have a tinge of yellow. Barbels are present.

The sexes appear very much alike, the black markings in the male
(at left) appearing to be just a little more brilliant.

This species is particularly adept at eating its own eggs, so that those
who hope to breed it must be clever enough to outwit the fish. Breeding
temperature about 75 degrees, which is also their top for comfortable
living. They may go down to 65 degrees without distress, being one of
those exotics which is not necessarily a "tropical."

The illustration represents the maximum size, which they seldom attain.
Ordinarily aquarium size is about 2/3 as large as shown here.

A special effort should be made to keep up the strength of small fishes
by occasional feedings of live foods, such as Daphnia, Enchytrae and
Tubifex worms. *B. gelius* is included among the small fishes.

Bärbus oligolèpis (BLEEKER)

Pronounced Bar'bus ol'i-go-lee"pis (ol'i-gol"ee-pis is allowable)

MEANING OF NAME: *oligolepis*, having few scales

Sumatra   Eastern Location Map E35 to J40   Length, 2 inches

THE beautiful black-bordered orange dorsal identifies this fish instantly. No other known Barb is even slightly similar.

The lower fish is the female of the trio. Usually the double dark line on the side of the males does not show so strongly nor regularly on the female as it does here. In addition, the sexes are easily distinguished by the differences in color. The species has a small pair of barbels.

At breeding time the orange in the dorsal of the male is intensified and he becomes suffused with black, through which sparkles many a scale of blue and green. Breeding as per other Barbs. There are about 200 eggs to a spawning and the young, which hatch in 60 hours at 78 degrees, are very small and translucent, requiring the finest sizes of live food, in addition to green water.

It has been found that where several females are ripe at the same time they may be bred together with an equal or a greater number of males.

The species sometimes, but seldom, reaches the size shown.

A male Honey Dwarf Gourami, **Colisa chuna**, in all the glory of its gorgeous breeding colors. Photo by R. Zukal.

The Opaline or Cosby Gourami, **Trichogaster trichopterus**, showed up originally as a "sport" in a brood of Blue Gouramis. Photo by Harald Schultz.

A pair of **Cichlasoma facetum**, more commonly known as the White Convict Cichlid, attacking Miracle Worms (freeze-dried tubifex) in a feeding bell. (Below) The Leopard Ctenopoma acutirostre. Photo by Hilmar Hansen.

A member of the small family of Nandids is **Datniodes quadrifasciatus**.
Photo by Dr. Herbert R. Axelrod.

Telmatherina ladigesi, a fairly young specimen. Later the black first dorsal and anal rays become longer. Photo by Hansen.

The smallest of the Loach group is the Dwarf Loach, **Botia sidthimunki**, which gets to be only 1½ inches long. Photo by Dr. Herbert R. Axelrod.

Leporinus striatus, the Striped Leporinus. Photo by Dr. Herbert R. Axelrod.

Although **Brachydanio kerri** is a member of a very popular group, we seldom see it. Photo by Dr. Herbert R. Axelrod.

Another hybrid variety of **Brachydanio frankei**, the Leopard Danio. This variety has colored dorsal fins. Photo by Dr. Herbert R. Axelrod.

Capoeta (Barbus) melanampyx, the Ember Barb, develops a deep rosy flush when it is ready to spawn. It is native to India. Photo by Dr. Herbert R. Axelrod.

This is **Barbodes (Barbus) schwanenfeldi**. Its two widely used common names are Schwanenfeld's Barb and the Tinfoil Barb. It has a ravenous appetite and gets quite large.

Serrasalmus rhombeus is called the White Piranha because of the lack of red in its fins and body. This specimen is 6 months old and 3½ inches long. Photo by Dr. Herbert R. Axelrod.

This is the Red Piranha, Serrasalmus nattereri, one of the best known of that savage group. They must be very carefully handled, of course, with due respect to their razor-sharp teeth. Photo by Dr. Herbert R. Axelrod.

Metynnis schreitmuelleri, does not have the spots that characterize some of the other Metynnis species. The species has been spawned in captivity on a few occasions. Photo by Dr. Hansjoachim Franke.

Metynnis maculatus, the Spotted Metynnis, is a vegetarian as are the rest of the fishes in the genus. They should be given vegetable foods to nibble on. Photo by Dr. Hansjoachim Franke.

This is the **Chalceus macrolepidotus** collected and photographed by Dr. Axelrod in the Purus River system of Brazil. It differs from other varieties by the shoulder spot and the yellow color of the anal and ventral fins. (Below) The spotted **Prochilodus insignis**. As the fish grow older they lose the body markings. Photo by Dr. Herbert R. Axelrod.

This is the fish, **Catoprion mento**, which, because of its very high dorsal fin, was called the Wimple Piranha by the late Harald Schultz. It looks ferocious but lacks the razor-sharp teeth of the true Piranhas. Photo by Harald Schultz.

One of the more rare of the African dwarf cichlids is **Pelmatochromis klugei**. Photo by Hilmar Hansen.

Puntius (Barbus) filamentosus is becoming more and more popular. This is a young male; as the fish gets older, the dorsal rays get longer until they almost reach the tail. Photo by Gerhard Marcuse.

A new African cichlid, **Pelmatochromis thomasi**, collected and photographed by E. Roloff.

The Clown Knifefish, **Notopterus mikereedi,** from Thailand. Photo by Gerhard Marcuse.

The Indian Hatchetfish, **Laubuca laubuca,** has been known to the aquarium hobby for a long time but is still seldom seen. This may be because its body shape is not as bizzare as that of other hatchet fishes. Photo by Dr. Herbert R. Axelrod.

Nemacheilus (sometimes spelled **Noemachilus**) kuiperi, closely related to the Kuhli Loach. Photo by Hilmar Hansen.

Luciocephalus pulcher from the Malay Archipelago. Photo by Klaus Paysan.

Acanthophthalmus semicinctus is very much like and often confused with the Coolie Loach. Photo by Dr. Herbert R. Axelrod.

Acanthopsis choirorhynchus is easily recognized by its long snout which is responsible for its common name, the Long-Nosed Loach. Photo by Hansen.

This is the original Discus, **Symphysodon discus**, also known as the Red Discus. Photo by Dr. Herbert R. Axelrod.

The Green Discus, **Symphysodon aequifasciata aequifasciata**. You can see 11 fry feeding from the slime on the fish's side. Photo by Dr. Herbert R. Axelrod.

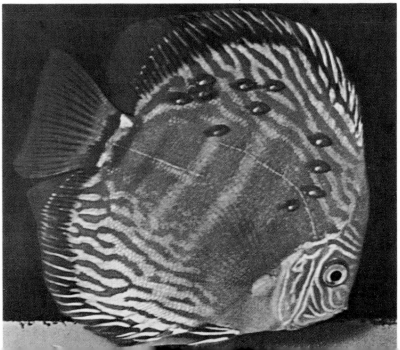

The Brown Discus, **Symphysodon aequifasciata axelrodi,** shows a lot of blue in its fins when ready to spawn. Photo by Dr. Eduard Schmidt.

Africa has given us many Cichlid species, and one of the most beautiful and popular is **Pelmatochromis kribensis,** male above, female below. Photo by Kremser.

Bärbus partipentazòna   FOWLER
Pronounced Bar'bus   par'tee-pen'ta-zo"na
MEANING OF NAME: *partipentazona,* partly five-zoned
First known to aquarists as *Barbus sumatranus* (incorrectly)
Siam and Malay Peninsula   Eastern Location Map X36 to F39   Length, 1¾ inches

THIS is one of those fishes whose misfortune (or is it the aquarist's?) it was to be introduced under the name of another species, *B. suma-tranus.* The error was one that was easily made, as the two fishes are fairly similar, but such mistakes are always difficult to correct even when the error has been rooted but a short time. The genuine *B. sumatranus* has seldom been imported.

B. partipentazona is a most pleasing Barb of small size. It has a silver body, slashed vertically with black bars as shown in the illustration. One feature the plate cannot show without the aid of colors is the very pretty streak of red in the dorsal fins, just in back of the black. This begins to show at a fairly early age, but does not reach its full depth and brilliance until maturity, which is in about a year. It is slightly brighter in the males, and, except for the shape, is the only outward indication of sex.

Like many of their Barb cousins, they do not seem to be at all "scary," and early learn to regard their owner as their friend.

They breed like other Barbs, but so far have not proven prolific. A detailed account of their breeding appears in "The Aquarium" for June, 1935. Temperature for them should average about 75 degrees.

Bärbus phutùnio   (HAMILTON-BUCHANAN)

Pronounced Bar'bus foo-too'nee-o   *Popular name,* Dwarf Barb
MEANING OF NAME: *phutunio,* after a native name, pungti phutuni
India   Eastern Location Map r28 to v33   Length, 1¼ inches

PRESENTING one of the most charming of diminutive fishes, and one that ideally qualifies for those aquarists who like small pets in small aquaria.

The species has in marked degree that silvery sparkle which characterizes so many of the Barbs. Photographs show something which the unaided eye scarcely detects. The sparkle for the most part is confined to vertical lines from the *centre* of the scales. In contrast with silvery sheen the dark dots of the photograph are black. The dark spot on the gill plate is not black, but translucent, exposing the pink of the gills. Fins, pale orange, slightly darker in the male. Sexes difficult to recognize, except by the time-honored method of noting the fuller body of the female, especially as breeding time approaches.

The species does not require a high temperature. Eggs hatch in 2 days at 75 degrees. Although small, they are not as difficult to rear as might be imagined. With these, as well as with other small fish babies, it is well to avoid the introduction of Cyclops among the living food.

The species is a very easy one to feed, and makes a good community fish, if not overshadowed by disproportionately large companions. Not especially difficult to spawn.

Our photograph is made just a little larger than life size, a fault we usually strive to avoid.

Bärbus semifasciolàtus GUENTHER
Pronounced Bar'bus sem'ee-fa'see-o-lay"tus
MEANING OF NAME: *semifasciolatus,* half-banded

S. China   Eastern Location Map p45; s43   Length, 2½ inches

*I*N OUR own lives we often find ourselves agreeably attached, not so much to persons of brilliance, as to those having good dispositions; those that endure much and ask little. So it is with *B. semifasciolatus,* a fish without any striking beauty that has for many years maintained a degree of popularity among aquarists.

Its half-dozen partly broken bands give the fish its outward identity. These cross a green-golden lateral line and a field of large, iridescent scales. The fins are tinted yellow. At mating time the belly of the male is moderately flushed with red. Barbels (2) very small.

They breed freely in the Barbus manner and may be kept with other exotic fishes without danger, at any reasonable temperature.

Barbus fasciolatus is a very similar species from West Africa, having about twice as many bars and exactly twice as many barbels, one pair of which is large. We have never seen that fish and can therefore offer no illustration. Sometimes dealers believe they have *B. fasciolatus,* but so far as this writer is concerned they have turned out to be *B. semifasciolatus* that happen to have a few extra bars.

Bärbus stòliczkànus DAY
Pronounced Bar'bus sto'licks-kay"nus
Named for Dr. Stoliczka

India   Eastern Location Map v34   Length, 2½ inches

W E HAVE here a fish not easily distinguished from one of its cousins, *B. ticto*. One of the principal differences, from the fanciers' standpoint, is that it is much rarer. Chief among the external appearances is that it has a more golden hue. Then, too, our photograph shows two other points which may or may not be of importance. Ichthyologists do not mention them. The forward body spot is much rounder and there is a suggestion at the tail base of a third spot, vaguely heart-shaped. Eye colors are not dependable characteristics, but these specimens have pale gold irises, while *B. ticto* has a red spot in the upper part of the eye.

The author has never seen the species bred, but it is said to be prolific, and as hardy as the better-known *B. ticto*.

Bärbus tèrio (HAMILTON-BUCHANAN)
Pronounced Bar'bus tee'ree-o
MEANING OF NAME: *terio,* after a native name
British India   Eastern Location Map ll9 to q29   Length, 2½ inches

ALTHOUGH this species looks a good deal like *B. conchonius,* there are several differences to be noted by the close observer. One is a reddish orange spot on the gill plate. Another is a faint dark line between the body spot and the base of the tail. Also the dorsal fin is more pointed.

The male may be identified by the fact that he is yellowish all over, and his anal and ventrals are touched with orange. The female is silver with clear fins. Breeding and care are the same as for *B. conchonius,* but the species does not spawn so readily. The male instead of turning crushed-strawberry red at mating time becomes a beautiful orange.

In connection with the above name, Hamilton-Buchanan, coupled with this and many other aquarium fishes, the reader may be interested to know that it is not, as is often supposed, the names of two men. It is the compound name of a most interesting Scottish scientist who had a colorful career in the Orient.

Bärbus ticto   (HAMILTON-BUCHANAN)
Pronounced Bar′bus tick′toe
MEANING OF NAME: *ticto,* after a native name
India   Eastern Location Map q17 to r29 and A20   Length, 3½ inches

A POPULAR Barb favorite, this fish. An arching reddish area about the middle of the dorsal is very pretty, and is set off by a dark spot in the fore part of that bright field. The other fins are light yellow. A golden circle edges the dark spot on the rear of the body. The forward spot is a vertical oval. No barbels. Eye, light red in upper part.

This species is quite as glittering as any of the genus, and makes an excellent community tank fish. Being a little smaller than the popular *B. conchonius,* and carrying color in the fins more consistently, it is, among many aquarists, even more popular than that seasoned favorite.

The female may be told by her clear dorsal fin. The variety is very hardy, tame and easily bred. See standard directions for Barbs.

Bärbus vittàtus   (DAY)
Pronounced Bar'bus   vi-tay'tus
MEANING OF NAME: *vittatus,* striped
India, Ceylon   Eastern Location Map q17 to A20, and C22   Length, 2 inches

ONE of the smaller Barbs is shown here. It is difficult to see where *vittatus* or "striped" applies, but it is too late to dispute with the namer, Dr. Day, about that. The body is warm silver, yellowish towards the rear, and in addition to the single black spots in the anal, caudal and dorsal regions, shown in the photograph, the sides are also peppered with small dark dots. Other writers find the fins to be yellow, but those photographed were clear, except the dorsal which we agree has an oblique, dark band as shown, producing a triangle with the front edge of the fin, and enclosing an area of orange. No barbels. Silver eye.

As a rule dealers do not carry this fish in stock, but it is not to be considered a rarity.

Mr. Holbein, a prominent New York aquarist, has one of the species which is over 10 years old.

This is a hardy little fish and a good breeder. It is quite inoffensive. Temperature range, 65 to 85 degrees. See standard breeding directions.

Cȳclocheilīchthys ápogon (CUVIER AND VALENCIENNES)
Pronounced Sigh'klo-kile-ick"thiss a'po-gon
MEANING OF NAME: *Cyclocheilichthys,* round mouthed fish; *apogon,* without barbels
Sumatra, Borneo, Malay Peninsula, Siam and Burma
Eastern Location Map x35 to w38 and F39; D34 to J41; L42 to M48; I45 to B50
Length—Aquarium size, 4½ inches; Nature, 20 inches

A FISH of which we know little as to its habits. It has been imported
on only a few occasions, yet when a fish withstands the trip from
the Malay Archipelago it must have the endurance that may some day
make it popular in the aquarium, especially when combined with a very
attractive appearance. Experience with the species was ended in each
instance by the fish jumping out, a point for future owners to keep in
mind.

In color it reminds one of the warm flush of the male Rosy Barb in
mating season. The dark parts shown in the fins are rosy. The brilliance
of the large scales is also similar to the Rosy Barb, as well as the strong
black spot at the base of the tail. However, the fish would not be mistaken for a Barb. It is easily cared for in all ways (except the one noted),
and gets along amiably with other fishes.

There is a recent importation of another fish having a general shape and
color resemblance to this one, but the dorsal is less pointed, and the base
of the fin is much longer from front to back. The first ray is more forward
on the body. The fish is *Osteocheilus hasseltii.* As yet we have no
photograph of it.

Osteocheìlus vittàtus   (CUVIER AND VALENCIENNES)
Pronounced Os'tee-o-kile"us vi-tay'tus
MEANING OF NAME: *Osteocheilus,* bony lips; *vittatus,* striped
Malay Peninsula, Siam, Indo China   Length, 2½ inches
Eastern Location Map G37 to J41; F39; S39; L42 to M48; I45 to B50

ONE is reminded by this fish of our own Black-nosed Dace (*Rhinich-thys atronasus*), but the black line in this species is, if possible, even more intense. From the scientific standpoint the resemblance is superficial only. The fins are differently located, while the fin ray and scale counts do not match at all with those of our pleasant little native fish.

Osteocheilus vittatus is another of those comparatively rare importations of which we know little, but would like to see more. It shows itself to be an active, good-natured aquarium fish with sides and belly of bright silver, the back being tinted olive. Close inspection will reveal small barbels, or "whiskers." The fins are all quite clear, except where the little spur of black enters the tail fin. Takes almost any kind of food. No external sex distinctions. Never bred. No differences in sex characteristics have been observed. A suitable temperature is about 75 degrees.

THE LOACHES
FAMILY COBITIDAE
Pronounced Co by′ ti dee

The Loaches are much like the Carps, but they differ from them in having 3 or more pairs of barbels. They never have jaw teeth. The Loaches are all from the Old World.

Acánthophthálmus kùhlii   (CUVIER AND VALENCIENNES)
Pronounced A-kan′thof-thal″muss kool′e-eye
MEANING OF NAME: *Acanthophthalmus*, with spine near eyes;
kuhlii, after the naturalist, D. Kuhl
Malay Peninsula and Archipelago   Length, 2¾ inches
Eastern Location Map x36 to F39; G38; L43; G44 to D48

AN odd little Loach, and rather pretty. Active, too. The body is a sort of salmon-pink. Markings across the back and sides, dark gray to black, being darker on the edges. The eye, occurring on one of the dark spots, is not easily seen. A rather comical set of bushy barbels adorns the mouth, looking like an obstinate little moustache.

The fish is a fair scavenger of rather limited capacity. It eats almost entirely at night, refusing even Daphnia in daytime. On the other hand, it has an advantage over most of the other Loaches of the aquarium, inasmuch as it never grows too large. The illustration represents its extreme size. Sometimes the fish will come to rest in an odd position among the leaves of the aquarium, when it is not combing the bottom for bits of food. A most difficult fish to catch in an aquarium, especially a planted one.

As we know nothing of its breeding habits and it has to be imported from a long distance, it is rather expensive, and is likely to remain so.

Cobìtis taènia LINNAEUS

Pronounced Ko-bite'iss tee'ne-a   *Popular name,* Spotted Weatherfish
MEANING OF NAME: *Cobitis,* meaning not certain; *tænia,* striped
Western Location Map k51 and b56 Eastward and Northward to edges of map
Eastern Location Map from h1 and a1 through Siberia to b51   Length, 4 inches

THIS fish, like Acanthophthalmus, has a movable spine below the eye. There are 3 pairs of barbels on the upper jaw. It is one of our best scavengers, and has the advantage that it does not grow over 4 inches in length. The dark markings are variable, and appear on a buff-colored background.

Like many of the Loaches, this fish is long-lived and can endure pretty bad conditions, as well as extremes of temperature.

The details of its breeding habits are not known with certainty, but we have reasons to believe that they are similar to those of the European *Cobitis fossilis.* We know of an authentic instance in which they bred in a lily pool during the late summer. The young wriggled out of the mud the next May, much to the surprise of the owner, especially as the winter had been a severe one.

Misgúrnus angùillicaudàtus (CANTOR)

Pronounced Mis-gur'nuss an-gwill'ee-caw-day"tus   *Popular name,* Japanese Weatherfish

MEANING OF NAME: *Misgurnus,* from Misgurn, old English name for Loach;
anguillicaudatus, meaning not known

Japan, China, etc.   Eastern Location Map e58   Length, up to 8 inches

THIS fish differs from Cobitis and Acanthophthalmus in the absence of the movable spine below the eye. It is light gray with irregular blotches of darker gray, while the European form, *Cobitis fossilis,* is light brown with several dark stripes along the body. They are virtually the same fish, both from the scientific and the aquarist's standpoints.

Before the merits of Corydoras as aquarium scavengers were so well known, the "Weatherfish," as well as other forms of Loaches, were much used for the purpose. Some aquarists still utilize them, but seldom in sizes over 4 inches in length. Their movements are wild and impredictable, somewhat "like a chicken with its head off." When size is added to the fish, these strange, lashing actions become unendurable to the aquarist, for the sediment is whipped into a state of suspension and sand is shifted without regard to scenic effect. It would not be correct to give the impression that this fish is always on the rampage. It is quiet for periods, often buried in the sand with its head looking out cutely. Then it will emerge and begin a peculiar, interesting action of "combing" the sand surface, in search of food. Sand and dirt are taken into the mouth and rapidly expelled through the gills.

Will stand temperature from 40 to 80 degrees and has seldom been bred. Wilhelm Schreitmüller has an interesting account of its breeding in "The Aquarium," Philadelphia, October, 1934. They spawn on the bottom and the young bury themselves for a long period, no doubt feeding on microscopic life and vegetal decomposition.

THE CATFISHES

The Catfishes or Siluroids used to be placed in a single family, Siluridæ, which is nowadays split up into several. We have used these newer family designations, but wish at this place to point out the distinguishing features of Catfishes as a whole. No Catfish ever has scales, though some of them are more or less completely covered with bony plates. The chief differences from the other families of the order Ostariophysi are internal, but there are not many Catfishes which are not immediately recognizable as such. All but a few obscure ones have barbels.

FAMILY DORADIDAE
Pronounced Do ray' di dee

The Doradids are heavy-bodied Catfishes which can easily be placed by the single row of bony plates, each bearing a spine, which runs along the middle of each side of the fish. In some species which we have had in our aquaria (such as *Acanthodoras spinosissimus*) there are smaller spiny supplementary plates, both above and below the main series. Such species might be confused with the Armored Cats, treated further on, but the Doradids never have a spine supporting the front of the adipose fin, as do the true Armored Cats. All the Doradids are from South America.

Acánthodòras spìnosíssimus (EIGENMANN AND EIGENMANN)
Pronounced A-kan'tho-do"ras spy'no-siss"i-mus   *Popular name,* Talking Catfish
MEANING OF NAME: *Acanthodoras,* spiny Doras; *spinosissimus,* very spiny
Amazon   Western Location Map H19; O19   Length, 4 inches

THIS recent introduction is one of the best-armed creatures we
know of. A larger fish picking it up as a morsel of food would
receive a sensation somewhat as though it had taken a chestnut burr
into its mouth. Besides the rows of erected spines visible in the photograph, there are many other small erectile ones over the body, to say
nothing of the menacing, stiff dorsal fin and a special contrivance now
to be described. It will be noticed that the side or pectoral fin is long
and powerfully constructed. Just above and parallel with it is a row
of strong spines on the body. When the powerful pectoral fin (a weak
affair in most fishes) closes on an enemy and holds it against the saw-
like sides, some flesh is going to receive quite a ripping in tearing itself
away from this touch-me-not fish.

This specimen did not flee the net when about to be caught, but braced
itself in some rockwork from which it was dislodged with difficulty.

The fish, in common with related species, makes a grunting noise
when out of water, hence the popular name, Talking Catfish. During
our observation it did not use its strange armor as a weapon of offense.
Easily kept, but not yet bred. Temperature, 75 degrees.

FAMILY SILURIDAE
Pronounced Si lu'ri dee

These Catfishes are easily identified by the *very* long anal fin and by the fact that the dorsal fin is either very small and far forward, or absent. All the Silurids are Old World fishes.

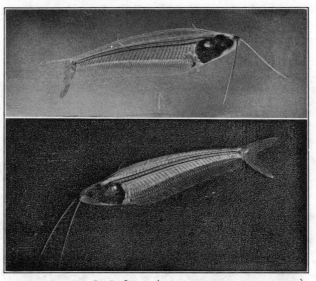

Kryptópterus bicírrhus   (CUVIER AND VALENCIENNES)
Pronounced Krip-top'te-rus by-si'riss
Popular name, Glass Catfish   *Native name,* "Limpak"
MEANING OF NAME: *Kryptopterus,* hidden fin, an allusion to the almost invisible
one-rayed dorsal fin; *bicirrhus,* with two hairs (whiskers)
Java, Borneo, Sumatra, Siam   Eastern Location Map   Aquarium size, 2½ inches

THIS is by far the most nearly transparent fish kept by aquarists. Were it not for the opaque, silvery sac containing the internal organs, it would really be difficult to see the fish at all. Its skeleton is fairly visible, but the flesh, from the intestines to the tail, is truly glasslike. When a light is held so as to shine *through* the body, it displays a wealth of prismatic colors. The illustration with dark background was lighted in that way.

One is impressed on examining the photograph by the fact that the internal organs are set forward about as far as it is possible for them to be. The vent is almost under the head.

Daphnia, Tubifex, Glassworms and Enchytrae are eagerly (although at first shyly) eaten. Harmless. Not bred. Temperature, 72-82 degrees.

FAMILY BAGRIDAE
Pronounced Bag'ri dee

The Bagrids are "ordinary" looking Catfishes, with dorsal fin present and of usual place and size, anal fin of moderate length, no "armor" on the body, and the "whiskers" usually long. All are from Africa or Asia. The differences between the Bagrids and the South American Pimelodids are small, and internal, so that, for the aquarist, the best distinguishing feature is the habitat.

Mystus tengàra (HAMILTON-BUCHANAN)
Pronounced Miss-tus ten-gay'ra

MEANING OF NAME: *Mystus,* meaning of name not clear; *tengara,* the native name in the Punjab is "ting ga rah"
Usually known to aquarists as *Macrones vittatus* (another species)
N. India, the Punjab and Assam   Length, 4 inches

THIS species, to be correct, should have 8 barbels, 2 of them nasal. Our photograph does not show that many, but otherwise the fish looks very much like correct figures of the species as listed above. It is not impossible that some of the barbels were out of view when the photograph was taken. At any rate, this illustration will serve to indicate the fish now being sold under the name. If not *Macrones vittatus,* it may even be a species of South American origin. In any case it is an interesting, attractive aquarium fish. Easily fed and cared for. Harmless. Seems happy at a temperature ranging at about 72-80 degrees.

FAMILY PIMELODIDAE
Pronounced Pim e lò di dee

The Pimelodids are Catfishes very similar in most features to the last family (Bagridæ) but come from South and Central America.

Pimelòdus clàrias   (BLOCH)
Pronounced Pim'el-o''dus klar'ee-as
MEANING OF NAME: *Pimelodus,* a fat fish; *clarias,* like the Indian catfish, Clarias
All of South America East of the Andes from Panama to Buenos Aires
Aquarium size, 4 inches and over

THIS is one of those fishes which is most attractive in its smaller sizes, but which when fully grown is neither good looking nor suited to the aquarium. Adults not only lose those stunning big spots, but reach a length of 10 to 12 inches. Only smaller specimens are imported and, in an ordinary sized aquarium, they retain both their dimensions and their dots. These decorative spots are dark brown, placed on a golden ground. Harmless, moderately active aquarium fishes having the novel qualities of the South American Catfishes, including that of being difficult to breed. We know nothing of its reproductive methods. It is a species which has for years been brought in only occasionally, and is, therefore, not often to be found in the stocks of dealers.

The temperature of the average warm-water aquarium suits it very well. Easily fed.

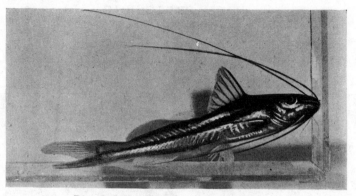

Pimelodélla gràcilis (VALENCIENNES)
Pronounced Pim'el-o-del''la gray'sil-iss
MEANING OF NAME: *Pimelodella*, a little Pimelodus; *gracilis*, slender
South America   Western Location Map A15 to V22   Length, 3½ inches

HERE are many very similar species of Pimelodella, and it is impossible to be certain of identification without alcohol specimens and having accurate locality data. The species illustrated is typical of most of those imported. It came in as *P. gracilis* (Valenciennes) but we are not at all sure that it really is that species. For the practical purposes of the aquarists, however, it seems that we had best continue to call the fish by its trade name until such time as we may know better.

It happens that in this illustration the extremely long barbels show very plainly, but this development is not at all unusual with this type of fish. What we would like to know about these thread-like extensions is their purpose, for it would seem there must be one, other than a decoration of doubtful beauty. As most catfishes are night prowlers, and even in daytime seek dimly lighted places and muddy bottoms, it is not at all unlikely that the barbels are sensory organs, to be used as a help to, or instead of eyes.

The fish from which this photograph was made had beautiful silvery sides with slight herring-bone depressions, divided about equally in half down the middle by a brilliant black line. A very active little fellow. The sexes appear to be exactly alike, and for that reason we show but one specimen.

Mìcroglànis parahỳbœ   (STEINDACHNER)

Pronounced My'kro-glay"niss par'a-high"bee

MEANING OF NAME: *Microglanis,* little catfish; *parahybœ,* from the Rio Parahyba, Brazil

Also known as *Pseudopimelodus parahybœ*

S. E. Brazil   Western Location Map S33 to U31   Length, 2 inches

A CHOICE little Catfish that has been with us in small numbers for a long time. Evidently they are not plentiful where collected, for the price has never been low.

The markings are pinkish gray on a background of dark brown. The illustration shows ventral and dorsal views as an aid to identification. It will be observed that there are 3 pairs of barbels. These alternate in light and dark sections. Never bred in captivity. A peaceful little fish, but not a particularly active one. Easily fed. Temperature range, 70-85 degrees.

FAMILY MALAPTERURIDAE
Pronounced Mal ap′ te ru″ ri dee

This family contains only one species, the African Electric Catfish. It has a large adipose fin, but no dorsal.

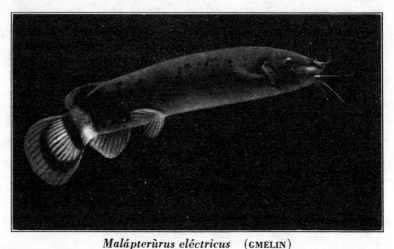

Malápterùrus eléctricus (GMELIN)

Pronounced Mal-ap-te-ru′rus e-lek′tree-kus   *Popular name,* Electric Catfish

MEANING OF NAME: *Malapterurus,* very doubtful, perhaps soft tail fin; *electricus,* electric
Most of Tropical Africa   Length, 6 inches
Western Location Map x45; A52; D59; L71; P68

TOO sausage-shaped to be graceful, but nevertheless very interesting. It is one of the side-shows of the aquarium, and a never-failing creator of publicity where advertising is wanted. Why not, when it can deliver an electric current strong enough to make a man jump as he would on accidentally touching an exposed wire carrying 110 volts? Just how this electricity is made, stored and discharged is not known, but any one having felt it remembers it as a very real thing. Just touch a finger tip to the still fish in water, or try to pick it out of a net, and the experimenter will get a free electrical treatment of the whole arm. It is not dangerous, but surprising.

Mr. Boulenger, of the Zoological Society's Aquarium in London, states that the shock of this fish causes other fishes to spit out their food, which the Catfish proceeds to eat.

Experiments at the Shedd Aquarium in Chicago have been inconclusive as to that point, because this fish, like other "Cats," carries on most of its life business at night, thus making observations difficult. Conclusions so far reached at that institution are that the fish in day-time does not show any predaceous qualities; that smaller species have a tendency to jump out of the tank containing these fishes; that those which do not escape occasionally disappear over night.

That they have plenty of power with which to stun a fish seems certain; or it could be used as a beautiful defense against enemies, somewhat after the idea of Mark Twain's yarn in his book, "A Yankee at King Arthur's Court," in which the Yankee paralyzes men in armor by connecting a dynamo with their suits of armor.

Too frequent use of the fish as a show-piece, or as a producer of practical jokes, runs down its storage battery and seems to shorten the life of the animal. At any rate, where the fish is used as a plaything, it does not last long, whereas under ordinary care it lives for years. It will thrive on a mixed diet.

In color it displays varying shades of gray and black, very much as in the illustration.

We have no record of any successful breeding of this remarkable aquarium oddity, nor do we know any external evidences by which the sexes may be recognized. Considering that it comes from tropical Africa, it is rather adaptable in the matter of temperature, being safe within 68-85 degrees.

FAMILY BUNOCEPHALIDAE
Pronounced Bu'no sef al''i dee

The Bunocephalids are small unarmored Catfishes with a very wide, flat head and a slender, elongated body. All are from South America.

Bunocéphalus bìcolor   STEINDACHNER
Pronounced Bew'no-seff''a-lus by'col-or

MEANING OF NAME: *Bunocephalus,* with hills (bumps) on the head; *bicolor,* two-colored
Amazon   Western Location Map K9 to G24   Length, 2½ inches

ANOTHER of those many Southern American Catfishes, not particularly outstanding. It was one of the early importations but is seen little at present. It has a very broad head and but a single pair of barbels, which are marked in alternating rings of light and dark color. When the tail fin is spread, which is seldom, it shows a rounded form, and is nicely spotted. From top to bottom the fish is very flat, but not in the same way as a Flounder. This would be difficult to tell from the illustrations, taken only from above and below. The dorsal fin, when up, is almost perpendicular. The illustration to the left indicates this somewhat. The same figure also shows the beady little eye, which is almost imperceptible. Looks disagreeable, but isn't. Never bred. In common with most of the Catfishes, it eats almost anything. Temperature range, 65-85 degrees.

FAMILY CALLICHTHYIDAE
Pronounced Call ick thy' i dee

The Smooth Armored Cats are just that. The body is encased in a coat of bony mail formed of two series of overlapping plates along each side. In no case is the armor completely covered with fine prickles and the mouth is never modified into a sucking disc. The adipose fin is supported by a spine. All the Smooth Armored Catfishes are South American.

Callichthys callichthys (LINNAEUS)

Pronounced Kal-lick'thiss kal-lick'thiss   *Popular name,* Armored Catfish

MEANING OF NAME: *Callichthys,* a fish having bumps or callouses

N. South America   Western Location Map y19 to F29 and V22   Length, 4½ inches

THE even rows of marks along the sides of the fishes in the illustration are the edges of overlapping armor plates, common to the so-called "Armored Cats." The fishes do not have ordinary scales.

The fish is quite a good scavenger; in fact, was one of the first used by aquarists in that capacity. It is harmless, and therefore well suited to the community tank.

Eggs are placed in bubble-nest in plants at the surface. Parents guard eggs and young. Breeding temperature about 80 degrees. Seldom bred.

THE CORYDORAS

*O*UR knowledge regarding the characteristics of the individual species of Corydoras is so limited that it seems advisable to consider them as a whole. They are all a genus of the family Callichthyidæ, popularly and not incorrectly known as South American Armored Catfishes. Instead of having ordinary scales, they are covered with two main rows of overlapping, bony laminations or plates. Many of these armored fishes reach a size that would make them quite impossible in a household aquarium, but, fortunately for us, Corydoras are the dwarfs of the family. We say *fortunately* because these fishes have proven themselves of great value and interest to aquarists.

They are droll, gnome-like little beings, going about their business of life in what seems to us a serio-comic fashion. This business, as far as the aquarist is concerned, is that of scavenger. It would hardly be going too far to give them the title of health officers, for their self-appointed task is going about the bottom of the aquarium, seeking bits of food that other fishes have overlooked, and which would soon contaminate the water. They go farther than this, as they consume dead leaves, dead snails and even dead Daphnia. However, one should not "work a willing horse to death." Their eating capacity is limited, and they cannot reasonably be expected to dispose of large amounts of surplus food carelessly placed in an aquarium.

Although many of us like these fishes for their own marked individualities and their contrast to other aquarium species, it is as scavengers that they have permanently established themselves in popular favor, having largely replaced snails for that purpose. True, they will not work on the side glasses as will snails, for they are strictly bottom-feeders. The important point is that no fish attacks a Corydoras of moderate size, whereas many of our exotic fishes make short work of snails. Then, again, snails eat fish eggs. Unless the eggs are on the bottom a Corydoras will not seek them out. Finally, snails once established are difficult to get rid of, which is not true of our little scavenger fish. However, under suitable circumstances, snails should be used as auxiliary cleaners. That is, in association with such fishes as will not kill them, and where the question of egg-eating does not arise, as among live-bearers.

This type of fish when first introduced into Germany was known as "Panzerwels," meaning plated or armored Catfish, and for some time continued under that name in the United States, after its importation from Germany, but that name has now become almost obsolete here. It originally had reference to *Callichthys callichthys*.

The first Corydoras to become well established among aquarists were *paleatus* and *nattereri*. They are still the most easily obtained and the ones we know most about, for we have very good accounts of their breeding habits, which at this time is more than can be said of most of the other species, although it is reasonably to be expected that their methods would be at least closely similar.

In the majority of species the female is somewhat the larger. We are sure that in *C. paleatus* the ventral fins are slightly more rounded in the female. Our accom-

panying illustration shows this difference. Not having seen other species breed, we do not know whether this applies to them all, but it probably does. As breeding approaches, the belly of the female takes on a reddish hue. Also the strong first ray of her pectoral fins reddens and thickens. In addition to these indications we have the old rule to select the more round and full-bodied fish as the female. It has long been claimed that the males have more pointed dorsal fins. Our observations do not confirm this.

The sexes can best be recognized by the shape of the ventral fins. Those of male are more pointed (lower fish). Inset shows eggs being held between ventral fins of females, just before they are attached to plants.

Still referring to *C. paleatus*, the first sign indicating that spawning is soon to follow is when the male persistently swims over the back of the female, bringing his barbels into occasional contact with the place where her neck ought to be, if she had one. Presently the pair comes to rest on the aquarium bottom, and assumes a strange position, not easily described. The male rolls over, nearly on his back. The female then clasps him at a right-angle position, crossing breasts. Her right-side barbels are caught beneath his left-side pectoral fin. In this position they remain still for about half a minute. Upon freeing themselves they swim independently of each other. It can then be seen that the female has pursed her ventral fins together, and that between them she is carrying 4 eggs. She searches for a suitable place to attach them, going up and down different plant leaves with her mouth. A firm Sagittaria leaf seems to please her most. In an upside-down position she clasps the leaf with her ventral fins and firmly presses the large eggs against the leaf, where they adhere tenaciously. First, 2 eggs are attached, and, in a few moments, 2 more. The process is repeated at intervals over a period of about 2 hours, at which time a large female will have deposited nearly 100 eggs. The curtain has fallen on the interesting show when the pair starts rooting in the sand.

The male does not follow the female when the eggs are deposited. Neither does he pay any attention to them. Certain it is there is no internal fertilization, as with live-bearers. It is stated by some that the female takes the male sperm in her mouth and applies it to the spot where the eggs are to be placed. From her actions in mouthing the plants this would seem reasonable. Observing the embrace in brilliant light we could see no possibility of her gathering the sperm in this way.

Unless parents provide some definite care for the young, we favor for all species their removal from the eggs and babies, regardless of possible well-established good reputations.

The young Corydoras soon take refuge in the natural sediment of the aquarium. These settlings should be at least a quarter inch deep. The babies make themselves scarce for about 2 weeks.

In a properly prepared aquarium they will not need to be fed at once. If there is not plenty of sediment for them to root through, a little paste from boiled oatmeal should be provided. At the same time snails should be introduced to eat the surplus oatmeal. There need be no hurry about supplying live Daphnia. Small sifted sizes may be provided in a month.

These spawnings occurred in slightly alkaline water (pH 7.4) and at temperatures of 74, 68 and 65 degrees. At the higher temperature a slight aeration was supplied. Eggs hatch in from 4 to 6 days, according to temperature.

Considering that so many thousands of Corydoras are now kept in aquariums, it is remarkable that one so seldom hears of their breeding. This may be because they are not considered in feeding, except as second-table guests, pursuing their humble occupation of taking left-overs. To place them in good breeding condition, they should have plenty of live Daphnia and Tubifex Worms. Like pigs, they do not *prefer* left-overs, but take what they can get.

Added to their chief merit of nosing about the obscure parts of the aquarium and clearing up sources of contamination, they also do a good service in keeping the surface of the sand loose and free from caking. At the same time they do not roil the water as do Weatherfish and Tadpoles. Many aquarists make a point of having one or two Corydoras in company with other fishes in every aquarium, except, of course, where breeders should be by themselves. They do not eat any young the size of live-bearers, and probably no others.

Sometimes Tubifex worms become established in the soil of an aquarium and present an unsightly appearance. Corydoras will dig them out.

No Corydoras knows the meaning of "fight." Even rival males at breeding time seem to be the best of friends. Most of them successfully endure a range of temperature from 62 to 82 degrees.

EGGS OF *Corydoras paleatus*, SLIGHTLY ENLARGED

They were on the under side of the leaves which were turned over for photographing by use of the glass rod seen in the front of the picture.

Còrydòras œnèus (GILL)

Pronounced Ko'ree-do"rass ee-nee'us

MEANING OF NAME: *Corydoras,* helmeted Doras (Doras is another genus of Catfishes);
œneus, bronzy

Trinidad   Western Location Map x between 19 and 20   Length, 2¾ inches

*A*VERY good scavenger fish, freely introduced in 1933. A popular method of distinguishing the species is by the diffused large dark area beginning just in back of the head, somewhat like an indistinct, horizontal oval. Also by the absence of any pattern markings on either body or fins.

Còrydòras ágassizi STEINDACHNER

Pronounced Ko'ree-do"rass ag"a-see-eye (not ag-a-see'zee)

MEANING OF NAME: *agassizi,* for Prof. Agassiz, whose name is pronounced Ag' a see

Amazon   Western Location Map 13 between H and I   Length, 3½ inches

A RATHER ungainly, large species of which we aquarists know little. It is distinguished by a very flat base line and a peculiar, shovel-like head. One of the two pairs of barbels is quite long. The front part of the dorsal fin is dark gray, and the tail is crossed by rows of spots, as seen in the illustration.

Còrydòras hastàtus EIGENMANN AND EIGENMANN

Pronounced Ko'ree-do"rass   hass-tay"tus

MEANING OF NAME: *hastatus,* with a spear, in reference to the spearhead-like
spot on tail root

Incorrectly known as Microcorydoras

The Amazon   Western Location Map G23   Length, 1¾ inches

℘OO bad this quite small Corydoras is not very hardy. It is interestingly individual. Its movements are unlike those of other Catfishes,
possibly excepting the Glass Catfish, *Kryptopterus bicirrhus.* It does not
grub about the bottom, but balances itself in the water by a rapid motion
of the pectoral and caudal fins, ready to dart quickly in any direction.

The body is translucent olive. Usually the dark stripe on the sides
is a little clearer than shown here. An easily outstanding feature for
identification is the white crescent at the base of the tail, standing out
all the more clearly on account of arching around a black spot.

A few large, single eggs are deposited on the sides of the glass. Neither
eggs nor young are eaten by the parents. The babies are about ¼ inch
long when hatched, and are easily raised on sifted Daphnia. Domestic-
raised specimens of this species seem to do better in the aquarium than
imported stock.

The fish takes ordinary food and breeds at about 75 degrees.

Còrydòras leopärdus MYERS

Pronounced Ko'ree-do''rass lee'o-par''dus   *Popular name,* Leopard Corydoras

MEANING OF NAME: *leopardus,* with leopard-like spots. Sometimes erroneously
sold as *Corydoras undulatus*

E. and N. E. Brazil   Amazon or nearby—Exact location not known   Length, 2½ inches

A DISTINCTIVE importation of 1933. They came in large numbers
and promptly gained many friends, who, for the most part, consider them to be the best of the Corydoras. This is because they are
prettily marked, very active, hardy and not too large. They can be
roughly recognized by the triple stripe on the sides, the black spot
above the centre of the dorsal fin, and the spots extending over the nose.

Còrydòras melanístius REGAN
Pronounced Ko'ree-do"rass mel'an-iss"tee-us
MEANING OF NAME: *melanistius,* black dorsal
Guianas and Venezuela   Western Location Map A15 to A22   Length, 2½ inches

ANOTHER spotted South American Catfish in which the spots extend over the nose. However, the two characteristic dark markings noted in the photograph are quite different from the ornamentations on *Corydoras leopardus,* and, besides, there is no side stripe. This interesting species has so far not been imported in large numbers. It appears to be hardy.

Còrydòras náttereri STEINDACHNER
Pronounced Ko'ree-do"rass nat'ter-er-eye
Named for Johann Natterer, its discoverer

E. Brazil   Western Location Map X28 to U31   Length, 2½ inches

A HIGHLY-REGARDED "scavenger fish," quite as good as the following, but not in such good supply. There is no pattern in the fairly clear fins. The ventrals are light, opaque yellow. High lights seen about the gill plates are green. Belly, yellowish. A pronounced dark stripe the length of the body suggests being deep in the somewhat translucent flesh. General color of the body is light, tending towards yellow. Eye, gold. Breeds per description.

Còrydòras pàleàtus (JENYNS)
Pronounced Ko'ree-do"rass pay'le-a"tus

MEANING OF NAME: *Corydoras,* helmet-doras, Doras, having darts, referring to the barbels;
paleatus, with dappled markings.

Argentina and S. E. Brazil   Western Location Map V22 to Z27   Length, 2¾ inches

PROBABLY this is the most generally used of the Armored Catfishes. It is hardy, low-priced and is nearly always obtainable.

The tail and dorsal fins are nearly clear, marked with a dark pattern. Pectorals (side fins) yellow; anal and ventrals, opaque ivory. The body is yellow, shot with a few green scales, especially about the head. The dark body markings in the photograph are black to bluish. Eye, light gold. Breeds per description, at temperature of about 65 degrees.

FAMILY LORICARIIDAE
Pronounced Lo' ri car i" i dee

The Spiny Armored Cats are elongate, flattened Catfishes with a full coating (except on the abdomen) of bony plates which are rough with a thick coating of fine prickles. The mouth forms a sucking disk under the head. The adipose fin, if present, is supported by a bony spine covered with fine prickles. The Spiny Armored Cats inhabit South America and northward to Nicaragua.

Hypóstomus plecóstomus (LINNAEUS)
Pronounced High-poss'tow-muss   ple-kos'tow-muss
MEANING OF NAME: *Hypostomus,* with mouth underneath; *plecostomus,* folded mouth
Known in the trade as *Plecostomus commersoni*
Nearly all of South America East of Andes   Length, 4 to 6 inches
Western Location Map y7 to V22

*W*ITH their peculiar mouths they can cling tenaciously to any smooth surface. They are well equipped for eating algae, which they do industriously, even going up and down Sagittaria leaves without injuring them. It is most active at night.

What appears in the illustration to be a very large mouth is only a marking. The mouth is like that shown on Otocinclus. Color, gray with brown markings. Eats prepared foods or cereals. Never bred. Temperature, 62 to 80 degrees.

Farlowélla species
Pronounced Far'low-el''la
Named for Prof. W. G. Farlow, of Harvard (Botany)
Amazon Basin and Guiana   Length, up to 8 inches

NOT a very satisfactory aquarium fish, but included here because it is occasionally imported and aquarists want to know something of it. At least 6 different species have been imported, but they are difficult to identify. Males of some of them differ from the females in having the snout covered with very fine spines.

Theoretically it should be a scavenger fish, as we look at the suckermouth resembling that of some of the Loricarias. In its native habitat it probably lives mainly on algae. In the aquarium it leads a life that is short but not merry. It is sluggish, seems out of place and soon takes its departure.

To those who wish to experiment with this oddity, we suggest trying to feed it on the paste from boiled oatmeal. Also we note that about 4-inch specimens seem to fare better than those of larger sizes.

Otocinclus áffinis STEINDACHNER

Pronounced O'to-sin"klus aff'in-iss

MEANING OF NAME: *Otocinclus,* sieve-ear, in allusion to the holes in the skull in the ear
region; *affinis,* similar to (another species of Otocinclus)

Rio de Janeiro, Brazil   Western Location Map U31   Length, 1¾ inches

A VERY interesting little "scavenger fish." It probably goes over leaves more thoroughly, above and below, than any other fish. When tired it seems to take a nap, perched in some odd posture, usually atop a leaf. The illustration is made with a view to showing the extended sucker organ, with which it goes about eating algæ or other food. This is really an extension of the lips. A peculiar thing the fish sometimes does is to swim upside down at the surface of the water, clinging to it like snails do, and apparently clearing it with its sucker mouth.

Unusual breeding habits have been described, which the author cannot vouch for, but which he has no reason to doubt. After some love-chasings, the female in an upside down position clasps the under-side of a leaf, such as Ludwigia, with her ventral fins, and presses a single egg in contact with it. The male quickly follows, and with the same kind of movement, fertilizes it. Only one egg is placed on a leaf. They hatch in a few days.

This species causes the large wholesaler many a financial grief, for when newly received and crowded in bare containers, lacking plant life, they die off like flies. Under the conditions supplied by the retail dealer and the aquarist, they are more at home, and live satisfactorily.

A most inoffensive fish, and, once acclimated, seems hardy. Temperature range, 72 to 85 degrees.

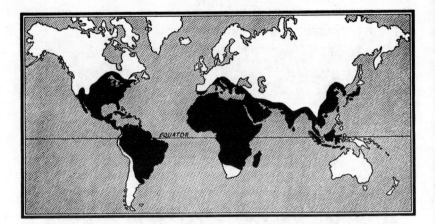

THE EGG-LAYING TOOTH-CARPS
FAMILY CYPRINODONTIDAE
Pronounced Sy prin o don'ti dee

The Egg-laying Tooth-carps (Killies or Top-minnows) belong to the order Cyprinodontes, together with their viviparous relatives. The Egg-laying Cyprinodonts are well distinguished from the Live-bearing Tooth-carps by the absence of the external sex organ, or modified anal fin, of the males.

The fishes of this family, covered in the following pages, belong to two subfamilies. The subfamily Cyprinodontinæ, which is distinguished by the three-pointed teeth, is represented only by Jordanella and Aphanius. All the other species mentioned belong to the subfamily Fundulinæ, and have one-pointed teeth.

There are over 200 species of Cyprinodontidæ known, most of them inhabiting Africa and South America. Southern Asia has only a few species.

Fúndulus chrysòtus HOLBROOK
Pronounced Fun'dew-lus kry-so'tus
MEANING OF NAME: *Fundulus,* bottom fish; *chrysotus,* golden-ear, with reference
to golden gill plates

S. E. United States   Western Location Map d26 to j26   Length, 3 inches

A LTHOUGH this peaceful fish is very variable, it is easily recognized. On its olive sides are a few spangles of green gold, usually mixed, on the male, with round red dots. Sometimes added to these are irregular islands of black. Extremely beautiful specimens are sometimes seen in which the red dots strongly predominate, while a deep reddish hue extends into all of the fins, even with the female, which in the ordinary form has them clear. The light spot shown on the gill plate is green to gold. Eyes, usually yellow. There is another strain that is spotted heavily with black, somewhat like a male *Gambusia holbrooki.*

The species is a typical egg-dropper, preferring such plants as Myriophyllum for spawning purposes. The eggs at 75 degrees hatch in about 12 days, and the young are easily reared. Female (above) has larger anal.

Although this is one of those fishes found in both fresh and salt waters, it is perfectly at home in the ordinary aquarium. One thing the aquarist should keep in mind regarding any salt-fresh-water species is that if for any reason salt treatment becomes necessary, plenty of it can be used if gradually added over a period of say two days.

The fish is highly regarded by European aquarists and even by some Americans, notwithstanding that it is a home product.

Chriòpeops goodei (JORDAN)

Pronounced Kry-o'pee-ops good'eye   Formerly *Fundulus goodei*
MEANING OF NAME: *Chriopeops,* similar to Chriope, a minnow;
goodei, for George Browne Goode
S. E. United States   Western Location Map f25 to i26   Length, 2 inches

*M*ANY of our beautiful small native fishes, especially those from
our extreme Southern states, have found recognition among
European aquarists when we ourselves have spurned them, probably
because "familiarity breeds contempt." In this instance we draw attention to one of our most delightful of aquarium fishes that has been only
feebly noticed, either here or abroad. Standard foreign books seldom
mention it, although, if we may say so, many species, totally devoid of
interest or value to the aquarist, are shown by them with time-honored
regularity.

This is not a flashy fish, except in a proper setting. Perhaps that is the
reason it is unappreciated. While the female is not by any means a drab
fish, it is the male that carries the color banner of the species. This consists mainly in flashing, iridescent, elusive blue in the dorsal and more
particularly in the wide-spread anal fin. Both fins are finely edged with
black. The fish in health always maintains a spirited carriage with the
fins showing to advantage. To be seen at their best it is quite necessary
that they be viewed by a strong light coming from the direction of the
observer. Direct sun is best, aided by a background of dark foliage.
There are two golden spots at the base of the tail, adjoining a flash
of red. The space below the dark lateral stripe and between the anal
fin and tail is golden in the male and purple in the female. Both sexes

have olive backs and golden eyes, pierced by a continuation of the black body line. Belly, bright silver. It may safely be said that this species has an individuality which at once sets it apart from all other known aquarium fishes.

The fish has what might be called an ideal aquarium disposition and can easily be bred. Adhesive eggs are dropped among the finely divided leaves of plants, much after the manner of the Barbs. They seem particularly fond of spawning against the sides of an aquarium from which long algæ is growing. Preferred spawning temperature, about 75 degrees. Temperature range, 60-82 degrees.

It does not need much reading between the lines to infer that this is one of the author's favorite fishes.

Cùbanichthys cubénsis (EIGENMANN)
Pronounced Kew'ban-ick"thiss ku-ben'sis
MEANING OF NAME: Cuban fish from Cuba
Cuba   Western Location Map 1 and m25 and 26   Length, 1¾ inches

THIS fish has not only some degree of individual beauty, but among known aquarium fishes it has a detail in breeding habits which is unique. The large eggs, as will be seen in the photograph, are suspended in a bunch at the end of a web-like thread. This thread withstands quite a bit of jerking about without breaking, but it finally catches in some aquarium plants, is torn loose from the fish and the eggs hatch where they hang. Possibly in Nature they continue to dangle from the fish until hatched. The fertilization has not been observed, but in common with nearly all other fish eggs it is quite probable they are fertilized immediately after being extruded. Fish eggs are at first slightly flattened, like a rubber ball that has been lightly pressed. As an egg quickly rounds itself into a sphere, it sucks in a little of the surrounding water which has just been charged with the sperm of the male fish, and so helps fertilize itself.

The lighter lines on the sides are electric blue. These lines, as will be observed, are considerably brighter in the male. The general color is olive.

The fish has not yet become freely distributed, but it no doubt will be, for it is interesting, it has been bred several times, the original source of supply is easily reached, it is peaceful and easily kept.

A range of 70-80 degrees suits it very well.

Leptolucània ommàta (JORDAN)

Pronounced Lep'toe-lew-cane''e-a om-may'ta

MEANING OF NAME: *Leptolucania,* slender; *ommata,* with eye-like spots

Also known as *Lucania ommata*

Okefmokee Swamp, Georgia and N. Florida   Length, 1½ inches

Western Location Map f25; h25

THESE fishes are moderately well-known to aquarists of Europe and America, especially to those who like to have comprehensive collections. They are not what would be called generally popular.

The male is a light but warm golden color, while the female is duller and verges towards green. Both have the long dark body stripe but in the male it is less clear towards the end and is traversed by light vertical bars. A difference in the sexes will also be noted in the shape of the fins.

This, as will be seen at the heading, is one of our native fishes, and is not new to the aquarium. The author has not found it to be very durable, but there are others who succeed with it.

The species spawns at a temperature of about 74 degrees, and likes to deposit eggs in thickets of fine plants. Incubation period, approximately 10 days. The babies are very small and at first require minute Infusoria.

A perfectly peaceful species. Although small, it should have plenty of room. Eats anything, but needs occasional feedings of live food. **Temperature range, 65 to 80 degrees.**

The Rivulus

*T*HE members of this genus have rather long, cylindrical bodies and it will be noticed that all their fins are rounded. The mouth is smaller than in the Panchax, and with regard to this difference one may make the correct assumption that they are less likely to eat small fishes.

The Rivulus are quaint little creatures, often standing still, perfectly balanced in some odd position for minutes at a time, as though waiting for something unusual to happen. While the expected event seldom occurs, they impress one as being quite ready for whatever it might be.

They breed at the top among plants, which should be thick enough to produce good shade. The single eggs are large and may be collected daily by lifting a bit of the attached plant, or the fish can be left with the accumulating eggs for a week and then taken out. With liberal feeding of live food, they will seldom eat their eggs. If eggs are removed they should be hatched in subdued light.

Temperature range, from 60 to 80 degrees; breeding usually at about 73 degrees. Clear water preferred. Eggs hatch in about 11 to 13 days.

Most of these fishes are not particularly popular, possibly on account of not moving about the aquarium very actively. Then, too, the majority of them are not very brightly colored.

They are great jumpers and have the power of sticking on the wet side or cover glass of the aquarium. It is said that in their native habitat they can travel short distances over the ground in moist weather and even catch land insects and worms.

In the aquarium they are easily fed, but if prepared food is used, it should contain a liberal proportion of animal matter.

The female in most species can be recognized by the spot at the upper part of the tail base.

Rívulus cylindràceus   POEY
Pronounced Riv'you-lus   sill'in-dray"see-us
MEANING OF NAME: *Rivulus,* river or brook; *cylindraceus,* cylindrical
Cuba   Western Location Map m25 to m27   Length, 2 inches

THIS species was introduced into aquaria in 1930 and at this writing it is the latest Rivulus to attain any degree of popularity. It is one of the prettiest and is the most active of these several species.

Coloration varies considerably according to conditions. No uncolored illustration can do it justice, yet this statement is not intended to convey the impression that it is one of those gorgeous, flashy fishes, for it is not. The belly is yellow to orange, becoming deeper under the throat. The irregular line along the sides is dark brown and continues half way through the tail fin. Just above this line the body is olive, overcast with green, while the back is usually brown. In the male the body is sprinkled irregularly with dark green spots and a few red ones. His dorsal is a strong greenish yellow, lightly margined at the top with white. The little dark spot in the photograph at the base of the last ray of his dorsal fin is in reality a bright red. The dark spots in his anal are also red, the lower area being yellow, and slightly edged black. Ventrals, yellow. Darker portions in the tail fin are greenish yellow, except the lower corner, which is black.

The female is somewhat drab compared with the male. It is easy to tell her sex by the usual female "Rivulus spot" at the upper edge of her tail base.

Breeding and care as described for the genus. Fairly prolific.

Rívulus härtii (BOULENGER)
Pronounced Riv'you-lus hart'e-eye
MEANING OF NAME: *hartii*, after the collector, Hart
Venezuela and Trinidad   Length, 3½ inches
Western Location Map x between 19 and 20; x18

SOMETIMES confused with *Rivulus urophthalmus*, but is not the same fish. It is one of the larger members of the family. Although one of the long-established favorites, and a fish that is attractive and easily bred, it has, for some reason, been omitted from most aquarium literature.

The body is warm gray to pinkish, overlaid with dots of red that form themselves into rows, as illustrated. The tail fin is yellow on the upper and lower edges, with black adjoining the yellow on the inside. The centre of the end of the fin is also black. Eye, light gold.

They breed like other Rivulus, and for several days deposit quite large eggs in fine grass. These they do not eat. Although not shown in the photograph, fine transparent dots will be seen in the tail fin of the male. These are absent in the female. In this species the usual ocellated spot at the upper base of the tail of the female (top fish in illustration) barely shows. Her color is more muddy and the red dots duller than in the male. Temperature range, 70 to 85 degrees.

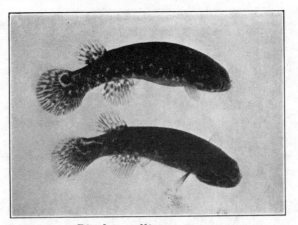

Rívulus ocellàtus   HENSEL
Pronounced Riv'you-lus   o-sell-a'tus
MEANING OF NAME: *ocellatus*, with eye-like spot
S. E. Brazil   Western Location Map V30   Length, 2½ inches

NEARLY all of the females of the different species of Rivulus have the "eye spot" near the upper base of the tail. In *ocellatus* it is particularly clear and attractive. Some writers claim that both sexes exhibit this spot, but this author fails to find any in the male, except perhaps a vague one.

Bright colors in this species are conspicuous by their absence. For all that the fish is not unattractive. The markings shown in the photograph are composed of harmonious shades of brown and gray. The only actual bit of color is in the anal fin, which is tinged yellow.

The position this pair has taken for their portrait is not out of keeping with the many comical angles at which they cock themselves—a true Rivulus habit.

They stand any reasonable temperature such as is usually provided for exotic fishes, an average of 70-76 suiting them quite well.

This is one of the species that is either very plentiful or very scarce. At this writing, the supply is low. The fish accepts almost any food.

A hardy, friendly species, easily kept and bred. In general appearance and actions it reminds one very much of our own Mud Trout (*Umbra pygmœa*).

Rívulus urophthálmus GUENTHER

Pronounced Riv'you-lus   your'off-thal''muss
MEANING OF NAME: *urophthalmus*, with eye-spot in tail
Popular names, Red Rivulus and Blue Rivulus   Also known as *Rivulus poeyi*
Amazon   Western Location Map H12 to G28   Length, 2½ inches

℧HE two color variations in this species are so widely different that it is difficult to be convinced that they are the same, especially as the red or golden form shown in our color plate carries no ocellated spot at the tail base of the female. The blue variety, loyal to Rivulus tradition, always has it. It is quite easy, however, to tell the sexes in the golden variety, for the male has all the red spots.

In color the "blue" variety is considerably darker and from a distance the color is rather nondescript. Closer examination shows alternating rows of red and green scales. The fins are grayish and in both sexes the 3 unpaired fins are spotted with red, more strongly in the male.

This species, in either color, is rather hardy and can stand a temperature range of 65-85. Breeding, at about 75 degrees. They are inclined to being cannibals with their young. Breeding and care as per description. Eggs hatch in 2 weeks at temperature of 75.

Rivulus strigàtus REGAN
Pronounced Riv'you-lus stry-gay'tus

MEANING OF NAME: *strigatus,* streaked   *Popular name,* Herring-bone Rivulus
Amazon   Exact locality not known   Length, 1½ inches

IF the reader will vision the dark lines of the herring-bone pattern on
the sides of the male as being a rich red, and the light parts a beautiful blue-green, he will have a good idea of the principal impression made
by this stunning little fish, as well as a sure method of identification, for
no other known aquarium species of Rivulus presents this particular
pattern.

While the colors in the female are the same, only in reduced degree,
the herring-bone design is absent or only vaguely suggested.

The centre of the tail fin suggests the same color scheme as the body,
but the upper and lower edges are yellow to orange. Ventrals and anal
in the male are yellow, tipped with red. Pectorals, yellow. Dorsal, light
yellow with a few red dots. Fins in the female are nearly clear, but she
shows the characteristic female Rivulus spot in the upper tail base. Eyes
in both sexes, pale with dark outer edge. The species is not so given to
the long holding of poses as are most of its cousins.

Rivulus .strigatus is rather touchy. It likes a temperature of about
75 and breeds at 80 degrees. Its breeding habits conform to the standard
description for the genus, and while it is one of the more difficult ones
to succeed with, it is by no means impossible, and is well worth the effort.

Cȳnolèbias bellóttii STEINDACHNER

Pronounced Sy'no-lee"be-ass bel-lot'ee-eye   *Popular name,* Argentine Pearl Fish
MEANING OF NAME: *Cynolebias,* dog-toothed Lebias; *bellottii,* after Dr. Bellotti, of Italy
Argentina   Western Location Map V21   Length, 3 inches

HERE is an elusive charm about *Cynolebias bellottii,* at least to the male fish, not easily described. It is even hard to pin him down to his principal color. So much depends upon his condition and the light he is in. At his best there is a strong touch of indigo about him, shading to olive. Sometimes he is olive to yellow. Our color plate shows him at his best, with his sides and fins ornamented by blue-white pearly dots. The female varies little in color, but she is so different from the male, not only in markings but in fin formation, that one wonders whether they are really identical species, but they *are.*

The illustration of the male shows a purplish crescent on the end of the tail fin. This effect is in some way produced in the photograph by dark colors in the background, showing through the transparent fin, and gives an impression that is not true to life.

As they are collected in small quantities from mud-holes in the plains of Argentina, and as their propagation is a tedious matter, there is little prospect of the beautiful species ever glutting the market.

The principal point in breeding them is in the preparation of the aquarium soil. This should be composed of sand and soft loam. The male digs a hole and then circles the female until she is over the depression. He then stands vertically with his nose in the prepared spot. She approaches, presses her body to his in the same position, and drops a single egg. The male covers the hole by a swish of his tail. This is repeated frequently over a period of several days, after which the breeders should be removed. A third of the water should be carefully changed once a week. Eggs hatch in 3 months. In their native habitat, the eggs are able to resist the drying out of the mud in which they are encased, and hatch when the friendly rains again fill the pools. Breeding temperature, 72 degrees.

The young grow quite rapidly. It is the belief of collectors that, at least in some situations, the parents die each year as the water-holes dry out, and that the continuance of the species is dependent upon the ability of their eggs to resist drying.

It is quite a feat to rear this fish in the aquarium or tank. Most of them that hatch are unable to rise from the bottom, apparently from defective air-bladders.

These Cynolebias are well equipped with teeth and prefer a diet of live food, but can be induced to eat a prepared article containing a large proportion of animal substance.

This species likes plenty of sun and does better in a changing temperature between 68-76 than in uniform heat. Not a safe community fish.

Another species, *Cynolebias wolterstorffi,* is described by other writers. It is a speckled fish and has never, to our knowledge, been brought to the United States. Therefore we have no illustration of it.

Aphyosèmion calliùrum   (BOULENGER)
Pronounced Aff'ee-o-see"me-on   kal'lee-you"rum
MEANING OF NAME: *Aphyosemion*, fish carrying a flag; *calliurum*, with beautiful tail
West Coast of Equatorial Africa   Western Location Map B48   Length, 2½ inches

THE following fish *(A. australe)* was originally named only as a color variation of above fish. While there is still doubt as to whether they are separate species, aquarists need a distinction, and since Myers and Ahl have classified them separately, we have good grounds for doing the same.

The principal color differences seem to be that *A. calliurum* is in general a lighter and more yellow-brown color, lacking somewhat in the bluish richness on the sides, and having more of a tendency to show fine vertical bars on the rear portion of the body. Also the fin points are a little shorter. They are said to be more tender, as well as more difficult to breed. Otherwise all remarks regarding one species apply to the other.

There is always a ready demand for both of these similar Aphyosemions. In addition to being most beautiful, they are also very peaceful.

To see them at their best (and it is indeed an impressive sight), the light should come from over one's shoulder. It is especially beautiful when struck by sun from that direction. The upper fish is the male.

The Aphyosemions ought to be fed on live food or fresh sea food, such as bits of crab meat. Daphnia or white worms are perfect for them. Prepared food will do "on a pinch."

Aphyosèmion austràle   (RACHOW)

Pronounced Aff'ee-o-see''me-on aws-tray'lee   *Popular name,* Lyretail
MEANING OF NAME: *Aphyosemion,* a fish with a banner; *australe,* southern
Known to American aquarists as "Cameronensis," in Germany as the "Kap Lopez"
Cape Lopez, Africa   Western Location Map E58   Length, 2½ inches

OUR color plate gives a true representation of this beautiful fish in health. When not kept in conditions to its liking, it "folds up," becomes narrower, does not spread its fins and is apt to resign from life altogether. In a favorable environment, it is not a delicate fish.

Considering that it comes from tropical Africa, it stands water of moderate temperature very well, 73 to 75 degrees suiting it admirably, although for breeding it should be kept warmer, say 78 to 80 degrees. What it is most particular about is *old* water, preferably a little acid, about pH 6.8. This is important in breeding.

Eggs are deposited, a few at a time, among such plants as Riccia. They are rather easily seen, but the parents do not touch them. Hatching period, about 14 to 16 days. There is no advantage, however, in keeping the breeders with the eggs, once they are through a spawning period, which is likely to last several days. On plenty of Infusoria, preferably from a pond, the young grow rapidly and soon require sifted Daphnia.

Aphyosèmion cámeronénse (BOULENGER)

Pronounced Aff'ee-o-see"me-on kam'er-on-en"see

MEANING OF NAME: *cameronense,* from Cameroon

Equatorial W. Africa   Length, 2¼ inches

Western Location Map F58 and 59; H60; C58 and 59

GIVING this fish its true name and place caused aquarists some mental irritation, for we had become confirmed in the habit of placing the name of "Cameronensis" on *A. australe*. It was some time after having this error drawn to our attention that the rightful claimant of the name appeared on the scene. This fish was only imported here in 1933, many years later than the one that was innocently parading under a false name.

Considering the outstanding beauty of the false *A. cameronense,* it was rather a let-down to see the real one, although it is rather attractive. The tail fin, as the illustration shows, is rounded instead of lyre-shape, and all the colors, by comparison, are pale. It is simply a light fish of a creamy shade, striped with red lines which are a series of dots. Between these dotted lines are stripes of a pretty metallic green, which at some angles change to blue. The spots and lines shown in the fins of the male are the same shade of red, surrounded by metallic blue borderings. On the outer edges of these fins, except the centre of the caudal, we find a pale lemon tint. Pectorals, edged blue. Eye, green. The female (lower fish) is barely dotted red. Breeds like other members of the genus.

Likes old, slightly acid water, and not much strong light.

The Fundulopanchax Group

THE group of species of Aphyosemion which were formerly known as Fundulopanchax differ externally from the 3 preceding species in the more forward position of the dorsal fin. It will be seen that their breeding habits also differ. This includes all the Aphyosemions that follow.

Although these several species come from equatorial Africa, it is well to remember that they naturally inhabit well-shaded, still pools where the temperature does not rise excessively. Many capable aquarists have failed with these several fishes, because of the fixed idea that all exotic fishes must be kept at a high temperature, an error brought about by a too inflexible interpretation of the word "tropical" as applied to aquarium fishes.

It is said that their natural breeding season in their native waters is from November to March, and that best results in the aquarium will be in that period. Perhaps they follow the persistence of rhythm, the same as the habit of that beautiful household plant, the Lorraine Begonia, which, when transferred from its native southern hemisphere to our northern, where the seasons are reversed, refuses to adapt itself to the change, but blooms its best in our winter months.

Another peculiarity is the reversal of rules in regard to the effect of temperatures on the incubation period of the eggs. We usually expect an increase in heat to shorten the time. With most of these species the eggs hatch in about 7 weeks at a temperature of 70. At 78 it takes about 16 weeks!

While these fishes are among the more tedious to breed and difficult to handle, their great beauty makes the effort worth while and challenges our ability as aquarists. They are egg-droppers which mostly deposit their spawn on or in the sand and sediment of the bottom. A few place their eggs on bushy plants at the bottom. These will be mentioned last in the descriptive list to follow. At present we dwell only on what might be called the "soil breeders," including those in the fore part of the following descriptions of the different species of Fundulopanchax.

The breeding aquarium should be at least 10-gallon size, but 15 is better. Water ought to be—*must* be—old, and about 7 inches deep. If available, use one part of marine to 20 parts of this water. Otherwise one ounce of genuine sea salt to 8 gallons of water. Bottom: sand, with a top layer of natural sediment. Temperature, 74. Use floating vegetation for a light screen and plenty of growing, bushy plants on the light side of the aquarium for the same purpose. These may also serve as a refuge for the female if the male becomes too boisterous.

While the courtship is not elaborate, the spawning is peculiar. After the pair comes to an understanding they select a spot at the bottom, take a side-by-side position, interlock fins, tremble, deliver and fertilize a single egg and deposit it on or in the dirt or sand. Stoye records an observation in which the female forces the egg into the sand by the use of a chute made by cupping her ventral fins together. A pair will deposit about 25 eggs per day for a period of 5 days, after which the male should be removed. After a week he may be returned to the same aquarium to resume operations, for if the eggs are properly buried and the female has been well fed, there is no danger of the eggs being eaten. So far as the safety of the eggs is concerned, the spawning may be repeated over a period of 5 weeks, at which time both breeders should be removed, for the young, soon to appear, would be devoured. By this plan the young will vary proportionately in size with their different ages, and as they are very carnivorous, separation into sizes is necessary. If one is content to handle a week's spawning as a unit, this precaution may not be necessary.

So used have these fishes become to subdued light that any eggs not properly covered will not hatch if left in strong light.

For general maintenance these species do well in a temperature range from 68 to 78 degrees, with 71 to 74 as ideal. Every effort should be made to feed them on a carnivorous diet, preferably living, even to the extent of young live-bearers, if Daphnia and mosquito larvæ cannot be had. Chopped earthworms, excellent. The best substitutes are bits of fish, shrimp, crab, oyster, etc.

And remember, *they jump.*

Aphyosèmion gärdneri (BOULENGER)

Pronounced Aff'ee-o-see''me-on gard'ner-eye   *Popular name,* Fundulus from Togo

MEANING OF NAME: *Aphyosemion,* a small fish with a banner (referring to colorful tail fins); *gardneri,* for its collector, Captain Gardner

Togoland, Africa   Length—male, 2¼ inches; female, 1½ inches

Western Location Map A55; B57

ONE of the most brilliant and bizarre of a beautiful family of fishes. Unfortunately it is rare, delicate and difficult to breed.

It is suffused with light blue, strikingly overlaid with brown and deep crimson markings, represented by the dark parts of the illustration. The most intense crimson markings are those about the head, the large spots on the anal and the wavy line going through the lower part of the tail fin. The upper and lower edges of this fin are light yellow, while the centre carries an extension of the color effect in the body. Both the anal and dorsal fins shade from blue to yellow and both are naturally fringed. Eye, light green to blue. Should be kept at 70 degrees or higher.

The female is considerably the smaller of the pair, reaching a size of only about 1½ inches. Her fins, as will be observed, are very different in shape, as well as color, from those of the male. She is of a plain, light olive shade, over which, and into the dorsal and anal fins, are pale red dots. Eggs hatch in 2 weeks.

From reliable European authorities we are informed that they spawn on fine-leaved plants near the bottom. Never bred here.

Aphyosèmion bivittàtum (LOENNBERG)
Pronounced Aff'ee-o-see"me-on by'vi-tay"tum
MEANING OF NAME: *bivittatum,* two-striped
Also formerly known as *Fundulus bivittatus* and *Fundulopanchax bivittatus*
Tropical W. Africa   Western Location Map B58; C58; D59   Length, 2½ inches

PROBABLY printing inks on this plate do as well as might be expected. They are approximately correct, but miss a delicate, translucent beauty which the fish possess. The fish itself varies considerably in color, only showing its best in old water in a well-planted aquarium, in not too much light. Live food is important to it.

Its manner of moving about the aquarium is peculiar. It darts and then stands still, balanced by a continuous movement of the pectoral fins.

Like other members of the family, it deposits eggs among plant thickets. These hatch in about 12 days, at a temperature of 72 degrees. The young vary much in size and should be graded to prevent cannibalism.

By nature the species is suited to living with other fishes, but it is very particular about the quality of water, especially as to not being placed in water that is even slightly new. On the whole, we would say that this is one of the "touchy" species, requiring skilled handling.

Aphyosèmion cœrùleum   (BOULENGER)

Pronounced Aff'ee-o-see''me-on see-rue'lee-um   *Popular name,* Blue Gularis
MEANING OF NAME: *cœruleum,* blue
The "Blue Gularis" of aquarists, also known as *Fundulopanchax cœruleum*
Equatorial W. Africa   Western Location Map C59; B56; A56   Length, 4 inches

⟨T⟩HIS is not only one of the handsomest members of its family, but is probably in the best supply commercially. For all that, it can scarcely be said to be a popular fish. This may be for one or all of several reasons. It is cannibalistic towards fishes small enough to be swallowed, but is not quarrelsome, nor a fin-ripper, although the male may mutilate the female at breeding time. A strong jumper that must always be closely covered. Has decided preference for live foods, but will take dried ones. Stands still with a slow weaving motion and makes sudden dashes. Needs old water, plenty of plants, not much light, and a temperature of about 72 degrees. Breeds best at 68 to 72 degrees. Individuals vary, especially in the length of fins and also in coloration. The intensity of the brownish red in the lower portion of the tail fin is especially variable.

Our photograph, taken by the natural color process (this plate made in 1920, being the first aquarium fish ever recorded by that method), gives a sufficiently good idea of the fish, so that further elaboration is unnecessary. The illustration is of a male fish. The female has a rounded tail fin as in the following illustration, and but little color.

The fish is hardier than might be imagined, but few of them dying on their long voyages of importation, although on arrival their colors are apt to be poor.

Eggs are deposited singly on or near the bottom, take a long time to hatch and the young are easily raised. They breed true to type as previously described for the family. Temperature range, 68-82 degrees.

Aphyosèmion gulàre   (BOULENGER)

Pronounced Aff'ee-o-see"me-on   gew-lay'ree   *Popular name,* Yellow Gularis

MEANING OF NAME: *gulare,* concerning the throat

Previously *Fundulus gularis* and *Fundulopanchax gularis*

Equatorial W. Africa   Western Location Map B57   Length, 2½ inches

THIS fish is found in much the same habitat as the foregoing and is usually regarded as a color variation of the same species. There is some doubt on this point. It is smaller, less hardy, rarer and more difficult to breed than *A. cœruleum.* The general overcast color is yellow instead of blue. With those exceptions, all other remarks regarding both species apply equally.

Aphyosèmion sjoestedti   (LOENNBERG)
Pronounced Aff'ee-o-see"me-on   shuss'ted-eye (not so-jess'tedy)
Named for its Swedish discoverer, Sjoestedt   Formerly known as *Fundulus sjoestedti*
Tropical W. Africa   Length, 3 inches
Western Location Map B57, between A46 and z47; CD59

*B*Y many this is considered the most beautiful of the Aphyosemions. In health and mature size (and in the right light) it is a truly gorgeous sight. The dominating color on the sides is a rich, reddish brown. The irregular parts of the dark over-pattern are dark red, adding to the general red effect. There is nothing, however, of the bright red about the fish. It is more of a warm, glowing mahogany, which is enriched and set off by blue scales shown in the illustration above the anal region, and by a startling indigo blue on the throat and lower half of the gill plate in the male. Reversing the usual order of things, the anal fin in the female is the deeper. However, the male may easily be distinguished by the reddish brown pattern in his tail fin. The dorsal is blue in the upper part, while the lower half is yellow, spotted red. The pectorals are edged blue-white. Eyes in both sexes, gold and black. In age the fish becomes generally deeper in the body than shown here. From what has been stated, it will be seen that the male is the fish to the left.

Does very well under suitable conditions, but cannot adapt itself to an unfavorable environment. A fish for the experienced fancier having the best of conditions in a situation under a rather subdued light. Not a species for the community tank. Live food preferred.

Breeding and care as under "Fundulopanchax Group."

Aphyosèmion spléndopleùris (MEINKEN)
Pronounced Aff'ee-o-see"me-on splen'do-plew"riss
MEANING OF NAME: *Aphyosemion*, a small fish with a banner (referring to colorful tail fins); *splendopleuris*, splendid sides
Also known as *Fundulopanchax splendopleuris*
Tropical W. Africa   Western Location Map C59; B58   Length, 2 inches

☞HIS species appears somewhat like a yellow edition of the better known *Aphyosemion bivittatum*, although the body is more slender and the fins of the male are shaped differently. Also it is quite lacking those delightful blue tints and reddish markings. The female is remarkably similar to that of the species mentioned, but the reddish markings on the body are absent. The only warmth of color in the species is the reddish brown dots in the dorsal fin of the male. His tail fin is a pretty yellow in the ends, finally tipped white. The yellow anal fin is finely edged black. Body, yellow to golden brown. As shown in the photograph, the two dark horizontal lines on the female are much stronger than on the male. The species is very similar to *Aphyosemion loenbergii*.

Breeds like other species, laying eggs among floating top plants, but is seldom propagated for the reason that the stock is scarce. Eggs hatch in about 2 weeks.

Nothobránchius rachòvii AHL

Pronounced No'tho-brank"ee-us ra-ko'vee-eye   Erroneously called *Adiniops rachovii*
MEANING OF NAME: *Nothobranchius,* with pseudobranchiae (inside gill cover);
rachovii, after Arthur Rachow
Portuguese East Africa   Western Location Map P71   Length, 1¾ inches

SOMETIMES a fish is difficult to describe on account of the complexity
and delicacy of its coloring. The color pattern of the male of this
species is quite simple, but the intensity is so overpowering that words
fail to paint the picture. It is our intention to later attempt a color
photograph of this little gem, knowing that it must fall far short of the
mark. It is easy to state that the outer edge of the tail fin is an intense
black crescent, bordered on the inside by another crescent of brilliant
orange; that the dark markings of the fish are red and the light parts
blue, but the vivid richness of these contrasts must be seen to be appreciated. The female, smaller and more slender than the male, is as drab
as he is gorgeous.

They are difficult to breed. Spawning takes place at the bottom of the
aquarium, somewhat like that of Fundulopanchax, but the eggs are
actually buried in the sand, and take about 70 days to hatch. The young
are tiny, but once past the infant stage they are quickly reared. Their
first food should be green water or small Infusoria from a pond. A commercial harvest awaits breeders who can produce this little beauty in
quantity. At present the stock is costly, and is nearly all imported.

Live food is recommended and a temperature of about 74-82 degrees,
with not too much light. This is a species that must have conditions to
its liking. Given them, it is not delicate. Old water is one of the essentials.

The Panchax Group

*A*S the species of Panchax, Pachypanchax, and Epiplatys to be described are very much alike in their life and breeding habits, a few general observations will be in order.

These Pike-like little fishes are all very expert jumpers, and make their aerial dashes suddenly. That is equivalent to saying they should be carefully covered.

With the exception of *P. playfairii,* which will be noted later, all are peaceable enough, provided their companions are not of a convenient size to be eaten. No mean picking or petty snapping at fins. The question with them is "to swallow or not to swallow."

All of the Panchax are of the egg-laying type, needing loose floating plants in which to spawn. The males are vigorous drivers, capable of courting several females at one time, which seems to be the best arrangement. A female drops only one egg at a time, totalling perhaps 20 in a day. This is repeated for about a week and may be considered to constitute a spawning, after which time the breeders and eggs should be separated. The fishes usually will not eat the eggs, but the young would be in danger.

The eggs are about the size of a pin head, which is considered fairly large, and consequently produce fry of good size, needing Infusoria for only a short time before graduating to sifted Daphnia. Growth from that point on is rather rapid.

The large babies sometimes eat the small ones. While the dwarfs of any large hatching of fishes may as well be disposed of in that way, it must be remembered that there is usually a week's difference in age of a lot of Panchax young and it would not be fair to assume that the small ones are runts. To save the little fellows through their infancy they should be occasionally sorted for size. A female may produce 400 eggs during a breeding season. The eggs at a temperature of 75 degrees hatch in 2 weeks or a little more.

These species seem to be stimulated by a rise in temperature from 70 at night to 77 in the day. Such a change, however, should not be brought about by the addition of new water.

The species are all easily fed, but should be given a fair preponderance of animal food such as live Daphnia, mosquito larvæ or bits of minced fish, shrimp, etc.

They are rather long-lived and are apparently happy in the aquarium, seldom contracting disease.

Páchypánchax plàyfairii (GUENTHER)
Pronounced Pack′ee-pan″chax play-fair′e-eye   Known also as *Panchax playfairii*
Named for its discoverer, R. L. Playfair
Seychelles Islands, Zanzibar and E. Africa   Length, 3½ inches
Western Location Map H-I74 and LM6 on Eastern Location Map

*M*ANY of our aquarium fishes are so nearly alike that trained observers have difficulty in distinguishing species, and a writer has double trouble in naming some simple points of identification for his readers. It is with pleasure that we pounce upon *P. playfairii*, for here is a fish that literally could be identified by a blind man. The scales, especially in the male, stand out slightly on end, like in a fish having the disease called dropsy. It is the only aquarium fish known to the writer having this peculiarity.

The general color of the species is yellow, being deeper in the male. The irregular dark dots on the upper fish (female) are red, and the dark spot in her dorsal is black. Her fins are otherwise clear, with a slight yellow shade. The male is richly colored with bright shades of yellow and orange, in both body and fins, with 5 rows of red dots on his sides. The dark edge of the anal fin is red, the same color showing in a fine line on the upper and lower edges of his tail fin. The dots in his anal and dorsal fins are metallic green.

The fish has an interesting appearance, but is known as "a bad actor." It picks on other fishes and eats its own eggs and young. For breeding it requires extra thick planting and early separation of breeders and their eggs. Temperature, 72-85 degrees. Rather carnivorous.

Epiplàtys cháperi (SAUVAGE)

Pronounced Ep'ee-play"tiss chap"er-eye (not cha-peer'ee)

MEANING OF NAME: *Epiplatys,* very flat, with reference to the head; *chaperi,* after M. Chaper, its discoverer

Sometimes known to aquarists as *Haplochilus* or *Panchax chaperi*

Gaboon, W. Africa   Western Location Map y47; B52   Length, 2 inches

ONE of the true old favorites, and while of recent years it has been crowded by more showy species, it holds a place in many collections. It is fairly hardy and of a popular size.

A small but very individual color characteristic of the male is the fiery appearance of the lower lip and throat, best seen from the front view. Another peculiarity of the species which makes it easy to recognize, and at the same time tell the sex, is the pointed extension, in the male, of the lower part of the tail fin. The vertical bars in the photograph stand out against a background of olive to brown overlaid by a blue-green iridescence, the scales on the back being delicately edged with red. The pectoral fins are orange, while the others are yellow. The anal and tail fins in the male are handsomely edged with black. The dark portion of the anal fin shown in the female is black. There are dark dots in the dorsal fin of the male.

The species can live in a temperature range from 65 to 90, and breeds at about 75 degrees, being quite prolific.

Epiplàtys fásciolàtus (GUENTHER)
Pronounced Ep'ee-play"tiss fas'see-o-lay"tus
MEANING OF NAME: *fasciolatus,* with bands on side
Also known as *Haplochilus* or *Panchax fasciolatus*

Sierra Leone   Western Location Map z47   Length, 3 inches

SEVERAL writers have stated that this species is difficult to distinguish from *E. sexfasciatus.* While it is true that the greenish-brown color in both species is somewhat similar, there are characteristics which should make distinction easy. It will be seen that the dark markings in the dorsal, tail and anal fins in *E. fasciolatus* are lacking in *E. sexfasciatus.* Also the female in *E. fasciolatus* has a yellow edging to the anal fin, whereas in *E. sexfasciatus* it is clear.

Under too strong a light or in water that is too fresh or too cool, the fish is an insipid yellowish color, almost devoid of markings, but when in old, warm water and it comes out into the light from a position well shaded by plants, it is a very beautiful fish. The ground color is olive-yellow, the light spots are green, while the dark body line and the pattern and dots in the fins are maroon. Fins in the male, greenish yellow; in female, nearly clear. About 10 light bars sometimes appear on the sides. Breeding and habits as described for the group. Temperature, about 75 degrees. The species is somewhat difficult to procure commercially.

Epiplàtys màcrostígma (BOULENGER)
Pronounced Ep'ee-play"tiss mack'row-stig"ma
MEANING OF NAME: *macrostigma,* with large spots
Known also as *Haplochilus* or *Panchax macrostigma*
Cameroon, W. Africa   Western Location Map G59; H60   Length, 2¼ inches

ONE of the rarer and more delicate of the Epiplatys species. It comes about second in size to *Panchax blockii.* The lower half of the sides is blue-green, which shades up to brown-olive on the back. The feature which to the aquarist gives it its individuality is the large, deep carmine or wine-colored dots on the sides. In the male the dots extend into a blue-green field in the 3 single fins. The back edge of the gill plate in the female is transparent, and shows the rosy tint of the gills. Her ventrals and anal are tipped light blue-green.

A color variation having the lips bordered with red and having other slight color differences was for a time listed as *E. grahami.* This is now recognized as *E. macrostigma.*

A charming fish which is not seen as often as could be wished for.

While not a fighting fish, it nevertheless belongs in an aquarium with only its own kind. It does not seem to be happy nor at home in a tank of mixed fishes. Should occasionally have live food, especially Daphnia or White Worms.

The species is rather difficult to spawn, although its breeding habits conform to those of its near relatives. Needs old water and a temperature of 72-82 degrees.

Epiplàtys séxfasciàtus GILL

Pronounced Ep'ee-play"tiss sex'fas-see-a"tus

MEANING OF NAME: *Epiplatys,* very flat, with reference to the head;
sexfasciatus, with six bands

Also known as *Haplochilus sexfasciatus* and *Panchax sexfasciatus*

Tropical W. Africa   Western Location Map A47; E59; F59; E62   Length, 4 inches

THE first and substantially correct impression one gets of this species is a greenish yellow, strongly barred fish. Although in size and general characteristics it resembles *Panchax lineatus,* it has none of the sparkle of that distinguished member of the genus. The spots on the sides between the bars are dark, but are occasionally relieved by a few flashes of metallic green. Fins of the female (upper fish), clear or tinged yellow; in the male, strong greenish yellow, except the ventrals, which are orange-gray. The tail fin is faintly tipped with red. A black lower lip presents a rather unusual appearance. Both sexes have pale gold eyes.

While the male does not have the decidedly pointed fins of some of the species, nevertheless his strong color and considerable breadth of anal fin are characteristics by which the sex can easily be told.

The fish is not especially difficult to breed, but few seem interested in propagating it. For that reason the stock is rather scarce. Temperature, about 75-80 degrees.

Like most of its relatives, it is a jumper. Cover at all times.

Pánchax blóckii (ARNOLD)

Pronounced Pan'chax block'ee-eye   *Popular name,* Haplochilus from Madras

MEANING OF NAME: *Panchax,* after a native name, Pang-chax;
blockii, after Capt. Block, the original collector

More usually known in the trade and by American aquarists as *P. parvus*

S. India and Ceylon   Eastern Location Map A19; x22   Length, 1¾ inches

𝒯HIS is the smallest Panchax we aquarists know, and one of the prettiest. To be fully appreciated, its sparkling facets should be bathed in direct sunlight. Olive sides, darkening towards the top, furnish good backgrounds for the dazzling regular rows of red dots which alternate with sparkling scales of greenish-yellow tone. The spots in the fins of the fish to the right, which will be recognized as the male, are warm brown. The dark edging of his fins represents yellow. It will be observed that the female has an oblique dark bar in the dorsal fin just at its base. Her colors are merely a pale suggestion of those in the male. When the photograph was taken her anal fin was folded, giving an erroneous impression of its form. Gill plates transparent, showing the rosy color of the gills. The eyes of both sexes are pale gold. Specimens are seldom quite as large as our illustration.

The fish is a good breeder and an aquarium of 3-gallon capacity is sufficiently large for it to spawn in. One should always remember, however, that young fishes grow better in large aquariums than in small ones. They breed like the other Panchax. Temperature range, 70-84 degrees.

Pánchax pánchax   (HAMILTON-BUCHANAN)
Pronounced Pan'chax   pan'chax
MEANING OF NAME: *Panchax,* after a native name, Pang-chax
India and Malayan region   Length, 2¾ inches
Eastern Location Map q17 to F39; H38; M45; H46

*W*HEN a scientific name is doubled, as in this one, it is called a
"tautonym." Fishes are seldom originally so named. The situation
is caused by the species having first been placed in a wrong genus (indicated by the first name). When transferred to its proper genus, the
specific (last) name remains. It sometimes occurs that these names are
the same, as has happened here, and with *Badis badis,* and a few other
aquarium fishes.

A medium-sized fish which is easily recognized by the double bordered
and oval tail fin of the male. This edging is black on the outside and
anything from lemon-yellow to brilliant orange-red showing as a thin,
clear-cut line just inside the black. The dorsal contains colors to match,
with the addition of a black spot at the base. The fins are in varying
shades of yellow.

So variable is this species that at one time 3 color varieties were
recognized—yellow, red and blue, the latter being sprinkled with small
indigo blue spots. However, as none of these variants breed strictly true
to color, efforts to maintain these sub-divisions have largely been aban-
doned. The basic color of the body is olive in different shades. Females
rather colorless.

This is one of those species with which it is practically impossible for
the aquarist to go astray in the matter of identification.

Fairly peaceful and a good breeder. Temperature range, 70-84 degrees.

Pánchax lineàtus   CUVIER AND VALENCIENNES
Pronounced Pan'chax linn'e-a"tus
MEANING OF NAME: *lineatus,* striped
Formerly and still to some extent known as *Haplochilus rubrostigma*
India   Eastern Location Map z19   Length, 3½ to 4 inches

THE colors of this species vary so much according to the light in
which it is placed that no one picture can show a composite of
the truth. Our color plate is the best of many we have made of this
difficult subject, but it is lacking that important metallic sparkle which
has so far eluded the arts of the photographer and the photo-engraver.
At times the lines of metallic scales seem like rows of tiny mirrors of
burnished gold. Again both fishes may be of a uniform, pale green color,
but the female always has more and stronger vertical bars and very few
red dots. The black spot at the base of the dorsal also identifies her. The
white markings on the upper and lower edges of the tail fin are absent in
some individuals.

   This is the best known of the Panchax species, as well as the easiest
to breed. It has a mouth of considerable capacity and in its larger sizes
the fish can suddenly dispose of a half-grown Guppy.

Aplocheilíchthys mácrophthálmus MEINKEN

Pronounced Ap'low-kile-ick"thiss mack'roff-thal"muss *Popular name,* Lamp-eyes
MEANING OF NAME: *Aplocheilíchthys,* similar to Aplocheilus;
macrophthalmus, with big eyes
Incorrectly introduced as *Panchax luxophthalmus*

Logos, Nigeria   Western Location Map A55   Length, 1¼ inches

A NOVELTY introduction of 1931, this interesting species has had several subsequent importations which were rapidly disposed of. It has been occasionally propagated by a few breeders in this country. This is one of those species which is reasonably hardy if kept under favorable conditions. One of the conditions they require is old water.

The name "Lamp-eyes" proved a good selling label for the fish. No matter what merit a species may have, a name cleverly capitalizing its outstanding characteristic has a popularizing effect. Our little exotic here has sufficient merit to sell itself, but an interesting or imaginative interpretation of its striking peculiarity gives an added charm.

This peculiarity lies in the eyes. The upper part of the eye-ball is a light metallic green, which, when played upon by a top light, and especially with a dark background, reminds one of the mysterious lamp-eyes of the deep-sea fishes. However much they may appear to give forth a light of their own, they really do not, for in darkness they show nothing. The pale green translucent body offers the eyes no competitive brilliance, the only other outstanding feature being the dotted metallic line down the side, which, instead of taking away effect from the "lamp," only adds to it by giving the fish the appearance of a miniature comet. The dorsal, anal and tail fins are flushed with delicate blue, the latter fin also being lightly dotted with red.

The sexes may be distinguished by the fact that the dorsal and ventral fins of the male are more pointed than those of the female.

The species likes a temperature of 72-80. Eggs are placed singly in thickets, are not eaten and hatch in about 10 days at a temperature of 80.

Aplocheïlus látipes   (SCHLEGEL)

Pronounced Ap'low-kyle''us   lat'i-pees

MEANING OF NAME: *Aplocheilus,* simple lip; *latipes,* broad-foot—this connection rather obscure

Popular names, Medaka, Rice Fish or Cold Water Haplochilus

Japan, China and Korea Eastern Location Map e57; g54; d51 to l39 Length, 1¾ inches

NATURE'S infinite variety is strikingly shown in the many breeding methods of fishes. This demure little fish, having no great beauty, offers us one of the spawning novelties. In the Spring and early Summer the males chase the females in conventional custom, but instead of the eggs scattering, they stick to her vent like a miniature bunch of tiny glass eggs, where they are fertilized by the males. The eggs do not long remain in this position. Within a day they are brushed off, seemingly by accident, on aquarium plants, where they remain from a week to 10 days before hatching. The parents do not eat either eggs or young, which makes their breeding a simple matter for beginners.

The species stands a temperature range of from 40 to 80 degrees, and breeds at about 64 to 68. It likes plenty of sun.

The color of the original wild strain is olive, with silvery, white belly. In the cultivated stock a pale gold replaces the olive, but the light belly remains unchanged. There is said to be a deeper orange stock which the writer has never seen.

While the colors of the sexes are the same, the male is easily distinguished by his longer dorsal, with the last ray somewhat separated from the others, and by a much broader anal fin. Both sexes have light green eyes and perfectly clear fins.

These are among the most peaceful fishes known to aquarists. Any food.

Aplocheìlus javánicus
Pronounced Ap'low-kyle"us   ja-van'e-kuss
MEANING OF NAME: *javanicus,* from Java
Java   Eastern Location Map F39; L44   Length, 1½ inches

UERY much the same as the foregoing except that it is smaller in size and deeper in proportion to length. The fin difference in the sexes does not appear to be as great as in the Medaka. The species comes from Java, and is more uncommon as an aquarium fish.

Aphànius sòphiœ (HECKEL)
Pronounced A-fain'e-us so'fee-ee
MEANING OF NAME: *Aphanius,* indistinct; *sophiœ,* after Sofia, Persia
Persia   Western Location Map o81 to m71   Length, 1½ inches

THE male of this species is one of the most beautifully spotted fishes in the aquarium. The regular small spots in the fins and the large, slightly irregular ones on the body are light blue to white, and stand out like pearls against a dark setting, the body being olive-brown and the fins blue. This color description, it will be at once seen, fits only the male. As is usual with fishes, the female gets the worst of it as far as fine raiment is concerned.

This is one of those species which can live in ordinary aquarium water, but does better with a little sea water added, as in directions for some of the Aphyosemion species—enough to stimulate the fish, but not to kill ordinary aquatic plants.

They breed among plant thickets, and as the male is an aggressive driver when breeding, plenty of refuge should be available to the female. She deposits clear eggs which hatch in about 10 days at a temperature of about 75 degrees. These fishes have a great preference for live food, and ordinarily will not touch their eggs unless pressed by hunger. As there is no point to leaving the babies with the parents, they may as well be separated in the beginning.

Fishes of the genus Aphanius have a wide temperature tolerance, ranging from 60 to 90, but do best at 72 to 76 degrees.

An active, beautiful aquarium fish, unfortunately not always available. It should be more extensively cultivated. It likes sun.

Aphànius ibèrus (CUVIER AND VALENCIENNES)
Pronounced A-fain'e-us eye-bee'rus
MEANING OF NAME: *iberus,* from the Spanish peninsula, Iberia
Spain and Morocco   Western Location Map k52; 152   Length, 1½ inches

THIS fish may briefly be described as a striped edition of the foregoing. All comments regarding breeding and temperature are ditto.
In place of the 12 silver-blue bars of the male, the female has about the
same number of dark dots along her sides. As will be seen, the fish is of
a slightly more slender build than *A. sophiæ.* Some writers describe
4 curved, gray bars in the tail fin, but our specimens do not show these.
Minor variations in fish markings, for many reasons, must not be taken
too seriously.

Both species of Aphanius get along well with other small fishes. Very
quick in their movements. Like any food.

Jordanélla flòridæ   GOODE AND BEAN

Pronounced Jor'dan-el''la   flo'ri-dee   *Popular name,* Flag Fish

Named for David Starr Jordan and the State of Florida

Florida   Western Location Map g25 to j26   Length, 2 inches

AQUARISTS have not always been as successful with this beautiful and interesting species as they could have been had the food requirements been better understood. There seems to be an impression that Jordanella is a sunfish, and that it is strictly carnivorous. Both beliefs are wrong and it is largely the lack of algæ as food that is responsible for failures.

Then the fish comes from too near home to be fully appreciated. Few ever try it, although it is highly esteemed by European aquarists.

With the aid of the photographic illustration, the colors are easily described. The dark lines on the sides and the dots in the fins are deep red, while the light, separating dotted stripes are metallic green. The strong central spot on the male is dark, but overcast with glossy green. Colors in the female are similar but fainter. She has a small dark area at the end of her dorsal fin. It is the only species of its genus, and is not likely to be confused with any other fish.

Spawn is deposited in depressions or among rootlets at the bottom, and is cared for by the male, who proves himself an excellent parent. The eggs hatch in a week at 74 degrees, and are easily raised.

The species can usually be had from the stocks of Florida dealers.

Live-bearers

NOT many years ago the author was often in receipt of letters, usually to "settle a bet," asking whether fishes really have their young born alive. The popularity of exotic fishes has become so general that the public now accepts the phenomenon of viviparous or live-bearing fishes without surprise. No more letters on that point are received.

However, there is some basis of truth in the idea that only mammals give birth to their young, for, while many of our aquarium fishes do indeed present developed young to the world, apparently without going through the egg period, this is not precisely true. Fully formed eggs are in the egg duct of the female, where they become fertilized, are hatched and grown to the same point of maturity as the young of egg-laying fishes which have absorbed their yolk-sacs and are ready to swim freely. In other words, the eggs of viviparous fishes have the protective advantage of hatching where no harm can come to them, and of entering the world well equipped to meet life on a competitive basis.

While it is true that an egg is the medium through which all live-bearing animals (whether warm or cold-blooded) transmits the spark of life, there is a great difference between the internal process in mammals and fishes. In mammals, the ovum or egg after fertilization becomes attached to and is part of the mother. Its life streams proceed from her. These things do not occur in fishes. As before stated, the female merely furnishes within her body a well-protected hatching place for her eggs.

Period of Development She has no definite period of gestation as do warm-blooded animals. The young develop according to temperature, and after maturity are delivered at somewhat variable times, dependent upon conditions. Possibly the whim of the mother is a factor, for we know that if one fish is selected from a number of apparently "ripe" females and placed in fresh water, she is liable, through stimulation or excitement, to deliver within an hour. The babies are likely to be just as perfect as those coming from the other females several days later, indicating that they have been well formed for some time.

In the mother they lie folded once, with head and tail meeting, and are delivered in this form, one at a time, or occasionally two. Very soon they straighten out and swim for the best refuge they can find. The young when first introduced to the world are about a quarter inch long, which is considerably larger than those from species whose eggs hatch externally.

As has been stated, temperature has a bearing on the period of incubation, but to give the reader an approximate idea of what to expect from average conditions, it may be said that at 75 degrees the time from fertilization to delivery is about 4 to 5 weeks. The time may be greatly protracted by a few degrees less temperature. At 67 degrees it may be as long as 12 weeks. As with the egg-layers, however, it is believed that fairly rapid incubation produces the stronger young.

Repeated Broods Owing to physiological reasons not fully understood, a female may have 4 or even 5 lots of young from a single fertilization. These will be about the same distance apart in time as the time between fertilization and the first delivery.

Maturity Age Different species vary considerably in this respect, and all species vary according to the conditions under which they are reared. A young Guppy, male or female, raised at an average temperature of 75 to 80, given plenty of room and live food, will be ready for breeding in 6 to 8 weeks. Platies are almost as rapid, while the minimum time for the maturity of Mollienisias is approximately twice as long.

Fertilization Interesting as are the facts already related regarding the live-bearers, they would be incomplete without an account of the fertilization itself. Those not already acquainted with the process will find it instructive. Many aquarist friends have found the theme of reproduction of live-bearing fishes to be an easy and natural medium of preparing the young for the "facts of life."

To outward appearances the sexes are the same at birth. In a few weeks the anal fin of the male fish becomes just a trifle more pointed. As time for maturity approaches, it rapidly lengthens into a straight, rod-like projection, carried backward and parallel to the body, and usually close to it, although capable of being quickly moved at any angle, forward or sideways. All appearances of a fin have disappeared. This is now called the gonopodium. In appearance it varies much with different fishes. In Platies it is small and not always easily seen. In Guppies and Gambusia it is unmistakable, while in such genera as Phallichthys and Pœcilistes it is quite obvious. However, as only the tip is inserted in the egg-duct of the female, that is the important part, especially as the tip in various species differs in shape, thus mechanically determining the possibility or impossibility of cross-breeding between species. The opening of the egg-duct is at the vent of the female.

The male in courting grandly spreads all fins and excitedly approaches the female, usually parallel to her and a little from the rear. He may circle her, all the while on the *qui vive*, ready to make a quick thrust from a position of vantage. The act is over in a second. The female never seems to be flattered by these attentions. Perhaps she dimly realizes, with true world-old feminine instinct, that she is only his desire of the moment. At any rate the author has never seen nor heard report of her willingly accepting his attentions, nor of responding to them. Nevertheless, "love finds a way," and live-bearing fishes continue to multiply even faster than the rapidly increasing ranks of aquarists.

The live-bearers do not mate in the sense that the Cichlids do, nor the nest-builders. They are not even polygamous, but strictly promiscuous. Reproduction with them is conducted on a basis of what might be termed *impersonal opportunism.*

Saving the Young
With all prolific animals Nature seems to set up some barrier so they do not overrun the world. With live-bearing fishes in the aquarium, it is cannibalism on the part of parents. Aquarists can easily circumvent this tendency and save the babies.

First of all, the fewer fishes present at the time of delivery, the better. This excludes the male also, his function having been completed weeks previously.

There are two general methods of saving the young. One is by providing them with hiding places, such as plant thickets, and the other is by the use of some mechanical contrivance which prevents the mother from getting at her babies.

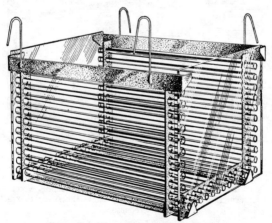

GLASS-BAR MATERNITY FOR LIVE-BEARERS
This is suspended and partially submerged in an aquarium

Many such mechanical devices have been developed for the preservation of newly-delivered baby fishes. They have their points of merit. The central idea, with all of them, is to confine the ripe female in a space where she can live and which provides a small opening (or openings) through which the young fall or swim, and through which they cannot well return. The first of these devices was perhaps the poorest. It was a glass funnel suspended in the water with the stem cut off near the apex. A bit of wire was inserted in the opening to prevent the female becoming wedged in the hole if she dove downwards in fright. This will work, but unless the funnel is a very large one, it provides only a small space for the mother fish, and no facilities for feeding her, except with live food.

Other arrangements consist of oblong boxes composed of glass bars or of perforated metal. In these it is possible to place a small feeding tray, so that the food does not fall through.

V-shaped arrangements of sheets of glass in aquaria, with the bottom of the V slightly open can be used in a large way for a number of ripe females at one time. Also a single sheet of sloping glass with the lower edge nearly against one side of the aquarium glass is another variation.

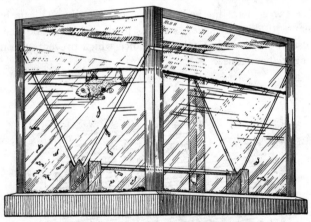

V-TRAP FOR SAVING YOUNG LIVE-BEARERS

This may be quite large, according to the size of the aquarium. A number of ripe females can be placed in it at the same time. Some wholesale breeders use this method. If prepared food is used, snails should be present to eat any surplus which falls through the slot. The water level should be low enough to allow the snails to reach the air at the side edges.

These various mechanical devices have their uses, especially if the aquarist is not in a position to place the expectant mother in a thickly planted tank. It will be found, however, that in well-equipped establishments, where the breeding of live-bearers is conducted on a large scale, they are seldom used. Preference is given to the other method, utilizing thickets of plants as hiding places. The ideal aquarium for the purpose is an oblong one of from 3- to 8-gallon capacity, one-half of which is planted thickly across the narrow way with either *Sagittaria natans* or *subulata*. Loosely among the plants and at the surface should be some floating aquatics such as Riccia or *Utricularia minor*. Any other planting which provides a thicket is satisfactory, such, for instance, as masses of Anacharis or Myriophyllum.

The planted side of the aquarium should be *towards the light,* as this is the natural direction for the young to take. The parent will not give chase among the plants, or will do so only feebly. The young sense their danger and are pretty cute at dodging.

There are several advantages to this plan of delivery. The female can be placed alone in the aquarium well in advance of expected appearance of young, thereby avoiding a certain amount of danger in handling her at a later time which might cause injury, but more probably premature birth. In such an aquarium she can be well fed and kept in fine condition. With the aid of the open space she can easily be caught and removed after the completion of her duty to her species—and to her owner. By this scheme practically no young are lost and they grow well when left in the planted aquarium.

Shallow water seems best adapted to the needs of the young of the live-bearing species. From birth to 2 weeks old they are safer in depths of 7 inches or less.

Keeping Species Separate   As a matter of avoiding later confusion, it is best to keep the young of all similar fishes separate. This is particularly true of the live-bearers. Many of them not only look alike before maturity, but they are liable to breed much earlier than would be expected.

Hybridization between different species is not very likely to occur in an aquarium of mixed fishes, but undesired crosses are quite liable to happen between different color strains of the same species, such, for instance, as between red and blue Platies. This causes a degeneracy of pure types. When crosses are wanted, they should be deliberate.

Feeding Young Live-bearers   Young live-bearers remove from the aquarist one of his burdens. Being born a good size, it is not necessary to fuss about live microscopic food for them. They can take small sifted Daphnia at once, or will do fairly well on finely powdered fish food of almost any kind. Manufacturers have grades especially for them, but this is only a matter of size. Any granular food can be pulverized for the purpose. Size of food can be increased as the babies grow.

At a reasonably high temperature, say about 75 degrees, they should be fed from 2 to 4 times daily. Whether the food be prepared or living, there should be only enough of it to last a quarter hour. Excess prepared food fouls the water. Too many Daphnia reduce the oxygen content. Snails dispose of prepared food the fishes have not taken. For this reason *it is advisable to have them with young fishes of all kinds that are being raised on prepared foods.* As the fishes grow, some species will kill the snails. If there is evidence of this, the snails may as well be removed and Corydoras substituted.

Sometimes beginner aquarists write that their baby fishes have not grown appreciably in several months. This state of affairs is likely to end in permanently stunting them, even though better conditions are later provided. The causes of retarding growth are: too small aquariums, too many fishes, too low temperature, too little food, too little live food. See paragraph on "Forcing Growth."

When May Young Be Placed with Adults? The answer to this question depends much on the size of the parents. Large parents of a given species do not have larger young than small parents, but they can swallow bigger fishes. The offspring of average parents are safe to place with the parents when the young have tripled their length, which should be in a month, with correct feeding. When placing *any* small fish in *any* aquarium, consider what the largest fish in that aquarium might be able to do to the little stranger. Can the big fish swallow the little fish?

Live-bearers seem to be quite impersonal as to their own particular young or the young of their own species. They are neither more nor less liable to eat them than the young of other parents or of other species. Their own appetites and the size of the proposed victim are the only considerations.

Generally speaking, the live-bearers will not eat young fishes if they have a continuous supply of live Daphnia for themselves. And, while generally speaking, it should be said that any fish introduced into an aquarium is apt to fare better if its hosts and future companions are in that mellow humor which is produced by having had a good meal, particularly if the new arrival happens to be small!

When Is a Female "Ripe"? Except with those few live-bearers which are black, or nearly so, there is a contrasting dark area on the body, just forward of the vent. It varies in shape and clearness in different species, but tends towards a crescent form, or sometimes a triangle. This is called the "gravid spot," and is directly over the place where the eggs or young are carried. In some of the more translucent fishes, the eggs or embryos can be seen through the skin at this point. As the embryos develop, the gravid spot becomes larger and clearer. Still more important, the sides of the fish bulge, particularly when viewed looking down on the back. A little experience will give an idea of how far matters have progressed. With fishes we have not all the guiding facts that help our own medicos to make their computations in timing human births, but sometimes our guess is just as good!

Subsequent Fertilization   Here is a subject of which we know little, but we have an idea. As previously stated, a single fertilization is sufficient for 4 or 5 broods. Immediately after a female has delivered her young, the males are intensely attracted to her and double their attentions. Although she is probably able to deliver another brood without further male contact, the question is whether such subsequent contact would result in part or all of the young inheriting the characteristics of the last male mate. This is brought up for the reason that if a fish breeder wishes to establish the characteristics of a certain male in its descendants, such, for instance, as particularly attractive markings in a Guppy, he would not be safe in assuming that the first 4 or 5 broods are necessarily fertilized by him if the female has, prior to the fifth delivery, been exposed to another male. That presents an interesting subject for research.

It is, of course, also a possibility that a second male contact any time after the first delivery of young, but before the fifth, would have no influence on the first 5 broods, but might fertilize later ones.

Number of Young   Broods may be as few as 3 in number, or as high as 300. A fair average for a grown fish to deliver is 40 to 50. Anything over 100 is considered unusual. Some species have fewer and larger young than others. As previously stated, while the size of the female greatly influences the number of young she delivers, it has no effect on the size of the babies.

Mollienisias   In some respects the breeding of Mollienisias requires separate directions. These are given under the heading for that genus.

FAMILY GOODEIDAE
Pronounced Good'i dee

Viviparous fishes, but the males lack the long gonopodium common to the Poeciliidae, having, instead, the first rays of the anal fin stiffened and slightly separated into a point. Confined to Central Mexico.

Skiffia bilineàta (BEAN)
Pronounced Skiff'e-a by'linn-e-a"ta
MEANING OF NAME: *Skiffia,* after F. J. V. Skiff, formerly director of the
Field Museum; *bilineata,* with 2 lines

Rio Lerma, Mexico ⸱ Length—male, 1½ inches; female, 2 inches
Western Location Map o12

ONE of the most interesting introductions of 1935. A live-bearer which does not look like one—according to what aquarists have come to expect. Instead of the anal fin of the male changing into a rod-like gonopodium, it is unusually full and broad, with just a suggestion of a notch, made by the first few rays. This is large enough to be seen in the illustration. It is the organ of fertilization.

They are different from other live-bearers in that the female requires a new fertilization for each brood of young. Under favorable conditions there are 5 broods per year, numbering from 5 to 40, according to the size of the female. The parents do not eat their young and are not fighters. Maturity takes place in from 3 to 6 months.

The species is silvery with gray in the fins as shown. An interesting blue-green arched line divides the belly of the female from the upper body. Best temperature, 70 to 77 degrees.

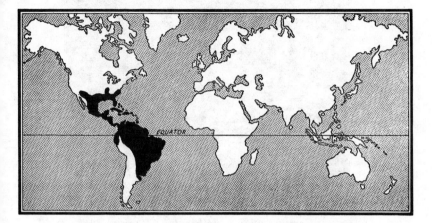

THE LIVE-BEARING TOOTH-CARPS
FAMILY POECILIIDAE
Pronounced Pee'sill ee''i dee

The Pœciliids, or Live-bearing Tooth-carps, are the live-bearers of the aquarist. They are easily distinguished from the Egg-laying Tooth-carps by the elongated gonopodium or intromittent anal fin of the male. It is largely by the microscopic structure of this organ that the various genera are classified. As will be seen from the accompanying map, all the Pœciliids are from the New World, the greatest number of genera and species occurring in Central America and the West Indies.

Certain prolific fishes of this family, due to their liking for mosquito larvæ, have been of great service to man in the fight against mosquito-borne diseases of the tropics, such as malaria and yellow fever. Gambusia and Guppy have been carried far and wide over the earth in this work. Although one may nowadays find Gambusia from Spain to Palestine and the Philippines, only the original, natural distribution of the family is shown on our map.

Gambùsia áffinis hólbrookii (GIRARD)

Pronounced Gam-bew'see-a aff'in-iss hol'brook-ee-eye

MEANING OF NAME: *Gambusia,* worthless; *affinis,* related; *holbrookii,* after J. E. Holbrook

Atlantic Coast States, Delaware to Florida　　　　Length—males, 1½ in.; females, 2½ in.

Western Location Map a28 to j26 and f21

The western form, *Gambusia affinis* (Baird and Girard), extends from b20 to f21 and o15

To many aquarists, at least in the United States, *Gambusia affinis* represents the beginning of an epoch. It was our first live-bearer. The species was advertised by dealers as the eighth wonder of the world. All flocked with their $2 per pair to prove or disprove for themselves the claims for this strange fish. All placed them in with fancy lace-tail Goldfish. Soon the beautiful fins of the Goldfish were in shreds and the Gambusias were banished. But they were kept long enough to prove that they have their young born alive, and to demonstrate that they bred faster than purchasers could be found. This is not surprising, for in appearance they have no merit sufficient to offset the disadvantage of their destructive natures. Like other efficient fighters, they give no notice of attack.

G. affinis is a justly famed fish, for it has saved many human lives by eating mosquito larvæ. It has been introduced into many parts of the world for this purpose, but its chief service to man has been in destroying the larvæ of the mosquito which carries the germs of malarial and yellow fevers. In tropical countries in situations where the draining of mosquito ditches is impossible or too expensive, the little fish has been successfully brought into service. Its practical value is enhanced because it can live in good or bad water, and will stand a temperature range from 40 to 100 degrees. Success in building and maintaining the Panama Canal depended partly on the solution of the fever problem. *G. affinis* was and still is largely responsible for making Panama habitable to the white man.

There is much confusion in the minds of aquarists about the differences between the 2 common forms of Gambusia in our southern states. The worst error, and the hardest to eradicate, is the idea that the black-spotted Gambusias form a distinct species, *holbrookii*. *The black spotting has nothing whatsoever to do with separating the two forms!* The facts of the case are these: In the southern United States (excluding Texas for the moment), there are two forms of Gambusia, an eastern and a western, practically identical in color, form, size and habits. The eastern form *(holbrookii)*, which is found in lowland streams of the eastern seaboard from Delaware to Florida and Alabama, has 8 rays in the dorsal fin and the third ray of the gonopodium shows a deep split when examined under the microscope. The western form *(affinis)* occurs in lowland streams from Alabama to southern Illinois and south in the Texas coastal region to Tampico, Mexico. It has only 7 rays in the dorsal fin and the microscopic split in the third ray of the gonopodium is absent. In Alabama the eastern and western forms meet and merge their distinctive features so that certain individuals from this area cannot be placed definitely as one or the other form. Hence they are not nowadays regarded as distinct species, the western one being known as *G. affinis* and the eastern one as a variety of it, *G. affinis holbrookii*.

Both sexes of both *affinis* and *holbrookii* are ordinarily pale gray fishes often with faint bluish metallic reflections. The dorsal and tail are usually marked with rows of tiny dark dots. The dots in the tail easily distinguish the plain females from female Guppies. Otherwise they look much alike.

The velvet black spotting or blotching which is prized in aquarium specimens may be present in either *affinis* or *holbrookii*. Dr. George Myers, who has collected *affinis* wild in North Carolina, says: "Schools of several hundred Gambusias were to be seen swimming in shallow water near shore. In every second or third school a single, or at most 2, black males were observed; they were very conspicuous among their pale brothers. The original collectors who sent Gambusias north used to catch out these colored 'freaks' with a dip net, pair them with any large females caught in the schools, and ship them as a different species, the so-called '*G. holbrookii.*' These black freaks seem in many cases to breed true, and at least some of our southern dealers seem to have developed strains which breed fairly true. Wild black-blotched females are extremely rare, but in the course of man's selective breeding for black fish, a proportion of fairly dark females appear. So far as available data go, the black blotching of either sex occurs about as frequently in the western *affinis* as in the eastern *holbrookii*, but the black color, as can be seen from the foregoing, no more indicates specific difference than does the black color of the black Molly."

Our 2 illustrations do not include a normal pale-colored male of either variety, since these are almost never shipped by the southern dealers. The first figure shows a normal female and a partially black-spotted male of the same form.

For breeding in the aquarium, it prefers a temperature of about 75 degrees. It conforms to the usual type of breeding described for "Live-bearers," but is one of the species which is particularly likely to eat its young if given the opportunity. Since they multiply with such tremendous rapidity when in the wild state, it must be that the young very quickly take themselves off to good hiding places. With plenty of natural food they soon develop to a size which is too large to be swallowed by the parents.

In the matter of food they are easily suited. While preferring animal substance, they will take any of the prepared articles.

The species is very seldom attacked by any kind of disease.

In some of the streams of southern and western Texas there are 3 or 4 other, very different species of Gambusia, only one of which, the golden Gambusia *(G. nobilis),* has ever found its way into aquariums.

Gambusia (*affinis* or *holbrookii*)
Black-spotted male and female

Gambùsia punctàta POEY

Pronounced Gam-bew'see-a punk-tay'ta   *Popular name,* Blue Gambusia

MEANING OF NAME: *punctata*, dotted

Cuba   Western Location Map m25 to m29   Length—male, 2 inches; female, 3 inches

THE writer hesitates to express his full admiration of this species, for it is a fish which must be seen in the right light in order to be appreciated, and at best its beauty is not of the showy sort. For that reason an enthusiastic description might easily lead the reader to disappointment through expecting too much. The beauty of the fish is quite simple. It consists almost entirely of a delicate suffusion of a rich light blue over a gray to olive body color. The blue is also in the lower part of the tail fin, the first ray of the anal, the gonopodium of the male, and is intensified about the head, reaching a point of actual brilliance in the violet-colored eye. This blue eye is unique among all the aquarium fishes known to the writer. The dorsal is pale yellow, edged black. Rows of dark brown dots further adorn the male.

The illustration of the male might give the reader an incorrect idea as to the form of his tail fin. It happened to be photographed in movement. In reality it is shaped as shown on the female.

To see this fish properly the light must come from the direction of the observer and strike on the side of the fish. A dark background is best.

While this is a hardy live-bearer, the temperature on it should not drop below 68.

Breeding temperature, 75. Quite apt to eat young. Not prolific.

A satisfactory fish in the community aquarium.

Belonèsox belizànus KNER
Pronounced Bel'on-ee''sox bel-i-zay'nus
MEANING OF NAME: Gar-pike, from Belize

British Honduras   Length—male, 4 inches; female, 6 inches
Western Location Map p15 to s21

THIS is a once-seen-always-recognized fish. Although not closely related, it looks like a young pike, and shows a half-concealed, menacing double row of teeth in a long mouth that is "all the better to eat you with." A very, very carnivorous fish, which demands the daily sacrifice of smaller fishes. Daphnia and even newly-born Guppies are beneath the notice of adult specimens. Half-grown live-bearers suit better. They can sometimes be induced to take a few tadpoles or bits of worms, or in some instances prepared food composed almost wholly of animal matter, but to prosper and have living young, these live-bearers must have live fish to eat. This makes them expensive to maintain. Then most of us are shocked to witness cannibalism, *especially if it is against our interests!* We are unconcerned with the well-known fact that nearly every fish in the ocean is carnivorous, but we have a great horror of the unspeakable shark that makes a meal of a man who has himself been well fed on beef, birds and fishes. And so, if *B. belizanus* would consent to eating Daphnia and live things other than our fishes, we would feel better about it. But it won't. Therefore the fish, though often listed by dealers, is seldom seen, and when kept is usually hollow-bellied from insufficient food.

A temperature of 72-85 suits them. Live-bearing fishes, the young of which are ¾ inch long when delivered, and are ready for eating full sized Daphnia at once.

Clear old water is desirable, and should contain a bit of salt as described under the heading "The Fundulopanchax Group."

Except for blue-green iridescent high-lights about the head and near the centre of the body, we have here an olive fish with clear black dots as shown.

Heterándria formòsa AGASSIZ

Pronounced Het′er-an″dree-a for-mo′sa   *Popular name,* Mosquito Fish
MEANING OF NAME: *Heterandria,* male different from female; *formosa,* comely
North Carolina to Florida   Length—male, ¾ inch; female, 1⅛ inches
Western Location Map c27 to i26

THIS tiny fish is unquestionably the smallest of the aquarium live-bearers. The male is of breeding size when only a half inch long, while the female is not much larger.

There seem to be 3 fishes bearing the popular name "Mosquito Fish," 2 of them (Guppy and Gambusia) because they are extensively used for the extermination of mosquitoes by eating their aquatic larvæ. The name is also applied to the present subject, *Heterandria formosa,* possibly because the male is not much bigger than a large mosquito.

The coloring is not bright, but pleasant. Ground color, olive, with the rather clear, horizontal dark line. Vertical bars in the photograph are black. Below the long dark line the belly is bright white. An interesting touch of color is a red spot just above the black spot in the dorsal. The female has a slight dark mark in the anal fin, but as they are live-bearers, the sex is usually distinguished by the physiological formation of the males.

In breeding they are different from the usual type, inasmuch that a brood of young is not all delivered within a few hours, but over a period of a week to 10 days. Each day for that time the tiny mother will drop 2 or 3 young. Among plenty of floating plants they do not need to be removed from parents, but require smaller food than the larger live-bearers. Temperature range, 55 to 85. Breeds at about 70 degrees.

The species in general is very active, a good little aquarium fish, and not expensive. In its native haunts it inhabits thick, matted growths of fine-leaved plants. It is our opinion that this diminutive species should be kept only among its own kind.

Pseùdoxíphophòrus bimaculàtus   (HECKEL)

Pronounced Soo'do-ziff-o-fo"rus by-mac'you-lay"tus (Soo'do-zif-fof"o-rus is allowable)

MEANING OF NAME: *Pseudoxiphophorus,* false Xiphophorus; *bimaculatus,* with 2 spots

Central America   Length—male, 1¾ inches; female, 3½ inches

Western Location Map p15 to s21

ALTHOUGH this species was commonly kept in the early days of exotic aquariums when anything that was a live-bearer was considered good, it is being gradually crowded out by more attractive and better-tempered fishes.

Our subject here is just a live-bearer with a rather savage nature. The female, twice as large as the male, usually vents her temper on him, with fatal results. Possibly she has more sense than most fishes and realizes the trouble he causes her. The young when delivered are about half an inch long, and grow rapidly. Temperature range, 70-85 degrees.

In color the fish is an olive-brown on the back, shading down to a yellow-white belly. There are flashes of metallic green about the head and along the back. Scales are edged black, and rather attractive. The 2 black dots for which the fish gets its specific name are not particularly conspicuous. They will be seen in the photograph just in back of the gill plate and at the base of the tail. Also the illustration gives a good idea of a female live-bearer that has just delivered her young.

Should have live food, but will take prepared ones.

This is a fish for any of those ardent fanciers who take pride in possessing a large number of species. Temperature range, 68-82 degrees.

Phallóceros caudomaculàtus (HENSEL)

Pronounced Fal-los'ser-os   caw'do-mac'you-lay"tus

MEANING OF NAME: *Phalloceros,* with hooked gonopodium; *caudomaculatus,*
with spot on caudal peduncle

Also known as *Girardinus reticulatus* and *Girardinus januarius*

S. E. Brazil   Length—male, 1¼ inches; female, 2½ inches

Western Location Map U31 to V22

THERE are two recognized strains of this species, the plain and
the spotted, known as *reticulatus.* Our illustration is of the spotted
variety, but serves for either.

The fish was one of the earliest introductions among the live-bearers,
and in Germany excited the same comment that *Gambusia affinis* did in
the United States.

In the matter of color, the plain variety has little to boast of. The
spotted strain is rather attractive. The background color of both is a
greenish gray, shading lighter towards the belly, which is nearly white.
There is a little green under the throat. Eye, pale green to gold. Good
breeders and fairly hardy. It will be noticed that in this species the
gonopodium turns sharply downward at the very end. An average temperature of 72 suits it very well. Any food. Will not molest other fishes.

Phallíchthys isthménsis (REGAN)

Pronounced Fal-lick'thiss isth-men'sis   Also known as *Phallichthys pittieri*

MEANING OF NAME: *Phallichthys,* fish with a phallus, or gonopodium;
isthmensis, isthmus (of Panama)

Panama   Western Location Map w25   Length—male, 1½ inches; female, 2½ inches

WHILE this agreeable live-bearer has no marked or outstanding
characteristics which at once reveal its identity, a closer look will
show a combination of points which make it readily recognized. It is
interesting to see how far careful amateur observation can go in the
absence of exact measurements and the records of tooth, scale and fin
counts of ichthyologists. Looking at the plate, we see that the extremely
long gonopodium reaches almost to the tail fin. It is turned slightly
downwards at the end. The first ray of the dorsal fin is almost at the
highest point of the body. The dorsal of the female is nearly as large
as the male's. There is a black line running through the eye and extending just below it, giving the effect of a clown's make-up. An observer of
the fish in life would see that the dorsal fin is edged orange with another
line of black just inside the orange; that the anal fin of the female is
yellow at the rear edge; that the ventrals of both sexes are edged pale
blue; that the tail fin is clear; that the scales are edged black. Enough
points for a reasonably good identification of *Phallichthys isthmensis.*

A moderately fertile live-bearer, preferring a temperature range between 70 and 80 degrees. Easily fed and is a satisfactory fish in the
company of other species.

Pœcilistes pleurospïlus (GUENTHER)
Pronounced Pee'sil-iss"tees plu'row-spy"lus
MEANING OF NAME: *Pœcilistes*, like Pœcilia; *pleurospilus*, spotted sides
Also known as *Pœciliopsis pleurospilus*

Central America   Length—male, 1½ inches; female, 2 inches
Western Location Map p15 to s20

SIX or seven dark spots evenly spaced along the sides where they interrupt a thin line of high light, give this attractive live-bearer its character. The body is in color what might be called "fish olive," while the fins have a faint tinge of brown. In the tail fin will be observed two delicately dark vertical bars.

Not a well-known live-bearing species, but one that is well established and likely to remain with us, for in addition to being something out of the ordinary in appearance, it is also a fairly good breeder. A peaceful, desirable fish. Temperature, 70-84 degrees.

Girardìnus metállicus   POEY
Pronounced Jir'ar-dy″nus   me-tal'li-cus
MEANING OF NAME: *Girardinus,* after the French-American ichthyologist,
Charles Girard; *metallicus,* metallic
Cuba   Western Location Map m25   Length—male, 2 inches; female, 3 inches

WHILE this fish is possessed of a fairly bright metallic sheen, it is not so outstanding that one would expect the characteristic to be incorporated in the name of the species. About 15 back-slanting silvery bars cross the sides, the intervening spaces being darker. Small, greenish dots are sprinkled under the eyes and on the gill plates. The dorsal fin in both sexes displays a dark dot where the base joins the body. The sex organ of the male is double-pointed and the longer point is slightly hooked. If the tail fin of the female appears to be double-pointed, this is due to its curved position.

An active, hardy species. Eats anything, including its new-born young, but this danger can be kept to a minimum, as with other live-bearers, by providing the mother with plenty of good food and the young with effective hiding places. In general, a satisfactory fish, requiring a temperature of between 68 and 84 degrees.

Quintàna atrizòna HUBBS

Pronounced Quin-tay'na at'ri-zo''na   Erroneously known as *Limia eptomaculata lara*

MEANING OF NAME: *Quintana,* pertaining to the fifth (referring to the peculiar fifth
ray of the gonopodium); *atrizona,* divided into zones (by the black bars)

Cuba (Baracoa)   Length—male, 1 inch; female, 1¾ inches
Western Location Map m 31

A PLEASING little live-bearer of comparatively recent introduction. In general color it is olive. The dark bars shown in the illustration are dark gray to black. The dorsal is rather attractive, the centre being lemon color, while the front and back edges are dark. The prettiest feature, however, is a pleasing pale metallic blue in the ventrals and particularly in the anal fin of the female. She is considerably larger than the male. Somewhat the same sort of blue sometimes flashes from the gill covers. The upper part of the eye is golden.

These fishes are pleasingly active in the aquarium when kept at a temperature of about 73-80 degrees. On the average they have about 20 young at a delivery. They are easily raised and make excellent growth if kept at a temperature of 75 degrees or higher, and given alternating meals of live and prepared foods. It is possible to mature them to breeding size in 16 weeks. To accomplish this the same thing is necessary that we find with most of our young fishes. That is, they ought to have frequent, small meals—several a day.

The species lives at peace with other fishes.

Poecilia vivipara BLOCH AND SCHNEIDER
Pronounced Pee-sill'e-a   vi-vip'a-ra
MEANING OF NAME: *Poecilia,* a fish with reticulated markings; *vivipara,* live-bearing
N. South America, Porto Rico, Leeward Islands   Length—male, 1½ in.; female, 2¾ in.
Western Location Map x42; w37; E38; v42

*A*S with so many of the live-bearing species, the male is comically smaller than the female, but what he lacks in size he makes up with bristling activity and a color superiority.

This is not, however, one of the brilliant species, even with the male. His dorsal fin is attractively colored, being a variable orange shade, darkest at the base. It has two dark, arching bands, one of them at the outer edge of the fin. The spot shown on the side of the body is dark with a golden border at the rear. A dark patch (not a gravid spot) appears on the belly just above the ventral fins. This is more prominent in the female. The general body color is silver and olive, with a bluish over-tone. Different strains of the species vary considerably, especially in the richness of the dorsal tints of the male, and with some there is a distinct brassiness about the throat.

A very satisfactory live-bearer, and a peaceful one, easily fed and managed. Temperature range, 68-82 degrees.

Lìmia caudofasciàta   REGAN

Pronounced Ly'mee-a   caw'do-fas'see-a"ta   *Popular name,* Blue Pœcilia

MEANING OF NAME: *Limia,* a coined name without meaning; *caudofasciata,*
banded tail, referring to bars near tail fin

Incorrectly, *Limia arnoldi*

Jamaica   Length—male, 1¾ inches; female, 2½ inches

Western Location Map o and p29 and 30

A FISH flecked with blue fire. The vertical small highlights shown
in the illustration are spangles of sapphire. These no doubt give
the fish its popular name, for there is no other blue coloration. The
general background is olive, but with sufficient dark markings along the
sides to make the metallic scales even more vivid by contrast. Fins in
the female are clear, except for a faint tinge of orange at the base of the
dorsal. In the male this is stronger, and has a black spot in the centre
of the orange, next to the body. Tail fin in male, orange shading to
clear. The male also has a somewhat golden belly. Both sexes have
golden eyes.

Breeders find the fish rather keen on eating its young. Care should
be taken to protect the babies, for this is a species well worth cultivating.
A properly lighted aquarium containing a number of *L. caudofasciata*
is beautiful. They should be seen by reflected light, as described for
other species.

Live-bearers. Breeding temperature, 75 degrees.

Limia tricolor STOYE
Pronounced try-color
MEANING OF NAME: *tricolor,* having three colors
Jamaica   Length—female, 2½ inches; male, 2 inches
Western Location Map, just above p30

SOME question exists as to whether this is the same species as the
foregoing, *L. caudofasciata.* Certainly to the eye of the aquarist
there are distinct differences. The most obvious one is the very large
and very clear gravid spot near the vent of *L. tricolor.* The spot in
L. caudofasciata barely shows. Otherwise the markings are similar.
L. tricolor we observe to be of a more lively disposition.

The photographs of the two species might lead the reader to expect
them to be of different sizes. They are not. This is due to the difference
in the specimens themselves.

The species when crossed with *Limia nigrofasciata* produces an interesting hybrid, shown under the heading "Hybridizing."

Lìmia nìgrofasciàta REGAN
Pronounced Ly'mee-a ny'grow-fas'see-a"ta
MEANING OF NAME: *nigrofasciata*, black banded

Haiti   Western Location Map n to o33 to 34   Length, 2 inches

A NUMBER of fishes appreciably change shape with age, but with this species it is very marked in the male. As he reaches towards his full size, the forward part of his back humps in a very pronounced degree. This certainly does not improve the appearance of the fish, but here the law of compensation again comes into evidence, for while the back acquires a sort of old-man's-hump, the dorsal fin develops in size until it is a thing to be proud of, and as he spreads it roundly in courting the female, he is quite a dandy.

The outer half of the dorsal is black, while the base is slightly yellow. Tail fin and belly, yellow in male; lighter in female.

About 10 dark bars on the body account for the specific name. The body is gray and somewhat translucent, so that the spine can be seen.

This fish, a live-bearer, is hardy and easily bred at a temperature of about 72 to 75.

The species crosses readily with *Limia tricolor,* giving very interesting and attractive hybrids. A large number of these offspring have been produced commercially.

Lìmia vittàta (GUICHENOT)

Pronounced Ly'mee-a   vi-tay'ta   Formerly known as *Limia cubensis*

MEANING OF NAME: *vittata,* with a band

Cuba   Western Location Map m25 to n30   Length—male, 2½ inches; female, 3¾ inches

A RATHER robust species, as the photograph indicates. Not brightly colored in any respect, but the scales are delicately overcast with a pleasing light blue. Body color, olive-brown. In the female this is overlaid with about 4 dark dotted lines, going lengthwise, while the male has rather irregular, dark, broken vertical bars. These are variable, and may be absent. Dorsal and tail fins in both sexes are slightly yellow. In the male both these fins are dotted, but in the female the tail fin is clear.

The light dots on the female are photographic high lights, and do not represent metallic scales. Eye, silver.

Not a showy fish, but a friendly one. The rather generous dorsal of the male is a feature.

Breeds freely at about 74 degrees. Easily cared for.

Móllienísia velífera REGAN
Pronounced Moll'le-en-iss''ia   vel-if'era
MEANING OF NAME: *Mollienisia,* named for M. Mollien; *velifera,* sail bearer
Yucatan   Western Location Map o20 to n22   Length, 5 inches

THERE are those who proclaim this fish to be endowed with triple royalty: King of the Mollienisias, King of the Live-bearers, and King of Aquarium Fishes. The first claim seems the soundest. A proud dorsal fin always arouses admiration for any aquarium fish, the same as we thrill to the high-arching neck of a spirited horse. When the male of *M. velifera* fully expands his fins (we could wish he would do it oftener) he is a truly wonderful sight, especially if one be so fortunate as to witness this with direct sunlight playing on him. The dominating dorsal has and needs no bright colors. When it is spread the delicate tracings, overlaid by a touch of blue iridescence and a gorgeous row of dark markings, high on the fin, are sufficiently rich in themselves. A detail which should be observed when the dorsal is spread is that the numerous small light spots are *rounded* and encircled by dark borders. In *M. latipinna,* as will be noted by a comparative study of the photographic illustrations, the markings are dark *streaks* which do not enclose circular centres.

Of the three most important species of Mollienisia the dorsal fin in *M. velifera* is not only the largest, but is set the farthest forward, a most important point in identification. Although aquarists can seldom count the fin rays of living fishes, it may be of value to know that in this species the dorsal fin count runs between 16 and 19, whereas in *M. latipinna*, its nearest relative, the count is between 12 and 16. Again, *M. velifera* is considerably larger, has a different geographical distribution, does not readily interbreed with *M. latipinna*, and lastly, while in *M. latipinna* only certain strains and individuals attain typical sail-fins, with *M. velifera* it is virtually universal.

It is very, very difficult to secure a photograph of any Mollienisia with its fins fully spread, especially the sail-fin types. We are, therefore, much favored in being permitted to use the photograph of a freshly preserved specimen, taken by Dr. Carl L. Hubbs, especially as Dr. Hubbs is a leading authority who has made a special study of Mollienisias.

A number of erroneous impressions regarding the different species of Mollienisias have gained foothold. Among them is the belief that *M. velifera* is only a glorified strain of *M. latipinna*.

Although *M. velifera* is much more difficult to obtain, and we consequently have less experience with it, it seems from our observations that it stands aquarium life better than *M. latipinna*. Its young are quite large, being about half an inch in length. One difference, not so favorable to *M. velifera*, is that it is more apt to eat its young. Broods may run over 100 in number. Temperature, 72-84 degrees.

Except for the colors being a little stronger and richer in *M. velifera*, they are much the same as described for *M. latipinna*.

Móllienísia látipínna   LE SUEUR

Pronounced Moll′le-en-iss″ia lat′i-pin″na   *Popular names,* Sail-fin and Mollie

MEANING OF NAME: *latipinna,* broad-fin

Gulf States and N. E. Mexico   Length, 3¾ inches

Western Location Map c27 to j26, h20 and o15

THIS is the usual "Mollie" of commerce. Coming from a considerable geographic range, it varies correspondingly in appearance,
especially in that point of importance—the dorsal fin. This varies so
greatly that it may class the individual either as a super-fish or as simply
"another Mollie." In a highly developed specimen, his resplendent dorsal
fin is truly a crown of glory. To witness this "sail" fully exhibited in
its royal splendor is to see something unforgettable—at least to an appre-
ciative fish fancier or ichthyologist. Naturally his best display is put on
either in a sham battle with another male (they seldom come to blows),
or before what might be called his lady of the moment. With all sails
set he comes alongside her with insinuating motions, and then takes a
position across her path as if, with a flurry of quivering fins, to prevent
her escape. The colors displayed in these rapid and tense actions do

not seem to be produced by excitement. It is merely an unfolding of the hidden tints which are always present but displayed only on occasions. The dorsal shows a gentle blue iridescence, but it is in the tail fin that the real color display takes place. The upper and lower thirds become a flashing, light metallic blue, while the centre is a beautiful golden yellow. Yellow also covers the forward part of the belly.

The body of the fish is olive, with 5 narrow brown stripes, joined by rows of a lighter, sawtooth pattern.

Mollienisias require more care in breeding than most of the live-bearing species, but that extra attention bears fruit. They must have plenty of room, a temperature close to 78 degrees and plenty of the right kind of food. Salt or brackish water is not necessary. The fish is by nature largely vegetarian and, being active, it eats often, especially in the matter of nibbling at algæ, which it does almost constantly. For this reason alone the fish should be in a large, well-lighted aquarium, which is conducive to the growth of algæ. If there is insufficient of this growth for the purpose, some should be scraped from other aquariums. If this is impossible, then they ought to occasionally have a little chopped boiled spinach, or finely chopped crisp lettuce. Ground shrimp or boiled foods containing shrimp and spinach in addition to a cereal, form good staple diets. Live Daphnia, or mosquito larvæ should be given frequently but not constantly. Feeding 4 to 6 times in 24 hours is desirable, provided each meal is entirely consumed within 10 minutes. This frequent feeding is important both to breeding stock and the growing young. Prepared food should be in quite small sizes.

At the first sign that a female is ripening, she should be removed to a well-planted delivery tank of about 10 or more gallons capacity. Gravid females of all Mollienisias are adversely affected by handling, and the results are reflected in the young being born dead or defective in some respect, usually too heavy to leave the bottom. In fact, Mollienisias in general and *M. latipinna* in particular, had best be handled and moved from one aquarium to another as little as possible. If things are going well with them, a good motto is "Let good enough alone." If only a single pair is being bred, it is preferable to keep the expectant female where she is and remove the male as a matter of precaution, although in the majority of cases, *M. latipinna* does not eat its young.

No female Mollienisia should ever be placed in a small breeding trap. They need room and plenty of greens.

The one puzzle no one has so far been able to overcome is the fact that in aquariums it is seldom possible to raise Sail-fin young from Sail-fin stock.

Orange-tail Varieties of *Móllienísia sphènops*
(CUVIER AND VALENCIENNES)
Pronounced Moll'le-en-iss''ia   sfee'nops
MEANING OF NAME: *sphenops*, wedge-face
Gulf Coast to Venezuela   Western Location Map y8 to x16   Length, 2 to 4 inches

ONE of the major Mollienisia errors is to call the black breed of *M. latipinna* by the name of *M. sphenops*. Fortunately it is only done by a few misinformed aquarists and dealers. At this writing a black *sphenops* is in the making, but is not yet perfected.

While *M. sphenops* is a widely distributed and extremely variable fish, it is clearly a species. Although some specimens have quite good dorsal fins, they are considered to belong to what is called the short-finned Mollies. In addition to the dorsal fin being shorter, it has less rays. (The dorsal ray count is 8 to 10.) What is equally important from the standpoint of identification, especially by the aquarist, is that the first ray of the fin starts *well back on the body,* just past the centre hump.

Usually the wild specimens are without black marks or color, but the species is very variable. Beautiful strains occur in Nature, including those shown here, as well as "Liberty Mollies" and others.

Black Mollienisias or Midnight Mollies
(Not *M. sphenops*)

*B*LACKS are nearly always a race of *M. latipinna,* produced by line-breeding from stock showing a tendency towards black. This, by the way, is a pathological condition called melanism. The strain has been continuously improved for about 10 years and we now have many specimens which are a perfect midnight black, so velvety that the scales can scarcely be seen. Not infrequently a genuine Sail-fin appears among the blacks. Such individuals, to the minds of many aquarists, represent the grandest development among all aquarium fishes, especially when there is a thin line of golden yellow along the top edge of the dorsal fin. This feature in our illustration is a little richer than we ordinarily find. The black Mollienisia is at present in great demand, and show-specimens of black Sail-fins bring high prices, and will probably continue to do so.

When young from blacks are born, some are light and some dark. All become light in a few weeks, and when about an inch long they begin spotting black. Some become black in 6 months, some in 2 years, and some, never. It is a common belief that once they become black, they grow very little more. One of our biggest breeders of blacks does not consider this to be true.

It is also believed by some that those few blacks which are originally found in Nature occur only in salt water. Large collectors assure us this is incorrect. Certainly we know that salt or brackish aquarium water is not necessary to breeding blacks. Nearly all species of Mollienisias are, however, found in fresh and salt water and in all intermediate degrees of salinity. They do best in alkaline water, ranging from pH 7.4 to 7.8.

The tendency towards black is not confined exclusively to *M. latipinna*. A race of *M. sphenops* with this peculiarity has been discovered and is now being worked on. Our color illustration of the speckled *M. sphenops* shows a very interesting and promising prospect in that direction.

It has thoughtlessly been stated that Mollienisias are the only black fishes in the aquarium. Our old friend *Gambusia affinis* comes quite black, but as an aquarium fish it in no way compares with Mollienisia, which is not only a peaceful community fish and a beauty in its own right, but it enhances by contrast the brilliant colors of all other species.

Móllienísia látipunctàta (MEEK)
Pronounced Moll'le-en-iss''ia   lat'i-punk-tay''ta
MEANING OF NAME: *latipunctata,* broad-spotted

Mexico   Western Location Map n14   Length, 2½ inches

ONE of the smaller, newly introduced species of Mollienisia. Males may be recognized by the black vertical bars on the mid-sides, and by the rows of orange spots along the lower sides of the body. The rather large dorsal and tail fins are strongly sprinkled with small, irregularly placed black dots. Females always show a line of black spots along the sides. The young are few, but are large at birth.

Lebístes retículàtus (PETERS)

Pronounced Le-biss"tees re-tik'you-lay"tus   *Popular names,* Guppy and Rainbow Fish
MEANING OF NAME: *Lebistes,* meaning not known; *reticulatus,* netted
Also known as *Girardinus reticulatus, Girardinus guppyi* and *Pœcilia reticulata*
Trinidad, Guiana and Venezuela   Length—male, 1⅛ inches; female, 2¼ inches
Western Location Map x19 to A24
Artificially introduced into many other locations

"MISSIONARY FISH" would be a fitting name for this little
beauty, for it far exceeds any other species in the number of
convert aquarists it has made. And many of these converts who branched
out and became aquarists in a big way still keep Guppies, and still feel
that, with their infinite variety of colors, they are the most interesting
of all aquarium fishes. Each male is as individual as a thumbprint. Look
as you will, no two will be found exactly alike. Hours can be spent
in the pleasant pursuit of trying to disprove that statement. The only
result will be added admiration.

Besides its beauty the Guppy has other great merits. Scarcely any
other fish combines so many cardinal points in such degree. It is a live-
bearer, the most popular type of fish. It is an extremely fertile as well
as a dependable breeder. It is unusually active. It will thrive in close

confinement. It can stand foul water. It has an extreme temperature range of 35 degrees, from 65 to 100. It will take any kind of food. It does not fight. It is not timid. It matures rapidly, an important point for those aquarists breeding for definite color patterns. It is subject to few diseases. It can be had everywhere at prices available to everybody.

The specimens chosen for use in our color plate were selected with the idea of illustrating certain features. Perhaps the subject can be presented most briefly and easily by referring to them. The central figure, of course, is the female. The dark area, or gravid spot, near her anal fin indicates that she is carrying young, and the bulging line of the belly intimates that delivery is near, especially when the sharp fullness extends to the forward part of the body near the head. Unlike most animals, the males of live-bearing fishes continue to court fertilized females. That is fortunate so far as this picture is concerned, for the gentleman approaching from the rear is in typical position for action, with his gonopodium brought forward for an instantaneous thrust. The three other males nearest her head are also in characteristic attitudes of paying court, but are not yet in a position of vantage.

The tail fins of Guppies often appear to be oddly shaped or sometimes partially clipped. This is usually due to the opaque color markings being placed on fins which are so transparent that it is almost impossible to see them. The spear-shaped design on the fish at the lower right corner and the clipped edge on the one at the lower left demonstrate that the tail fins are not actually the shape which they appear to the eye.

By patient selective line breeding certain fin and color characteristics have become fairly well fixed in strains of Guppies. Five of these established features are shown. The fish just below the head of the female displays two of them. He has a "lyre-tail" and also the "peacock" or "lace" design in the tail. This pattern is not necessarily or even usually combined with the lyre-tail shape. The fish in the lower left corner also embodies two definite points. First it is a "Chain Guppy." This refers to the irregular dark line from the head through the body. The eye in the dorsal also makes it a "Birdseye Guppy." An extremely long, pointed dorsal fin is a choice feature embodied in some strains. It is well shown in the partially hidden fish with its tail projecting to the extreme right. So-called "Swordtail" Guppies (not hybrids) possess pointed extensions of the lower or upper ends of the tail fin. Further interesting developments are open to experimenters.

While the Guppy has become so cheap as to be unprofitable to breeders, there is always a demand at good prices for super-strains embodying size, fin, and special color developments.

While a wide temperature toleration for the species has been given, it should not be assumed that the fish is well off at the extremes. A favorable range is 74-82 degrees. Breeding and "gestation," so called, are much slowed down at 68 and greatly accelerated at 78 degrees. Many aquarists (including the author) sometimes leave their fishes outdoors a little too long in the autumn. When the water drops to the low sixties, the Guppies are among the first to die. In this way they are good danger signals, like Canary Birds used for detecting poisonous gases.

A variation in food suits them best, and in the absence of Daphnia they should sometimes have shrimp, finely chopped earthworms, etc.

In the matter of breeding, they conform perfectly to the description under "Live-bearers." Owing to their ability to stand cramped quarters, they are perhaps better adapted to the use of breeding traps than most species. Young females throw as few as half a dozen young in a litter, while a fish of the size in our color plate will have perhaps 60 or more. Many breeders try to bring the male Guppy to a more robust size. This can only be done by continuous rapid growth under the influence of the magic 3 of fish culture—right temperature, plenty of room per fish and plenty of live food.

It is an interesting fact that "Guppy" is the only name among exotic fishes that has found its way into popular usage. Persons with no knowledge of the aquarium use it to designate all kinds of aquarium fishes other than the Goldfish. It is also used to express the diminutive, so that instead of referring to a small person as a "shrimp" it would now be understood if he were called a "Guppy"!

The species was first introduced to aquarists from Kingston, Jamaica, in 1912, by our distinguished contemporary, Dr. E. Bade. Like rings in a pond, its fame is still spreading.

A LARGE "LACETAIL" MALE GUPPY

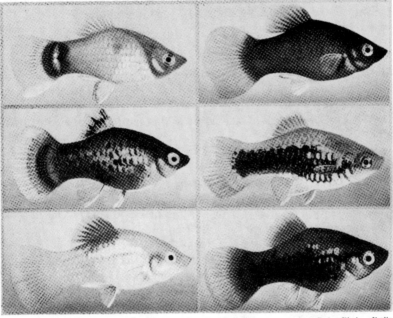

Blue — Variegated — Golden

Some Color Varieties of Platy Fish

Red — Black — Berlin

Plátypœcílus maculàtus GUENTHER

Pronounced Pla'tee-pee-sill''us mac'you-lay''tus (Pla'tee-pee''sill-us is also correct)

MEANING OF NAME: *Platypœcilus,* deep-bodied Pœcilia; *maculatus,* spotted

Popular names, Moonfish, Platy

Rio Papaloapan, S. Mexico   Length—male, 1½ inches; female, 2 inches

Western Location Map q16

*B*EYOND doubt, the general awakening of public interest in exotic aquarium fishes is due in large measure to the outstanding characteristics of a few species. The Platy Fish is one of the true early leaders, and one, through its many good points, that has retained favor while others have come and gone. The Platy, in addition to being one of the most attractive and generally satisfactory fishes in its own right, has contributed to the aquarium a most interesting assortment of hybrids. It may be safely stated that no other fish has made possible such elaborate studies in the inheritance of characteristics. This valuable quality, however, is beginning to overwhelm us with complications and many finely-drawn distinctions, so that it now seems as though aquarists should seek to simplify the Platy situation, rather than further complicate it by the recognition of more and more sub-divisions of the species and of its hybrids. It is with that thought in mind that the writer here intends touching only on the straight Platy and its well-recognized variations.

The reason the species is known as "Moonfish" is because in many of the specimens first imported, there was a dark, moon-shaped mark at the base of the tail. This, however, proved to be one of the most variable points in the fish, and few are now found having a true moon. Dr. Myron Gordon, a leading student of this subject, has recorded literally dozens of combinations of dark markings on wild specimens. These consist mainly of dots, crescents and moons of different sizes and shapes in various combinations, mostly at the base of the tail. It is the appearance of these various markings, combined with any of the many color variations, that threaten to overrun us with sub-sub-divisions of the Platy. The motive will usually be found in the desire to commercialize some chance combination, which is of little, if any, importance. Societies at their competitive exhibitions can help check this tendency by not recognizing as separate classes such Platies as have only hair-splitting differences, and which have a head-splitting effect upon the judges.

The original wild stock is a grayish brown or olive, with a tendency towards a blue and green iridescence. The body is peppered with fine black dots and the dorsal fin contains a fair amount of brick red; not a brilliant color. Through much patient effort in line breeding, aided by the sporty strain in the species, wonderful changes in color have been wrought and well fixed by breeders. Some of the principal ones are shown in our color plate. They are all based on 3 principal lines of development: the black, the red and the gold.

BLUE PLATY

"Blue" embraces quite a range of shades in the Platy. Most of the wild stock, as has just been stated, has a tendency towards a blue or green gloss. This has been brought out in cultivated stock, and in the latest development nothing but blue appears. When lifted in the net, this fish is a distinct indigo color. Such specimens usually have no red in the dorsal fin. In the writer's opinion, this is the most beautiful type of blue Platy, especially when it possesses a true crescent in the tail, such as is shown in the illustration. Some specimens are deeper in blue than pictured here. The type as yet is not any too well fixed, the tendency towards green being difficult to eliminate. However, the preference for solid blue is only a matter of personal choice. The usual standard for judging blues calls for dull red in the dorsal fin. Partial green on the body is allowable.

RED PLATY

For long after a deep red strain was brought into existence, it was peppered or stippled with the same kind of black dots that characterize the wild Platies. These marks have now been bred out and we have a modern strain of pure blood-reds, such as in the specimen used for our illustration. It is indeed a beautiful fish and has been bred in immense quantities in an effort to keep up with the demand. The color becomes deeper with age, usually ending in a mahogany red. For some reason the blood-reds are not quite as hardy as the others, nor as long-lived. It has been found that they do best in slightly acid water, and that they find aeration welcome.

BLACK PLATY

A broad black stripe extends along the body of this well-known variety. The remaining parts, above and below, are neutral shades, tending towards

New Black Platy

green or yellow. A strain has recently come into existence which is nearly all black, except for the fins, which retain the blue-white front rays on the ventral and anal fins and the lower part of the tail, and which in this variety stand out in strong contrast with the black of the body. These ornamental white rays, prominent in the original stock, have persisted through most of the cultivated strains.

GOLDEN PLATY

Some years ago a German aquarist discovered a "sport" among his Platies, and from this break has been developed a popular line known as "golden." The shade is a rich yellow, scarcely deep enough to be called gold, yet better than our illustration, which is a little weak. The fish is somewhat translucent. They all have red dorsal fins and some, like our illustration, have red saddles on the back. A great difference of opinion exists as to whether this should be present in the variety, but as there is no recognized body of fish fanciers to settle this purely fanciers' problem, it will have to remain a matter of choice. Personally, the writer thinks the saddle makes the fish more attractive. The saddle in the males is the larger. It should not be deeper in shape than shown. It sometimes covers nearly half the fish.

PLATY CROSS-BREEDS

The definitely established color strains which have been described have been crossed to make sub-varieties. An obvious instance of this is the figure in the color plate at the lower right, plainly a combination of the two types above it, and a pretty one, too, if the red remains pure, which it often fails to do. This is known as the Berlin Platy, or erroneously as the "Berlin Hybrid."

The Variegated Platy at the left centre presents a sparkling array of rich colors. This is a mixture of several strains, the result being a beautiful fish, which, in the opinion of the writer, has not yet come into its own in the matter of general appreciation and commercial possibilities.

Among recent Platy developments is a strain which is a translucent white with irregularly placed areas of red. Along this same line a correspondent advises us that he has a number of Platies with white bodies and red heads.

And so it will be seen that we have not reached the end of color effects with this singularly obliging species.

SPOTTED PLATY

The Spotted Platy, illustrated herewith, an interesting black-and-white fish, has an individuality worthy of notice.

Fishes with markings like these, and also with smaller specks, or stipplings, are among the most common wild types.

An interesting fact that can scarcely be accounted for is that there is much less difference in the comparative sizes of male and female cultivated Platies than there is in the wild stock. The male has increased and the female diminished in size.

BREEDING PLATIES

It should be remembered that all color strains or varieties of the species *Platypœcilus maculatus* are still the same species, and that they themselves in breeding pay no attention whatever to the colors of their mates. In practical application this means that if the aquarist is interested in maintaining pure strains he should keep all breeders of each variety in aquariums containing only their own kind.

Crosses between color varieties of any species are cross-breeds. The cross between the red and the black, shown on our color plate, is erroneously known in some trade circles as the "Berlin Hybrid." It is no hybrid, but a color variation of *Platypœcilus maculatus*.

Platies are bred very much the same as Guppies, except that they are a little less likely to eat their young. Also they do not take very kindly to the breeding trap, but should be placed in thickly planted aquaria and fed liberally when young are expected. They have a temperature range from 65 to 90, but do best at about 74 degrees. They are among those fishes that like to pick at algæ, and it should be supplied them if possible. All Platies are good community tank fishes.

Always on the move, they give a pleasant liveliness to the aquarium. If their tank is well planted and they are not disturbed they will seldom leap from the water.

Plátypœcílus vàriàtus MEEK
Pronounced vay'ree-a"tus

MEANING OF NAME: *variatus,* varied or variable   *Popular name,* Variatus
Rio Panuco to Rio Cazones, E. Mexico   Length, 2 inches
Western Location Map m13 to n14

THE specific name of this fish, *variatus,* is surely appropriate. In coloration it is one of the most variable of aquarium fishes. For this reason it offers aquarists interesting problems in fixing the most attractive color forms. Just which are the best is a matter of personal taste, so let each work on the line that appeals to him.

The darker markings on the sides are much the same in them all, but there are two principal color strains—one with yellowish sides, brilliant canary-yellow dorsal and deep yellow-to-reddish tail fin. The other has considerable blue on the body, yellow in the dorsal and a deep red tail fin. They are respectively referred to as "yellows" and "blues." All imaginable intermediate variations occur. Among the later developments are solid reds, solid blues and blues with red heads. Some have a large, deep blue dot at the base of the tail fin. The males carry the colors, which begin to show at about 4 months, and are fully developed in a year.

This species is quite hardy and for short periods can stand a temperature as low as 50 degrees. It is a prolific live-bearer. If well fed with live Daphnia the parents are not likely to eat their young. At present only a small proportion of them show strong red in the tail fins. This is the type which is in the greatest commercial demand. Breeding temperature, about 75 degrees. Good community fish.

Xíphophòrus héllerii HECKEL

Pronounced Zi'fo-fo"rus hel'ler-e-eye (Zi-fof"o-rus also correct)

MEANING OF NAME: *Xiphophorus,* sword-carrier; *hellerii,* after the collector, Carl Heller

Popular names, Swordtail and Helleri

Eastern Mexico   Length, exclusive of tail spike, 2¾ inches

Western Location Map q16 to s21

ONE of the most important of aquarium fishes. Its striking appearance, interesting habits and lively ways have made many an aquarium convert of those who saw it by chance. Then its variable colors, combined with the fact that it is a good breeder, have made it useful in discovering certain laws of inheritance. We have been able to create new strains and new hybrids of great beauty.

The original imported stock, selling at the then fancy price of 10 dollars per pair, was strongly overcast with iridescent green and had metallic green in the tail spike. The saw-tooth line along the centre of the body was red and distinctly formed. The tail spikes were straight and long. Only a small proportion of the stock now available has these original characteristics in full measure. That variable quality which has made the Swordtail a good subject for experimentation has also made it

difficult as to stability, so that clearly-drawn lines in varieties for purposes of competition in aquarium shows are hard, if not impossible, to
maintain.

The principal color classifications are green body with green spike
(called Green), green body with orange spike (called Orange), and a
translucent yellow-brown fish with black-edged scales and a yellowish
spike (called Golden). A sub-division of this latter class with an orange-
red spike is now being developed.

In addition to the described main color divisions, there are markings
to consider. One is a black crescent at the tail base and the other is a
pair of separated dots similarly located. Dr. Myron Gordon, who has
made a special study of the species, finds wild specimens comparable
to all of the described variations except the Golden. In nearly all specimens, of whatever strains or crossings, the black edging of the spike
remains, particularly the lower one. The Golden is an exception.

Our color plate shows the Orange variety, in which the reddish stripe
along the side is broader and less clear-cut than in the original imported
Green stock.

For purposes of competitive exhibitions it is better to adhere to the
few main classes and not become involved in endless sub-divisions.

The several Swordtails, in addition to being showy, are good aquarium
fishes, but a few special characteristics should be remembered. They
are wonderful jumpers, especially the males. Males are apt to bully
one another, so it is best policy to have but one male in an aquarium.
Like Mollienisias, they like to pick at algæ. It should be supplied them,
if possible, even if it has to be scraped off another tank. In its absence
a little finely chopped lettuce is desirable. It is a species that feels the
effect of a single chilling for a long time and may never recover from
the "Shimmies" resulting from that cause. They should have an average
temperature of 72-80 degrees.

Otherwise, breeding and care as per standard description. The sexes
at first look alike, but as the male develops to maturity not only does
his anal fin change into an organ of sex, but the lower rays of the tail
fin elongate into the well-known spike. If this change occurs while the
fish is still small, it will never grow much more. Good-sized males are
secured only by growing them rapidly while young. This calls for plenty
of room (aquarium of 10 gallons or more), no overcrowding, a warm
temperature and plenty of live food. The species likes a flood of light,
and shows best in it.

A large female is liable to deliver from 100 to 200 young. The highest
authentic record (at Shedd Aquarium) is 242.

Xiphophòrus móntezùmœ JORDAN AND SNYDER

Pronounced Zi'fo-fo"rus   mon'te-zu"mee

MEANING OF NAME: *Xiphophorus,* bearing a sword; *montezumœ,*
after Montezuma, King of the Aztecs

Mexico   Length, exclusive of tail spike—female, 2¼ in.; male, 1¾ in.

Western Location Map n14

℉OR some years a large yellow-red fish with dark, regular markings
was popularly known as the "Montezuma Swordtail." Scientists
told us that this was not the true *montezumœ*. As the genuine in almost
all articles is better than the spurious, we waited hopefully for the real
montezumœ to appear. When the fish was finally imported (1932) we
were greatly disappointed, for it proved to be lacking in color and style,
the same situation that we described regarding *Aphyosemion australe* and
A. cameronense.

The species, gray-green in color, considered by itself, is not without a
quiet sort of attractiveness. Only a few have thus far been bred, and as
the demand is not likely to be heavy, not much of an aquarium future
can be expected for the species. An interesting novelty for the ambitious
aquarist. Temperature, about 70 to 80 degrees.

The more popular hybrid Montezuma follows immediately, so that the
reader may get an idea of the difference. A distinctly interesting hybrid
between this species and *Platypoecilus variatus* has been produced, showing a high, rounded dorsal fin, numerous black bars on the sides and a
slight tendency towards a spike-tail. This is shown under the heading
"Hybridizing."

Montezumæ Hybrids

JUST what this cross is, no one seems to know, aside from the fact that it resembles the general Swordtail x Platy type. It is not one of the simple, original well-known crosses, but has probably been bred back again with the Golden Swordtail. There is a surprising but well-recognized uniformity to the strain, the principal variation being in the size of the tail-spike of the males. This may be anything in size from a mere suggestion to something quite ornamental, like the one shown in our illustration.

In general color the fish is a warm yellowish red, with brown-to-black markings.

It is more fertile than most hybrids, and, like several of them, grows to a very large size. A length of 4½ inches, exclusive of the spike, is not unusual.

Red Swordtail Hybrids

A BEAUTIFUL fish, similar to the upper one in our illustration, appeared as the result of an unknown Red Platy-Swordtail cross, in the aquarium of a gentleman in New York City in 1922, or thereabout. He succeeded in fixing the strain and astounded the aquarium world by showing 20 perfect specimens at an exhibition where the author was a judge. Only some of the individuals were fertile, but the breed persisted and came into general use.

Another strain appeared in about 1930, of a beautiful translucent red color, with a good spike and a tendency to a white belly. This whiteness has largely been bred out. The strain is extremely prolific, which gave ground for the argument that the fish is not a hybrid, but a straight Red Swordtail, under which name it is known in trade. This argument by itself is not very sound, as fertile hybrids can be had by several re-crossings with one of the parent stocks. The lower fish in our color plate represents this later strain, but we find it impossible to reproduce its beautiful translucent quality.

There is still variation in the tail spike as to length and as to the presence of its black margin. The strain has proven extremely popular.

Variegated Hybrids

HYBRIDS of this very variable and interesting type are usually the results of crosses between some color variety of *Platypœcilus maculatus* and *Xiphophorus hellerii*. Some are produced by various crossings of the hybrids themselves, and by back-crossings with one side or the other of the parent stock.

Truth to tell, much of it is done by chance, without any deliberate application of the Mendelian laws to attain a given objective.

Of the 3 shown, the upper fish, called the Black Spangled, is the most definitely established. It is produced by crossing the Niger variety of the Platyfish with a Green Swordtail. Those specimens in which the blue-green scales are carried evenly over the body, and into the head, are the most highly prized.

The ancestry of the centre fish, called the Calico, or Variegated Hybrid, is unknown to the writer, and probably to the owner as well. From appearances it easily could be the result of a cross between the Black Spangled fish and a hybrid Red Swordtail.

THE HALF-BEAKS
FAMILY HEMIRHAMPHIDAE
Pronounced Hem i ram'fi dee

The Half-beaks live up to their name, for the easiest distinguishing feature of these peculiar fishes is the long lower jaw, prolonged into a beak. The true Bill-fishes or Gars have *both* jaws prolonged. The Half-beaks are mostly salt-water fishes, but a few in the East Indies are from fresh water. These fresh-water forms are nearly all viviparous, in contradistinction to the salt-water species.

Dérmogénys pùsillus VAN HASSELT
Pronounced Der'mo-gen''iss pew'sill-us
Popular name, Half-beak
MEANING OF NAME: *Dermogenys,* with skin-like cheeks; *pusillus,* small, or weak
Known also as *Hemiramphus fluviatilis*
Siam to Java, Sumatra and Borneo   Length—male, 2 inches; female, 3 inches
Eastern Location Map x36 to 39; I40; L42 to M47; H45

USED as we are to thinking of conventional types of live-bearers, such as Platies, Swordtails and Mollienisias, it comes almost as a shock to learn that this odd fish, with a head like a Humming Bird, also delivers its young alive. In color the fish is interesting but not flashy. Back, olive-brown; sides, lighter; belly, nearly white. Fins, especially the ventrals, are reddish, more so in the female. Breeding temperature, 75 degrees.

Many of the young are born dead. The addition of a teaspoonful of salt to the gallon improves chances of success. Shallow water is advisable for breeding.

THE STICKLEBACKS
FAMILY GASTEROSTEIDAE
Pronounced Gas'ter os tee'i dee

The Sticklebacks are well-known nest-builders of the temperate and sub-arctic parts of the Northern Hemisphere, their chief distinguishing feature is the series (2 to 15 or more) of free spines along the back in front of the dorsal fin.

Gásterósteus acùleàtus LINNAEUS

Pronounced Gas'ter-os''tee-us ak-you'lee-a''tus *Popular name,* Three-spined Stickleback

MEANING OF NAME: *Gasterosteus,* with bony belly; *aculeatus,* sharp

Brackish and fresh coastal waters of the N. Atlantic and N. Pacific, South to New Jersey and Lower California   Length, 2½ inches

THE most showy of the Sticklebacks and the surest one to breed in a tank. Specimens secured in the early spring months and kept at a temperature of about 65 to 70 degrees are almost certain to put on their breeding "act." They should never be kept warmer than 75 degrees.

The male wears his best scarlet vest, from his chin to the end of his belly. In contrast with the marbled green of his sides it is truly brilliant. He builds a shallow nest with raised edges, as shown.

Males fan and guard eggs, which hatch in 3 days. Both adults and young need live food. Not a community fish.

Apéltes quadràcus (MITCHILL)

Pronounced A-pel'tees quad-ray'kus   *Popular name,* Four-spined Stickleback
MEANING OF NAME: *Apeltes,* without plates or armor (which are formed on the sides of most Sticklebacks); *quadracus,* four-spined.
Atlantic coast streams of United States, South to Virginia
Length—male, 1½ inches; female, 2 inches

REALLY a marine fish that comes up fresh-water rivers and creeks of the Atlantic seaboard to spawn. They appear in large numbers in these streams in the early spring, about March. If netted at this time they are fairly sure to spawn in an aquarium. The water should be at about 65 to 70 degrees. Eastern dealers have them in season, at low prices.

The male builds a nest between the leaves of such plants as Vallisneria or Sagittaria, using bits of aquarium rubble for the purpose. Broken bits of Myriophyllum are ideal for his use. At the breeding season the male exudes from special glands in his body a sort of sticky cobweb, with which he glues the nest together and anchors it to nearby leaves. The nest is usually open at the top and has a hole in the side, insuring circulation of water as he blows into it during the several days of the hatching period. He does not eat the young. Sometimes several females will deposit their eggs in one nest.

The young must have Infusoria, followed by sifted Daphnia. Adults also need live food, preferably Daphnia.

Sticklebacks are pugnacious and should not be kept with other fishes. They cannot stand much heat. In breeding season the ventral fins of the male are brilliant red. With this species the parents do not usually live long after breeding is over.

THE SILVERSIDES
FAMILY ATHERINIDAE
Pronounced Ath er in'i dee

The Silversides are common salt-water fishes found on nearly all tropical and temperate coasts. A few permanently inhabit fresh water. The separate spiny dorsal fin and the Cyprinodont-like mouth will identify fishes of this family.

Melànotaènia nìgrans (RICHARDSON)

Pronounced Me-lay'no-tee'nee-a ny'grans   *Popular name,* Australian Rainbow Fish
MEANING OF NAME: *Melanotaenia,* with black band; *nigrans,* black
Australia   Eastern Location Map S56; R61; Q61   Length, 3 to 4 inches

THIS is probably the most beautiful and generally satisfactory of the rather few aquarium fishes that have been brought from Australia. Under favorable conditions it is so prolific that it is liable to cause overproduction. Those conditions are that a number of them be placed outdoors in summer in a concrete tank crowded with fine-leaved plants; that they be fed continuously with live food and left alone. Nature will do the rest. The young need not be separated from the old. Or a pair may be spawned in a large aquarium in the same manner as ordinary egg-droppers.

The striking feature of the species is a brilliant array of red and yellow stripes on the sides. The apparently dark spot on the gill plate is fiery red. The male (above) is smaller, slimmer and more brilliant. Very peaceful, hardy and easily fed. Temperature range, 60 to 90 degrees.

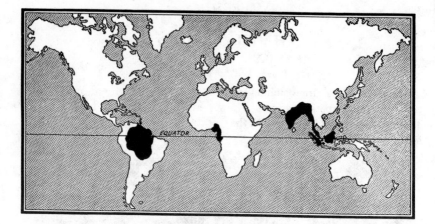

THE NANDIDS
FAMILY NANDIDAE
Pronounced Nan'di dee

Most spiny-rayed fishes are found in salt water and very few families of this type are restricted entirely to fresh water. The Cichlids, Sun-fishes, true Perches, and Gouramis are among such fresh-water families. The Nandids also share this distinction, and of all such groups they are the most widely scattered in range.

Monocirrhus (one species) is found over most of the Amazon Basin and in the Essequibo River, British Guiana.

Polycentrus (one species) is restricted to Guiana and the island of Trinidad.

Polycentropsis (one species) alone represents the family in Africa, where it is confined to a relatively small area about the mouth of the Niger. In India there is *Nandus* (two or three species) and *Badis* (two species). It is interesting to speculate on what tremendous past changes in the earth's crust caused this wide scattering of the members of this little family.

The Nandids differ technically from other related families chiefly in features of the skeleton. All of them (except *Badis*, which may have to be placed in a separate family) have large mouths which can be opened out to a tremendous extent (see photo of *Monocirrhus*) and all (except *Badis* again) have the peculiar feature of having the tail fin and the rear ends of the dorsal and anal fins so transparent as to be hardly visible in the live fish. The transparent dorsal and anal fin ends are almost constantly in motion.

329

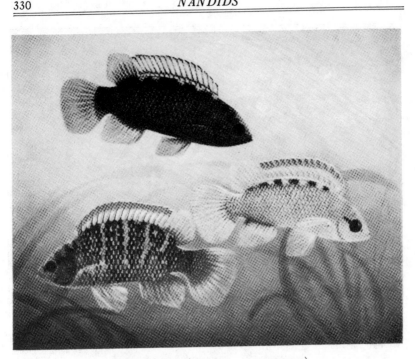

Badis badis   (HAMILTON-BUCHANAN)
(Pronounced as spelled, either with the broad a as in ah or long a as in bay)
Name is based on a native name

India   Eastern Location Map m19 to p31   Length, 2¾ inches

ANY of our exotic fishes have extensive wardrobes of colored garments which they wear according to whim and occasion, and an author attempting descriptions feels that he is helplessly repeating himself in saying very much the same thing about a number of species. However, *Badis badis* is one of the extreme cases. Our color plate saves words. The reader may imagine any intermediate shades he pleases and not be far wrong. The usual color is brown with black or red bars in a chain-like pattern. The clearness of the pattern as shown is not exaggerated.

Sexes cannot be told positively, but the males are more hollow-bellied and are apt to be darker and larger. Their fins are larger, too.

They usually spawn upside down on the inside of a flower-pot. Temperature around 80 is preferred, at which point the eggs hatch in 2 days. The male guards them and protects the young for a short period.

This is one of those species that stands still in peculiar positions. It will eat live food only. Safer in community tank than in pairs.

Pólycentrópsis abbrèviàta BOULENGER

Pronounced Pol'lee-sen-trop"sis   ab-bree'vee-a"ta

MEANING OF NAME: *Polycentropsis*, resembling *Polycentrus; abbreviata*, abbreviated,
referring to the illusion that the fish has no tail fin

From a small area about Gulf of Guinea—See preceding family map

Western Location Map A55; B56   Length, 3 inches

*J*NTRODUCING one of the very select fishes of the aquarium; a
recluse not often met with, one long honored by European aquarists;
a fish with an aura of mystery about it, and likely never to become common; it is even less known to ichthyologists.

The species in the main resembles the better-known *Polycentrus schomburgkii,* to which it is related, but the transparency of the soft-rayed fins is even more striking. It takes a second look to be certain they have not been sharply amputated.

There are no bright colors, only varying and changing shades of brown, irregularly spotted black. The eye is the hub of 3 radiating dark lines, seen in several Nandid species. Mouth very, very large and well adapted to its particular pleasure of eating smaller fishes. It will take worms, mosquito larvæ and the larger water insects, but to be placed in breeding condition it should have fish. Along with Belonesox and *Hoplias malabaricus,* this species offers a solution for the disposal of surplus fishes, an ever increasing problem with the amateur breeder; only with Polycentropsis the outcome of the breeding should be the more profitable, either from the standpoint of sales or trading.

Sex indications very slight. The breast line of the female is a trifle fuller.

The spawning resembles that of the Bubble-nest Builders but is not the same. The male makes bubbles among the tops of leaves such as Cabomba, and the female deposits about 100 eggs singly on the plant among the bubbles. Female should then be removed. Eggs hatch in 3 days at 80 degrees and the young hang on plants from sticky threads until the yolk-sac is absorbed. They then drop to the bottom to a place which has been cleared by the male. Shallow water and uniform temperature are required. Difficult to raise.

Although carnivorous and rather savage looking, these fishes are not much of fighters. They stand still for long periods, prefer subdued light and are nocturnal.

Pólycéntrus schómbúrgkii (MUELLER AND TROSCHEL)
Pronounced Pol'lee-sen"trus shom-burk'e-eye
MEANING OF NAME: *Polycentrus,* many-spined; *schomburgkii,* after the
naturalist, Richard Schomburgk
Trinidad and Guiana   Length, 2½ inches
Western Location Map x between 19 and 20; A between 21 and 22

*I*N abrupt contrast with an ordinarily dark body, the transparent ends
of the dorsal and anal and the entire tail fin produce a startling effect.
Like most Nandids this species undergoes the most extreme changes in
color, from light brown to blue-black. The black dots in irregular vertical
rows shown in the photograph may entirely disappear, but usually they
are strong, and give character to the otherwise plain brown shades of the
fish. Four dark oblique bars are sometimes seen. The light spots are
also variable and may disappear. Usually they stand out best when the
fish is in one of its dark moods. Except where the fins are transparent,
they harmoniously take on the general colors of the body. Eye, dark dull
gold. The spiny rays of the dorsal and anal fins are tipped white.

A number of aquarists succeed each year in multiplying the fish, but
it cannot be said to be easily bred. The pair should be in an aquarium
that is partially shaded and having, in addition, a plentiful screen of

growing aquatic plants. They like to spawn *inside* a flower-pot that has been laid on its side, the opening *away* from the aquarist's view, and *towards* a darkened corner. Female should be removed when spawning is completed. Male fans eggs, which hatch in 4 days at a temperature of 77 degrees. He, also, should then be removed.

The species is strictly carnivorous but may be kept in a community aquarium, provided there are no fishes present of a size that would tempt it as food. Temperature range is 70 to 85 degrees. Very deliberate in its movements and often stands stone still, but not in a sluggish way. It is rather on the *qui vive*, waiting to make a dash for some morsel of live food. They do well on worms.

The sexes are difficult to tell, but the male is usually the darker fish.

Mónocírrhus pólyacánthus HECKEL

Pronounced Mon'o-sir"rus   pol'lee-a-kan"thuss   *Popular name,* Leaf Fish
MEANING OF NAME: *Monocirrhus,* with one whisker; *polyacanthus,* many spined
Amazon and Guiana   Western Location Map A 21 to H12 and G28   Length, 2½ inches
Evidently found over the whole Amazon Basin

ALTHOUGH this extremely odd fish was first described by Heckel as long ago as 1840, the type specimens in the Vienna Museum for many years remained the only ones of which we had any knowledge. In an interesting reprint from the "Biological Bulletin" for November, 1921, Dr. W. R. Allen describes a sluggish brook, overhung with tropical vegetation, from which he captured 3 specimens. The bottom was matted with fallen leaves. The fishes, of a leaf-brown, irregularly mottled color, were difficult to see. They moved about peculiarly like drifting leaves, and would not have been seen, except that the collector thought it strange that leaves should move at all in such sluggish water.

The species is most peculiar, and is a real novelty of decided exotic character. To begin with, the leafy color is much more apparent in life than a black-and-white photograph can show. It is really quite striking, and is not confined to any particular shade of brown, but changes greatly.

Whether this is a chameleon-like power of protective coloration, we can only surmise. The eyes are difficult to distinguish, owing to the dark lines radiating from them. Usually the fins are spread, their saw-edges contributing much to the leaf-like effect. The beard on the male adds a stem to the leaf. Even the natives call the species the Leaf Fish.

They move about sedately and pose themselves at unusual angles, frequently head-down, as we see in the illustration. They do not seem to be particularly bored with life, but they gape or yawn prodigiously. Many fishes do this moderately, but the Leaf Fish puts on a startling act. The mouth seems to unfold from within itself until it becomes a veritable trumpet. Our camera caught the lower fish in the act.

They deposit, fertilize and fan their eggs somewhat like Cichlids, but their paternal care is not nearly so intense. The first spawn of this pair, placed in a dark vertical corner where the aquarium glasses join, was the most successful. Those later placed in pots did not do so well. The youngsters varied greatly in size, and after 3 weeks commenced disappearing. Removed from the parents and graded for size, the trouble ended. They have barbels for the first months, and when quite small are covered with tiny white dots which look like the parasitic disease, Ichthyophthirius. This is common to a number of kinds of very young fishes, and is probably protective coloration.

Although *Monocirrhus polyacanthus* likes small fishes as food, it is not pugnacious, either with its mates or other species. It will eat prepared foods containing a liberal percentage of animal matter. Considering that the species comes from an equatorial part of the world, it is rather surprising to find it breeding at about 78 degrees.

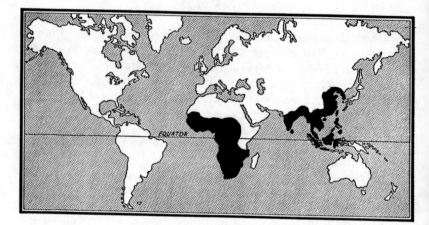

THE ANABANTIDS
FAMILY ANABANTIDAE
Pronounced An a ban'ti dee

The Anabantids include the Climbing Perches and Gouramis. The family belongs to the order Labyrinthici, which is characterized by the presence of a chamber above the gills for the retention of air for breathing. The Anabantids differ from the Snakeheads in the spiny fins and in the more complicated breathing chamber structure. All of them are from Southern Asia and Africa.

The family is not a large one. The species and genera are most numerous and varied in the Asiatic part of their range, only 3 or 4 genera inhabiting Africa. Nearly all the species are useful in their native haunts as destroyers of mosquito larvæ. Since only 2 or 3 are large enough to be considered as food fishes, it will be seen that most Anabantids are good aquarium material.

NUPTIAL EMBRACE OF PARADISE FISH

The Labyrinth Bubble-nest Builders

LABYRINTH fishes are those having an auxiliary breathing apparatus in addition to the ordinary gills. Although not capable of independent muscular action, this organ is comparable to the lung of an air-breathing animal, and serves the same purpose. It is called a labyrinth on account of its involved structure which brings a great many fine capillaries into contact with the air forced through it. These capillaries absorb oxygen from the air and deliver it directly into the blood stream of the fish. The air, however, does not pass through the labyrinth in the same manner as we humans breathe, but is taken at intervals by the fish at the surface of the water. Simultaneously a new bubble is taken in the mouth and the old one is forced out through the edge of the gill covers, having first passed through the oxygen-absorbing labyrinth. This is in the head.

These fishes use the regular gills for oxygenating the blood to a much greater extent than is generally believed. Accurate experiments have been carried out in which a species of labyrinth fishes (Paradise Fish) was sealed in a bottle of water in which there was no air surface. The fishes showed discomfort, but, contrary to what might be expected, they did not suffocate in 12 hours. Furthermore, measurements showed that they extracted almost as much oxygen from the water as did other species without labyrinths. On the other hand it is a great advantage to a fish to be equipped with both kinds of breathers, for in situations where the oxygen in the water is so deficient as to suffocate ordinary species, the labyrinth fishes maintain life without apparent distress. From this it will be seen why they may be kept in comparatively small containers.

The intervals at which air in the labyrinth is changed varies with species and conditions. When excited the fish may come to the surface several times a minute, but at other times, especially in cool water, it may remain below for several minutes at a time.

Nearly all of the labyrinth fishes are what are known as "bubble-nest builders." As the description of this peculiar method of breeding applies to the several species under this heading, it will not be needlessly repeated in each instance, but where individual characteristics vary from the following description, they will be pointed out as occasion requires.

The outstanding feature of the breeding of this family of fishes is the floating nest of bubbles which they construct and in which the eggs are placed, hatched and the young tended. These bubbles are formed by the male as he comes to the surface, draws a little air in his mouth and envelops it in a film-like saliva. When released, the globule naturally floats to the surface. Endless repetition of this act piles up what looks like a little mound of very fine soap bubbles. They often select a building spot just under some floating aquatic leaves or a large single leaf.

When a male starts building a nest, even in a small way, it indicates that he is about ready for breeding. Unless a female is already present, it is the proper time to bring a pair together. It is better to move the male into the aquarium occupied by the female. Most of these fishes are quite harmless to species other than their own, but at breeding time there is danger of one being killed, usually the female. For this reason it is desirable to have plenty of room and a liberal supply of refuge plants, which, by the way, they never injure. The courting is conducted by a grand spreading of fins, first of the male, with ultimate response by the female if his suit is successful. His best holiday attire is used in courtship, and in most species they are masterpieces of color.

The male is often an impatient courtier. After the nest is built, he drives the female towards it. If she is not ready for spawning her response will be slow, and it is then that he is liable to attack her, tearing her fins or perhaps killing her outright with a single head-on blow, delivered against her side. It is at this time that the aquarist needs to be something of a strategist, as well as a diplomat, for the pair should not be separated at the very first sign of trouble. Like the wise judge at a Domestic Relations Court, he should give the contestants a reasonable chance to adjust their difficulties themselves. If, on the other hand, matters grow worse, the strong arm of the aquarist should intervene, and give the parties an enforced separation. A later trial mating may prove more successful.

But let us assume, as we should, that the courtship has been a normal one, and that the pair is ready for the Business of Life. She follows him to a position just below the prepared nest. He bends his body into a crescent which encircles her. As they slowly sink through the water, rolling over, she drops several eggs which are immediately fertilized during the embrace of the male. He releases himself, picks up the eggs in his mouth, encloses them in a bubble and floats them upward into the nest. This act is repeated for perhaps an hour, at the end of which time there may be from 100 to 500 eggs in the nest. The male then asserts his rights as a father (in fish language) that is unmistakable. He drives the female to the farthest limits of the aquarium and assumes full charge of the nest. At this point she should be removed as soon as possible, for she is likely to be killed, especially if the aquarium is a small one, say under 15 gallons.

With the presence of the eggs in the nest the male redoubles his efforts in producing bubbles, for the old ones gradually burst. In order to retard this evaporation, and for another reason to be explained shortly, the aquarium should be kept well covered with glass. The bubble-nest, originally about 3 inches wide and half an inch high, becomes perhaps an inch high and spreads out to 4 inches. The small eggs between the bubble suds can be seen, but sharp eyes are needed.

These labyrinth fishes like a breeding temperature of 78 to 82 degrees. The eggs hatch in about 2 days. At first they are like microscopic tadpoles among the foam, and are quite helpless. As they fall out of the nest through the water, the vigilant father gathers them up in his mouth, and, attaching them to an ever-ready bubble, floats them back into their watery cradle. This continues about 3 days, the nest gradually becoming shallower and the young taking a position at the surface of the water just below it. By the time the young have absorbed the yolk sac and gained their balance it is nearly gone. Some observers have claimed that the male blows it to pieces, but this is doubtful, for it soon disintegrates without constant repairs. The babies now move about in a school. No schoolmaster ever had a busier time looking after his charges and no children could have a more vigilant caretaker. He looks after the wanderers with an eagle eye, ever alert and willing to give his life in their defense. In perhaps 3 weeks he considers his task done and that the young should be able to protect themselves. So thoroughly does he seem to enter into this idea that he is liable to start eating them himself! Perhaps this is Nature's method of eliminating those that can be caught. In the wild state his protection is no doubt necessary, but in an aquarium in which there are no fish enemies there is no reason to keep the father with the young after they are free-swimming. After all, our main object is to raise fish.

There are several points of practical value in raising bubble-nest builders which may be covered briefly. It is a very, very common experience for beginners to become enthusiastic over prospects of raising a nest of these young, only to have them die off at an age of from 2 to 4 weeks. The principal reason for this is insufficient food of the right kind, and the causes in back of this are aquaria that are *too small* and *too clean*. These small fishes require a considerable amount of microscopic food, which can only be developed and maintained in old water. The proper aquarium for this purpose should be at the very least 15 gallons in size, well planted, containing old water from 6 to 8 inches deep, and with a fair amount of natural sediment on the bottom. The presence of a few decaying aquarium plants is desirable. No snails should be used. When the eggs are laid it is advisable to sprinkle a little dried and crumbled lettuce leaves on the water, and also a very little of any finely powdered fish food. The decomposition of these organic substances keeps up the culture of microscopic life which will later be needed. It is a fact that very small fishes of this character have been raised on a fine flour made of fish food, but it is quite likely that the resulting Infusoria which feed on the decomposition of this substance have something to do with the success attained. At any rate, while it is a good idea to have a separate source of Infusoria culture, as elsewhere explained (under "Fishfoods"), it is also desirable to cultivate a natural supply of it along with the baby fishes, especially when they are of a species which are extremely small. Aside from this suggested aquarium preparation, the young of labyrinth fishes may be raised as per the regular formula for egg-droppers. A little green water is good for them in the early stages. Daphnia should not be given until they are large enough to take finely sifted sizes.

The other cause for losses is the failure to keep the aquarium well covered with glass during the critical period when the labyrinth is forming, for this organ does not begin to develop until the fish is about 3 weeks old. At this time they are particularly sensitive to draughts and temperature changes. Also at this time if the surface of the water is at all dirty or filmy, it should be frequently cleaned by drawing a piece of newspaper across it.

The writer has, with marked success, bred 4 kinds of labyrinth fishes outdoors in a 6-foot lily pool, one species each season. Nests were always placed by the fish under a lily pad. Temperature ranged from 60 to 90 degrees, averaging 73. Females were never killed. Several overlapping nestings per season were raised, none interfering with or apparently eating the others. Sometimes 2 pairs of breeders were used. No artificial culture of Infusoria was used. Daphnia occasionally. This was soon cleaned up by the parents or the young which were large enough to eat it. Never tried Bettas in the pool. The reader should not assume that conclusions from pond breeding are applicable to aquarium culture.

The labyrinth fishes are by nature carnivorous, living principally on small crustacea and insects which fall on the water. They can easily be trained to taking ordinary prepared dried foods, but this should often be supplemented by fresh animal diet, such as Daphnia, chopped worms, bits of fish, shrimp or crab meat.

They are all suited to life in a community tank with fishes of approximately their own size, provided others of *their own species* are *not* present. Most of them, except Bettas, get along very well in tanks containing a *large number* of their own kind, apparently being content to ward off attacks from the rear.

Labyrinth fishes all come from Asia and Africa. There are many kinds, however, from different parts of the world having other forms of auxiliary breathing apparatus.

Mácropòdus operculàris (LINNAEUS)

Pronounced Mak′ro-po″dŭs oh-per′ku-lay″riss   *Popular name,* Paradise Fish

MEANING OF NAME: *Macropodus,* large foot (fin), in reference to dorsal and anal fins; *opercularis,* with spot on the gill cover

Formerly known as *Macropodus viridi-auratus*

Eastern Location Map s39 and s43 to l46 and d51   Length, 3 inches

F ancient lineage is the true basis for aristocracy, then the Paradise Fish is undoubtedly the Exalted Potentate of all tropical aquarium fishes. It was introduced into Paris in 1868 by Carbonnier. This introduction undoubtedly marks the beginning of the study of fresh-warm-water aquarium fishes as we have it today, and if any future enthusiasts wish to observe centenaries of the occasion, that is the year on which to base them. Goldfish and a few cold-water species, both fresh and marine, had been kept in European and American aquariums some years previously. It is now difficult to realize that in about 1850-60, especially in England, the household aquarium was a new and fashionable fad, and that many books appeared on the subject. Judging from the now comical misinformation contained in most of them, it is little wonder that the mushroom growth soon passed and left no trace, except for a few musty books. One of the earliest of them (Warrington, 1850) contained the first correct statement of the principles of the "balanced aquarium," indeed an epoch in itself, and one worthy of commemoration.

For many years following its introduction into America in 1876 by the famous Adolphus Busch, of St. Louis, the Paradise Fish was regarded as an aquarium novelty of doubtful value, for owners of Lace-tail Goldfishes rightly feared the presence of this menacing stranger among their

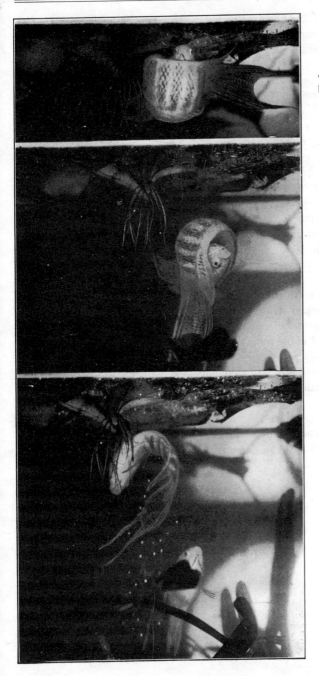

EMBRACE

White Paradise Fish beginning to spawn.

BARREL ROLL

At this moment the eggs are extruded and fertilized, the female being in an upside-down position.

RELEASE

The male now trembles a few seconds and then gathers the slowly sinking eggs in his mouth, soon floating them into the bubble-nest, which is over the plants.

highly developed but defenseless beauties. The Goldfish fins usually suffered when it was tried.

Because the Paradise Fish is so easily bred and can live in water down to 50 degrees, it is held cheaply. If rare it would be considered a great beauty. When the male's fins are at their best, the long, sweeping filaments at the tail-ends are blue white at the ends. The females have shorter fin tips.

The color-plate of a pair in breeding embrace gives a good idea of the intensified mating colors of the male, and of the reverse paleness of the female. When not excited they are more nearly of a color, the female not so pale and the male not so bright.

In contrast with Goldfish this species early acquired a reputation as a fighter, but in comparison with many other exotic fishes he is really quite a mild fellow in the company of other species.

A true albino strain of Paradise Fish with pink eyes was introduced from Germany in 1933. The bars on the sides are pinkish, becoming more red as the fish ages. Otherwise it is white, or cream color. It breeds true and is prolific. What little fight there is in the original stock seems to have disappeared in the albino, the male not even attacking the female after she has finished spawning.

Macropodus opercularis, or Paradise Fish, breeds true to standard form as described for Bubble-nest Builders. It is particularly suited to pond culture, as it is not injured by moderate chilly spells.

This fish is very tame, will take any food, will live in dirty water and is a good community tank occupant. It lives for years.

The species has been the subject of an unusual amount of scientific discussion, having undergone, since its first description by Linnaeus in 1758, nearly a dozen names, and been the subject of many hundred papers by ichthyologists and aquarists.

Mácropòdus chinénsis (BLOCH)

Pronounced Mak'ro-po''dus chi-nen'siss   *Popular name,* Round-tail Paradise Fish
MEANING OF NAME: *chinensis,* from China
Sometimes incorrectly known as *Macropodus opercularis*
E. China   Eastern Location Map c45 to k43 and h47   Length, 2½ inches

℣HIS Paradise Fish is easily recognized by its rounded tail fin, as
compared with the forked fin of the better-known *Macropodus
opercularis* (formerly *Macropodus viridi-auratus*). To aquarists it is a
much later introduction. While there is a fair amount of reddish color
in the tail fin of the male, it largely lacks the red and green fire flashed by
the body of the older favorite. It is also slightly smaller. Easily but not
often bred, as the demand is limited.

The two species are different, but the care and breeding conditions
are the same for each.

Mácropòdus cupànus dàyi (KOEHLER)

Pronounced Mak'ro-po"dus kew-pay'nus day'eye   Also known as *Polyacanthus dayi*

MEANING OF NAME: *cupanus,* after a river in India; *dayi,* for F. Day

Eastern Location Map c22 and z19 to q29   Length, 2¾ inches

HE *dayi* part of the name of this fish probably only represents a race of *Macropodus cupanus,* slightly larger in size and a bit more intense in color. The true *cupanus* is a much paler, grayish fish, usually lacking the lateral stripes, and showing as its chief color the red ventral fins of the male. The edges of the fins are a peculiar white that might be called phosphorescent.

The body has 2 dark horizontal bands, the lower one being the stronger. Throat and belly reddish. Tip of anal, red. General body color is in shades of brown. A hardy species which accommodates itself to temperatures between 60 and 90 degrees. Breeds at 75 to 80. It prefers old water.

This is rather more of a jumper than most bubble-nest builders, and should be kept covered.

The majority of aquarists consider it to be a good community aquarium fish, but experiences in this matter often differ.

It is a good breeder and is not shy. The fish in the photograph with the longer fins and shallower body is the male. At the moment of the photograph, however, his tail fin was not spread. Breeding habits as per description under "The Labyrinth Bubble-nest Builders."

Trichópsis vittàtus (CUVIER AND VALENCIENNES)
Pronounced Try-kop'sis vy-tay'tus
MEANING OF NAME: *Trichopsis,* similar to *Trichogaster; vittatus,* striped
Known also as *Osphromenus vittatus, Osphromenus striatus,* and *Ctenops vittatus*
Popular names, Croaking Gourami and Purring Gourami
Malayan region Eastern Location Map z41; w37; M45; H39 and 45 Length, 2½ inches

NOT a rare fish, but an unusual one in a collection. It is known
chiefly for a peculiar sound it makes at breeding time, produced by
vibrating the air in the labyrinth, the male making a sharper sound than
does the female. The sound is made mostly at night.

In point of appearance the most attractive feature is the very beautiful
eye. The dark parts of the iris are deep red, the light inner circle being
a brilliant blue. The body is not especially colorful, being a brownish
olive, faintly striped with broad horizontal lines, which become clearer
through the head. The tip of the dorsal and the 2 indistinct spots on the
tail fin of the male are somewhat red.

While these fishes are bubble-nest builders, they are not either master
builders or very solicitous parents, but they do have the individual
peculiarity that the female, as well as the male, floats the heavier-than-
water eggs in the nest. At their favorite breeding temperature of 80, the
young hatch in about 36 hours. They are exceedingly small, but in a
large, well-planted aquarium do not need to be separated from their
parents. The water should be 6 inches deep and it is most important to
keep a uniform temperature and a cover on while the fry are young. The
cover should not be lifted if the room temperature is several degrees
lower than in the aquarium.

Bétta spléndens   REGAN

Pronounced Bet'ta splen'dens   *Popular name,* Siamese Fighting Fish

MEANING OF NAME: *Betta,* after a local native name, Ikan bettah; *splendens,* brilliant
Siam   Eastern Location Map x37; y39; v36   Length, 2½ inches

*W*ITH all due respect to the Guppy for having aroused the interest of an enormous number of persons in aquarium study, there seems little doubt that the modern Veiltail Betta launched the hobby in a big way in America. Its extraordinary, spectacular beauty made instantaneous conquests among those who would never have looked twice at any other fish, but who are now dyed-in-the-wool fanciers and doing all in their power to interest others in the hobby.

But let us leave superlatives for a moment and have a look at the humble ancestor of this flashy fish. It is shown further on as Original *Betta splendens.* The body is yellowish brown with a few indistinct horizontal bands. At breeding time the male becomes darker and rows of metallic green scales on his sides become plainer. Dorsal, metallic green tipped with red; anal, red tipped blue. Ventrals always fiery red, tipped white. All fins of moderate size, tail fin being rounded.

Suddenly there appeared in our aquarium world a new comet—a cream-colored Betta with fiery, flowing fins. Two varieties, a dark and a light one, were in the shipment. These were brought into San Francisco in 1927 from Siam. Thinking he had a new species, Mr. Locke, the consignee who received and bred the fishes, called the light one *Betta cambodia*. This has since been proven, as have all the now numerous color variants, to be a race of *Betta splendens*. Other importations in varying colors soon followed, some of them coming through Germany. Breeders aimed for the darker colors and soon established the famous "Cornflower Blue," and finally a solid, rich purplish blue. There are now so many shades of this fish in blues, lavenders, greens and reds that a decorator could almost find specimens to match the color scheme of any room, but nearly all of them hold to the pair of drooping, fiery red anal fins.

The specimens used in the color illustration are by no means the highest form of fin development reached by these fishes, probably not by 50 per cent.

Much misinformation exists as to the fighting qualities of this fish, some of it so amusing that we present it, even at risk of too much length.

Dr. Hugh M. Smith, prominent ichthyologist and writer, former U. S. Commissioner of Fisheries and recently Adviser in Fisheries to the Siamese Government, is qualified to speak on this fish from any standpoint, especially as he has taken a particular interest in the species and personally brought to the United States some of the original Veiltail Betta stock. In response to a letter asking him to settle the point as to whether the fishes are especially bred for fighting or are caught from the wild for the purpose, the following extracts from his interesting and amusing reply should decide the matter finally, not only for newspaper columnists, but for aquarium writers, too.

"The literature of Betta as a fighting fish is replete with inaccuracies and absurdities. An unusually large number of these occur in a short paragraph in the article entitled 'The Heavenly-Royal City of Siam' by Florence Burgess Meehan (Asia, March, 1921).

" 'The fighting fish are about the size of goldfish. You catch one and put it into a bottle. Your neighbor does likewise. You put your bottle close to your neighbor's. Your fish becomes enraged. So does your neighbor's fish. They both flash all colors of the rainbow. They swell up. You bet on your fish. Your friends back you. After a time one fish or the other, hurling itself against the glass in a vain effort to reach its adversary, becomes so angry that it literally bursts. If it is your neighbor's fish that bursts, you win. If it is yours, you lose.'

"The writer of this paragraph certainly never saw what she was writing about, and the untrustworthiness of the account may be judged from the following facts:

"The Siamese fighting fish cannot properly be described as 'about the size of a goldfish,' whatever may be the meaning of the expression. The fish are not matched while in separate 'bottles,' and when not fighting are usually kept in special rectangular jars about 4 inches square and 10 inches high, and a little larger at the top than at the bottom. When fighting, the fish do not 'flash all colors of the rainbow,' do not 'swell up,' do not 'hurl themselves against the glass,' and do not 'literally burst.'

"With these exceptions, the account quoted is nearly correct, but not quite. For instance, the impression is conveyed that if you wish to stage a fight, you and your neighbor go out and catch wild fish, whereas practically all the combats are between domesticated fish. Fighting fish have been cultivated and domesticated among the Siamese for many years, and all of the noteworthy combats on which sums of money are wagered are with selected, often pedigreed, stock. They have short tail fins.

"There are in Bangkok 10 or 12 persons who breed fighting fish for sale, and about 1,000 persons who raise fighting fish for their own use. A dealer whom I recently visited reports an annual production of 50,000 young, but only a small percentage of these are carried to the fighting age and sold. For the best males the current retail price per fish is 1 to 2 ticals, females half price (1 tical equals 44 cents gold). There are 10 licensed places where public fighting fish combats and betting thereon are permitted. The sums wagered in such places range from 10 ticals to 100 ticals per fight, but much larger sums may be staked on private matches.

"The native wild fishes from which the ordinary cultivated fish has been derived rarely exceed 2 inches for the males, the females being smaller. The cultivated fish reach a length of 2½ inches for the males.

"The way in which the male fish are matched and their method of fighting are well known. It will suffice to state that the combatants are placed together in a bowl or jar and quickly come to close quarters, expanding their fins and branchial membranes and displaying the gorgeous red, blue and green shades that have made the fighting fish famous. They approach one another quietly and may remain in close relation, side by side, for 10 to 15 seconds, or longer, without action. Then, in quick succession, or simultaneously, they launch an attack almost too swift for the observer's eye to follow, and this is repeated at short intervals during the continuance of the combat. The effect of the fierce onslaughts begins to be seen in the mutilation of the fins, which may soon present a ragged appearance and considerable loss of fin substance may occur. The branchial region (gills) may come in for attack, and blood may exceptionally be drawn. On two separate occasions my own fish locked jaws and remained in that position for a number of minutes. That fish is adjudged the victor which is ready to continue to fight while its opponent is no longer eager for the fray and tries to avoid coming to close quarters.

"The effect of cultivation and selective breeding on the fighting qualities of Bettas is remarkable. Wild male fish will readily fight in captivity as soon as they become somewhat accustomed to their surroundings, say in the course of 2 or 3 days, but they lack stamina and rarely continue their attacks for longer than 15 minutes and usually quit much sooner. Cultivated fish that will not fight actively for 60 minutes are regarded as failures, and the best stock will continue to attack up to 6 hours."

Dr. Smith's reference to the courage of the cultivated breed of *Bettas* may account for their truly remarkable absence of fear under a certain circumstance which frightens and intimidates nearly all other fishes, especially the fighting sorts. This is the sudden confinement of the fish in a very small space such, for instance, as a glass photographing cell, or a half-pint jar. Placed in such a situation he calmly surveys his miniature prison, makes a few eel-like turns in it, apparently to see whether it can be done, and is then ready for each or both of his twin interests in life— breeding and fighting.

Owing to this intense fighting passion of the males, it is necessary, at the age of about 3 months, to rear them in individual jars or aquaria. This is the way all fine specimens are produced, for although their fins recover from injuries, scars remain and the fish is never again perfect. For this reason the price of fine specimens will always remain fairly high.

Bettas conform to the described habits for bubble-nest builders. They like acid water, about 6.8, and do best in a well-planted aquarium with liberal light. Water should be clear, but with plenty of natural sediment on the bottom.

These Veiltail *Betta splendens* are at their best appearance and vigor between the ages of 10 months and 2 years, and should be bred during that period. Prior to one year it is difficult to select the best specimens, and after 2 years they age rapidly.

The species is subject to a disease called "cotton-mouth," in which a white fungus forms at the lips. Possibly this is an infection from a bruise, but it is liable to become epidemic, and is usually fatal. Affected individuals should be immediately isolated. For treatment, see "Diseases."

This fish is almost as adaptable to foods as it is to its surroundings, but nevertheless it does best on animal substances such as Daphnia, mosquito larvæ, chopped worms, bits of fish, crab, shrimp, etc.

A single male may be placed in a community aquarium, and possibly a female also, if the tank is a large one. In general the sexes should be kept separated; the males singly or else spread around so that 2 of the species are not in the same tank. Males placed in small adjoining aquariums with a cardboard divider between will always spread themselves when the board is removed. It is a show for visitors that never fails.

No special feeding has any effect in developing long fins. This is dependent upon heredity. They breed best at a temperature of about 78, but can stand a range of from 68 to 90 degrees.

ORIGINAL *Betta splendens*

Bétta brèderi MYERS
Pronounced Bree′der-eye
Named for Chas. M. Breder, Jr., of the Battery Park Aquarium
Malay region   Eastern Location Map, about F40   Length, 3½ inches

THIS or a very similar large, heavy Betta has reached us twice previously and was labeled *Betta pugnax,* no doubt in error. When a shipment of them arrived in 1934 it was apparent they were not *B. pugnax,* and were named as above.

The very large eggs are dropped and fertilized in the usual Betta manner, but apparently only one at a time. This is picked up in the mouth of one fish and shot towards the other, who receives and returns it. After repeating this tossing several times, the egg comes to rest in the mouth of what we believe to be the male. Unfortunately, our observations end here, for the scientific ardor of the dealer who owned the pair was not strong enough to resist an offer of a fat price for them. They were taken away, eggs and all, and soon lost.

The species is rather sluggish, and has little color, excepting for the blue spangled rows of scales on the male (lower fish). The general color is warm brown. It does not appear to be much of a fighter.

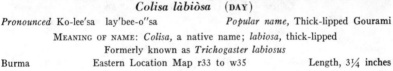

Colisa làbiòsa   (DAY)

Pronounced Ko-lee'sa lay'bee-o''sa   *Popular name,* Thick-lipped Gourami

MEANING OF NAME: *Colisa,* a native name; *labiosa,* thick-lipped

Formerly known as *Trichogaster labiosus*

Burma   Eastern Location Map r33 to w35   Length, 3¼ inches

THIS is the middle size among the Colisas. The light markings on the sides are blue-green, while the irregular dark bars are orange-brown. The projecting rays of the dorsal and anal fins are tipped blood-red. In the anal fin these fiery tips are supported by a narrow line of intense, deep blue. Tail fin, light warm brown. Thread fins in male, red; in female, colorless. The rear end of the anal fin in the female is red, while in the male it is blue. The lips of the male, as will be noted in the photograph, are thicker and more prominent than those of the female. Also his head over the eye is depressed, where hers is raised.

Breeding temperature, 80. Their glass-clear eggs float up to the nest. Seldom spawn.

Colisa lália   (HAMILTON-BUCHANAN)

Pronounced Ko-lee′sa lal′e-a   *Popular name,* Dwarf Gourami

The scientific name is based on two native names

Formerly known as *Trichogaster lalius*

Bengal   Eastern Location Map o15 to r39 and o30   Length, 2 inches

*C*OLISA LALIA is the smallest of its near relatives, and certainly one
of the most beautiful. A highly satisfactory and interesting aquarium
fish with but a single fault. It is apt to be timid and hide away in the
foliage. It is too beautiful a flower to be allowed to blush unseen. By
associating it with more forward fishes that rush to their master for food,
this little beauty soon overcomes its shyness.

In breeding habits this species varies from the type description for
bubble-nest builders in one interesting particular. Bits of plant are
incorporated into the nest, such as the fine leaves of Myriophyllum; also
the female helps build it. In addition to his much brighter colors, the
male may be distinguished by his orange-red "feelers." Temperature
range, 68 to 84 degrees. Breed at about 80. A species easily cared for.
Males sometimes kill females in mating. Otherwise very peaceable.

The Black Ghost Knifefish, **Sternarchus albifrons**, from the Amazon River system.
Photo by Dr. Herbert R. Axelrod.

For many years aquarium publications have referred erroneously to one of our beautiful small Tetra species as **Hemigrammus ulreyi**. Below is the true **Hemigrammus ulreyi**. Photo by Dr. Herbert R. Axelrod.

The Green Aruana, **Osteoglossum bicirrhosum**, showing the yolk sac. Other fishes will attack the yolk sac, so young specimens must be kept isolated. This fish is about 3½ inches long. Photo by Dr. Herbert R. Axelrod.

The Golden Emperor Tetra, **Nematobrycon amphiloxus**, is lighter in color than the more common Emperor Tetra. It comes from the Calima region of Colombia. Photo by Dr. Herbert R. Axelrod.

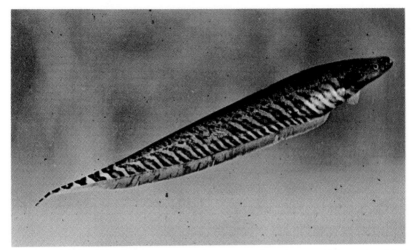

The Banded Knife Fish, **Gymnotus carapo**, is a very agile swimmer which can travel just as easily backward as forward. Photo by Dr. Herbert R. Axelrod.

This is a head study of the Black Ghost, **Sternarchus albifrons**. This species becomes quite tame in captivity. Photo by Harald Schultz.

A fairly new introduction is **Dianema urostriata, the Stripe-Tailed Catfish.**
Photo by Dr. Herbert R. Axelrod.

Corydoras metae looks as if it were wearing a black mask over its eyes, therefore the popular name, Masked Catfish. Photo by Dr. Herbert R. Axelrod.

Here are some beautiful examples of fine fancy guppies, **Lebistes reticulatus**. Top, the Leopard-Tailed Veiltail - photo by Dr. Eduard Schmidt. Center, the "King Cobra" Snake-skin Veiltail - photo by Dr. Herbert R. Axelrod. Bottom, a Half-Black Red-Tailed Veiltail - Photo by S. Golub.

The famous lyretailed variety of the Marbled Molly, **Mollienesia sphenops**.
Photo by Dr. Herbert R. Axelrod.

The Sailfin Molly, **Mollienesia latipinna**, has also been developed with the lyre tail.
Photo by Dr. Herbert R. Axelrod.

A source in Africa which is rich in unusual Cichlid species is Lake Nyasa. This is one of those species, **Pseudotropheus auratus**. Photo by W. Hoppe.

The Golden Nyasa Cichlid, shown here, is **Pseudotropheus tropheops.** The larger fish in the foreground is the male. Photo by W. Hoppe.

No difficulty recognizing the sexes in **Pseudotropheus trewavasae**. Their coloration is so different that at first they were thought to be two different species. The upper fish is the male. Photo by Dr. Herbert R. Axelrod.

This is the Zebra Nyasa Cichlid, **Pseudotropheus zebra**. Photo by W. Hoppe.

Nyasa cichlids became very much "in vogue" during 1965 and 1966 when Mr. Griem of Aquarium Hamburg in Germany was able to establish contact with a collector in that area. Many of the cichlids Griem imported were very beautiful, while others were more common. These three are "average." Top: Pseudotropheus fuscus. Center: **Pseudotropheus elongatus.** Bottom: **Petrotilapia tridentiger.** Photos by W. Hoppe.

A beauty from Lake Tanganyika is **Tropheus moorei.** This lake is very rich in Cichlid species. Photo by Dr. Herbert R. Axelrod.

Julidochromis ornatus, one of Africa's sparkling cichlids. Photo by Hilmar Hansen.

Lamprologus leleupi, the Lemon Cichlid, seems to be native only to Lake Tanganyika, in Africa. Photo by Dr. Herbert R. Axelrod.

The Red Devil from Nicaragua, Cichlasoma erythraeum. Every fish is differently colored, from a splotched red and black to a pure golden yellow. Photo by Mervin F. Roberts.

The Lyretail Swordtail was developed by Don Adams of Florida when he found a few appearing in the pools of Wolff's Fish Farm. This fish was crossed with the Simpson Hi-Fin (below) and all combinations of finnage and colors are now available. Photos by Dr. Herbert R. Axelrod.

Cynolebias nigripinnis, the Black-Finned Pearl Fish, is a beauty that comes to us from Argentina. This is a male. Photo by Hansen.

Aphyosemion sjoestedti, a population hybrid, whose father came from Central Sierra Leone and whose mother came from Eastern Sierra Leone. Photo by Col. J. Scheel.

Nothobranchius melanospilus, which comes from the vicinity of Beira, Portuguese East Africa. Photo by E. Roloff.

The killifishes include some of the most beautiful of all tropicals. Top, **Aphyosemion calliurum ahli** - photo by Dr. Walter Foersch. Center, **Epiplatys annulatus** - photo by E. Roloff. Bottom, **Aphyosemion australe hjerresenii** - photo by Hansen.

The Black Aruana, **Osteoglossum ferrerai**, from the Rio Negro in Brazil. This is a very young specimen about 4 inches long. Photo by Dr. Herbert R. Axelrod.

Because of its luminous white stripe on a black background, this beauty, **Hyphessorbrycon herbertaxelrodi**, has been named the Black Neon Tetra. Photo by Dr. Herbert R. Axelrod.

The Black Phantom Tetra, **Megalamphodus megalopterus** has an unusual characteristic which makes it very easy to recognize sexes: the males have big, all-black fins, while the females have a tiny red adipose fin and a red anal fin. Photo by Hilmar Hansen.

The Black Catfish from Thailand, **Pangasius sutchi.** Photo by Dr. Herbert R. Axelrod.

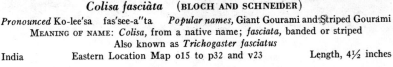

Colisa fasciàta (BLOCH AND SCHNEIDER)

Pronounced Ko-lee'sa fas'see-a"ta   *Popular names,* Giant Gourami and Striped Gourami
MEANING OF NAME: *Colisa,* from a native name; *fasciata,* banded or striped
Also known as *Trichogaster fasciatus*

India   Eastern Location Map o15 to p32 and v23   Length, 4½ inches

HILE the breeding habits of this Colisa are in general the same as for the family, there are differences. It does not build a very definitely formed nest, but blows a few scattered bubbles, preferably under a large leaf. The eggs are lighter than water and float to the surface, where they are more or less scattered. For some reason which we are not even able to surmise, the male takes mouthfuls of sand and blows it among the eggs.

In the meantime, both before and after the hatching of the eggs, the male takes several gulps of air in his mouth, proceeds to a point below the surface and expels a fine mist of air bubbles backward through his gills, scattering it with his pectoral fins. For a moment it seems as though the bubbles are coming from all over his body. He busies himself with this procedure in all parts of the aquarium. We believe this is the first record of these facts.

Eggs hatch in 2 days at 78 degrees. Remove female after spawning and male 3 days after eggs hatch. A peaceful species, easily fed.

Trichogáster trichópterus (PALLAS)

Pronounced Try'ko-gas"ter try-kop'te-rus

MEANING OF NAME: *Trichogaster,* hair belly; *trichopterus,* hair fin

Also known as *Trichopodus trichopterus* and *Osphromenus trichopterus*

Popular name, Three-spot Gourami (the third spot being the eye)

India, Malay Peninsula, Indo-China   Length, 5 inches

Eastern Location Map v37 to 40 to F39; L43; F46

A SILVERY fish, overlaid with a wavy pattern, and overcast with olive, which becomes dark on the back. The 2 black dots on the body stand out boldly. The long, broad anal fin is beautifully dotted with orange. The thread-like ventrals are yellow in the male. Colors in the male are a little deeper and the fins much longer and broader, especially the dorsal, as shown on the lower fish. The anal fin of the female is partly folded, and makes the difference appear to be greater than it really is.

The species is well disposed and easily kept. A bubble-nest builder that breeds about 3 times a year, its temperature range for this purpose being preferably 78 to 80 degrees. Occasional light feedings of chopped lettuce are taken with relish. *When hungry it will eat Hydra, a tremendous point in its favor.* (See "Hydra.")

Trìchogáster leèri (BLEEKER)

Pronounced Try'ko-gas"ter leer'eye *Popular name,* Pearl Gourami
Named for Leer
Siam, Malay Peninsula, Sumatra Length, 4 inches
Eastern Location Map D36 to F39; F37 to J41

A DELIGHTFULLY beautiful fish of recent introduction, its chief charm lying in an even pattern of pearly dots all over the body and the 3 single fins. There is a marked appearance of elegance about it.

The dorsal, anal, tail and even the pectoral fins are shaded yellow. Throat and belly, clear satiny white. The dark line running through the eye and down along the body to the base of the tail is black. There is a beautiful iridescence over the whole body, ranging from violet to green, according to the angle of the light. At breeding time the breast of the male is so brilliant that he can be compared with a Robin Red Breast.

The upper fish is the male. This bubble-nest builder was introduced in 1933. The species is particularly gentle. The male only mildly drives the female away from the nest. Neither of them eat the young. Temperature range, 68 to 85 degrees. Eats Hydra when hungry.

With increasing maturity the rays protrude through the back edges of the dorsal and anal fins, especially in the male fish.

Osphronèmus gorämy (LACÉPÈDE)

Pronounced Os'fro-nee"mus go-rah'mee   Also known as *Osphromenus olfax*

MEANING OF NAME: *Osphronemus* erroneously refers to the feelers as organs of smell;
goramy, after the native name

E. Indies   Length—aquarium specimens, 3 to 5 inches; in nature, 24 inches
Eastern Location Map M46; F37; E46

THIS is the only true Gourami and is certainly the real Giant
Gourami. In its native waters it is a food fish growing to a length of
2 feet. It will, however, breed in the aquarium at a 5-inch size.

Although the tail fin has a stumpy, ungraceful appearance, the fish is
not bad to look at. The dark spot, flanked forward and back by brilliant
cream white scales makes an interesting feature. A second black spot
near the ventrals is described by Rachow, but our photograph did not
pick up any such marking, nor does the writer remember any. Perhaps
this occurs in still younger specimens.

The fish has a reddish brown cast, with bluish throat and a white
ventral region. With age it loses its redeeming markings and becomes just
a food fish.

They are bubble-nest builders, but seldom breed. Temperature range,
68 to 90 degrees.

As importations are received only about every other year, and not
many come in at a time, the fish is not likely to become a problem.

Helóstoma témmincki CUVIER AND VALENCIENNES

Pronounced Hel-os'to-ma tem'mink-eye   *Popular name,* Kissing Gourami
MEANING OF NAME: *Helostoma,* with turn-back mouth, referring to the thick re-curved
lips, which are provided with series of small teeth; *temmincki,* for
C. Temminck, of Leiden
Malay region, Java, Borneo, etc.   Length, up to 12 inches
Eastern Location Map x38; F36; L43; G44, etc.

ALTHOUGH we know little about this fish, what we do know entitles it to the well-known label, "most peculiar." When not engaged in kissing another of its kind (or even its own image in a reflecting glass, like Narcissus), its mouth is not particularly unusual. It looks somewhat like the mouth in our illustration of *Prochilodus insignis.* During its favorite occupations of being sociable or eating algae from plants or stones, its lips curve back, morning-glory-like. Such pleasures consume much of its time. The kissing with another fish does not appear to have the sexual significance that it does with the Cichlids. It seems to be rather impersonal.

Probably the reason we know nothing of its breeding habits is because the 3-to-4-inch ones we receive for our aquariums are too small to breed. In its own part of the world it is a food fish, growing to a fair size.

It is silvery to greenish, with thin longitudinal lines along the sides, with the scales somewhat raised into ridges. Rather peaceful. Eats prepared foods. Temperature, 70 to 82 degrees.

Anabas téstudíneus (BLOCH)

Pronounced An'a-bas tes'tu-din"e-us   *Popular name,* Climbing Perch

MEANING OF NAME: *Anabas,* climber; *testudineus,* turtle-like

Formerly known as *Anabas scandens*

India, Malay Region and Philippines   Length, 6 to 10 inches in wild specimens

Eastern Location Map u23; r27; C22; I52; G58; w51

*A*S surely as a monkey in a window attracts attention, just so surely does any kind of a "walking fish" at an aquarium show draw the crowds. Attendants in charge of these pleasant affairs will tell the same story of panting persons who want to know, "Where is the walking fish?"

The Climbing Perch does the show-off job very well and doesn't seem to mind. The fish has spiny edges on its gill plates. By extending the plates and using a clumsy rocking motion, it can make fairly good progress out of water. In its native habitat it is said to travel overland in search of a new pond if its own dries up.

These are labyrinth fishes, but do not make any bubble-nest. Their eggs float at the surface of the water. Breeding habits not clearly known.

As to color, there is not much to describe. The body is a brassy brown. The fins are brownish and sometimes the tail fin is an attractive dark red. They are ravenous eaters and will take anything, preferably in chunks. They are pugnacious and should be kept alone. Temperature range, 65 to 90 degrees.

THE SNAKEHEADS
FAMILY CHANNIDAE
Pronounced Kan'ni dee

The Snakeheads are long, slim, snaky, air-breathing fishes from Africa and Asia, having no spines in the fins. In this they differ from their close relatives, the Anabantids. The Snakeheads are important food fishes in the Orient. They are tough and stand transport in tubs with little or no water. Chinese fishmongers can chop a good many steaks off the end of a fish before it sees fit to expire.

Chánna àsiática   (LINNAEUS)
Pronounced Chan'na   a'see-at"i-ka
MEANING OF NAME: *Channa*, meaning unknown; *asiatica*, Asiatic
Incorrectly called *Channa fasciata*

China   Length, 8 inches

*W*HILE the length of this peculiar fish is given as above, it is more apt to average about 5 to 6 inches in the aquarium. Their mouths are enormous; appetites to match. Bad company for other fishes.

The dotted zigzag lines on the sides divide a greenish color above from a gray tone below. Rather attractive. It has no ventral fins.

Eggs float at the surface and receive no attention, nor are they eaten. They hatch in about 4 days at a temperature of 80 degrees. The young are easily raised on Daphnia. Temperature range, 65 to 85 degrees.

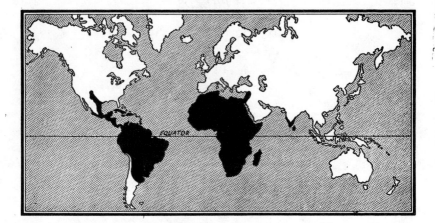

THE CICHLIDS
FAMILY CICHLIDAE
Pronounced Sick'li dee

The Cichlids are spiny-rayed fishes agreeing with the Pomacentrids in having only one nostril on each side of the snout, instead of the usual two. The Cichlids differ from the Pomacentrids in lacking the shelf of bone which supports the eye socket in the latter group. All the Cichlids are found in Africa, Madagascar, and Tropical Americas, north to the Rio Grande in Texas, with the sole exception of Etroplus, two species of which inhabit southern India.

In general the Cichlids are the big fishes of the aquarium. They are well represented by such species as the Chanchito *(Cichlasoma facetum)*, Jack Dempsey *(Cichlasoma biocellatum)* and the Jewel Fish *(Hemichromis bimaculatus)*. Rather long fishes with slightly flattened, moderately deep bodies. The head, generally of good size, is armed with a strong, jutting lower jaw, well suited not only to battle, but to the requirements of their remarkable habits in breeding, as we shall shortly see.

While a few of the Cichlids are peaceable citizens, most of them fight, especially with members of their own species, and more especially with those of the opposite sex. These battles mostly occur during courtship—terrific lovers' quarrels, as it were. Occasionally it is between mated pairs, as will be observed later.

No doubt feeling confident of taking care of themselves in open battle, most of the larger species tear out plants as possible hiding places for enemies, especially at breeding time.

Breeding With the unique exception of the mouthbreeders (whose habits will be described under their own headings), the

Cichlids breed so nearly alike that a general description will fit nearly all of them. The few traits that may be peculiar to a species will be noted under its own special text. For example, that popular ruling favorite, *Pterophyllum scalare*, requires separate consideration.

The typical breeding actions of Cichlids are certainly the most interesting and highly organized of any known aquarium fishes, especially when the habits of mouthbreeders are added to that which now follows.

Mating itself is with them no hit-or-miss affair. At the very beginning the ancient law of the survival of the fittest is put into practical operation. If left to themselves in a large group, pairs will mate themselves by natural affinity, which is one of the best ways of discovering pairs if one has the room and stock to carry out this plan. The usual procedure in trying to mate a pair with a minimum of risk is to place them in a large aquarium with a glass partition between. That is their formal introduction. One fish is usually ready to mate before the other, and as flirtation through windows is nothing new in the world, one of them makes the opening advances. As again in our world, it may be either the male or the female to make the first move. This consists in a wagging of the body, spreading of the fins and a variety of changes in coloring. When the "party of the second part" returns these salutations and shows signs of approval, it is time to take out the partition and note what happens. Usually the courtship continues and it is not long before the kissing stage develops. This is where one of the uses of strong jaws comes in. They grasp each other by interlocking the lips and then begins the first real test. Each tugs and twists the other, apparently in a test of strength. They may go through the performance several times. If they do this repeatedly without either losing its "nerve," they may be considered to be as well mated as though they have a marriage certificate. But it often happens that one of them takes fright and beats a retreat after one of those vigorous kisses. Fear is fatal, and the victim of it is liable to get killed unless a safe retreat is found, or a kind Fate in the person of the owner separates them.

Sometimes a subsequent trial will prove more successful, but it is advisable to try some other pairing, if substitutes are on hand. Certain fishes will reject or kill several proposed mates before meeting an agreeable affinity.

Owing to the physical tussle which takes place, an effort is usually made by the aquarist to match the candidates in size, but there are many instances of happy unions between fishes where disparity in this respect is great. *Whether or not both fishes are ready to mate is the important thing*. Their courtship promotes the elimination of the unfit.

This matter of the mating having been gone into so thoroughly by the contracting parties, one naturally expects that a good old-fashioned, non-divorce marriage is in the making, and for the most part that is true. It may be taken for granted that a water lily pool 5 feet square or larger is equivalent to natural conditions. In mild climates most Cichlids placed in such a pool in the beginning of summer will, if well fed, breed throughout the warm season. From this it is fair to assume that in their native tropical habitat, where there is no cold or even cool season, the mating lasts indefinitely, as with pigeons. The actions of animals in the usual restricted space provided in captivity are seldom entirely normal. It is therefore not surprising that in the average aquarium these matings sometimes come to an abrupt end—usually in a quarrel over domestic matters.

To return to the actual business of breeding—let us consider the proper conditions which should be provided. Success is more likely in large aquaria. Among the larger species, 3 inches is about minimum breeding size. Such fishes should be bred in an aquarium of not less than 10 gallons. Twenty would be better. As size of the pair increases, follow with proportionate room. It will pay.

Water should be old and at a temperature between 75 and 85 degrees. The best bottom covering is approximately 2 inches of well-washed sand. Any moderately good light is satisfactory. Omit plants for most species. Exceptions in this respect will be noted.

For a few days prior to breeding, the fishes dig holes in the sand. They also start cleaning a surface which they regard as suitable to the reception of their adhesive eggs. This spot may be the side of the aquarium, a large stone, the inside or outside of a flower-pot laid on its side, or even a spot on the bottom of the aquarium from which the sand has been fanned away. It has been observed that a light-colored surface is preferred to dark. For this reason some of our fish breeders place a piece of marble or other light-colored stone in the aquarium with mated Cichlids.

The breeding pair takes nothing for granted as to cleanliness. Regardless of whether they select a mossy side of the aquarium or a piece of marble fresh from the quarry, the sacred spot to receive their eggs must be painstakingly gone over to insure its absolute cleanliness. They bite, scrape and polish it with their mouths until no flaw can be found. No Dutch housewife could make it cleaner.

A day or two prior to the actual spawning both fish develop from the vent a breeding tube, or ovipositor. It first appears as a very small point or nipple. Whether it is a Cichlid or certain other species which deposit their eggs in a like manner, the appearance of the nipple is regarded as a sure sign that the fish is ripe for breeding. The tube shortly before spawning increases in length. In large specimens it may be as long as a half inch.

All things now being in readiness, the female approaches the prepared breeding spot and touches it lightly with the breeding tube, depositing one or more eggs. The male immediately follows and with a like action sprays the eggs with his fertilizing fluid. This is repeated many times over a period of perhaps 2 hours, when finally there may be from 100 to 500 eggs laid in close formation. As this whole operation is carried on by a sense of touch and the eggs adhere very lightly, it is quite remarkable how few are lost or knocked off.

The spawning operation being completed, each fish takes turns fanning the eggs with the breast fins or tail. They relieve each other every few minutes. It is a popular idea that this fanning is to supply oxygen to the embryo within the egg, but it seems unlikely that oxygen could penetrate the firm skin in which it is enveloped. As fungus is the great enemy of the eggs and the parents go to no end of trouble to have everything immaculate, presumably to avoid this danger, it seems quite likely they are preventing fungus-bearing particles of dirt from settling on·the spawn. Sometimes, despite care, fungus develops on a few eggs. It attacks all infertile eggs. Apparently sensing the danger of its spread, the fishes eat the affected eggs. This sometimes ends in all the eggs, good and bad, being eaten.

At a temperature of 80 degrees the eggs hatch in about 4 days. Now begins the next of the several remarkable stages in the breeding habits of these fishes. Either just before or just after the egg hatches it is carried in the mouth of either of the parents and deposited in a depression in the sand. It may be newly dug or one left from the home-building connected with the early part of mating. The parents alternate in making the trips between the hatching place and the depression until all are transferred. In some instances the fishes set up a system so that neither end of the line is left unguarded. Each stands guard at one end and as everything is in readiness for the transfer of young, a signal is given in fish language and they dash past each other to the opposite terminus.

The young in the depression look like a vibrating, jelly-like mass not very easy to see. For several days they are moved from one depression to another, gently carried in the mouths of the parents. While it is generally conceded that the lower animals do not reason things out, the result is often the same as though they do. What they do "by instinct" is often wiser than our actions guided by reason. Whether the apparent reasoning in the actions of animals is of their own creation or is a reflection of the Master Mind in Nature makes little difference. Reasons for everything exist. It is interesting to speculate on them, and if we attribute higher thinking powers to our friends the fishes than they actually possess, we are only giving them the benefit of the doubt.

Cichlids have not only the most highly developed breeding habits from the social standpoint, but combine with them a seeming understanding of certain scientific principles which, as far as man is concerned, were discovered but yesterday. These are the recognition of the dangers from bacteria, and of their control through cleanliness. Reference has already been made to the scrupulous care in cleansing the spawning surface and to the eating of such eggs as have been attacked by fungus. Various interpretations may be placed on the practice of moving the young from one hole to another. As this is begun before the babies are old enough to eat anything, it cannot be to provide new pastures. One hole would be as safe from enemies as any other. Besides, in the open places where these fishes breed, they are absolutely fearless in the defense of their young, so the theory of safety may be dismissed. The theory which is in line with their other actions points to cleanliness as the motive—*scientific* cleanliness if you will. The babies are picked up in the mouth, a few at a time, and apparently chewed. They are only rolled around harmlessly and discharged into the next depression. Every last one is so treated. It is the fish's baby bath. Each one emerges perfectly cleansed of any particles. By using a series of depressions for the purpose, the parents are absolutely certain that all babies were "scrubbed," of which they could not be sure if they were kept in one place.

After 8 to 14 days the yolk-sacs of the young have been absorbed and they swim up in a cloud with the parents, usually in formation, headed one way. Stragglers are gathered up in the mouths of the parents and shot back into the school. This family unity is very beautiful to see and gives the aquarist one of his biggest and most lasting thrills. How long the parents and young should be left together is a question largely of sentiment. In the wild the parents undoubtedly can be of much use to the young by protecting them after they are swimming about, but in the aquarium their usefulness ends at that point. The pleasure of seeing the parents and young together is the only reason for not separating them at once. No hen could be more solicitous for her flock than are these devoted fish-parents for their fry. In their defense they are the very embodiment of savage fury, no matter what or how large the real or imaginary enemy. The owner himself had better not poke his nose too close to the water when peering into the domestic affairs of a large pair of Cichlids unless he wishes to have it shortened.

The young of the larger Cichlids are a fair size by the time the yolk-sac is absorbed and for the most part can get along without Infusoria if finely sifted Daphnia is to be had. The smaller varieties will, of course, need to be put through the regular routine described under "Spawning the Egg-layers."

Theoretically these interesting fishes divide every domestic duty equally. It sometimes turns out that one is a better parent than the other, but resentment is clearly shown by the mate on which the heavier part of the burden is shifted. An effort is made to drive the negligent parent to its duty. This failing, open warfare is liable to occur, resulting in the breaking up of matrimonial arrangements, the eating of eggs or young and the death of the principal at fault. In other words, these fishes seem to have and to carry out a sense of justice. Otherwise we may look at it as the elimination both of the unfit parent and of its progeny. The eating of the eggs by either fish is, for the same cause, liable to end in the same way. Here, as elsewhere in animal life, defective individuals are eliminated by normal ones. It sounds hard, but it is the salvation of life.

With many Cichlids it is possible and even advisable to hatch and rear the young away from the parents. This method is described under the heading of *"Pterophyllum scalare."*

Some tact should be shown in approaching an aquarium containing eggs or young, as the parents are liable to misinterpret the intentions of the interested owner and eat their young in preference to having them captured.

When the young and parents are finally separated it is well to keep an eye on the old couple, as each may suspect the other of being responsible for the disappearance of the babies, and open an attack in reprisal.

Cichlids all tend towards carnivorous appetites, but few of them insist upon a diet exclusively of meats. While they do very well on worms, flies, larvæ, chopped clam, scraped meat, oyster, shrimp or fish (cooked or uncooked), Daphnia, etc., they will take either a mush composed of oatmeal cooked with shredded fish or shrimp, or a dried food containing mixed ingredients. The fishes in a warm temperature—75 to 85 degrees—are heavy eaters, and should be fed not less than twice daily.

Most of them will stand a reasonably wide range of temperature, about 65 to 90 degrees, although with valued specimens it might be unwise to risk anything below 68 degrees.

In general it is not easy telling the sexes. In older specimens the males often have longer pointed dorsal and anal fins. Where there is any distinctive difference in markings, this will be described in connection with the species. When the females are ripe, they are slightly fuller, but not in such a decided way as in some of the smaller fishes. It will be found that the breeding tube of the female is slightly blunt, whereas in the male it is pointed. However, this can only be discovered after it is too late to be of much value.

Large Cichlids live long. It is nothing uncommon for them to reach 10 years, although after 5 years they are likely to develop certain signs of age not connected with feebleness. There are 3 such points which may be noted. The mouth does not close completely in breathing; a spinal hump forms just in back of the head (as in the colored illustration of *Cichlasoma biocellatum*); the colors become more fixed and permanent; the colors do not change so readily under excitement.

Cichlids are commonly not good community fishes, although a number of big ones in a very large tank get along without trouble.

This is a life-size picture of a pair of young "Dempseys" with their babies. It is seldom they breed while so young. As yet no difference has developed in the fins of the sexes, and it would be hard telling them apart. Also from the picture it would be difficult to judge whether they are kissing or fighting. The appearance of the nipple at the vent of the fish to the right would indicate that another brood of young is in prospect.

Apistogramma agassizi   (STEINDACHNER)

The Dwarf Cichlids
The Nannacara and the Apistogramma species

ℭHERE are a number of interesting dwarf Cichlids which are puz-zling to correctly name, because ichthyologists have done so little work with them and we do not know the locations from which commercial specimens have been collected. The accompanying illustrations give a good idea of the general types and their sizes. We use the names under which they are sold, which will have to serve for the present.

It is the belief of the writer that the merits of these charming little fishes have largely been overlooked by aquarists. Many persons will not keep the ordinary run of Cichlids because of their large size and a general propensity to fight and to tear out plants. The dwarfs have neither of these faults. They are beautiful, but a little shy.

Their breeding methods, so far as we know them, are like those of their larger cousins, except for the fact that the female takes charge of the eggs and young, and assumes all domestic obligations, driving the male away. If the male is taken out, the female may be depended upon to take excellent care of her young family, and at no time to eat them.

One great advantage about these little Cichlids is that they can be successfully bred in an aquarium of about 3-gallon size.

As to temperature they are very well satisfied within a range of 70 to 80 degrees.

One of the best known and probably the handsomest of these miniature Cichlids is the one sold in the trade as *Apistogramma agassizi*. It is also the largest of the dwarfs, so to speak. There are at least 2 species passing under the same name, the other one being deeper of body than our illustration, especially about the fore part, while the dorsal, although handsome, is not as high in proportion to the depth of the body. However, the colors of both species are the same, so far as a description goes. The outstanding feature is the interesting color design in the tail fin. The illusion of a white spearhead is increased by the almost bloody streak along its lower half, indicated by the dark portion in the photograph. The lower fins are rich orange, while the dorsal is brilliantly topped off with blood red. Typical blue-to-green spangles ornament the body. Seen with its fins spread in the sun, this fish is a rare sight.

"*Apistogramma pertense*" is a sort of quiet little mouse. It is one of the smallest of Cichlids and one of the least colorful; yet it is attractive. The high lights about the head are blue, the body bars are gray on a green brown background, and the dark spot at the base of the tail is black.

Apistogramma pertense (?)   (HASEMANN)

Until comparatively recently no Apistogramma had been seen having a

Apistogramma "U2"

double-pointed or lyre-shaped tail fin. Now there are 2 known species. When the first of these arrived, rather than saddle the fish with a name that must later be forgotten, and at the same time to give it a better identity than one of the many "Apistogramma species," the writer proposed giving it a temporary symbol "Apistogramma U2," the letter U standing for "unidentified."

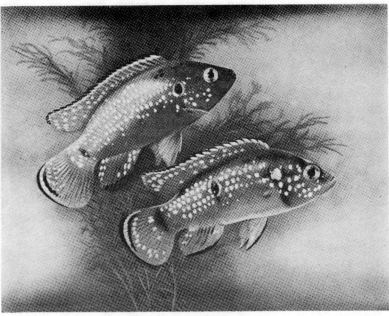

Hémichròmis bimáculàtus   GILL

Pronounced Hem'mee-crow"miss by-mak'you-lay"tus   *Popular name,* Jewel Fish

MEANING OF NAME: *Hemichromis,* half colored; *bimaculatus,* two spotted

Most of Tropical Africa   Length, 4 inches

Western Location Map A56; C59; D64; W70; W45; A52

ONE of the typical savage Cichlids. It needs several redeeming traits to justify being kept, and it has them. A temperamental fish, a good parent, fairly hardy and at times gorgeously beautiful.

Although the fins and general coloration are the same in male and female, the sex is easily determined. The male has more and larger jewels on the gill plate, while those in the tail fin extend farther and form themselves into a crescent. From this it will be seen that the upper fish in the illustration is the female, but the general difference in body color means nothing. At other times the male will be the brighter. It is true, however, that in her maximum redness the female is a little brighter than the male, reversing the usual order of things. During courtship the colors change rapidly, dark spots become light or disappear altogether, the jewel facets enlarge.

Out of breeding season both fishes are of a rather dark, nondescript color, lightly lined with blue jewelled scales and displaying a dark spot

Hemichromis bimaculatus FANNING EGGS

near the centre of the body, one on the gill plate and one at the tail base. It is hard to understand why the specific name of the fish is not *trimaculatus*.

Mating time is difficult and dangerous. Whether the group natural selection method is used or when there are only 2 fishes to work with, it is advisable with this species to have plenty of refuge places for the one getting the worst of it. In addition to the flower-pot for receiving the spawn, there should be heavy plants like Giant Sagittaria or some large stones placed in formation for recesses.

The eggs of this species, if in clean conditions, can be satisfactorily hatched and reared if the parents are removed, but then the aquarist loses one of his greatest pleasures by not witnessing the instructive and touching family life of the fishes.

The young grow rapidly and when about 6 weeks old begin attacking each other. For this reason they should be kept in an aquarium of at least 10-gallon capacity.

Temperature range, 60 to 90 degrees. Breeding at 80.

A scientific detailed study of the embryology and life habits of this species is reported in THE AQUARIUM for February, 1933, by Messrs. Solberg and Brinley, of North Dakota State College.

Hémichròmis fasciàtus PETERS

Pronounced Hem'mee-krow"miss fas'see-a"tus

MEANING OF NAME: *Hemichromis*, half Chromide; *fasciatus*, banded

Central W. Africa   Western Location Map x45 to P65   Length, 6 to 10 inches

*W*E sometimes find a species that is suited to the aquarium if the fish is not allowed to expand too much. *Hemichromis fasciatus* if kept in an aquarium of 10-gallon size can be held down to 5 or 6 inches, but if in a large tank, it reaches a length of 10 inches. As it is a bad digger, it can do a lot of damage when this size.

Contrary to *H. bimaculatus*, the colors are not bright. A brassy yellow or olive overlaid with 5 to 6 variable vertical bands constitutes the **main** pattern. Dorsal and tail fins, blue-black with narrow red edge. **Ventral** fins, clear to yellow; eye, brown. Black spot on opercle. At breeding **time** the forward part of the body becomes black and the belly pure **white.** The nose takes on a mahogany-red color, while the anal and tail fins become red. Breeds like *H. bimaculatus*. The fish is inclined to be savage.

The specimen from which the illustration was made had been purchased as *Tilapia nilotica*.

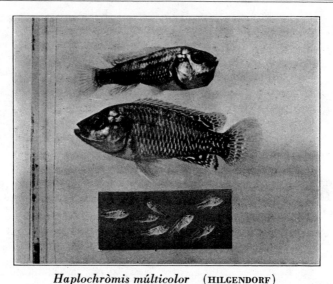

Haplochròmis múlticolor (HILGENDORF)

Pronounced Hap'low-krow"miss mul"te-col'or *Popular name,* Egyptian Mouthbreeder
MEANING OF NAME: *Haplochromis,* plain chromide; *multicolor,* many-colored
Also known as *Haplochromis strigigena* and *Paratilapia multicolor*

Egypt Western Location Map o68; r70; v70 Length, 2½ inches

MOUTHBREEDERS! What whim of Nature have we here? It is not so much a whim as it is one of Nature's most unusual bits of ingenuity for the protection of the eggs and young of certain species, of which this happens to be one. There is nothing very unusual about t first part of the courtship. The male fans a depression in the sand abc 3 inches in diameter and induces the female to circle with him over t̠ ̠ shallow pit, during which action a few eggs are dropped and fertiliㅈ ꓒ from time to time. The eggs of each deposit are quickly picked up ꓲ the capacious mouth of the female and kept there, not only until they are hatched, but until the yolk-sac is fully absorbed. The whole process takes about 15 days. As the eggs resemble small mustard seed both in size and color, and as there may be as many as 100 of them in the mouth of this small fish, it will be seen that she undertakes quite a burden, even though she is liberally equipped with mouth capacity. The bony structure of the head of the female is noticeably larger in proportion than that of the male. This is somewhat exaggerated in appearance as she approaches the end of her maternal duties, for during the entire period of carrying the eggs and young, she steadfastly refuses food, thus becoming thin and wasted about the body. The upper fish in the photograph character-istically shows the bulged head and shrunken body of a female near the end of her heroic, self-imposed task.

This aversion to food during the carrying period is no doubt Nature's provision against either accidental or intentional swallowing of eggs, for one of a fish's greatest delicacies is fish eggs. Many of them, as we have numerously noted elsewhere, do not stop at eating the eggs of other fishes, but also consume their own. What self-control the Cichlids must display in order to propagate their own kind, for practically all of them take their eggs into their mouths at some time; but especially the mouth-breeders whose temptation is multiplied by hunger!

The tenacity of this small species in caring for the eggs and young is remarkable in another way. If caught and roughly handled in a net and exposed to the air, they will not divulge their secret, but will keep their mouths tightly locked.

During the period of incubation and development of the young, all mouthbreeders use a peculiar chewing motion of the jaws to give a circu-lation of water among their charges. There is, no doubt, also sufficient friction used to keep them clean and free from dirt which might produce fungus. At the same time it can be noted that the lips are not opened as freely as when they are out of the carrying period. By getting a favorably lighted direct view into the mouth, the eggs can be seen.

It is best to remove the male after the spawning is completed.

The young are at first only allowed to leave the mother's mouth for short periods. At the least sign of danger they all rush back. This inti-mate care only ends when the babies get too big to crowd into their refuge.

Although this species and the three following are considerably different from the usual Cichlids in their life habits and nature, they are true Cichlids and their young should be fed in the same way.

Haplochromis multicolor is a beautiful fish, especially the male, and particularly when in direct sun. The name "multicolor" is rather good, for, indeed, it offers an array of many colors. The general color of the body is metallic green, but closer observation shows the centre of the scales to be brownish orange with light green edges. The lighter parts of the dorsal and anal fins are metallic blue, while the darker parts of the photograph showing these fins, and in the base of the tail fin, are a rich, burnt orange. Eye, gold and red, intersected with a vertical black bar. The spot at the tip of the anal fin in the male is bright orange.

A fairly peaceful fish, liking a temperature from 68 to 84 degrees.

Tilàpia macrocéphala (BLEEKER)

Pronounced Ti-lay'pee-a mak'row-sef"a-la   *Popular name,* Large Mouthbreeder

MEANING OF NAME: *macrocephala,* large headed; meaning of *Tilapia* is unknown

Incorrect name, *Tilapia heudeloti* (another species)

Gold Coast to S. Nigeria   Western Location Map B51 to 52   Length, 7 inches

THE habits of this fish are very much the same as the preceding, except that the male is the nursemaid. Also he does not hold the eggs with such bulldog tenacity. If caught in a net he will spit them all out and will not pick them up again. Under these circumstances one need not give up hope of hatching the eggs. Place them in clear, shallow water and stir them around a bit with a spoon several times a day. In about a week tiny fish will be found attached to the eggs, much smaller than the eggs themselves. The fry grow by absorbing the egg.

Sexes can not be told before the fishes are about 3 inches long, at which time the gill plate of the male becomes brassy yellow in the centre, whereas in the female it is a delicate, translucent pink.

A large species of Tilapia, still native in Lake Galilee, may very well have been caught by fishermen of Biblical times. Inset shows young.

The two outstanding features of the fish are the very black throat which sometimes develops, and the rosy glow in the fins, especially in the broad tail. The body is silvery, variably marked at times with black.

A gluttonous, good-natured fish. Temperature range, 68 to 85 degrees.

Tilàpia natalénsis   WEBER
Pronounced Ti-lay′pee-a   nay′tal-en″sis
Named for Natal, South Africa
Natal, S. E. Africa up to Zanzibar   Western Location Map X65 to H74   Length, 4 inches

A MOUTHBREEDER that has seldom been bred. We are not certain as to which parent carries the eggs during incubation.

The species is distinguished by a broad orange end of the tail fin, which is brighter in the male. Under excitement the body turns very dark, at which time about 4 light spots (shown in upper fish) appear. The male is farther distinguished when in his dark phase by the lower portion of his jaw becoming nearly white, this area being flecked with a few dark spots. Out of breeding season the general background tone is a mildly glinting metallic green, on which are laid irregular dark dots and stripes. The species is hardy, stands close confinement and a temperature range of 65 to 85 degrees without trouble. Not a fighter, except in mating.

Pelmátochròmis guentheri (SAUVAGE)
Pronounced Pel-ma′to-krow″miss gin′ther-eye
MEANING OF NAME: *Pelmatochromis,* Sole-chromide, referring to a peculiar internal
formation of the gill structure; *guentheri,* after the naturalist, Guenther
Trade name (incorrectly) *Pelmatochromis belladorsalis*
Equatorial W. Africa coastal rivers   Length, 4 inches
Western Location Map F58 to B51

THE dorsal fin on this fish is most striking, and entirely different from that of any other known aquarium fish. The light portions shown in the fins are much like applied gold leaf. As the body is a plain drab, of purplish hue, devoid of pattern, the startling fins have the field to themselves. The fish is peaceful and will eat anything.

At the time they were introduced (1933) they were believed to be mouthbreeders. This proved to be the case. They breed like *Tilapia macrocephala,* and on several occasions have reared their broods in small aquariums with both parents present. When the young first emerge, they are large. At the slightest sign of danger, they continue to use the mouth of the father as a refuge, even after they have reached a length of ⅝ inch. It is quite an amusing sight to see them scamper in, especially when their size makes it impossible for all to enter. It is like a hen who is no longer able to hide all her chicks under her feathers. Temperature, 70 to 82.

Pelmátochròmis annéctens BOULENGER
Pronounced Pel-ma'to-krow''miss an-nec'tens
MEANING OF NAME: *annectens,* connecting, no doubt meaning a connecting
link between species
Lower Niger   Western Location Map A to B on 56   Length, 4 inches

IN commercial circles this fish has been handled both as *Pelmatochromis
arnoldi* and *Pelmatochromis fasciatus.* Mr. J. R. Norman, the leading
authority on this group of fishes, says that our photograph closely resembles *P. annectens,* as here listed, and as Stoye has an elaborate description
of the species under this name, and that description accurately fits the fish
photographed, we feel reasonably certain it is correct.

A small but distinguishing feature is the bright white spot just above
the vent in the female. This barely shows in the male. There are 6 vertical bars and sometimes 3 horizontal stripes. Dorsal and tail fins
tipped red. The dorsal of the male (upper fish) is not usually as long as
shown in this specimen. Geometric blue dots in ends of dorsal, tail and
anal fins. Gorgeous in mating colors. Not a mouthbreeder.

For breeding, needs a large aquarium and a temperature of about 80
degrees. Does not destroy plants. Temperature range, 68 to 85 degrees.

For some reason it is difficult to induce this species to spawn.

Gèophàgus brasiliénsis HECKEL

Pronounced Jee′o-fay″gus bra′sil′ee-en″sis (Gee-off′a-gus allowable)

MEANING OF NAME: *Geophagus,* earth-eater; *brasiliensis,* from Brazil

Brazil　　　　　Western Location Map L37 to ★26　　　　　Length, 6 inches

SOME Cichlids might well be the envy of mere man, for they become handsomer with age. *G. brasiliensis* is one of that kind. The picture demonstrates the point. The high lights on the body and fins are electric blue-green and it will be seen in the illustration how much better they are developed in the older and larger fish. The dark central body spot is larger and more showy than the photograph indicates. The base color of the body is a varying shade of olive, while the fins are dark orange. Dorsal edge not as bright a red as in some other Cichlids—for instance, the "Dempsey."

The fish is rather easily distinguished from the other popular Cichlids by the outline of its body. The head is large and the body tapers off sharply where it joins the tail fin. This end of the body is called the "caudal peduncle." The eye is dark gold and black.

And, by the way, the picture shows a happily mated pair, despite the difference in size, and that the male is the larger. It is a common belief that there is less likely to be trouble if the female is the larger of the two.

The truth seems to be that affinity is more important than size, many apparently ill-assorted couples breeding beautifully.

G. brasiliensis is a fighter among its own kind, but can be kept with large fishes of other species. Ordinarily it is kept singly.

The fish withstands a liberal range of temperature, 65 degrees being about the bottom limit. It is fond of sunshine and likes to dig. Only strong plants such as Giant Sagittaria should be placed with it.

The eggs hatch in about 5 days and the young are guarded by the parents for quite a period. While it is a pleasure to witness this delightful family life, it is the best policy, as elsewhere stated, to separate parents and young after the babies are fully able to shift for themselves. Remember, however, that in this forcible separation the parents are liable to suspect each other of responsibility for the loss of the young, and to quarrel fatally. Either separate or watch them through this critical period. This applies to nearly all Cichlids except the mouthbreeders.

Found in stagnant waters and coastal streams, in some instances in slightly salt water.

In nature the fish reaches a length of 10 inches, but in the aquarium 6 inches is considered a good size.

Gèophàgus jùrupäri HECKEL
Pronounced Jee'o-fay"gus ju'ru-pär"ee
MEANING OF NAME: *jurupari,* after a native name
The Amazon   Western Location Map A21 to J9 and F29   Length, 5 inches

ONE of the newer Cichlids, rather plentiful at the present writing (1934), owing to recent importations. It is peculiar in the possession of a particularly long, pointed head, and in having a dorsal fin that is quite high along its entire length. The long, downward arching profile of the snout makes the lower part of the head and body seem somewhat flat. The eyes are very large and are placed high. Owing to the long snout they also seem to be set far back, giving the fish an odd look.

Like all other Cichlids, their color and markings vary greatly. The average background is a rather light golden color, while the light pattern on the body and in the fins is metallic blue.

The upper fish is the male, showing a longer point on the dorsal fin.

This is one of the more peaceful Cichlids, and does not tear out plants. Its breeding habits conform strictly to those described for the family.

Another species, *G. acuticeps,* is similar, but has extensions on the ends of the ventral fins, similar to those in the adult *Cichlasoma festivum.*

Heríchthys cyanoguttàtus

Pronounced Her-ik'thiss sy-an'o-gut-tay"tus   *Popular name,* Texas Cichlid
MEANING OF NAME: *Heríchthys,* fish like Heros; *cyanoguttatus,* blue spotted
Incorrectly, *Neetroplus carpintis*
Mexico and Texas   Western Location Map i14 to n14   Length, 7 to 9 inches

IN point of distribution this is the most northerly of all Cichlids. Through the Rio Grande and its tributaries it actually extends into Texas, and is the only member of the genus found in the United States.

Although without pronounced coloration, the fish is easily recognized. It is of a grayish tone, thickly sprinkled with small, light, round dots, extending well into the dorsal fin. These dots are smaller and more numerous than in any other Cichlid we know of. It is a species that is fairly well known to aquarists, but is not extensively kept.

At breeding season it develops interesting brown markings and patterns.

As may be assumed from its natural distribution, this fish can stand lower temperatures than most of the species, although it likes to breed at about 78 degrees.

The chief objection to the fish is that in a large aquarium it grows to an inordinate size. The species is not troublesome in company with other large fishes. Temperature range, 65-82 degrees.

Cíchlasòma còryphœnòides (HECKEL)

Pronounced Sick'la-so"ma ko'ree-fee-no"i-dees   *Popular name,* Chocolate Cichlid
MEANING OF NAME: *coryphœnoides,* dolphin-like
Near Manaos, Brazil   Western Location Map G20   Length, 4 inches

A SPECIES which has been imported from time to time, but of which we know little. For a year after its introduction it was temporarily labelled Cichlasoma U2, the letter U standing for "unidentified." We are now reasonably sure that the above identification is correct.

Even for a Cichlid the fish is remarkable for its extremes of color changes, and the speed with which they take place. The author, being responsible for the popular name, Chocolate Cichlid, does not feel that this was a very happy choice. Although one of its color phases is a purplish chocolate shade, a better name would have been Marbled Cichlasoma, for the light markings in the illustration, being of a warm ivory shade, often appear in marbled patterns against a most variable dark background, frequently a purplish brown, flushed with rose, if such a combination is thinkable! It is interesting to observe the color changes which take place if a light is turned on these fishes when they have been in darkness.

Efforts at breeding have thus far ended only in killings, but the survivors of the battles remain beautiful and interesting exhibition fishes. Temperature requirements, 70-85 degrees.

Cichlasòma cútteri   FOWLER

Pronounced Sick'la-so''ma   cut'ter-eye   Named for Mr. Cutter, the collector

Honduras   Western Location Map s23   Length, 3½ inches

*T*HE dominant feature of this fish is its 7 to 8 dark bars against a pale background, faintly suffused with blue. These bars at breeding time become stronger in the female, while her throat and belly take on a brown or black appearance. The third bar tends to extend into the dorsal fin, and at times ends in a peacock spot. Contrary to the female, the male loses most of his bars at the breeding season and his body becomes brown to olive green. The eye is attractively flashed with blue-green.

Unusually good care is provided by the parents, especially by the mother, who seems to be the *charge d'affairs*. One pair of these fishes raised its brood in a community tank without loss either of babies or damage to the other inhabitants, a performance calling for an unusual degree of firmness and tact.

The species is easily confused with the true *C. nigrofasciatum*, which averages darker and greener in color, and has a golden brown eye.

C. cutteri may be regarded as one of the safe Cichlids, having little or none of the pugnacious qualities common to most of them.

Eggs hatch in 3 days at 80 degrees.

Cichlasòma facètum (JENYNS)

Pronounced Sick'la-so"ma fa-see'tum   *Popular name,* Chanchito

MEANING OF NAME: *Cichlasoma,* resembling the genus Cichla; *facetum,* attractive

Discarded scientific name, *Heros facetus*

Brazil   Western Location Map v22   Length, 7 inches

THE Chanchito is one of the older friends of modern aquarists, and one of the most dependable. It will stand a temperature of 60 without trouble, is a sure breeder, an excellent parent, a fish that lives long and is easy to feed. The first Cichlid domesticated—1884.

Perhaps not so showy as some other of the large Cichlids, it is a fish of distinction and of interesting variation in color. Usually the background is horn-color overlaid with the black pattern shown in the illustration. The body color sometimes becomes almost black. The eyes are strikingly red, but the depth of their color varies in individuals. This is one of the few Cichlids which does not show any metallic spangles.

Except at breeding time the Chanchito is not a pugnacious fish, although the larger specimens are too big for the average community tank.

In breeding and feeding habits it is typical of the description for the group. It is well suited to summer culture in pools in states of temperate climate. Large broods can be so raised with little attention.

Cíchlasòma meèki   (BRIND)

Pronounced Sick'la-so"ma   meek'eye   *Popular name,* Firemouth

Named for Prof. Seth Meek

Yucatan   Western Location Map n21   Length, 4 to 5 inches

NOT every fish has a pronounced individual characteristic marking. *C. meeki* has two: the green-edged spot at the base of the gill plate and a fiery orange color along the belly, and which extends *into the mouth.* This color is present at all times and is brighter in the male, but becomes most vivid during mating, especially in the *female.* The light spots in the illustration on the head, along the edges of the dorsal, the anal fins and slightly streaked into the tail fin are electric blue-green.

The specimens used in the illustration were about 3 inches long, and up to this size there are no external sex differences, except that the belly coloring on the male may be a shade brighter. Six months later, when the pair had grown another inch, the male developed the usual long point on the dorsal fin, common to most Cichlids.

Breeding temperature, about 80 degrees.

The fish was an outstanding introduction of 1933, although a few specimens had appeared and disappeared a number of years previously. It has now been successfully bred many times, and it seems likely to be with us permanently. The breeding habits are the same as with the other Cichlids. It is surely worthy of a place in any collection of fishes of this type.

Cíchlasòma tétracánthus (CUVIER AND VALENCIENNES)

Pronounced Sick'la-so'ma tet'ra-can"thus   *Popular name,* Cuban Cichlid

MEANING OF NAME: *tetracanthus,* many-spined

Cuba   Western Location Map m25 to m29   Length, 6 inches

CICHLASOMA TETRACANTHUS is one of our recent successful introductions.

The colors ordinarily are not of a brilliant nature. The ground color is chamois, which is overlaid with designs in dark gray or brown. The back and upper half of the head are suffused with blue-green. Fins, gray.

Even out of breeding season *C. tetracanthus* rips out plants, even large ones, so it is not worth while wasting them on this species. Breeding habits are in general similar to type, but the female does most of the courting. She is the upper fish in the picture.

Heavy eaters, with a preference for animal foods, earthworms being "pie" for them.

At breeding season these fishes show a surprising array of colors, at which time the usually obscure blues and greens come out with unexpected brilliance. Temperature, about 75 to 80 degrees.

Cichlasòma séverum (HECKEL)
Pronounced Sick'la-so'ma sev'e-rum
MEANING OF NAME: *severum*, severe
Formerly, and more popularly, *Heros spurius*
Amazon   Western Location Map A21 to I9 and O19, and F29   Length, 5 to 6 inches

REFERENCE has already been made to the great changeability in coloring and marking of the various Cichlids. This is particularly true of the *Cichlasoma severum*. The background color in any individual may, in a few seconds, change from pale gray to deep green, brown or nearly black, with any imagined intervening shades. Agitation of one kind or another usually causes the color changes. Fright, anger, sexual stimulation, temperature, feeding, produce different but not predictable effects. Lifting almost any Cichlid in a net from one aquarium to another will cause an instant change in color. As photographing is nearly always done in a special aquarium of small size, this makes great difficulty in selecting any special color effect for recording, as the fish cannot be kept in such a confined space long enough to wait for it to put on some desired color costume.

The usual color is perhaps just a trifle more brownish than our illustration. The connecting bar between the two dark spots in the fins is liable to disappear, but in general one may recognize this fish by the dumb-bell pattern extending vertically across the fish into the fins, near the tail. We know of no other aquarium fish with this characteristic marking. In its larger aquarium sizes, about 5 to 6 inches, this fish is a striking beauty, although it is also fairly attractive when smaller.

Certain aquarium fishes cannot safely be gorged with food. *Cichlasoma severum* is one of them. It is liable to die from an over-feeding, even of live food.

While the name *severum* means "severe," it is no more militant than the average large Cichlid.

Undoubtedly this is one of the more difficult Cichlids to breed. It should have a large aquarium, plenty of temperature (about 80 degrees) and be well fed on garden worms in order to induce mating and spawning. Otherwise the methods conform to standard. The sex is easily told. The male has the regular rows of dots on the side, whereas the female has few, if any.

Cíchlasòma féstivum   (HECKEL)

Pronounced Sick'la-so"ma   fes'ti-vum   Known as *Acara bandeira* in Brazil

MEANING OF NAME: *festivum,* gaily attractive, festive

Also known as *Mesonauta insignis*

Amazon   Western Location Map A21 to O19 and F29   Aquarium size, 4 inches

A FISH of marked individuality. The strong oblique stripe traversing
the body from the mouth to the upper tip of the dorsal fin is unique
among our aquarium fishes, and makes identification of the species easy.
As in many fishes having threadlike extensions of fins, this characteristic
does not appear until the fish is well developed in size. This, of course,
refers to the "feelers" on the ventral fins. The general color of the body
is silvery, with a green cast. The fins have none of the color markings
common to many species of the genus. The magnificent upward oblique
bar is in itself a sufficient gift from Nature for any one fish. This fish is
at its best in a size of about 3 inches. When it gets larger the markings
are apt to become less distinct. Breeding temperature, about 82 degrees.

The fish is fairly hardy, especially as it becomes older and larger, but
it is difficult to mate. Although not a timid fish, it seems to prefer privacy
when mating and caring for its young.

Cíchlasòma bìocellàtum REGAN
Pronounced Sick'la-so"ma by'o-sell-a"tum *Popular name,* Jack Dempsey
MEANING OF NAME: *biocellatum,* with 2 spots, referring to the 2 ocellated
spots on the sides
South America, probably Brazil Length up to 7 inches

$\mathcal{B}$EFORE the reign of the Scalare, this fish, popularly and affectionately known as "Jack Dempsey," was the most popular of the Cichlids. Of its own type, with a long body and strong head, it is still the leader, for it has dazzling beauty, it is hardy, a good breeder and parent. A dependable show piece.

Our description of breeding of the Cichlids fits this species perfectly.

It was one of the earlier introductions into the aquarium, and for many years was known as *Cichlasoma nigrofasciatum,* a species we have described not far from this page.

With the Dempsey it is particularly true that with age the colors become more fixed, brilliant, and less likely to change under the influence of fear or other emotional excitement. Our illustration shows the hump-shaped nape, which in some Cichlids develops with age.

Often a large individual fish is kept as a pet in an aquarium by itself, where it soon learns to beg, in fish language, for morsels of food from its master. Lives for 10 years or longer. Temperature range, 65-90 degrees.

Etròplus maculàtus (BLOCH)

Pronounced E-tro′plus   mac′you-lay″tus   *Popular name,* Orange Chromide
MEANING OF NAME: *Etroplus,* with armored abdomen, referring to hard fin rays;
maculatus, spotted

India and Ceylon   Eastern Location Map y21; A22   Length, 3 inches

A VERY individual Cichlid, and a rather touchy one as to living conditions. Some of our best aquarists have given it up in despair, yet others have little trouble.

It is one of our very few Cichlids from India, and can stand plenty of temperature, being happiest in a range of from 75 to 82 degrees. The plate shows breeding colors. At other times the fish is not so deep a yellow, and the central body spot is black. The black in fins is less intense at other times. Upper fish is the male. Out of breeding season the male is just a little stronger in color and has more red in the eye.

Difficult to induce to spawn. Eggs are deposited preferably on the under-side of an arch or bridge, each egg hung by an individual thread. Care of young by parents as per usual Cichlid routine, except that the young follow the mother, while the father does police duty in keeping away enemies. They have been successfully bred in a community tank.

Cíchlasòma nìgrofasciàtum (GUENTHER)

Pronounced Sick'la-so"ma ny'gro-fas'see-a"tum

MEANING OF NAME: *Cichlasoma,* resembling Cichla; *nigrofasciatum,* black-banded
San Salvador, etc.   Western Location Map v24; t-u on 21   Aquarium size, 4 inches

IT should be stated that this fish is not the "Jack Dempsey," a much
better-known species incorrectly known as *C. nigrofasciatum.* This is a
smaller fish and is not adorned with the splendid spangles of the Dempsey.
It is much more of a fighter. The popular "Jack Dempsey" will be found
listed as *Cichlasoma biocellatum.*

While they breed like other Cichlids, it is more necessary to give
breeding pairs a large aquarium liberally supplied with refuges, such as
flower-pots or large stones arranged in arches or other forms providing
hiding places for the pursued. This is not necessarily the female. The
male sometimes gets the worst of it. It is usually the smaller fish that
in times of stress beats a retreat.

Cichlids which are highly strung change their colors rapidly. This
species belongs to that type. Our illustration shows 2 color phases.
The one to the right displays brilliant bottle-green in the bars and cheeks.
Tail spot, vivid black. To the left we have a creamy pale fish with gray
bars and a line of black dots on the side. These colors do not indicate sex.
That is shown by the pointed fins of the fish to the right, which is the
male. Temperature range, 70 to 85 degrees. Breeds best at 80.

(This page should have been placed to precede *Etroplus maculatus.*)

Æquidens látifrons   (STEINDACHNER)

Pronounced Ee'kwi-denz lat'i-frons   *Popular name,* Blue Acara

MEANING OF NAME: *Æquidens,* with teeth of same length; *latifrons,* broad forehead

Also known to aquarists as *Acara cœruleo-punctata, Acara pulchra* and
Cichlasoma cœruleopunctata

Panama and Colombia   Western Location Map x10   Length, 6 inches

A LONG established favorite of mild disposition. A prolific breeder. "Blue Acara" is a widely accepted name for the fish, but there is nothing distinctly blue about it. The body color is rather greenish, with the usual sprinkling of blue-green spangled scales and irregular markings on the head. Central body spot on the third bar is large. In strong, direct light, 3 purplish or plum-colored stripes show along the body. The scales on the upper part of the body have blue centres with brown edges, while the lower scales are exactly the reverse—brown centres with blue edges. Fins, dull orange, with blue-green markings. Sexes colored alike.

Temperature range, 70 to 85 degrees. Breeds at about 78. Peaceful.

Æquidens cúrviceps E. AHL
Pronounced Ee'kwi-denz kur'vi-seps
MEANING OF NAME: *curviceps,* with dome-shaped head
Commonly but incorrectly known as *Acara thayeri,* a fish not yet imported

Amazon	No exact locality known	Length, 3 inches

𝒯HERE are several points about this fish which destine it to remain among the aquarists' choice selections. It is not large, it is both beautiful and different in color, it is not savage and may be used in a community aquarium. Lastly, it can be bred, but not too easily.

This is one of the Cichlids which does not tear out plants. Otherwise there is no difference from the breeding habits described at the beginning of this section. They are prone to eat their eggs. It is believed that the eggs should not be exposed to direct sunlight. This is a rather shy fish and needs privacy. One aquarist devised a plan by which he places a card in front of the aquarium, perforated by a peep-hole for observation.

The illustration shows the breeding tubes just emerging. Sexes are very similar. There is often a dark spot in the centre of the dorsal fin where it joins the body. This does not indicate sex. Temperature, 74-78 deg.

Æquidens portalegrénsis (HENSEL)
Pronounced Ee′kwi-denz por′tal-e-gren″sis
Named for Porto Alegre, Brazil
Incorrect but popular scientific name, *Acara portalegrensis*
S. E. Brazil   Western Location Map ★26 to ‡21 and Q22   Length, 4 to 5 inches

USUALLY considered to be the most kindly of this general type and size of fish. Quite easily bred, even in aquaria that are too small. That is, it will manage in a 7-gallon aquarium, when it ought to have a 15 or larger.

The general color of the fish is a mixture of green and brown. A close examination of the scales shows them to be olive, edged black. The fins are dark yellow, the markings on them in the photograph being blue-green, the same blue-green also showing on the markings on the cheeks. The dark spot at the upper base of the tail is always present in adults, while the large spot in the centre of the body, as well as the stripes and bars, quickly come and go. Eyes are brown.

The fish has a decidedly blunt face, even more so than the photograph appears to convey. It seems to have been "up against it." It is by this characteristic appearance that the species can be recognized at a glance.

This is one of the more popular Cichlids, and is not difficult to secure commercially. Its safe temperature range is 68 to 85 degrees. Best breeding temperature, about 77 degrees.

Photograph shows spawning tubes almost ready for action. One of their favorite places on which to spawn is the inside of a flower-pot which has been placed in a horizontal position.

Cichlasòma bimaculàtum

Pronounced Sick′la-so″ma by′mak-you-lay″tum

Meaning of name: *bimaculatum*, two-spotted

Amazon and Guiana   Western Location Map A21 to F29 and H14

For the purposes of the aquarist the foregoing statement regarding the ease of identifying *Æquidens portalegrensis* is true enough, but it is not absolutely true. *Cichlasoma bimaculatum* is very similar, being distinguished by the presence of 4, instead of 3 spines in the anal fin.

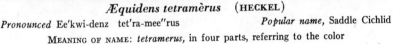

Æquidens tetramèrus   (HECKEL)

Pronounced Ee'kwi-denz   tet'ra-mee"rus   *Popular name,* Saddle Cichlid

MEANING OF NAME: *tetramerus,* in four parts, referring to the color

Amazon and Guiana   Western Location Map A21 to H14 and G28   Length, 7 to 8 inches

ONE of the rarer Cichlids, imported only occasionally and probably never bred in the United States. The distinguishing characteristic marking is the body spot, high on the side and usually going all the way across the back, forming a dark saddle. The scales on either side of the spot are somewhat golden. Regularly-spaced green-gold spots form lines along the lower sides. Not so many blue markings in the fins as in most Cichlids. Large eye is brown and gold. The fins of this species do not seem to develop flowing lines with age. The dorsal and anal rather get to curve inward at the ends as the fish attains size. Ultimately it reaches a length in the aquarium of about 7 inches, and is then a showy fish. Striped metallic markings about the head are particularly vivid. A fish worth cultivating when opportunity offers. Temperature, 70-85 degrees.

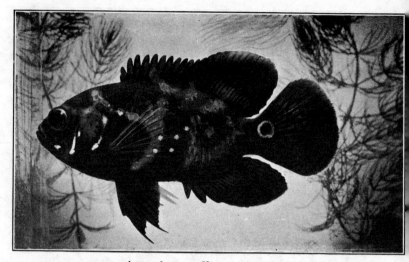

Astronòtus ocellàtus (AGASSIZ.)
Pronounced As'tro-no"tus os'el-lay"tus
MEANING OF NAME: *Astronotus,* marked with stars; *ocellatus,* with eye spot
Guiana, Amazon and Paraguay   Length, up to 8 inches
Western Location Map H12 to G28 and U22

*A*LLOW us to present a strange Cichlid, not only new to most aqua-rists, but of such odd appearance and ways that one could well believe it to belong in another family. The scales are not very visible, the fish seeming more to be clothed in a sort of olive suede leather, hand-somely decorated by a few fiery orange markings. These are represented in the photograph by the white areas, including the stunning ring of that brilliant color in the tail, which is further set off by an outside edge and a centre, both of black. The body markings are lighter shades of green-gray, or the fish may become nearly black. The fins are opaque.

When about 2 inches long the beautiful orange markings are not yet developed. They appear when the fish is about the size shown in the illustration. Again in larger sizes the colors change, but for the worse.

Their actions are peculiar. Two fish will assume a head-to-tail position very close to each other, wag their bodies in unison and go through a sort of sinuous, rolling motion. Apparently this has nothing to do with mating, and is more apt to occur when they are crowded.

Ordinarily two of these fishes get along beautifully together, but the aquarist should not take too much for granted. They may start fighting.

They are easily cared for and fed. Not yet bred. Temp., 72-82 deg.

Crénicíchla lepidòta   HECKEL

Pronounced Kren'i-sick"la   le'pi-do"ta   *Popular name,* Pike Cichlid

MEANING OF NAME: *Crenicichla,* Cichla with teeth; *lepidota,* with scales
on ear region (gill covers)

South America   Western Location Map U22 to v22 and ★26   Length, 4 to 5 inches

"*BAD* ACTOR" is a term applied by aquarists to fishes which are unneighborly in the community tank. Unfortunately it fits all the Crenicichlas, of which there are a number of species.

They follow the usual Cichlid method of breeding, but only the male looks after the eggs and young. He is a strict disciplinarian and requires the flock of young to follow him closely. Those that fail in this pay with their lives, for he eats them—his way of eliminating the unfit.

Although lacking brilliant coloring, they are decidedly attractive. The anal and lower part of the tail fin are shaded red, while all of the unpaired fins are interestingly dotted and lined with various shades of gray. The irregular markings on the back, observed in the photograph, are variable in their intensity. In this species it is the *female* which has the longer rays on the dorsal and anal fins.

None of the species of Crenicichla is often in supply commercially. They like a temperature of about 75 to 80 degrees, and do not tear out plants.

Pterophýllum scalàre CUVIER AND VALENCIENNES

Pronounced Ter'ro-fill"um sca-lay"ree   *Popular name,* Angel Fish

MEANING OF NAME: *Pterophyllum,* winged leaf; *scalare,* ladder-like, referring
to back edge of long fins

Amazon   Western Location Map A21 to I11 and F29   Length, 5 to 6 inches

THE true *Pterophyllum scalare* is seldom seen, and is difficult to breed. Most of our stock popularly passing as that species is *P. eimekei.* It is smaller than *P. scalare,* has a redder eye, more blue on the ventrals and has "fly-speck dots" on the sides.

The "Scalare" is the fish that nearly all beginners hope to graduate into owning, and perhaps breeding. After Guppies and Bettas it has probably done more to attract favorable attention to the exotic aquarium fish hobby than any other fish.

To the untrained eye, *P. scalare* does not look like a Cichlid, but nevertheless it *is* one. The typical Cichlid shape is seen in the younger stages in our illustrations on page 405, particularly in figure 4. It is also different from the type in nature and habits.

Except that it will eat small fishes of suitable size, it is quite a good "happy family" member. While the breeding habits are much the same

THE SCALARE NURSERY

The babies are in process of transfer from one leaf to the other. Those being examined so intently by the upper fish have just been sprayed where they are from his mouth. One is slipping off, but will be retrieved by the other parent.

as we look for in Cichlids, there are two distinct points of difference. Instead of depositing the spawn in or on such objects as flower-pots or stones, they prefer for this purpose a firm aquatic leaf, such as Giant Sagittaria, or some substitute that will approximate it. The color plate shows the beginning of a spawn on a leaf of Giant Vallisneria. They will accept a glass tube for the purpose, especially if there is something inside it. They seem to have no confidence in the clear glass. Sometimes a glass tube is slipped over the aquarium drain pipe. The tubing should be about an inch in diameter. A commercial article for the purpose consists of a strip of quarter-inch bakelite about an inch wide and 8 inches long, mounted in a cement base, sloping a few degrees off vertical. The chimneys of oil lamps have been successfully used, but here again they should be filled or else painted inside with a waterproof material. These mechanical substitutes have their advantages and are mentioned

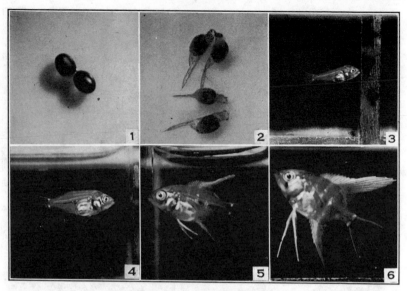

THE SCALARE, FROM EGG TO FISH

1. Eggs, light yellow in life, magnified 6 diameters. 2. Alevin at 3 days, same magnification. Shows attached yolk-sac. As with all baby fish, this is slowly absorbed, furnishing the first nourishment. 3, 4, 5 and 6, at 2-diameter magnification, represent ages 12, 20, 28 and 36 days. Note how figure 4 resembles the more usual Cichlid form, like *Tilapia macrocephala*.

here at some length because the big producers of Scalares use them. How it is done will be described after pointing out the following other important difference in breeding habits.

Unlike the great majority of Cichlids, the Scalare does not place its young in prepared holes in the sand. Wherever the baby Scalare hatches, there it adheres suspended from the head by a sticky thread, vibrating its tail vigorously. The mass of young produces an appreciable current in this way, thus getting both exercise and a rapid change of water. During this period the parents pick up mouthfuls of young, retain them a few moments and gently spray them on another leaf, repeating the operation at intervals of perhaps an hour, until the babies can swim freely, which is in about 2 days. During this period the parents are most solicitous, and use great care to pick up any of the young which did not adhere to a new location. Babies seldom reach the bottom before rescue arrives.

As to how long to keep the parents and young together—if at all—is a matter for each aquarist to decide. Leaving them all together is a

FULLY-FLEDGED YOUNG SCALARES

most interesting procedure if successful. The family of Scalares shown in the illustration remained together for 6 weeks, apparently without a loss, and were only separated because of signs of a new spawn. This new spawn, under apparently identical conditions, was eaten. As elsewhere stated, it is quite likely the parents may judge a spawning to be inferior in quality, and so destroy it.

If the main object is to rear fish, and one is willing to forego the pleasure of witnessing their interesting family life, then the best thing to do is to remove the eggs to a hatching tray or aquarium containing water not over 4 inches deep. The container and water should be perfectly clean, for the babies are not to be freed of dirt particles in the laundry-mouths of their natural parents. The water, of course, should be seasoned.

Returning to the subject of artificial spawn receivers, it will now be apparent where their use is a practical convenience, for they are easily lifted out of the aquarium and laid horizontally in the hatching tray. A light current of water about the eggs and young, produced by the mechanical liberation of air is desirable but not always necessary. By the time the young have absorbed all of the yolk-sac and become free-swimming, they are able to eat finely sifted Daphnia.

New hatched Scalares look nothing like their parents, but in a few weeks there is no mistaking their identity. Growth is rapid under the influence of liberal feeding and warmth.

A number of other Cichlids may be reared in this way. It is worth trying when parents persistently eat eggs or young.

Peculiarities of Scalares   Several things about Scalares require special consideration. Perhaps the most outstanding one is an unaccountable loss of appetite. Try a change of food. They are particularly fond of live mosquito larvæ, Daphnia, water boatmen (for large fishes), small or chopped earthworms, white worms and canned shrimp. If these fail to tempt, then try baby Guppies. Pretty bad case if these morsels fail to bring back the appetite. The only thing then left to do is to try a change of aquarium or of water in the present aquarium. Scalares seem to do best in slightly acid water, about pH 6.8. See paragraph on pH under "General Management."

There should be plants in the aquarium with Scalares. These tend to prevent dashing themselves to death against the glass when frightened.

Ordinarily when a fish lays over on its side on the bottom of the aquarium it is preparing to enter Fish Paradise. The Scalare is liable to do this from shock, fright or chill, and is quite likely to regain its equilibrium.

This fish is not very susceptible to Ichthyophthirius, but it is liable to a disease which causes the eyes to protrude. This sometimes leads to blindness and ends in death.

The young should be fed liberally, but never gorged, especially not on mosquito larvæ. Results apt to be fatal.

Sex in Scalares   This remains difficult to distinguish, but we can make a shrewd guess. Even mating is not a certain sign, for two females sometimes mate and have infertile eggs. In THE AQUARIUM for September, 1932, an illustrated article points out seven methods of discovering the sex in Scalares. Several of these are of doubtful value. The one in use by practical breeders has reference to the space at the lower edge of the body between the "feelers" and the beginning of the anal fin. In the female this portion of the body outline is longer and straighter. As with other Cichlids, the breeding tube, which appears in both sexes just before egg-laying, is more pointed in the male, and is carried at a more forward angle. This is well shown on the color plate, the fish in the rear position being the male. Also the female when filling with eggs looks fuller from an overhead view.

Symphỳsodon díscus   (HECKEL)
Pronounced Sim-fy'so-don   dis'kus (Sim'fy-so"don   allowable)
MEANING OF NAME: *Symphysodon,* with teeth at middle of lower jaw; *discus,* like a disc
Popular name, Pompadour Fish
Amazon   Western Location Map G17 to F29   Length, 5 to 6 inches

ONE of the spectacular introductions of 1933. It is of the "pancake" type, flattened like the Scalare. A show fish. Something that even the uninitiated remember. Its showy quality is increased by its rather large size.

The usual body color is warm golden, crossed by the dark vertical bars shown in the above illustration. These extend into the dorsal fin. The high lights on the fore part of the body and in the fins are a rich, deep metallic blue. The disc-like effect of the fish is enhanced by the dark circle extending through the dorsal, tail and anal fins. This is usually a deep blue (not metallic) color. There is considerable difference in the richness of marking in individuals. In the best specimens the upper dark arch of blue in the dorsal fin is followed, rainbow-like, with another arch of bright red. This color is repeated in the rear portion of the anal fin.

Outside of breeding season it is very difficult to tell the sexes, but as mating proceeds the male becomes darker, with brighter blue over-pattern, while the female gets more yellow. Some males, immediately before and after spawning, take on the most gorgeous raiment imaginable, equalling the gaudy marine fishes in brilliance. In the picture of the male fanning the eggs, the light part of the pattern is all a dazzling, metallic blue, while the dark streaks are a glowing, cherry-red.

MALE FANNING EGGS ON THE EDGE OF A BAR OF SLATE

The breeding methods are very much the same as with the Scalare, but the fish seldom spawns. Remove eggs from parents and aerate them. Eggs hatch in 3 days at a temperature of 84. They should be kept at this temperature in shallow, slightly acid water for a month, and be given mild aeration. We have seen a number of spawnings, and, in all cases except one, the parents have eaten the eggs or the young have died early. That one hatching proved successful.

A great drawback to the adult fish is that it will seldom eat anything except Tubifex worms, of which it is very fond. Temperature range, 70-84 degrees.

THE POMACENTRIDS
FAMILY POMACENTRIDAE
Pronounced Po ma sen'trid ee

The Pomacentrids, or Demoiselles, are like the Cichlids in having only one nostril on a side but differ in having an internal bony shelf to support the eye socket. Most of the species are marine coral reef fishes, but it has recently been found that at least some species can be acclimated to nearly or wholly fresh water. It is, however, very doubtful that they will ever breed or hatch their eggs in fresh water.

Dascýllus trimáculàtus (RUEPPELL)
Pronounced Das-sill'us tri-mac'you-lay"tus
MEANING OF NAME: *Dascyllus,* meaning not known; *trimaculatus,* three-spotted (banded)
Red Sea to East Indies and Hawaii (Marine)   Length, 2 inches

THE description and remarks regarding *Dascyllus aruanus* fit this variety very well, but it is not considered to be quite as durable. The intense white enamel spots on the sides and forehead are very vivid against the dark background.

It is best to keep marine aquaria out of strong daylight, as the water under the influence of sun is apt to rapidly turn green. Ocean water is much preferable to any synthetic article, but if the water must be made up artificially, one should be sure to use genuine evaporated sea salt.

Dascýllus aruànus (LINNAEUS)
Pronounced Das-sill'us ar-you-a'nus
MEANING OF NAME: *aruanus,* from the Aru Islands, E. Indies
East Indies to S. Pacific Islands (Marine)   Length, 2 inches

*A*S a marine fish to be kept in salt water in a home aquarium, this fish, considering all points, is unsurpassed by any that we know. It lives as well as the more dependable fresh-water fishes, is easily fed, is flashy in appearance and is always "on the go." Although it seems a bit scrappy, no damage seems to get done. To what extent it can be brought to fresh water is not known to the writer.

Although the markings are striking, they are extremely simple. They are just black-and-white, exactly as the picture shows. The white is brilliant. With fright the black parts become gray or nearly disappear.

This fish may commonly be seen in large public aquaria, but there is no reason why it cannot be kept privately in small space. Aeration desirable but not imperative. Breeding habits unknown.

Nearly all small sea-fishes enjoy and are benefited by a fair proportion of meals consisting of chopped clam.

Pomacéntrus fúscus CUVIER AND VALENCIENNES

Pronounced Po'ma-sen"trus fus'kus   *Popular names,* Blue Devil, Cockeyed Pilot
        MEANING OF NAME: *Pomacentrus,* with spiny gill cover; *fuscus,* dusky
Florida and West Indies (mostly Marine)   Length, up to 4½ inches
                    Western Location Map j25 to o37

THERE is considerable difference in the adaptability of those marine
fishes which can be kept in the fresh-water aquarium. Our subject
here is one of those which can be brought to the changed environment
by care—and it is worth all the patience that may be necessary. It is
a sparkling, vivacious little individual, darting about in a most sprightly
way, flashing its yellow rear fins and the geometric rows of deep sap-
phire-blue scales on the body. These scales and the head markings of
the same brilliant coloring are indicated by the white portions of the
photograph. The smaller fish, believed to be the male, displays more
rows of the sparkling scales. The body background is dark gray to
purplish.

   In Nature they deposit their eggs on the inside of large empty shells,
fan them and care for the young in the same manner followed by the
Cichlids.

   Those which were received were in 50% marine water. Some died,
but others were slowly changed to straight fresh water in about 6
months, and are living happily after nearly 2 years. They had best
be kept singly, or where good retreats are provided. (One should not
attempt to keep plants in brackish water.) Once established this fish
should be moved about as little as possible. Easy to feed. Temperature
requirements, 70 to 80 degrees.

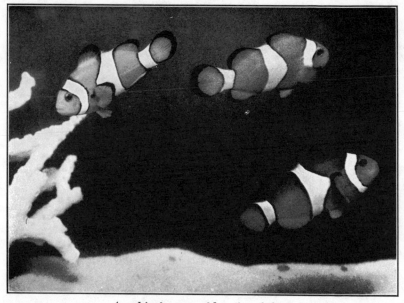

Amphiprion percùla (LACÉPÈDE)

Pronounced Am-fi-pry'on per-kew'la   *Popular name,* Clownfish
MEANING OF NAME: *Amphiprion,* both saws (referring to rough edges on sides of head);
percula, little Perch
On coral reefs   Eastern Location Map y35 to T71 and C82   Length, 2 inches

O F the several small marine fishes suited to the small home aquarium
this is one of the best, and is probably the most brilliantly colored.
Also the coloration is so different from any of our fresh-water fishes
that it is nothing short of startling. The gray portions of the fish as
shown by the photograph are a rich, brilliant yellow. The dark edgings
are black. In extreme contrast to these the 3 broad, irregular light
bands encircling the fish are pure white.

It is very lively, always busily on the move. In Nature it hovers about
Sea Anemones, ready to take shelter among their poisonous tentacles.
Probably the Anemone receives some benefit from this strange partner-
ship, but what it is, is not known, at least to this writer.

The Clownfish eats Brine Shrimp eagerly, and will also take bits of
raw scraped fish, or even ordinary prepared fishfood.

It needs marine water at a temperature of 70-75 degrees. Not bred.

At the time of this writing some of our leading dealers are making a
commendable effort to introduce this gorgeous fish to aquarists.

THE SUNFISHES
FAMILY CENTRARCHIDAE
Pronounced Cen trär'ki dee

This family contains the North American Sunfishes and Black Basses. They are found nowhere else. They are related to the Sea Basses but differ in various internal characters. Two nostrils on each side are present.

Elassòma éverglàdei JORDAN

Pronounced El'as-so"ma ev'er-glay"dee-eye   *Popular name,* Pigmy Sunfish
MEANING OF NAME: *Elassoma,* small body; *evergladei,* of the Everglades
North Carolina to Florida   Western Location Map f25 to i26   Length, 1 inch

THE male is rather smart-looking, with his big dorsal fin and vivacious manners. In the breeding season he becomes enveloped in velvety black, through which sparkle flecks of green and gold, a beautiful sight.

Out of breeding season the sexes can be distinguished by the male's larger fins. The dorsal is arched higher. All his fins are a darker gray.

The fishes build a simple nest of bits of plants at the bottom of the aquarium, into which the eggs are placed. These are guarded by the male, but he is so fond of his young that he may eat them.

The species seems to thrive only on living food. It is usually best to keep these little fishes by themselves.

Another species, *E. zonatum* Jordan, is sometimes shipped north. It is very similar to *evergladei.* Temperature range, 65-80 degrees.

THE AMBASSIDS
FAMILY AMBASSIDAE
Pronounced Am bass' i dee

The Ambassids are small, brackish and salt-water fishes of the Indian Ocean and Western Pacific. They are very much like the salt-water Cardinal Fishes but differ in having the spiny and soft dorsals connected at the base. Most of the species are translucent, this characteristic reaching its highest development in the little Glass-fish, *Ambassis lala.*

Ambássis buroénsis BLEEKER

Pronounced Am-bas'sis boo'ro-en"sis

MEANING OF NAME: *Ambassis,* from a native name; *buroensis,* from the island Boeru or Buru in the East Indies

Boeru in East Indies   Eastern Location Map J57; H53; W49; x73   Length, 2¼ inches

*L*ONGER and not quite so translucent as *A. lala* and lacking the blue edges on fins. It has been demonstrated that this species can be trained to eating shredded dried shrimp. Incidentally, this is one of the best foods for weaning live-food eaters over to prepared foods. This fish is a recent importation. It came in under the title of *Ambassis agassizi,* a name unknown to science.

Breeding habits are similar to those of *A. lala.* Although the species has been with us only a short time, it is found to be a very free breeder.

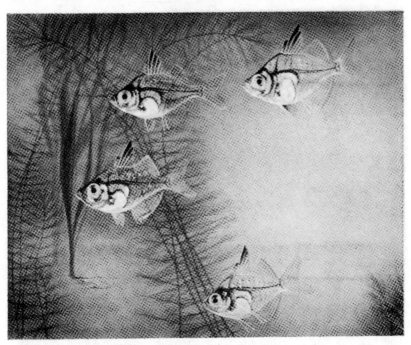

Ambássis lála   (HAMILTON-BUCHANAN)

Pronounced Am-bas'sis la'la   *Popular name,* Glassfish

After native names

India   Eastern Location Map s27; x22; t31; w32; y35   Length, 1½ inches

A NUMBER of our fishes are more or less translucent, but *A. lala* is very decidedly so. It is a very translucent fish that resembles a bit of crystal moving about the aquarium. Like crystal it will some-times catch the light in such a way that glints of prismatic colors—mostly bluish—are reflected by the scales. The slight natural tint of the body by transmitted light is yellow, the shade being slightly deeper in the male and considerably more apparent in both sexes at breeding time. Specimens of this fish which were kept in 50% sea water were of a rich amber shade, while the blue fin edgings stood out brightly.

The fish is so translucent that at first glance one would believe that the internal organs hold no secrets from the eye, but this is not so, for the reason that Nature has enclosed the viscera (except the plainly-seen swimming bladder) in an opaque, silvery sac.

The Ambassids belong to the Perch family, which is sufficient ground to assume that they are carnivorous. Daphnia is their ideal food. They may be fed Enchytræ (white worms), but should be given only small sizes or larger ones cut in half. So tiny is this fish that a partially swallowed white worm may reach around into the gills and strangle it.

While this tiny, very individual fish would seem to be delicate, owing to its approach to nothingness in size, together with its glass-like, fragile appearance, it really is not tender. It *does* like a temperature of about 75 and breeds at about 80. The fact that it so successfully endures the necessary weeks of travel from Asia to our own shores proves its tenacity of life.

Ambassis lala is not easily bred, but we know it can be done successfully, so that those who care to try will at least know they have a sporting chance. They should be in quite old water. For breeding purposes it ought to be about 4 inches (10 cm.) deep, the surface well crowded with Riccia.

The males are yellowish and have stronger vertical markings. Also the blue edging on the dorsal and anal fins is much brighter in the male. This is positive. Our illustration shows 3 males and one female.

At breeding time the fishes take a side-by-side position, quivering all the while, and turning to an upside down position, so that the eggs are discharged upward into the plants. They have also been known to spawn on Nitella or other finely divided plants on the bottom of the aquarium. The eggs, as might be imagined, are extremely minute and also transparent. The parents should be removed after spawning is complete. Instances are reported where they have not disturbed eggs nor young.

At a temperature of 82 the eggs have been known to hatch in 8 hours. The babies must be fed on the finest of Infusoria.

These fishes like a sunny situation. A little sea water or evaporated sea salt added to their aquarium is beneficial, but not enough of it to injure the plants.

Shocking as it seems to those of us who treasure this little gem of the aquarium, it occurs in such numbers in India and Burma that it is used as a fertilizer!

It is found in salt, brackish and fresh water.

Ambássis ambássis (LACÉPÈDE)

Pronounced Am-bas'sis am-bas'sis   *Popular name,* African Glass Perch

MEANING OF NAME: *Ambassis,* after native name

E. Coast of Africa to Australia Eastern Location Map F40; H40; K43 Length, 2½ inches

THERE are a number of kinds of Glassfish, but only a few of them are small enough for use in the household aquarium. We have here a variety distinctly larger than *A. lala* and different in what might be called personal style. This fish in contrast to the perky bearing of *A. lala,* is rather slovenly, seldom spreading its fins. In manner it is apt to be listless. It has not been bred in the aquarium and the 3 or 4 importations we have seen in as many years seem to have disappeared and left no trace.

It is considerably larger and more elongate than *A. lala,* and is therefore sufficiently different to add a note of novelty to a collection. The feeding habits are the same.

Our photograph was taken with a back light, which shows considerable of the internal structure of the fish, much the same as it looks in the aquarium when viewed by transmitted light.

THE THERAPONIDS
FAMILY THERAPONIDAE
Pronounced Ther a pon'i dee

The Theraponids are spiny-rayed salt-water fishes of the East Indies which frequently ascend rivers into fresh water. They have 2 nostrils on each side, but differ from most related families in the absence of the small scale-like flap at the base of the ventral fins.

Thérapon järbua (FORSKAL)
Pronounced Ther'a-pon jar'bua
MEANING OF NAME: *Therapon,* shield-bearer; *jarbua,* a native name
Red Sea, E. Coast Africa to China, N. Coast Australia   Length in nature, 10 inches

HE drooping concentric lines on a ground of shining silver are dark gray to black. In fact all the dark parts of the photograph are, in life, black or nearly black. The large spot in the dorsal is particularly intense, and adds to the already strange aspect of the fish.

Like the Ambassids, to which it is closely related, it is a marine fish which enters fresh water.

Unlike *Ambassis lala* and *Ambassis buroensis,* it has never been bred in captivity. It is one of the things to be hoped for.

The fish seems to be rather quarrelsome. It is easily kept in fresh water at a temperature of about 73 to 78 degrees. Seldom imported.

THE ARCHER FISHES
FAMILY TOXOTIDAE
Pronounced Tox o'ti dee

The Archer Fishes are a small family of 4 or 5 species from the East Indies. The head is flat above and pointed, the dorsal is set far back, and the soft dorsal and anal fins are scaly. Some of these scales can be seen in the illustration, especially on the anal fin.

An entirely different fish is, in some quarters, incorrectly credited with being the Archer Fish. It is one of the brilliant disk-like marine Chætodons (*Chelmo ostratus*), having a projecting mouth of tubular appearance. It would not be difficult to imagine this mouth to be a sort of rifle for shooting pellets of water. Natives believe that it shoots water at insects, but Bleeker, the great ichthyologist, who spent many years studying the fishes of India, says he has no reason to believe they do this. Nevertheless, like many other errors of tradition, the belief has become established and is kept alive by men like Ripley, who, in one of his Believe-it-or-Nots, shows this Chætodon in the sea, taking a shot at a fly in an overhead vine which is suspended from nowhere.
At any rate, we *know* that Archer Fishes exist, and that *Toxotes jaculator* is one of them.

Toxòtes jáculàtor ₍PALLAS₎

Pronounced Tox-o'tees jack'you-lay"tor   *Popular name,* Archer Fish
MEANING OF NAME: *Toxotes,* archer; *jaculator,* hurler
East Indies   Eastern Location Map r28; v33; w37; t48; N68   Length, 5 inches

*H*ERE is one of the unique showmen among aquarium fishes, and with the correct properties and settings supplied, it can be depended upon to do its act.

This is one of a few fishes that, from written descriptions, appealed to the author many years ago, and it was only recently that he had the thrill of seeing it in action (1933). The weird statement that a fish could accurately aim a mouthful of water as a missile with which to bring down a fly seemed to border on the fanciful. Aside from the mechanical difficulties of such a feat, anyone with a slight knowledge of optics knows that, due to surface refraction, objects do not appear in their true positions when looking into or out of water, unless, as might rarely happen, the line of vision or aim is vertical. A bullet from a rifle aimed at an angle to the water and apparently pointed at a small object below the surface could not hit it unless allowance were made for the optical "bend." The same thing is true from the *under* side of the surface, looking out, but the Archer Fish has learned the trick and will accurately splatter its prey from a distance of a foot or more, and usually bring it down.

It shoots a few drops at a high speed, capable of carrying 10 feet. If the first shot does not bring down the prey, it is followed by a rapid series until the insect falls. Few escape. The mouth is quite large, and the shooting is done while the lips are just above the surface of the water.

We are told that Toxotes varies considerably in color. Those shown here were silver with a slight overtone of yellow. Dorsal and anal fins are edged black. The 6 dark bars are gorgeous black, making the fish easy to remember by its striking appearance, as well as its original way of gaining a livelihood. It will eat live food which it has not knocked into the water. Meal worms seem to be particularly relished.

Nothing is known as to sex distinctions or breeding habits. A temperature of 75 degrees proves satisfactory.

This is one of those species coming from salt, brackish and fresh waters, and we believe a mixture of sea water, such as prescribed under the heading, "Fundulopanchax Group," is advisable.

They get along well together and even prove themselves sports by not quarreling when the shooter's victim is gobbled by another fish!

To our knowledge the species has been imported but a few times.

Like the various Electric and Walking Fishes, the Archer Fish is a star attraction at a public fish show, for it will "knock off" live flies as long as the spectators choose to supply them.

THE "SCATS"
FAMILY SCATOPHAGIDAE
Pronounced Scat'o fag"i dee

The "Scats" differ from the salt-water Butterfly-fishes, to which they are most closely allied in various technical internal features. They cannot be confused with any of the other groups of fresh-water aquarium fishes. The "Scats" are all from brackish water in the East Indies.

Scátophàgus ärgus (PALLAS)
Pronounced Scat'o-fay"gus ar'gus (Scat-off'a-gus allowable)
MEANING OF NAME: *Scatophagus,* offal eater; *argus,* many eyed (from the spots)
Popular name, Spotted Scat
Salt, brackish and sometimes fresh water of the East Indies
Length—Aquarium sizes, from 2 to 5 inches; in Nature, 10 inches

ALTHOUGH we are told that in Nature this fish comes in 10 and even 12 inch lengths, the usual size seen in the aquarium is from 2 to 4½ inches.

The fish is rather flat in form, or "laterally compressed," as it is called. In markings it is so variable that one would easily get the impression that the different patterns indicate various species. There are 3 principal types. First, those having large, round dark spots on a light background with green iridescence; second, those with small spots on a warm brown background; third, those with tiger stripes about the head and forward part of the body, and a few spots on the sides. This type often has orange or reddish areas along the back, and particularly about the top of the head. The name *rubrifrons* has been used to designate this variation. It is quite colorful. Sometimes these color differences are taken to denote the sexes. While we believe this to be a mistake, we have no other method to offer. The subject is not important anyhow, as we have little prospects of breeding the fish. It is chiefly ornamental and interesting in its exotic way.

Our illustration represents the second described type of markings. Also it averages somewhat larger in size than most aquarium specimens.

There has been much discussion as to whether the species can be successfully kept in fresh water. The answer definitely is that it can.

In Nature the fish is one of the real scavengers of the sea, inhabiting the mouths of rivers and the docks of various tropical seaports. It is therefore not surprising to find that it will eat anything, although it is hard to account for the fact that it is extremely fond of Duckweed. May be kept with other fishes, but seems happiest among its own kind. Temperature, about 73-78 degrees. Never cheap.

Scátophàgus tétracánthus LACÉPÈDE
Pronounced Scat'o-fay"gus tet'ra-kan"thus
MEANING OF NAME: *Scatophagus*, after a native name; *tetracanthus*, four-spined
(in allusion to the anal fin)
East Africa to East Indies to Australia   Length, 4 inches

A FEW aquarium fishes can live in either fresh or salt water. This
is one that can. Of course, if a change is made from one to the
other, it should be gradual.

The light portions in the illustration are brilliant, mirror-like silver,
showing to especial advantage under strong light. The darker portions
of the fish are black. No bright colors, nor even tints. Body flat, like
that of a Scalare.

Altogether it is a very satisfactory aquarium fish; certainly a showy
one. In the 2 years since the introduction of quite a shipment of them,
we have heard of no deaths.

Eats anything. Never bred. Suited to living with other fishes of about
its own size. Swims about the aquarium industriously, always on the
move. There is no known method of distinguishing the sexes. Temperature range, 70 to 80 degrees.

THE MONODACTYLIDS
FAMILY MONODACTYLIDAE
Pronounced Mon o dak ty'li dee

The deep form and the scaly fins will distinguish the Monodactylids from other aquarium fishes. They are brackish and salt-water fishes of the Old World.

Monodáctylus argénteus (LACÉPÈDE)
Pronounced Mon'o-dak"ty-lus ar-jen'tee-us (Mo'no-dak-ty"lus allowable)
MEANING OF NAME: *Monodactylus,* with one finger, referring to appearance of dorsal and anal fins; *argenteus,* silvery one
Indian Ocean   Vacated scientific name, *Psettus argenteus*   Length, 4 inches

NOT knowing that this is a marine fish, one would hardly suspect it. It is beautiful, but not with that gaudy display we have come to expect of marine tropicals.

The fish is extremely silvery, while the dark portions of the upper and lower fins represent a beautiful, rich yellow. Preference in purchase should be given to the younger specimens. They will grow rapidly in a large aquarium, *but should not be unnecessarily disturbed or moved about.* Salt water unnecessary. Never bred. Temperature, 75 degrees.

THE GOBIES

Three families of Gobies contribute species to our list.

FAMILY ELEOTRIDAE
Pronounced El e o'tri dee

These have the ventral fins entirely separate from one another, and *not* connected into a sucking disk.

Dòrmitàtor màculàtus (BLOCH)
Pronounced Dor'mi-tay"tor   mac'you-lay"tus
MEANING OF NAME: *Dormitator*, sleeper; *maculatus*, spotted
Coasts of Tropical America, Atlantic side, brackish water
Length—Aquarium size, 3 to 4 inches; in Nature, 10 inches
Western Location Map from d26 to w30 and y8 to F30

ALTHOUGH the species in color is a pattern of browns and grays, it is not lacking in character. The light spot in back of the gill plate is a sparkle of blue. The anal fin is ornamented with brown and blue spots, and is crisply edged with electric blue. A peculiarity is that in certain lights the centre of the eye is a blind, stony blue.

Notwithstanding its somewhat menacing appearance, the fish is quite harmless. Eats anything. Temperature range, 68-85 degrees. Never bred.

Oxyéleòtris märmoràtus   (BLEEKER)

Pronounced Ox'ee-el'e-o"tris mar'mo-ray"tus   *Popular name,* Marbled Goby

MEANING OF NAME: *Oxyeleotris,* sharp Eleotris; *marmoratus,* marbled

Better known as *Eleotris marmoratus*

Malay Peninsula   Eastern Location Map F39   Length, 6 inches

NATURE in providing for everything has not forgotten to give aquarists a few cannibal fishes which may be used for the disposal of small diseased or surplus specimens. This species, along with *Hoplias malabaricus,* performs the gruesome task with considerable satisfaction to itself, thus relieving the aquarist of a problem. Our subject here, with the aid of a very spacious mouth, will soon dispose of a fish almost half its own size.

Its pectoral fins are much larger than the photograph shows. We happened to get an edge view.

The marbled ivory markings against varying shades of brown are quite attractive. Most of the time the fish rests motionless, on or near the bottom, waiting for victims. Will eat earthworms or a porridge containing a large proportion of shrimp. Very hardy. The specimen here photographed has, at this writing, passed through 7 known ownerships in 2 years, and is in the best of health. Like most Gobies, it has not been bred, which will be good news to other aquarium fishes. Temperature range, 68-85 degrees.

Mogúrnda mogúrnda   (RICHARDSON)

Pronounced Mo-gurn'da   mo-gurn'da   *Popular name,* Purple Striped Gudgeon

MEANING OF NAME: *Mogurnda,* not known

Formerly known as *Krefftius adspersus*

Australia   Length, 2 inches

A PRETTY Australian fish and quite lively for a Goby; in fact, too lively in one respect, for it tears the fins of other fishes. As a community fish, it is one of the world's worst, being comparable in this respect to the much better known *Gambusia affinis.*

The spots on the body and fins are black and dark red, while the 3 light stripes on the cheek are purple, giving the fish its popular name.

Larger fins identify the male. Eggs are deposited on the glass of the aquarium in a space free from plants, usually on the near side where the aquarist may conveniently watch them. At a temperature of 72 degrees they hatch in 9 days. The male fans the eggs, but he should be removed after the eggs hatch.

Our friend, the late Wm. A. Poyser, first illustrated the species as *Krefftius adspersus* in "Aquatic Life" in 1918. There have been subsequent importations.

Temperature range, 60-80 degrees. Food preferably carnivorous. A desirable fish if kept only among its own kind, and rather pretty.

FAMILY GOBIIDAE
Pronounced Go bee'i dee

The true Gobies have the ventral fins united into a more or less perfect sucking disk by which the fishes adhere to solid objects.

Bráchygòbius dòriæ (GUENTHER)
Pronounced Brack'ee-go"bee-us do'ry-ee

MEANING OF NAME: *Brachygobius,* short goby; *doriæ,* after the Marquis G. Doria, Italian zoologist and explorer

Malay Peninsula and Borneo; exact locality not known   Length, 1½ inches

LIKE so many of the Gobies this little fish spends most of its time on the bottom of the aquarium, hopping about in a droll way. It can scarcely be called a scavenger fish, for scavengers eat anything, whereas this species has a distinct preference for Daphnia and white worms, although it will take dried food containing a large proportion of shrimp or other animal matter.

The very marked pattern shown in the illustration is mostly in shades of dark brown on a field of ivory or buff.

This little fish is often but not always to be had from the stocks of dealers. In common with most specimens from the Far East which have not been bred, it is never low-priced. Lives successfully and is perfectly harmless. Temperature range, 72-85 degrees.

Bráchygòbius xánthozònus   (BLEEKER)
Pronounced Brack'ee-go"be-us zan'tho-zo"nus

MEANING OF NAME: *Brachygobius,* short goby; *xanthozonus,* with yellow zones or bands
Malay Peninsula   Eastern Location Map E39; x41; L42   Length, 1¾ inches

THE remarks regarding *Brachygobius doriæ* apply to this species, except to add that this is a new introduction, is a little larger, and to state that the broad, light bands are a brilliant white to golden.

They live in rice swamps and in small, shallow, fresh-water pools. This species has been spawned on the inside of a flower-pot laid on its side, but the eggs disappeared after 10 days' fanning by the male. The female (lower fish) is fuller of body. Her pectoral fins during spawning become black. The species is hardy in almost any kind of aquarium water, and has an exceptional temperature range, 65-90 degrees. Does not fight.

FAMILY PERIOPHTHALMIDAE
Pronounced Pe'ree off thal''mi dee

These fishes differ from the Gobiidae in their projecting, movable eyes.

Périophthálmus bärbarus   LINNAEUS

Pronounced Pe'ree-off-thal''mus bar'ba-rus   *Popular name,* Mud Skipper

MEANING OF NAME: *Periophthalmus*, looking in every direction; *barbarus*, foreign. Not found in Europe, it being one of the few foreign Gobies known to Linnaeus

Also known as *Gobius kœlreuteri* and *Periophthalmus kœlreuteri*

Tropical Asiatic coastal waters from British India Eastward; also Polynesia

Length, 4 inches

BIOLOGISTS are pretty well united in the belief that life on the land crawled out of the water. The habits of this extraordinary fish make that very easy to believe. It is not only equipped with an efficient air-breathing mechanism, but the strong, muscular base of the pectoral fins enables it to use those fins as sturdy legs, while the eyes are finely adapted to vision above the water. It is easily conceivable that with a little further specialization of equipment many of these water animals could have permanently left their original environment to rove the land and undergo all manner of further changes.

Several importations have been made, but it is only recently that we learned how to keep them. They need ample space, not less than 3 feet square, and sandy flats rising from shallow, half-marine water, so that the fishes can be in any depth from 2 inches to nothing. Provisions should be made for them to climb to still higher levels and perch on rocks or sections of gnarled wood. The temperature ought to be at about 80, and it is important that their atmosphere be entirely enclosed, so as to keep it moist, as well as warm. The importance of moisture can be seen in their actions. They like to stand for long periods in about a quarter inch of water, but frequently they will roll over, somewhat like the action of a dog, to moisten themselves. Also using a pectoral fin like a paw they will wet their faces, no doubt in order to keep the eyes moist. They may be seen kept under ideal conditions at the Shedd Aquarium in Chicago, where they have even been taught to take dried food. Breeding habits unknown.

The following extract is from a most interesting article in THE AQUARIUM (November, 1932), by Henry W. Fowler, of the Academy of Natural Sciences in Philadelphia: "About the extensive mud flats of the Indo Australian Archipelago, Mud Skippers are met with in perhaps their greatest profusion. This is usually near lagoons or tidal estuaries, especially about or near mangrove flats. My first acquaintance with it was in the coral reef islands in the Java Sea. Though only a few were found at first, I saw perhaps more of its ability to skip about on land and over the water, than most any place visited. Its method of skipping over the surface of shallow pools, by leaping a foot or more, was most interesting. Each time it alighted on the surface of the water with a little splash and soon progressed from about 5 to 20 feet. Its objective was nearly always toward some goal above the water. Often it would finally alight on a mangrove root and then crawl or wriggle up until well above the water line. Sometimes it would jump from one root to another, often with fins expanded, though its movements through the air are so difficult to follow I was not always sure of this. On the soft, wet mud it would crawl, wriggle or skip about with apparent abandon, though doubtless in search of minute insects or crustaceans which were scarcely visible. Here it was found in numbers of a dozen or more, though appearing scattered and not in schools. About the mangrove roots it is usually impossible to catch any."

In color the fish is an olive brown with irregular, light blue markings, especially about the head. The colors of the front dorsal, beginning at the bottom, are blue, white and black. The rear dorsal is gray. A dark blue stripe, edged white, traverses it. The tail fin, usually being closed, looks unnatural spread as it is shown. Never bred.

THE BROAD-SOLES

FAMILY ACHIRIDAE
Pronounced A ky'ri dee

The Broad-Soles belong to the order Heterosomata or Flatfishes, all of which lie on one side and have both eyes on the upper side. The Soles differ from other Flatfishes in having a very twisted mouth. They are salt-brackish, or fresh-water fishes.

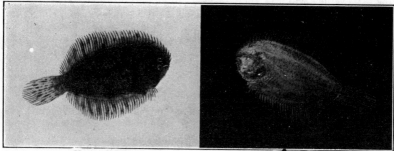

Upper Side   Lower Side

Trinéctes maculàtus (BLOCH)

Pronounced Try-neck'tees mac'you-lay"tus   *Popular name,* Fresh-water Sole

MEANING OF NAME: *Trinectes,* with 3 "swimmers" (fins); *maculatus,* spotted

Also known as *Achirus fasciatus,* Common Sole

Coastal waters from Cape Cod southward   Length, aquarium specimens, 2 inches

*W*E hesitated to include this fish in our list, but as there is a mild, persistent interest in it, we did so. It is really the young of a 5 to 6 inch fish related to the Flounders. Interest in it lies chiefly in its method of swimming. This is accomplished by an undulating movement of the fins at the edges of the body as the fish glides in a horizontal position, like a pancake being propelled through the water. All fishes of this type—and there are many of them—at first have eyes normally on each side of the head. At an early age, one of them moves over to the other side, so that eventually we see a fish blind on one side and with 2 raised eyes on the other. They lay in wait in the mud for small passing victims. In the aquarium they can be fed Daphnia or bits of chopped clam. They can stick quite firmly on the sides of the aquarium by body suction. Temperature, from 60 to 72 degrees.

In the aquarium they are not very active, spending much time either on or in the sand. On the whole we would say that they are more novel than satisfactory. Not safe with other fishes.

THE SPINY EELS
FAMILY MASTACEMBELIDAE
Pronounced Mas'ta sem bell"i dee

Rhŷnchobdélla acùleàta (BLOCH)
Pronounced Rin'kob-del"la ac-u'le-a"ta
MEANING OF NAME: *Rhynchobdella*, snout-sucker; *aculeata*, sharp
India and Burma   Length, 7 inches
Eastern Location Map o15 to r28 and F45 (in river mouths)

*A*N odd creature, seldom imported. We include it here because of its interesting appearance and the fact that it is the only member of this order which we have to show. It is one of the "spiny eels."

Like the Weatherfish, it spends much of its daytime buried in the sand, head peeping out. Probably the Weatherfish does this for protection, but with Rhynchobdella it is more likely a camouflage for attack, as it is a strictly carnivorous fish. At night it swims about the surface of the sand. In common with most nocturnal fishes it can be taught to eat in daytime, but as soon as it has had its meal of chopped earthworms it quickly returns to its sandy hide-out. Not interested in Daphnia or in raw meat. It will gladly take worms.

These fishes seem to like a temperature of about 78 degrees. After 2 years in the Shedd Aquarium, at Chicago, none of them have died. Neither have they bred.

THE PUFFERS
FAMILY TETRAODONTIDAE
Pronounced Tet'ra o don"ti dee

The Puffers are comical fishes. They can blow themselves up with air or water into a veritable balloon. No other fishes possess this remarkable feature. Like some other families in the order Plectognathi the fused teeth (2 above, 2 below) form a beak with which the larger species can give a dangerous nip. Most of the species are of good size and inhabit salt water throughout tropical and semi-tropical regions, but a few small ones inhabit fresh water.

Tétraodón flùviatìlis HAMILTON-BUCHANAN
Pronounced Tet'ra-o-don flu'vee-a-ty'lis   *Popular name,* Blow Fish
MEANING OF NAME: *Tetraodon,* four-toothed; *fluviatilis,* of the river
Most of India, Burma, Malay Peninsula   Length, 2 to 5 inches
Eastern Location Map y19 to F40

"*BLOW* FISH" in different species have a wide distribution throughout marine waters. This one occurs principally in fresh and brackish locations, and in aquarium trade circles is known as the Freshwater Tetraodon.

The background color is light, with a vivid sheen of green, interspersed with large, dark blotches and spots. Belly white, or nearly so.

Although a fish of clumsy, thick appearance, it is extremely active, never still a moment. It is also quite aggressive towards its own kind, but seems to do little harm.

The outstanding feature of these Blow Fishes is their ability to puff themselves up with air, balloon-like. They do this when frightened. Most

but not all specimens will do it when removed from the water, placed on the hand and tickled. Air is taken in at the mouth in about a dozen noisy gulps, until the belly is fully inflated and hard. As the internal pressure increases, little hollow spines are projected from the scale spots. Even the vent is blown inside out into a point. The fish is able to maintain this balloon form only about half a minute. When placed back on the water, as shown in one of the illustrations, the inflation soon collapses and the fish quickly swims to the bottom of the aquarium.

With ordinary care it will live well in the aquarium, preferably with its own kind. Eats anything. In Nature it is a scavenger. Never bred. Temperature, 70-80 degrees.

THE LUNG FISHES
FAMILY LEPIDOSIRENIDAE
Pronounced Le pid'o sir en"i dee

These peculiar fishes, which breathe by means of lungs, are much more primitive in their general make-up than the other fishes in this book, but their specialized breathing apparatus shows that they somewhat approach the amphibians.

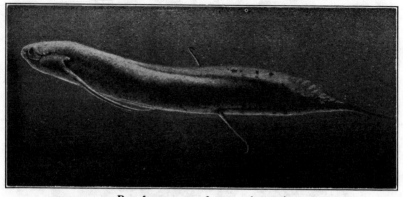

Protópterus annéctens (OWEN)
Pronounced Pro-top'te-rus an-neck'tens

MEANING OF NAME: *Protopterus,* before a fin, *i.e.,* with fins of primitive type; *annectens,* connecting (with reference to similarity to South American Lung Fish)
Tropical Africa   Length, 3 feet
Western Location Map (for 3 species) x46; z47; H69; B58; E71, etc.

WE include the species here on account of its extraordinary life habits, and the prominence it has been given in literature. It is a real "lung fish," encases itself deeply in mud as its pond dries, and can remain in this condition, breathing atmospheric air for a year or more, if necessary, awaiting the return of the rainy season.

Dr. Homer Smith, of New York, wrote a book called "Komongo," describing his search in Africa for this remarkable fish. It is so truly an air-breather that the first ones collected *drowned* in a container that was not deep enough for them to reach the surface with their mouths at the proper angle to enable them to take new air. Smaller lung fishes also occur in South America and in Australia. A few of 6-inch size are kept in small aquariums.

The fish is gray. The rope-like extensions on the sides are ventral fins, which they use in a circular rowing motion.

WHOLESALE BREEDING

$\mathcal{W}$HILE the principles governing the breeding of any fish must always depend upon the nature of the fish itself, there are special methods employed in quantity production. Again, the methods of wholesale breeders vary according to climatic conditions, as well as personal ideas.

A number of our very large breeders are in the Gulf States, for the obvious reason that heating expense there is reduced to a minimum. Whether this counterbalances the disadvantage of having to ship by a 3-day express haul to the main market (New York) is, and probably will remain, an open question. However, we are not so much concerned here with that commercial problem. What we are rather trying to do is to give our readers some idea of how and where the big producers carry on.

Regardless of location, one principle applies to nearly all of them. They specialize in only a few species, usually those for which there is the greatest popular demand. Ordinarily this comprises not over 5 or 6 species per establishment, and more likely not over 2 or 3. In the South the wholesale breeding is confined largely to Mollienisias, Platies, Swordtails and Bettas.

The majority of Southern fish farms (they can scarcely be called establishments) consist of a series of large pools in which breeder fishes are placed and fed, and from which several crops a year are netted. In many of them, especially those in the lowlands of Florida, it is impossible to drain off the pools except by the use of power pumps. This is owing to the high natural water level in the surrounding soil. Those pools that can be drained have a sloping bottom, so that the fish concentrate at the low point when the water is nearly out. Here they are easily caught.

The majority of these plants have no buildings, except perhaps a rude sort of shipping shed. This is a disadvantage, because it leaves the fish farmer with no control over excessive sun nor the chilly weather which is sometimes prevalent, even in the South.

Little or no effort is made at these simple farms to protect the fishes in ground level pools against their natural enemies. The idea seems to be to breed the fishes faster than they can be consumed by Dragon Fly larvæ, etc.

In such places the fishes are left to breed as best they can. Nature takes its course, with very little assistance. The only help they receive is enough food so that cannibalism is reduced to a minimum, and a reasonably good supply of plants in which the fishes can hide from each other and from their enemies. After all, this state of affairs approximates

Nature, and when Dragon Fly larvæ and Water Tigers are not too plentiful, the fish farmer harvests fairly large crops.

Most wholesale breeders have large pools in which they raise Daphnia. Mosquito larvæ are also important as food, especially in the South, where their natural season is very much longer.

Not all of the Southern fish-producing plants are conducted on the "let-Nature-do-it" scheme. There are a number of large and beautifully

SECTION OF BREEDING HOUSE WITH PARTIALLY SOLID ROOF

This is the generally approved design, especially in the South where there is an excess of light. A live-bearer section is shown here with aquariums for breeders and globes for deliveries of baby fish. The central section (below) contains large storage pools.

conducted establishments in which the pools, tanks and aquariums are housed over, assuring control of light and temperature. Scientific methods are in use. In such places a number of good strains of fishes have been developed by selective breeding.

In general, the wholesale breeding plant is *not* a greenhouse, especially in the South. The sides of the houses are solid and contain no glass. Openings in the roof comprise about one-third of the area. This admits sufficient light. Some houses are glazed where the roof openings occur,

and others are merely screened to keep out fish enemies, particularly
Dragon Flies and the flying bugs whose larvæ are Water Tigers.

The principle of using solid sides and roof, with all illumination coming
from overhead openings is one that it is well for all those to remember
who consider building a fish house or *aquiary*, as it has been well called,
especially where there is an abundance of light. Excess light and heat
can be a great detriment. Small greenhouses or "lean-tos" may be best
for city dwellers who are nearly or completely closed out of direct sun.
In the North the walls should not only be solid, but well insulated and

NORTHERN FISH AND PLANT PROPAGATING HOUSE

The side tanks are for propagating, while the big central ones are for increasing size.
In these are seen tall wooden dividers to separate species and to prevent their leaping into
another compartment. The fishes may jump into the alleys if they wish, but a careful
wholesale breeder would rather lose a fish than have it mixed with other species
or varieties. Although glass is whitewashed, this house admits too much light and heat.

air-spaced, for the saving in fuel will soon offset the slight extra expense
in construction.

In reference to heating, let us repeat that nowhere, either in home or
fish house, should any system be employed in which the product of

combustion is discharged indoors. This applies particularly to gas and oil, and more especially to "gas-water" heaters that do not take the burned gas out through a flue. There is no objection to gas and oil in themselves, so long as the gases formed by their combustion are carried out of the house directly from the fire. Portable oil stoves, gas logs and gas radiators are apt to be bad in that respect.

Besides the primitive principle of allowing the fishes to breed unattended, as it were, well-managed establishments have certain established and carefully followed procedures suited to different species. In a large Northern hatchery, for instance, all live-bearers and a number of species of egg-droppers are bred in wooden trays having ¼-inch mesh wire

BREEDING TRAYS WITH SCREEN BOTTOMS

bottom, through which eggs or young are dropped by the breeders. The trays are partially submerged and are supported on small inverted flower-pots. The tanks in which these breeding trays stand are shallow and very large. Our illustration pictures the general idea. To prevent loss of efficiency the wire screen must be occasionally scrubbed if it becomes choked with slimy algæ.

In other establishments, especially in the South, the live-bearing species are kept in large observation tanks, and as a female shows signs of early delivery, she is placed in an ordinary globe aquarium containing a sprig of Anacharis and more Mosquito larvæ than she can eat. A very small percentage of young is lost. A large establishment will be working several thousand globes simultaneously.

Thousands of globes are also necessary for the rearing of Bettas in wholesale quantities. The females may be placed in tanks together, but as soon as the males are nearly an inch long, each must have his own globe if he is to develop and retain perfect fins. Fine males are also shipped in individual jars.

Northern breeding establishments as a rule are not so large and are conducted more intensively. The Scalare is very important commercially. While many young are bred in Germany and sent to the United States and elsewhere, we produce great quantities of them here, mostly in one-man establishments within 100 miles of New York.

As to wholesale breeding of Scalares, a number of large ones are kept together in a big aquarium, and are allowed to mate naturally. Spawning is induced by frequent partial changes of water. Breeding pairs are not removed, but the eggs are taken out as soon as spawning is completed. Thousands of young can be reared to sufficient size for market in a small fish house in a few weeks if given aeration, room and plenty of live food. For details as to rearing, see *"Pterophyllum scalare."*

A recent development among large breeders is the use of refrigerator linings as tanks. These are "seconds" from refrigerator manufacturers, but to the breeder they are perfects. All they need is a piece of glass set in the open end. This is easily done and makes an extremely cheap tank of about 50-gallon capacity.

Feeding methods used in wholesale establishments are described under "Wholesale Feeding" in the section on "Feeding."

There are at present quite sufficient wholesale fish breeders to fully serve the needs of the trade. It is with sincere best wishes for all concerned that our invariable advice to those seeking it is *not* to go into fish breeding commercially, either in a small or a large way. There is much profit in the study of aquarium fishes, but the profit is seldom the kind that can be deposited in bank.

SHOW RULES AND PRACTICES

It would be very desirable to have national standards for judging competitive aquarium exhibitions. Efforts to organize societies so that this would be possible have so far not met with success. In the absence of nationally accepted standards, we publish the.rules of two prominent societies which cover most points, over a period of years, and which have been found generally acceptable.

The point system in use by The Pennsylvania Fish Culturists Association in judging fishes is as follows:

Condition and style	40 points
Color	40 points
Relative size, male and female	20 points
	100

Pairs always have precedence over single fish. Where sexes are difficult or impossible to recognize, 2 fish constitute a pair.

This society's practice with reference to household aquarium competitions is to have a committee of 3 examine the aquarium at the home of the owner. Awards are made on this basis:

AQUARIUM. Design, appearance and location	25 points
FISH. Condition and beauty of individuals	25 points
PLANTS. (Must be in growing condition.)	
Arrangement, condition, varieties	40 points
GENERAL APPEARANCE	10 points
	100

The aquarium competitions of the Boston Aquarium Society are held in conjunction with a large public exhibition. This to some extent changes their specifications, which follow:

Arrangement of Plants and Accessories	20 points
Variety and Rarity of Fish	20 points
Variety of Plant Material	15 points
General Artistic Effect	15 points
Design of Aquarium	10 points
Quality of Plant Material	10 points
Other Aquatic Fauna	10 points
	100

Competition in the show is confined to amateurs, but there is a special award for dealers. They are allowed to placard their aquariums, but the names of the owners in the amateur competition are not placed on the tanks until after the judging is completed.

INDEX OF FISHES

(Other subjects are under General Index)

Folio numbers with asterisk indicate color plates which are to be found following the page number indicated.

The names to the right are of those persons and firms who kindly loaned selected specimens for the illustrations.

446

447

CROSS INDEX OF GENERAL SUBJECTS